SARA,
    KEEP WRITING!
(AND THANKS FOR _____
                    Nick

Sara,
Thanks for
picking this up!
        Chuntin

PAST LIES

AN
AMY DEVLIN
MYSTERY

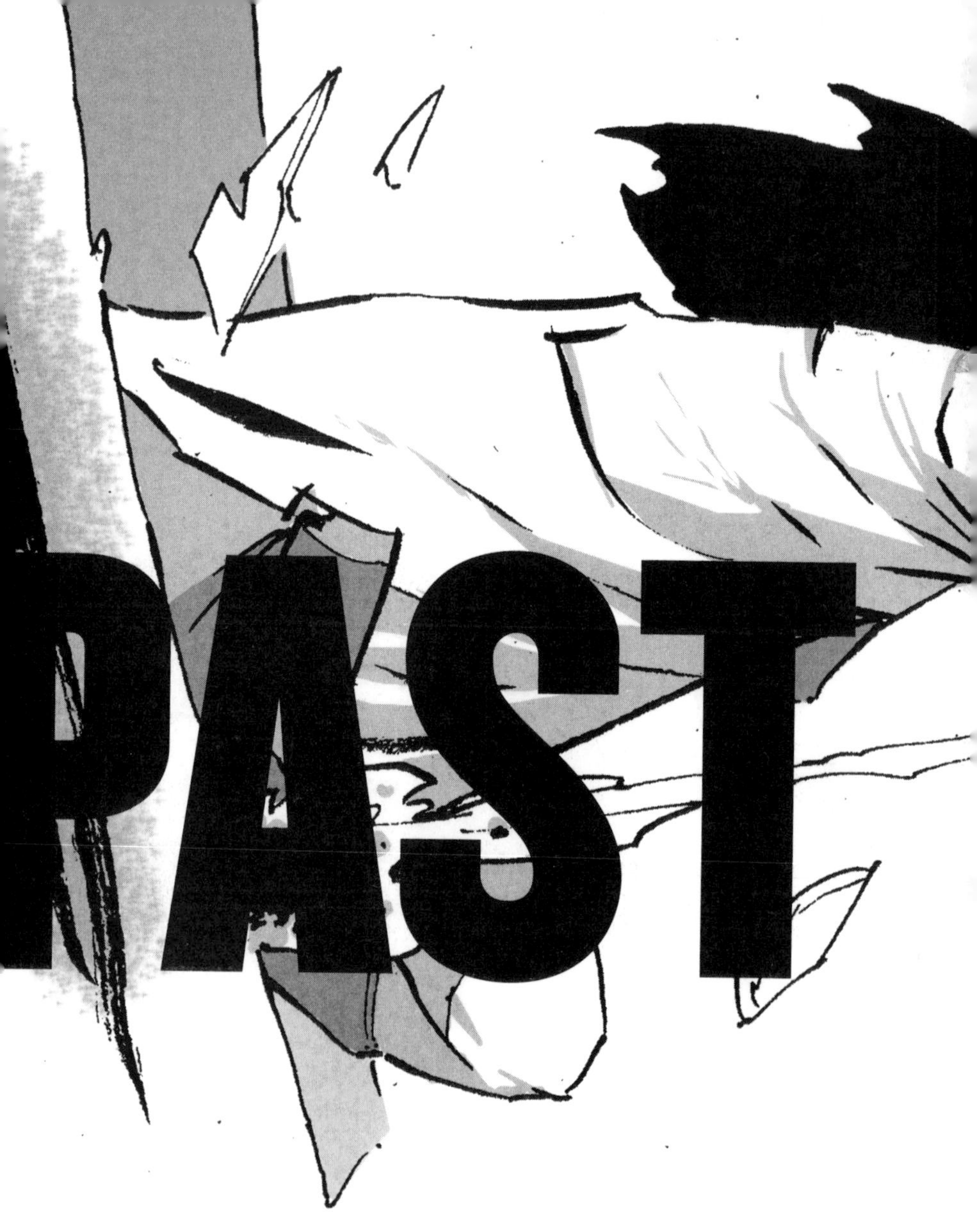
PAST

AN AMY DEVLIN MYSTERY

LIES

WRITTEN BY **CHRISTINA WEIR & NUNZIO DEFILIPPIS**
ILLUSTRATED BY **CHRISTOPHER MITTEN**

DESIGN BY **ERIC SKILLMAN**
COVER ART BY **CHRISTOPHER MITTEN**
EDITED BY **JAMES LUCAS JONES**

Published by Oni Press, Inc.
Joe Nozemack, publisher
James Lucas Jones, editor in chief
Keith Wood, art director
Cory Casoni, marketing director
George Rohac, operations director
Jill Beaton, associate editor
Charlie Chu, associate editor
Douglas E. Sherwood, production assistant

First Edition: July 2010

ISBN 978-1-934964-39-2

10 9 8 7 6 5 4 3 2 1

Oni Press, Inc.
1305 SE Martin Luther King Jr. Blvd.
Suite A
Portland, OR 97214

www.onipress.com

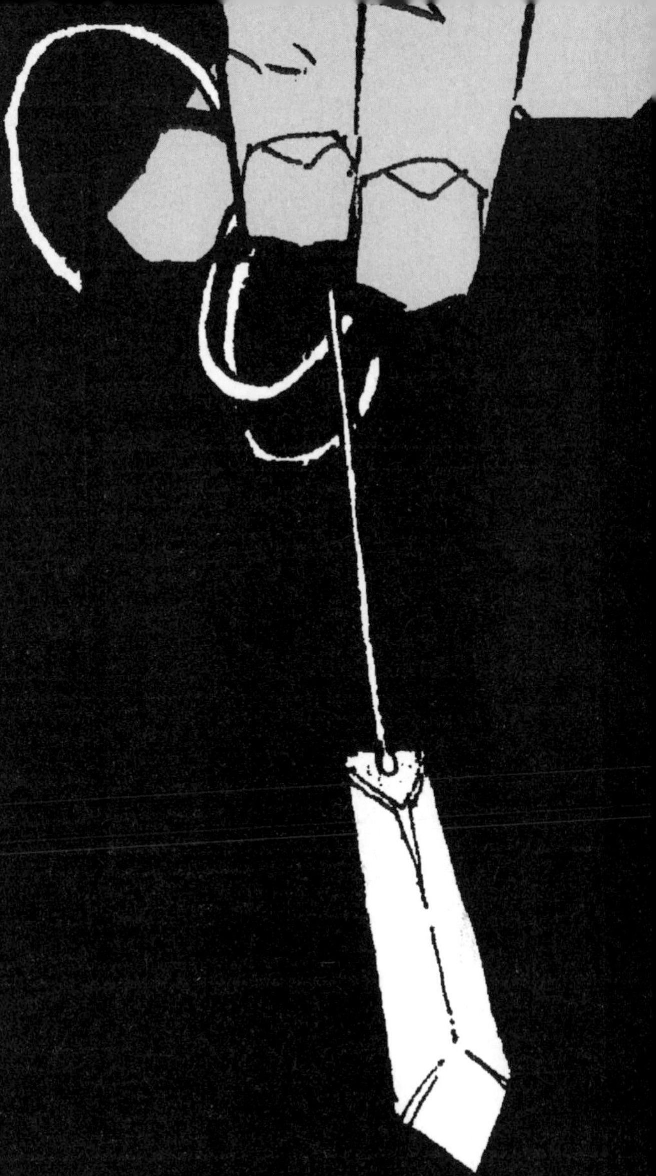

DEDICATED IN LOVING MEMORY TO GEOFFREY WEIR.

He was always our biggest fan, bringing our stories to every corner of the Weir universe. We'll miss him.

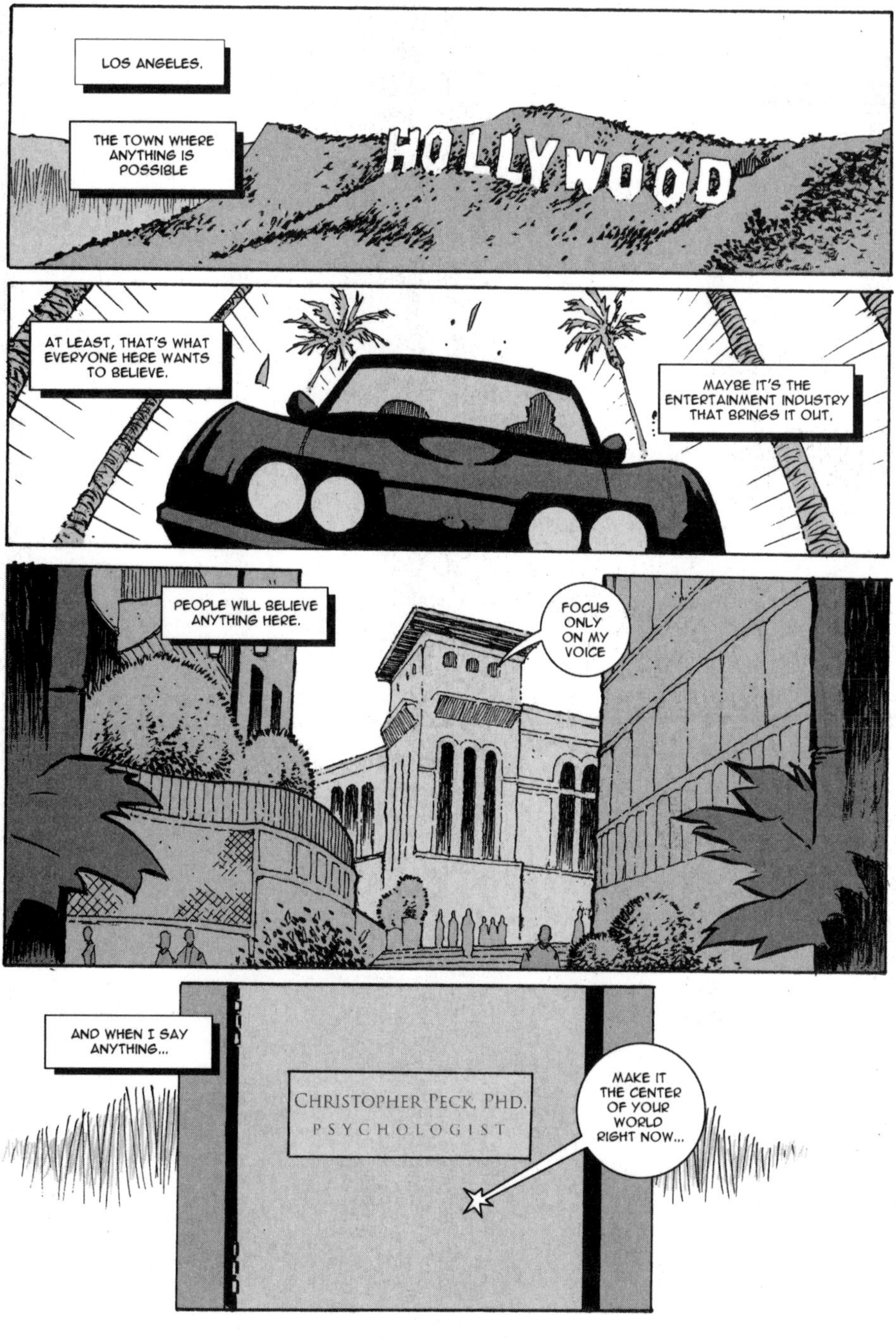
LOS ANGELES.
THE TOWN WHERE ANYTHING IS POSSIBLE
HOLLYWOOD
AT LEAST, THAT'S WHAT EVERYONE HERE WANTS TO BELIEVE.
MAYBE IT'S THE ENTERTAINMENT INDUSTRY THAT BRINGS IT OUT.
PEOPLE WILL BELIEVE ANYTHING HERE.
FOCUS ONLY ON MY VOICE
AND WHEN I SAY ANYTHING...
CHRISTOPHER PECK, PHD.
PSYCHOLOGIST
MAKE IT THE CENTER OF YOUR WORLD RIGHT NOW...

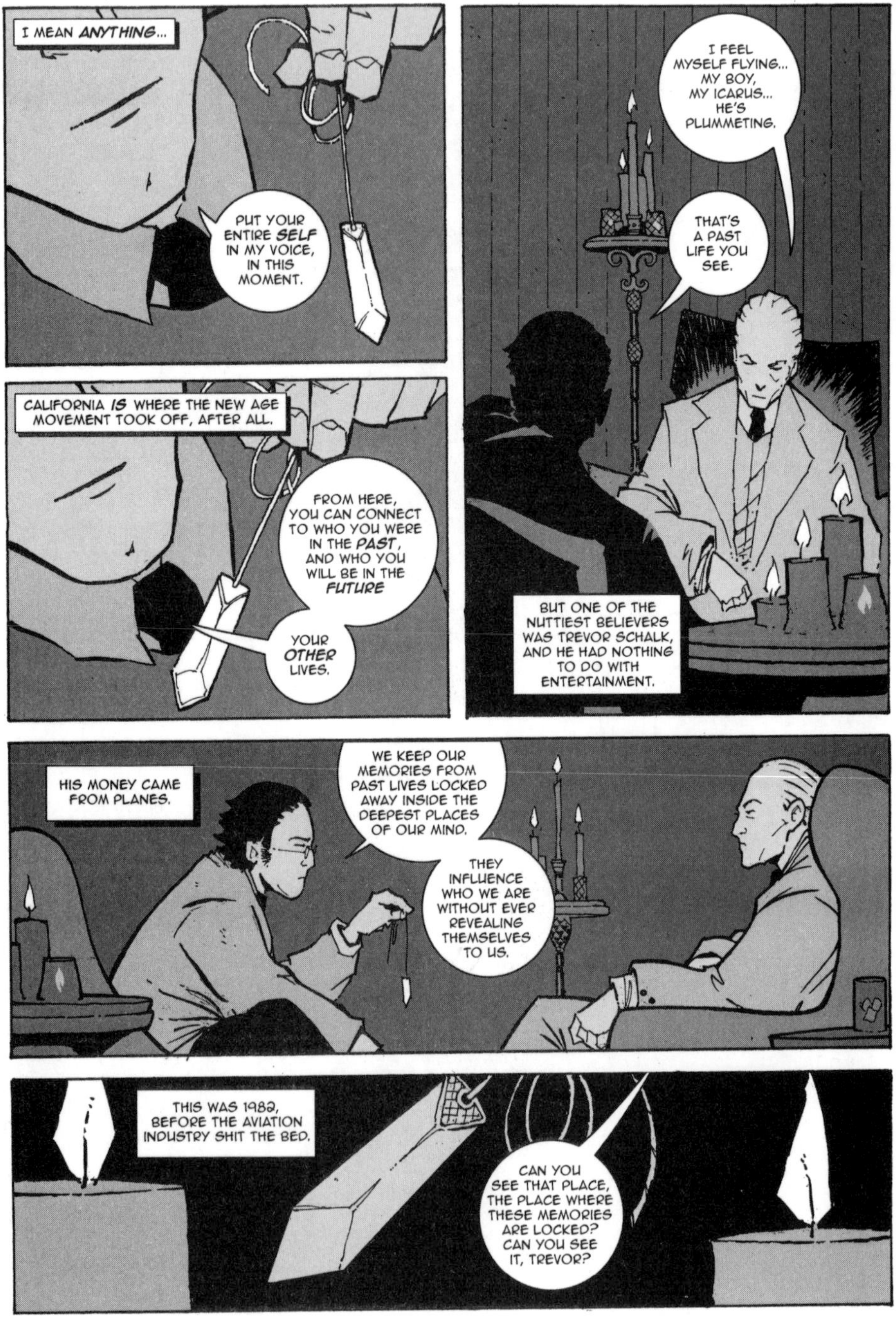
I MEAN ANYTHING...
PUT YOUR ENTIRE SELF IN MY VOICE, IN THIS MOMENT.
CALIFORNIA IS WHERE THE NEW AGE MOVEMENT TOOK OFF, AFTER ALL.
FROM HERE, YOU CAN CONNECT TO WHO YOU WERE IN THE PAST, AND WHO YOU WILL BE IN THE FUTURE
YOUR OTHER LIVES.
I FEEL MYSELF FLYING... MY BOY, MY ICARUS... HE'S PLUMMETING.
THAT'S A PAST LIFE YOU SEE.
BUT ONE OF THE NUTTIEST BELIEVERS WAS TREVOR SCHALK, AND HE HAD NOTHING TO DO WITH ENTERTAINMENT.
HIS MONEY CAME FROM PLANES.
WE KEEP OUR MEMORIES FROM PAST LIVES LOCKED AWAY INSIDE THE DEEPEST PLACES OF OUR MIND.
THEY INFLUENCE WHO WE ARE WITHOUT EVER REVEALING THEMSELVES TO US.
THIS WAS 1982, BEFORE THE AVIATION INDUSTRY SHIT THE BED.
CAN YOU SEE THAT PLACE, THE PLACE WHERE THESE MEMORIES ARE LOCKED? CAN YOU SEE IT, TREVOR?

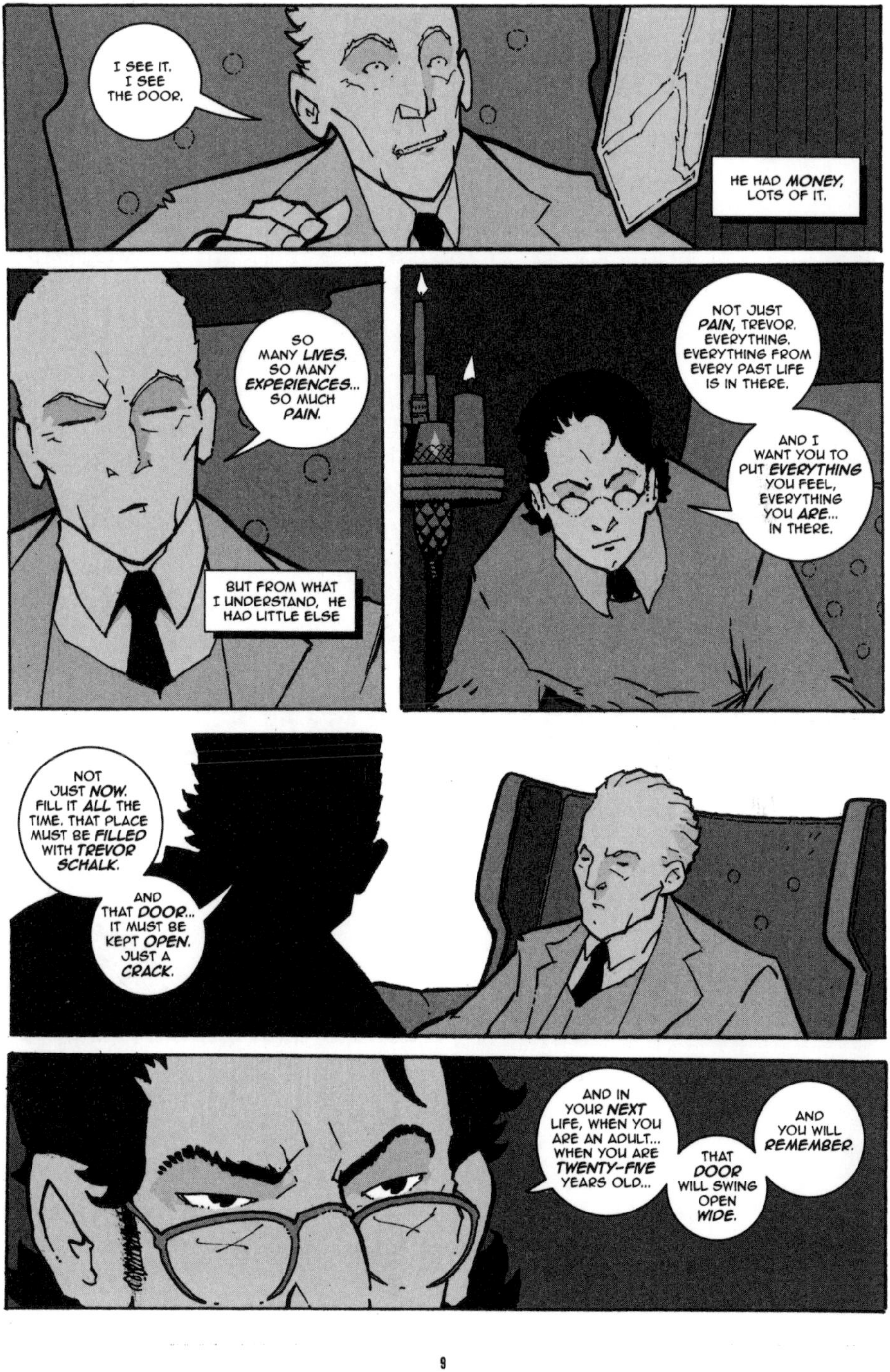

I SEE IT. I SEE THE DOOR.
HE HAD MONEY, LOTS OF IT.
SO MANY LIVES. SO MANY EXPERIENCES... SO MUCH PAIN.
BUT FROM WHAT I UNDERSTAND, HE HAD LITTLE ELSE
NOT JUST PAIN, TREVOR. EVERYTHING. EVERYTHING FROM EVERY PAST LIFE IS IN THERE.
AND I WANT YOU TO PUT EVERYTHING YOU FEEL, EVERYTHING YOU ARE... IN THERE.
NOT JUST NOW. FILL IT ALL THE TIME. THAT PLACE MUST BE FILLED WITH TREVOR SCHALK.
AND THAT DOOR... IT MUST BE KEPT OPEN. JUST A CRACK.
AND IN YOUR NEXT LIFE, WHEN YOU ARE AN ADULT... WHEN YOU ARE TWENTY-FIVE YEARS OLD...
THAT DOOR WILL SWING OPEN WIDE.
AND YOU WILL REMEMBER.

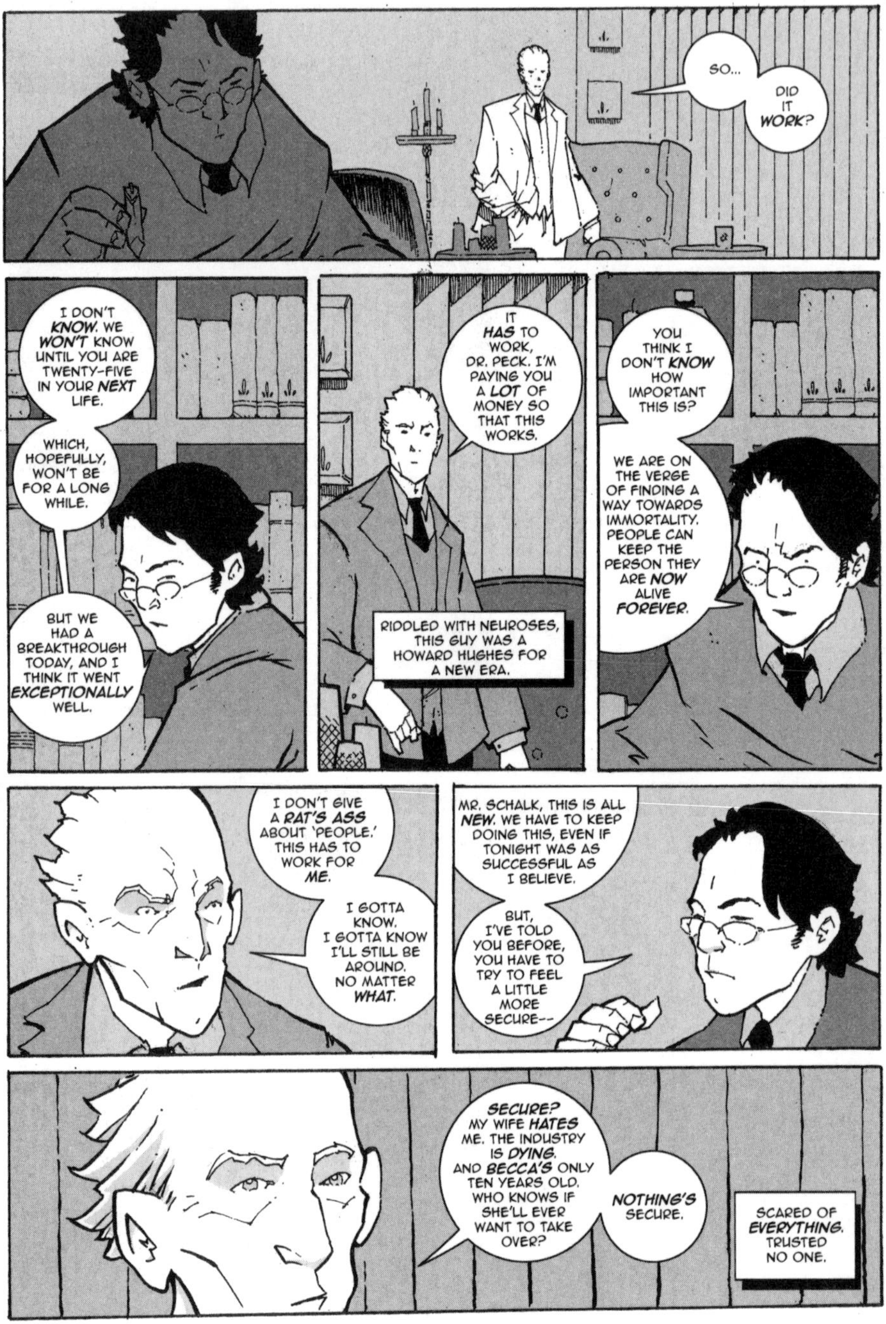

SO...
DID IT WORK?
I DON'T KNOW. WE WON'T KNOW UNTIL YOU ARE TWENTY-FIVE IN YOUR NEXT LIFE.
WHICH, HOPEFULLY, WON'T BE FOR A LONG WHILE.
BUT WE HAD A BREAKTHROUGH TODAY, AND I THINK IT WENT EXCEPTIONALLY WELL.
IT HAS TO WORK, DR. PECK. I'M PAYING YOU A LOT OF MONEY SO THAT THIS WORKS.
RIDDLED WITH NEUROSES, THIS GUY WAS A HOWARD HUGHES FOR A NEW ERA.
YOU THINK I DON'T KNOW HOW IMPORTANT THIS IS?
WE ARE ON THE VERGE OF FINDING A WAY TOWARDS IMMORTALITY. PEOPLE CAN KEEP THE PERSON THEY ARE NOW ALIVE FOREVER.
I DON'T GIVE A RAT'S ASS ABOUT 'PEOPLE.' THIS HAS TO WORK FOR ME.
I GOTTA KNOW. I GOTTA KNOW I'LL STILL BE AROUND. NO MATTER WHAT.
MR. SCHALK, THIS IS ALL NEW. WE HAVE TO KEEP DOING THIS, EVEN IF TONIGHT WAS AS SUCCESSFUL AS I BELIEVE.
BUT, I'VE TOLD YOU BEFORE, YOU HAVE TO TRY TO FEEL A LITTLE MORE SECURE--
SECURE? MY WIFE HATES ME. THE INDUSTRY IS DYING. AND BECCA'S ONLY TEN YEARS OLD. WHO KNOWS IF SHE'LL EVER WANT TO TAKE OVER?
NOTHING'S SECURE.
SCARED OF EVERYTHING. TRUSTED NO ONE.

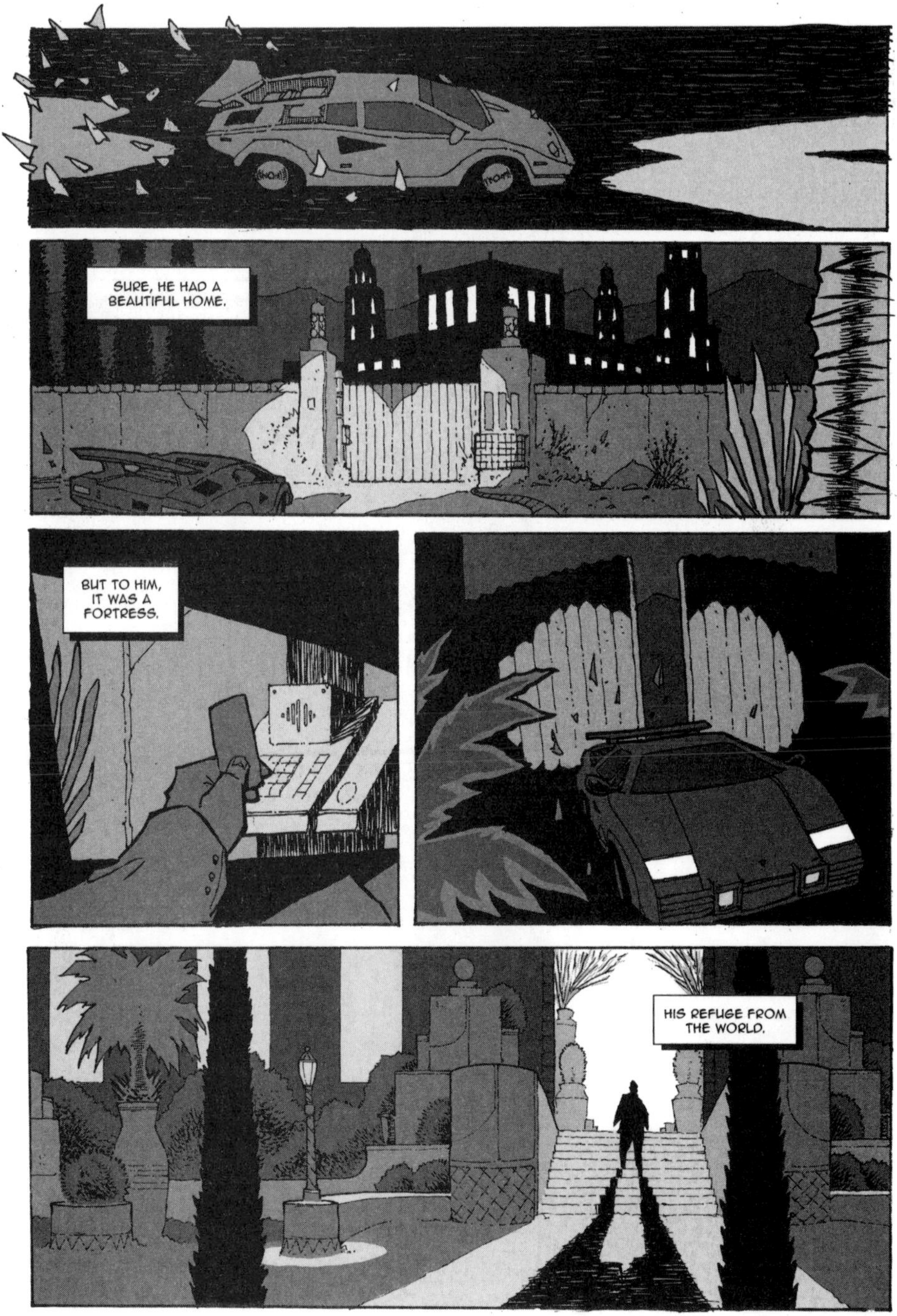
SURE, HE HAD A BEAUTIFUL HOME.
BUT TO HIM, IT WAS A FORTRESS.
HIS REFUGE FROM THE WORLD.

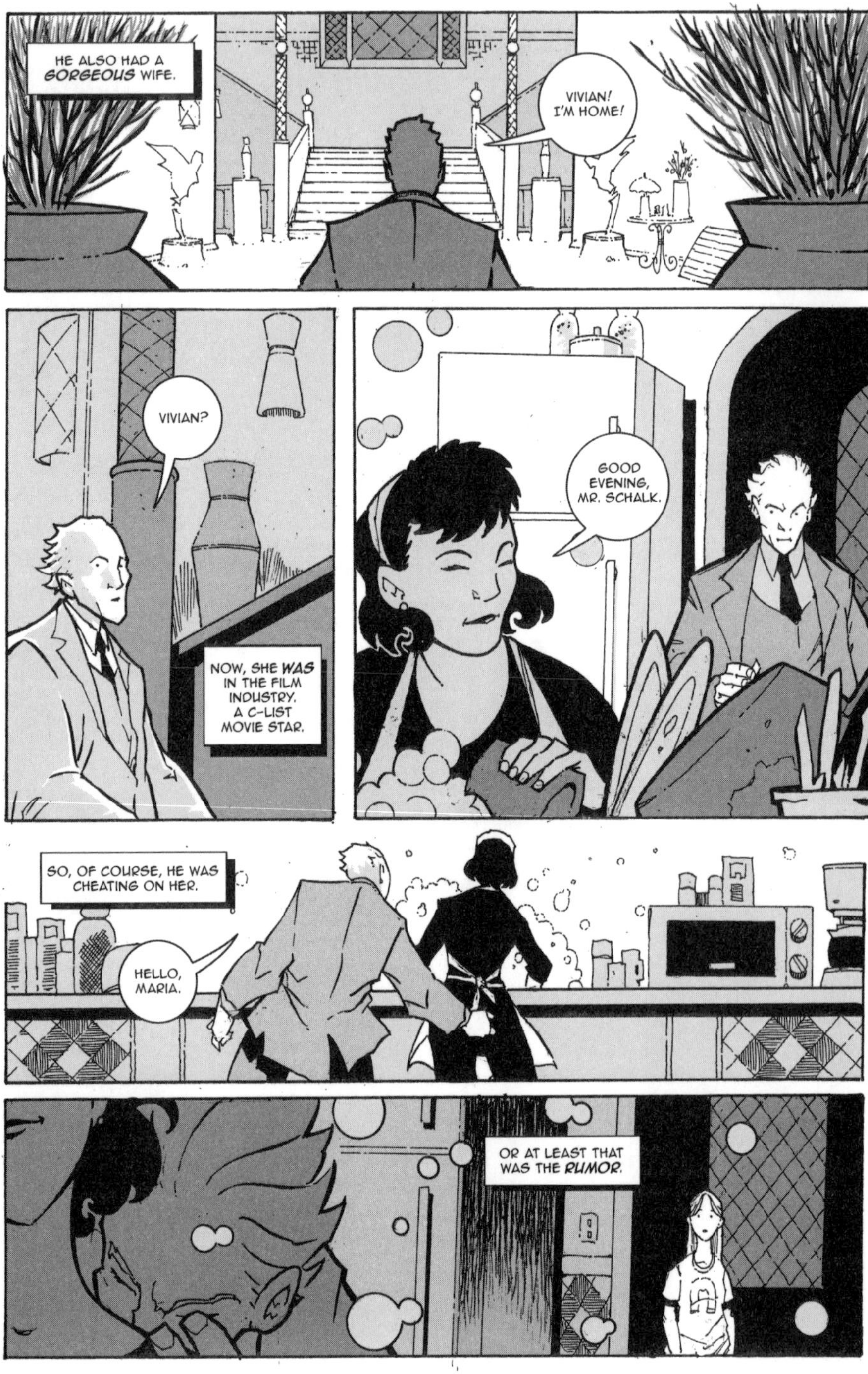
HE ALSO HAD A GORGEOUS WIFE.
VIVIAN! I'M HOME!
VIVIAN?
NOW, SHE WAS IN THE FILM INDUSTRY. A C-LIST MOVIE STAR.
GOOD EVENING, MR. SCHALK.
SO, OF COURSE, HE WAS CHEATING ON HER.
HELLO, MARIA.
OR AT LEAST THAT WAS THE RUMOR.

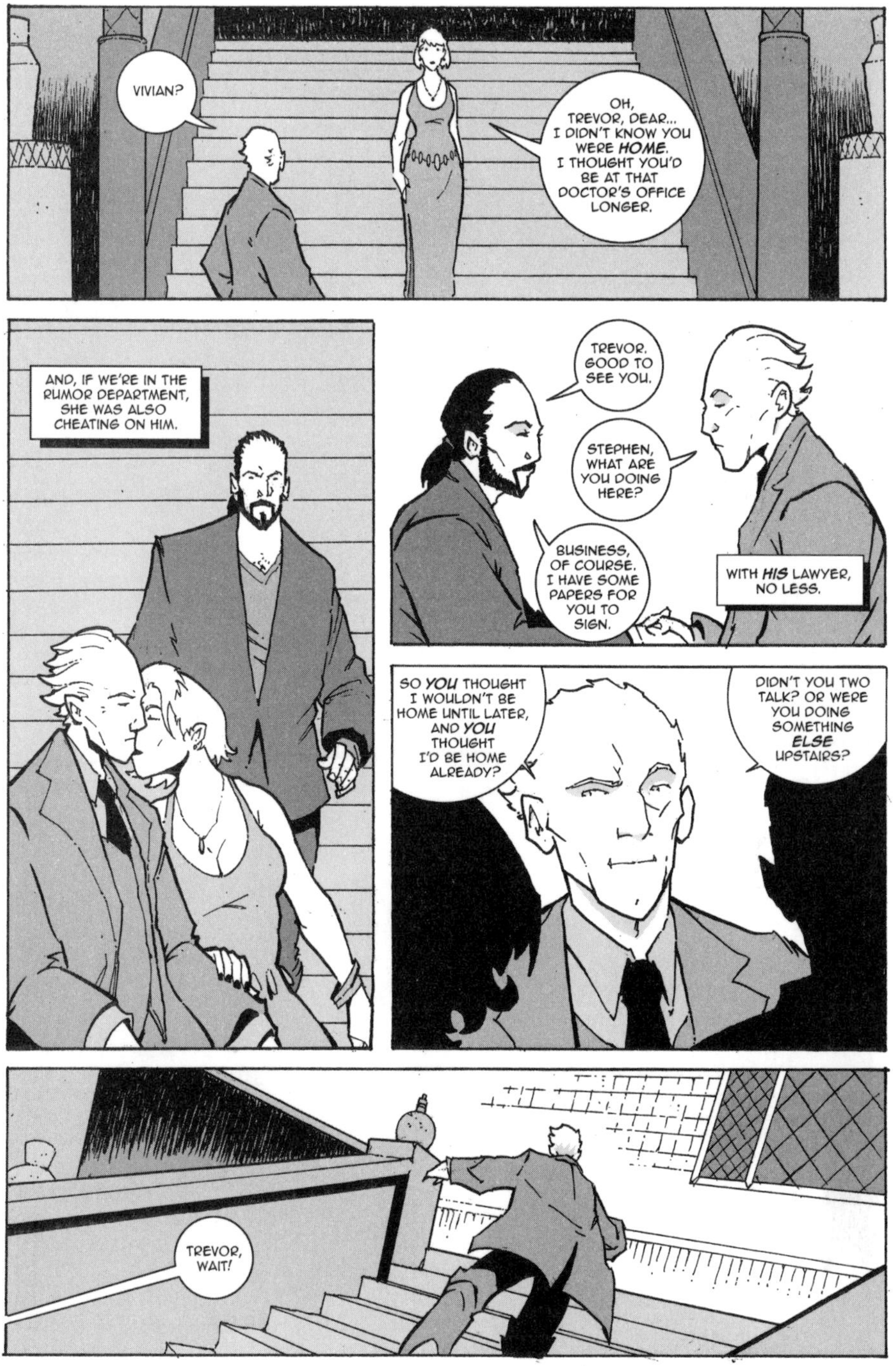
VIVIAN?
OH, TREVOR, DEAR... I DIDN'T KNOW YOU WERE HOME. I THOUGHT YOU'D BE AT THAT DOCTOR'S OFFICE LONGER.
AND, IF WE'RE IN THE RUMOR DEPARTMENT, SHE WAS ALSO CHEATING ON HIM.
TREVOR. GOOD TO SEE YOU.
STEPHEN, WHAT ARE YOU DOING HERE?
BUSINESS, OF COURSE. I HAVE SOME PAPERS FOR YOU TO SIGN.
WITH HIS LAWYER, NO LESS.
SO YOU THOUGHT I WOULDN'T BE HOME UNTIL LATER, AND YOU THOUGHT I'D BE HOME ALREADY?
DIDN'T YOU TWO TALK? OR WERE YOU DOING SOMETHING ELSE UPSTAIRS?
TREVOR, WAIT!

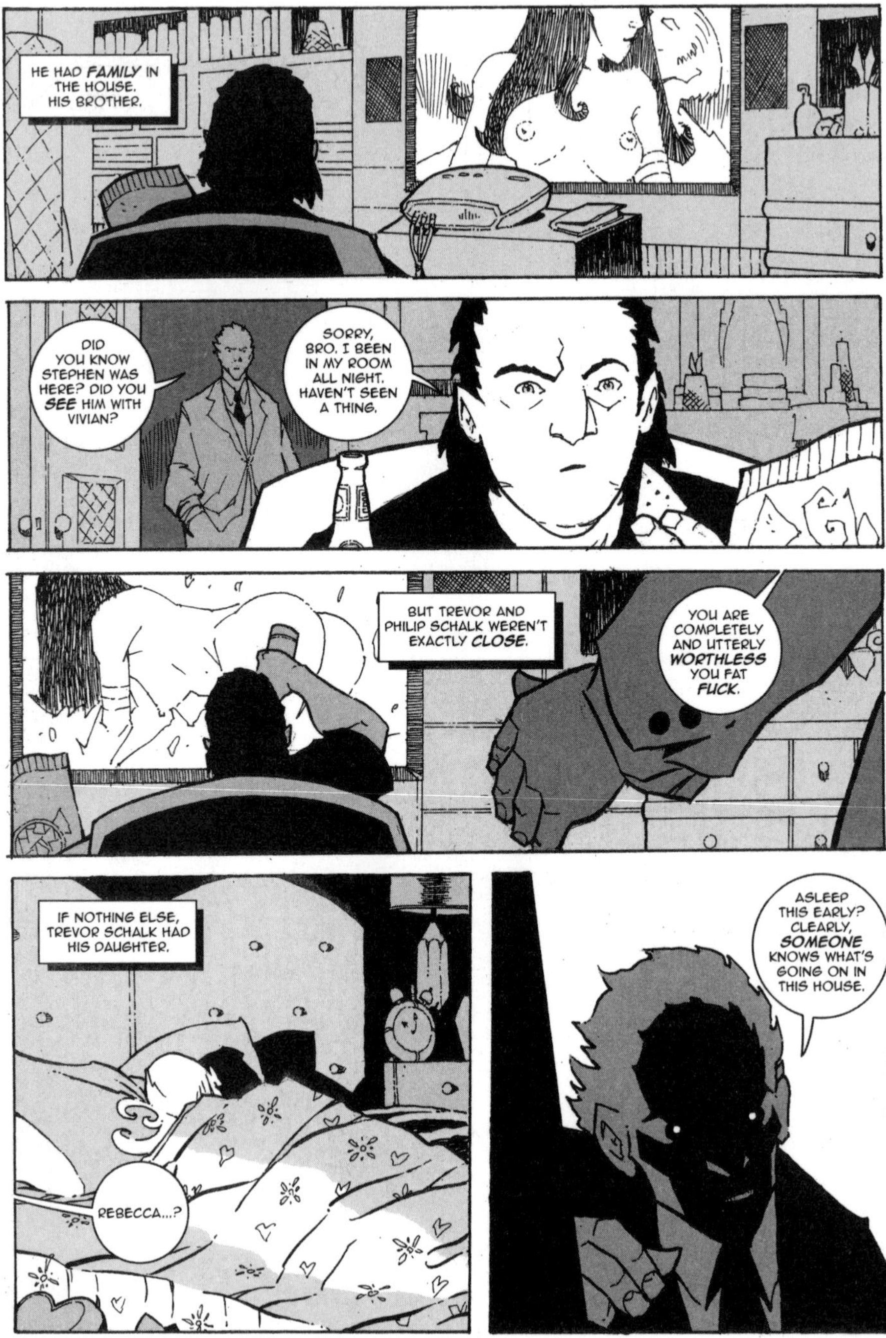
HE HAD FAMILY IN THE HOUSE. HIS BROTHER.
DID YOU KNOW STEPHEN WAS HERE? DID YOU SEE HIM WITH VIVIAN?
SORRY, BRO. I BEEN IN MY ROOM ALL NIGHT. HAVEN'T SEEN A THING.
BUT TREVOR AND PHILIP SCHALK WEREN'T EXACTLY CLOSE.
YOU ARE COMPLETELY AND UTTERLY WORTHLESS YOU FAT FUCK.
IF NOTHING ELSE, TREVOR SCHALK HAD HIS DAUGHTER.
REBECCA...?
ASLEEP THIS EARLY? CLEARLY, SOMEONE KNOWS WHAT'S GOING ON IN THIS HOUSE.

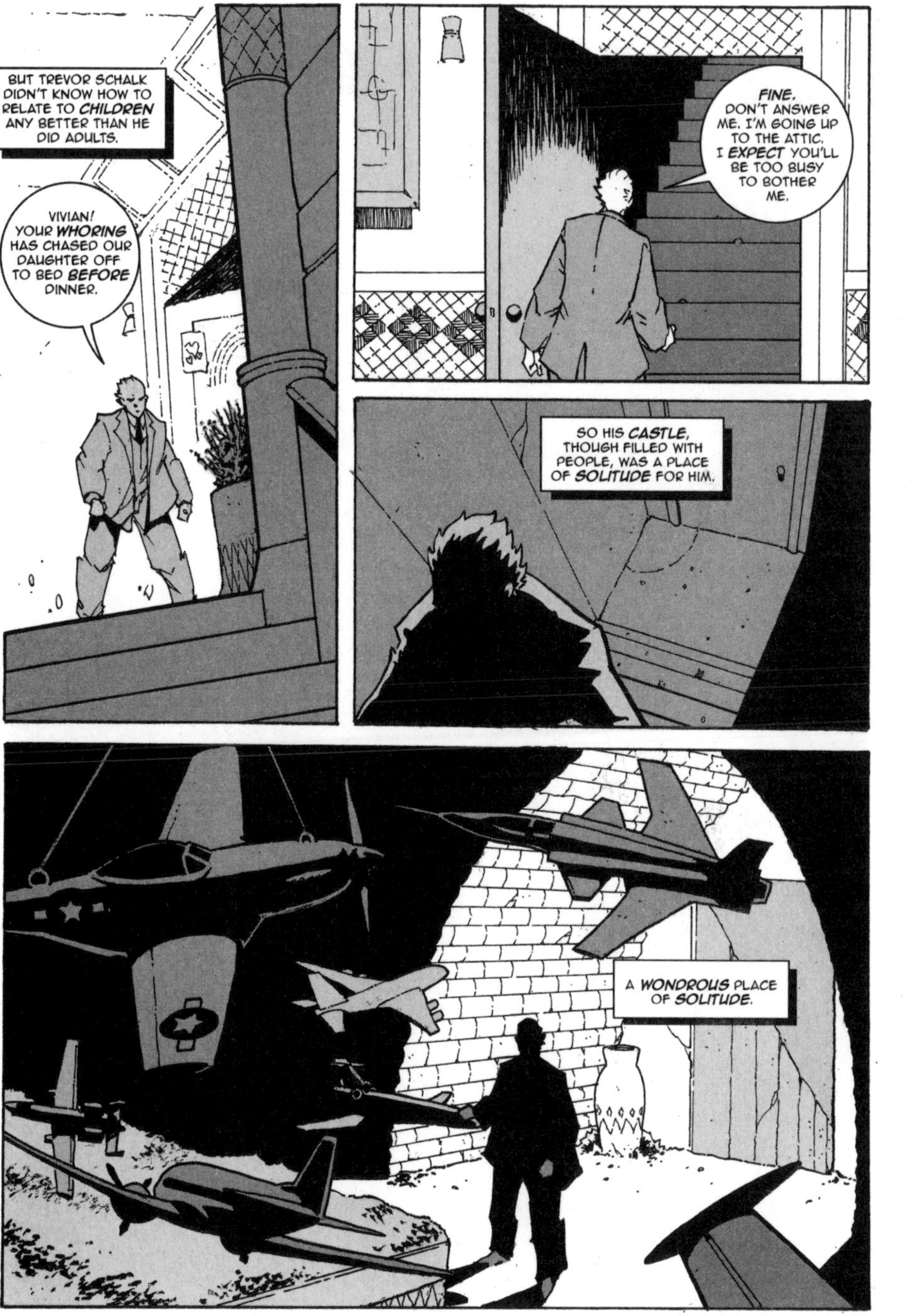
BUT TREVOR SCHALK DIDN'T KNOW HOW TO RELATE TO CHILDREN ANY BETTER THAN HE DID ADULTS.
VIVIAN! YOUR WHORING HAS CHASED OUR DAUGHTER OFF TO BED BEFORE DINNER.
FINE. DON'T ANSWER ME. I'M GOING UP TO THE ATTIC. I EXPECT YOU'LL BE TOO BUSY TO BOTHER ME.
SO HIS CASTLE, THOUGH FILLED WITH PEOPLE, WAS A PLACE OF SOLITUDE FOR HIM.
A WONDROUS PLACE OF SOLITUDE.

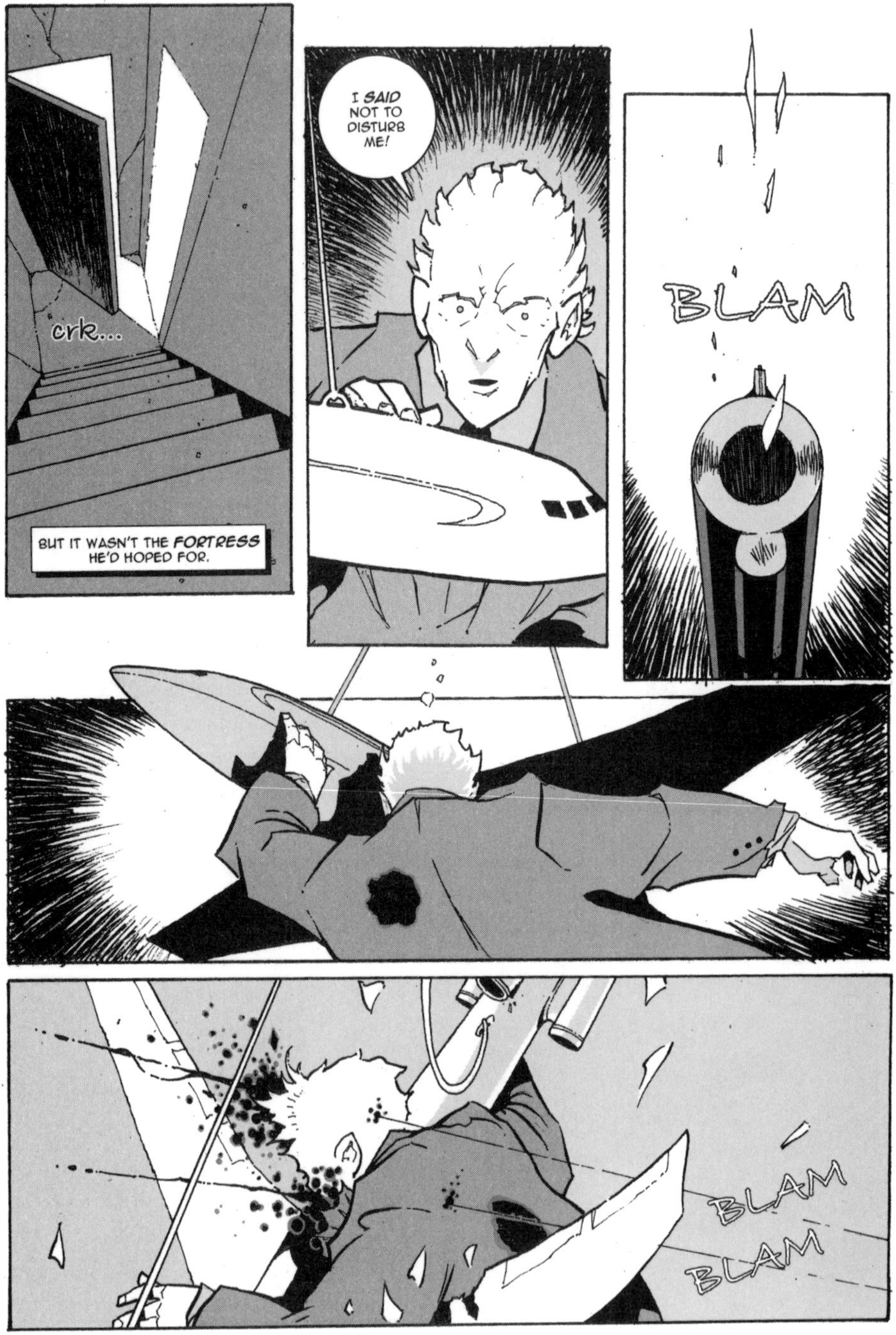
crk...
BUT IT WASN'T THE FORTRESS HE'D HOPED FOR.
I SAID NOT TO DISTURB ME!
BLAM
BLAM
BLAM

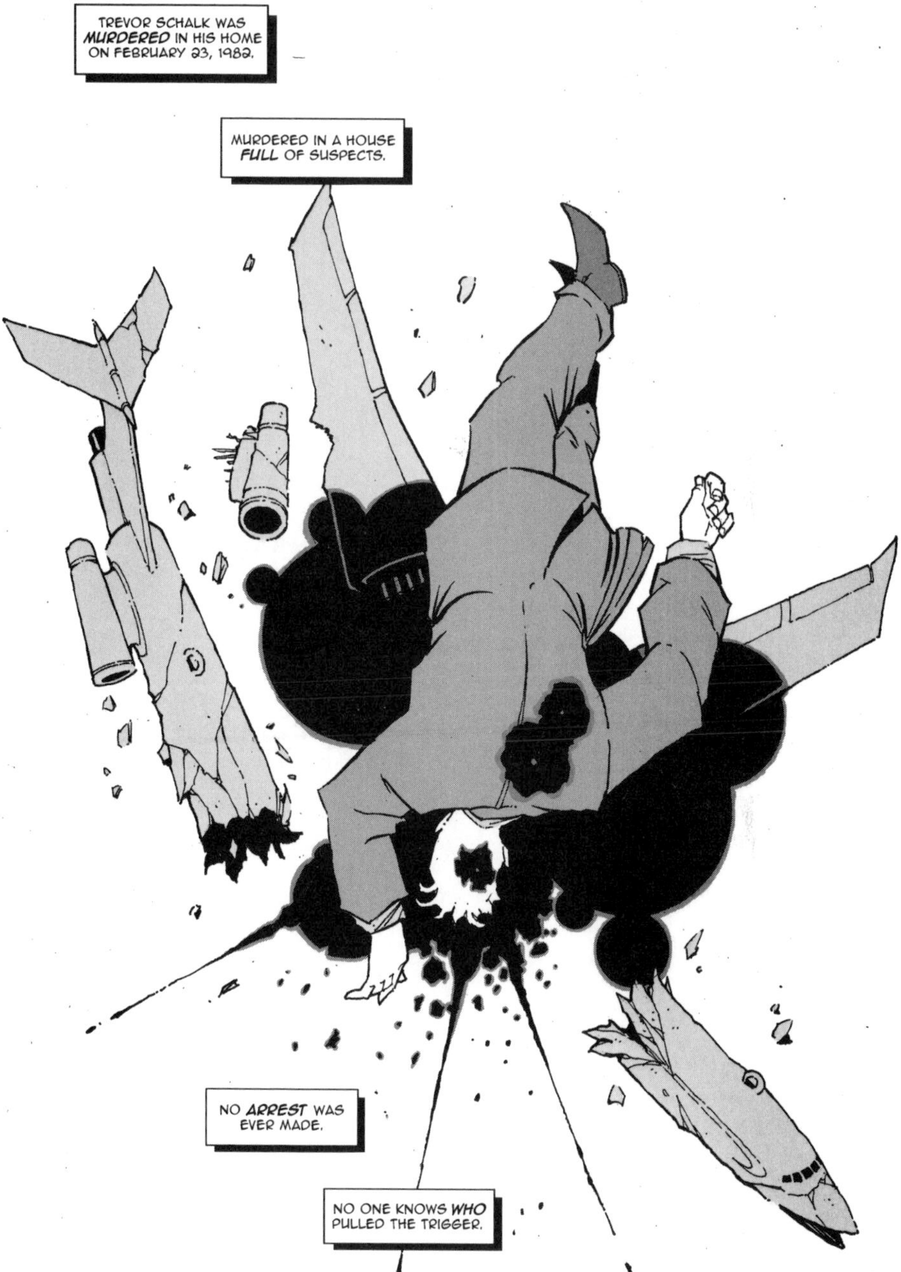
TREVOR SCHALK WAS MURDERED IN HIS HOME ON FEBRUARY 23, 1982.
MURDERED IN A HOUSE FULL OF SUSPECTS.
NO ARREST WAS EVER MADE.
NO ONE KNOWS WHO PULLED THE TRIGGER.

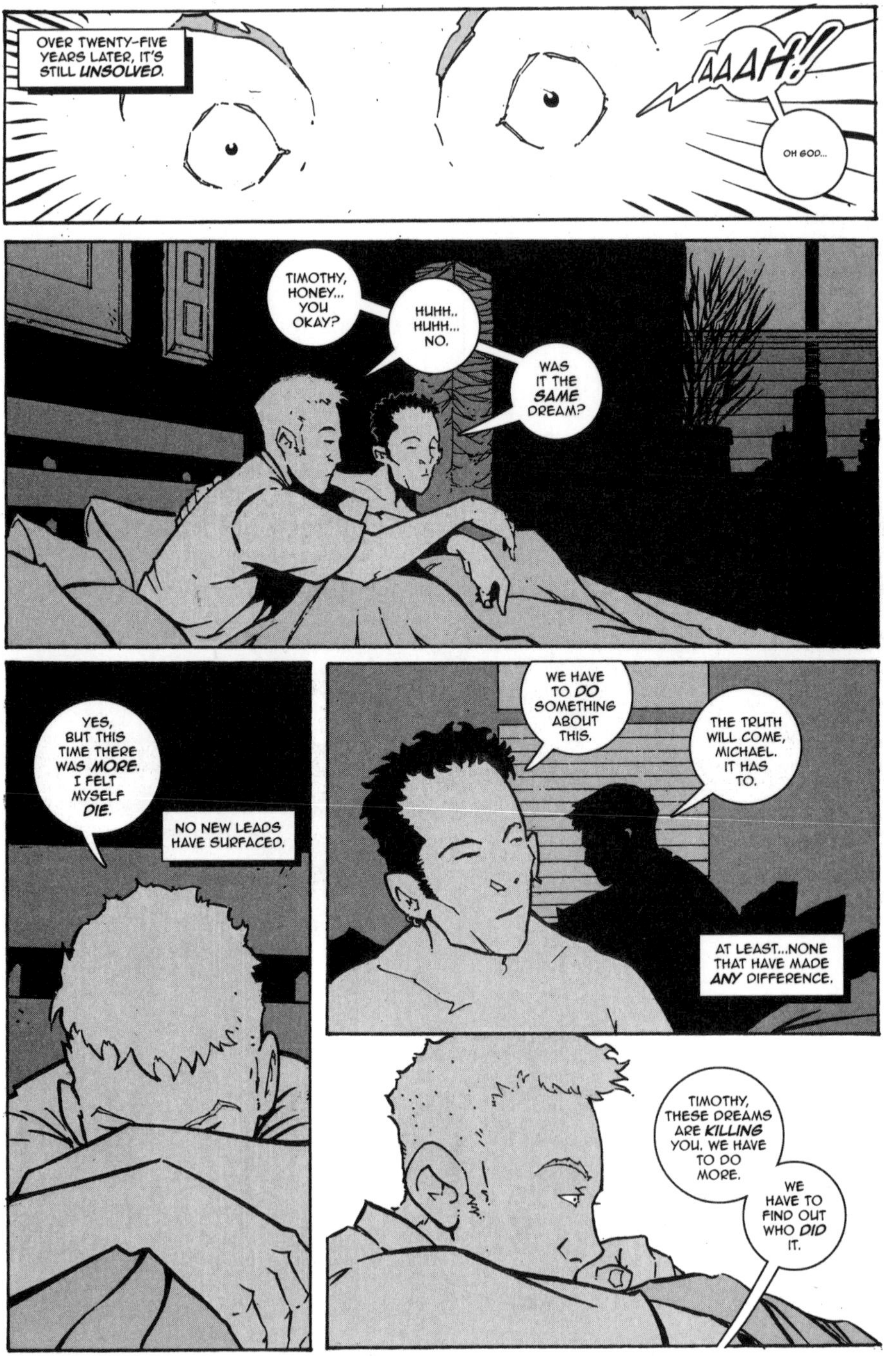
OVER TWENTY-FIVE YEARS LATER, IT'S STILL UNSOLVED.
AAAH!!
OH GOD...
TIMOTHY, HONEY... YOU OKAY?
HUHH.. HUHH... NO.
WAS IT THE SAME DREAM?
YES, BUT THIS TIME THERE WAS MORE. I FELT MYSELF DIE.
NO NEW LEADS HAVE SURFACED.
WE HAVE TO DO SOMETHING ABOUT THIS.
THE TRUTH WILL COME, MICHAEL. IT HAS TO.
AT LEAST...NONE THAT HAVE MADE ANY DIFFERENCE.
TIMOTHY, THESE DREAMS ARE KILLING YOU. WE HAVE TO DO MORE.
WE HAVE TO FIND OUT WHO DID IT.

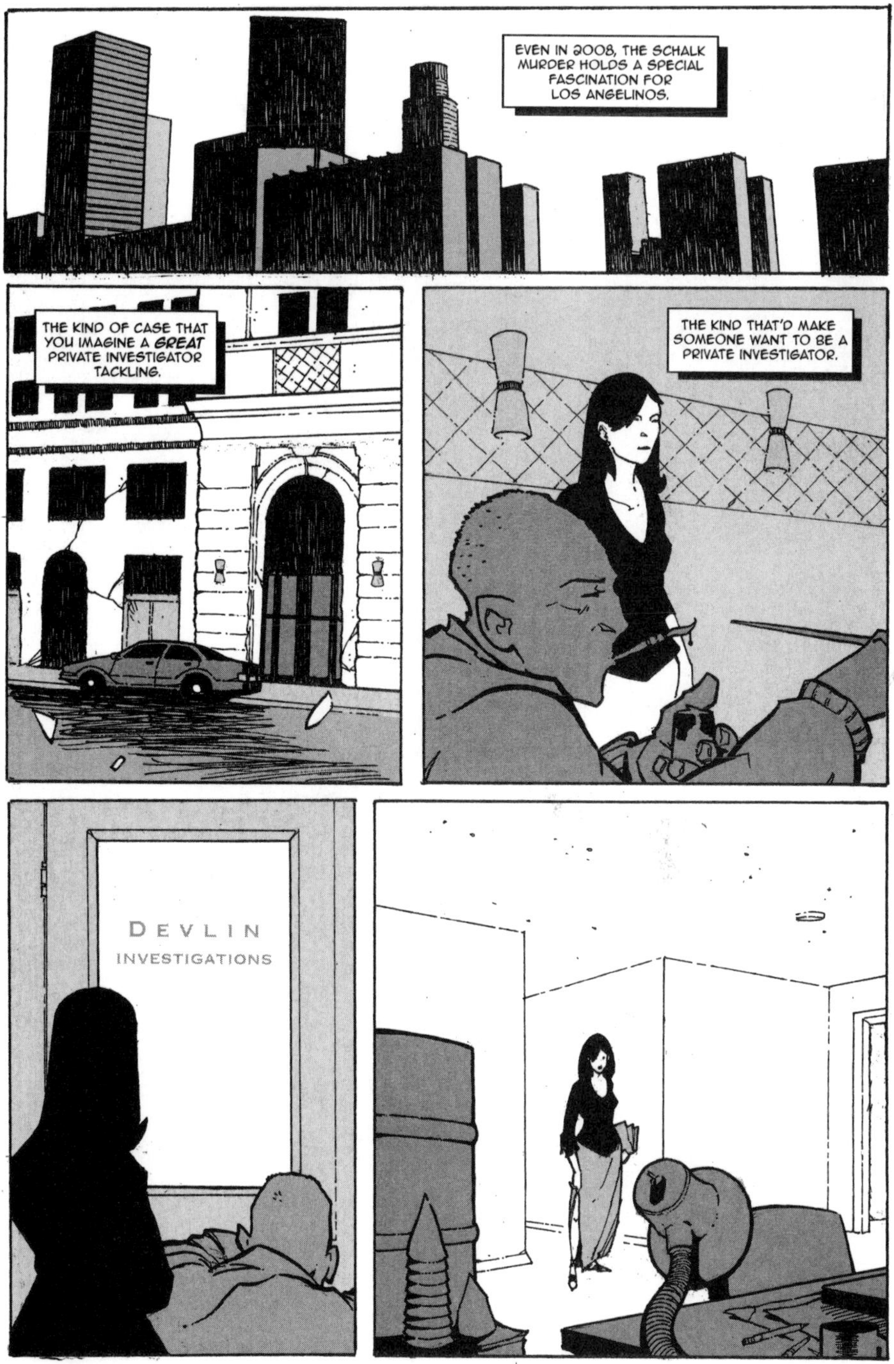
EVEN IN 2008, THE SCHALK MURDER HOLDS A SPECIAL FASCINATION FOR LOS ANGELINOS.
THE KIND OF CASE THAT YOU IMAGINE A GREAT PRIVATE INVESTIGATOR TACKLING.
THE KIND THAT'D MAKE SOMEONE WANT TO BE A PRIVATE INVESTIGATOR.
DEVLIN INVESTIGATIONS

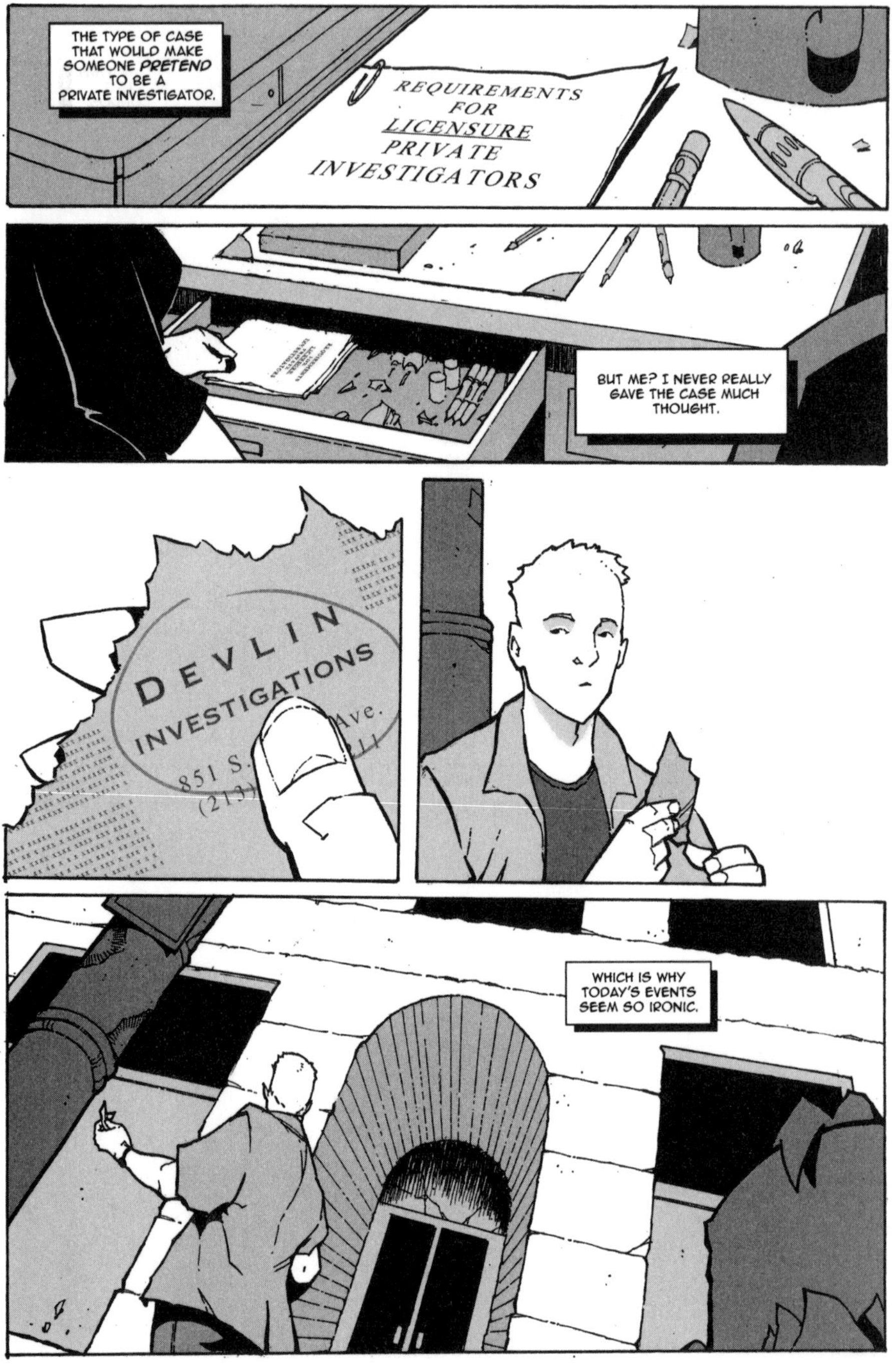
THE TYPE OF CASE THAT WOULD MAKE SOMEONE PRETEND TO BE A PRIVATE INVESTIGATOR.
REQUIREMENTS FOR LICENSURE PRIVATE INVESTIGATORS
BUT ME? I NEVER REALLY GAVE THE CASE MUCH THOUGHT.
DEVLIN INVESTIGATIONS
851 S. Ave.
(213)
WHICH IS WHY TODAY'S EVENTS SEEM SO IRONIC.

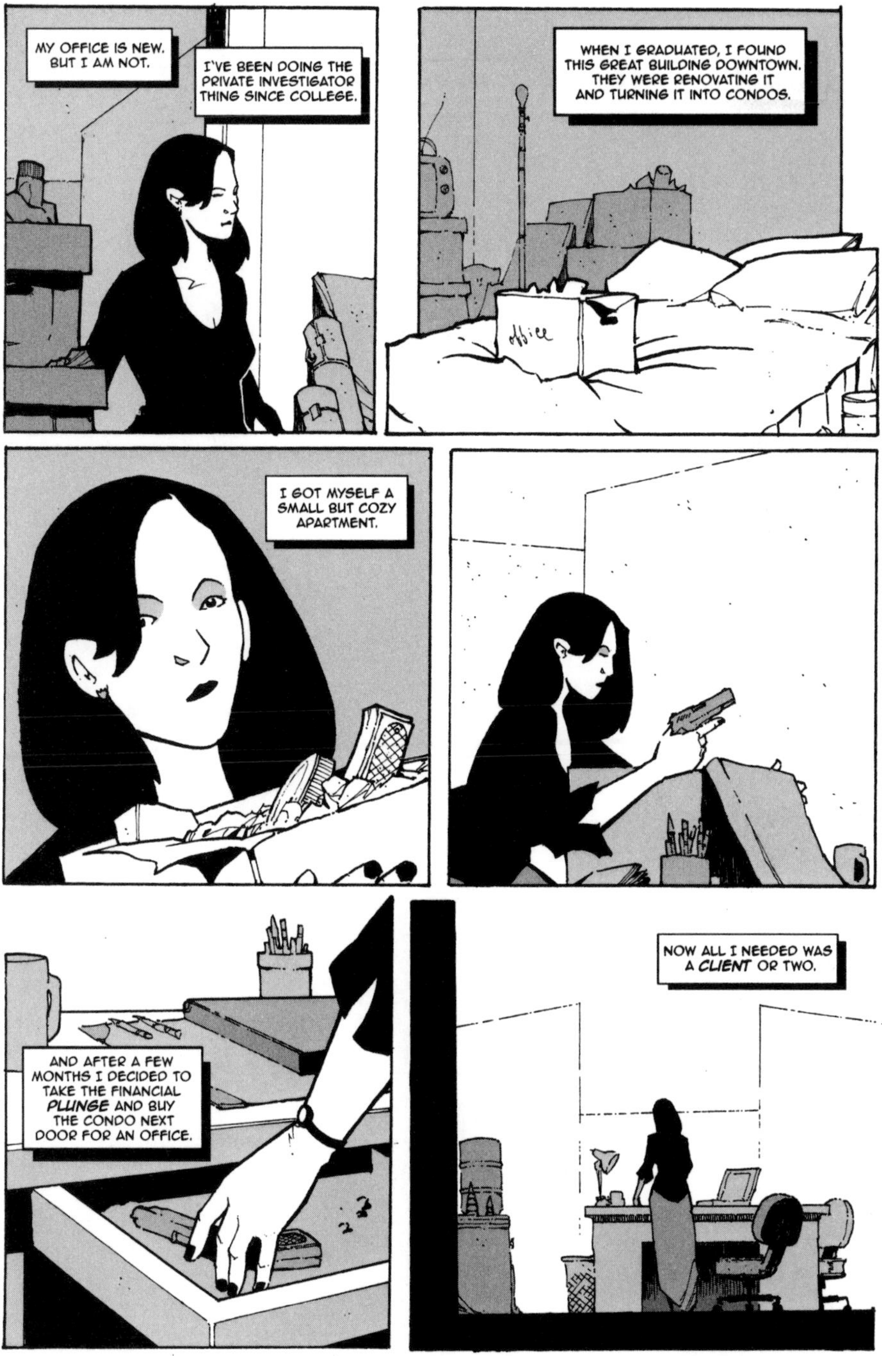
MY OFFICE IS NEW. BUT I AM NOT.
I'VE BEEN DOING THE PRIVATE INVESTIGATOR THING SINCE COLLEGE.
WHEN I GRADUATED, I FOUND THIS GREAT BUILDING DOWNTOWN. THEY WERE RENOVATING IT AND TURNING IT INTO CONDOS.
office
I GOT MYSELF A SMALL BUT COZY APARTMENT.
AND AFTER A FEW MONTHS I DECIDED TO TAKE THE FINANCIAL PLUNGE AND BUY THE CONDO NEXT DOOR FOR AN OFFICE.
NOW ALL I NEEDED WAS A CLIENT OR TWO.

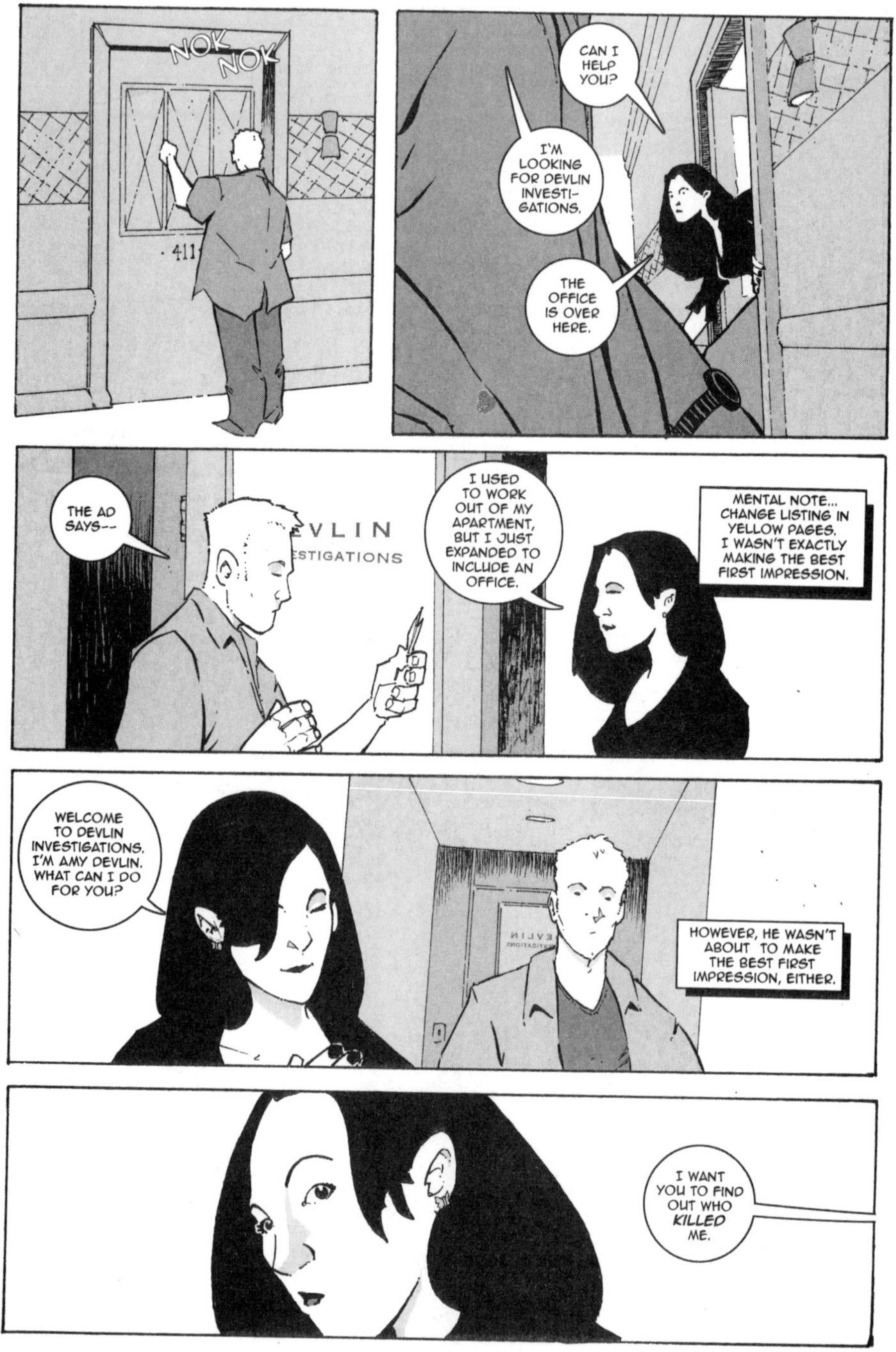
NOK NOK
CAN I HELP YOU?
I'M LOOKING FOR DEVLIN INVESTI-GATIONS.
THE OFFICE IS OVER HERE.
THE AD SAYS--
I USED TO WORK OUT OF MY APARTMENT, BUT I JUST EXPANDED TO INCLUDE AN OFFICE.
MENTAL NOTE... CHANGE LISTING IN YELLOW PAGES. I WASN'T EXACTLY MAKING THE BEST FIRST IMPRESSION.
WELCOME TO DEVLIN INVESTIGATIONS. I'M AMY DEVLIN. WHAT CAN I DO FOR YOU?
HOWEVER, HE WASN'T ABOUT TO MAKE THE BEST FIRST IMPRESSION, EITHER.
I WANT YOU TO FIND OUT WHO *KILLED* ME.

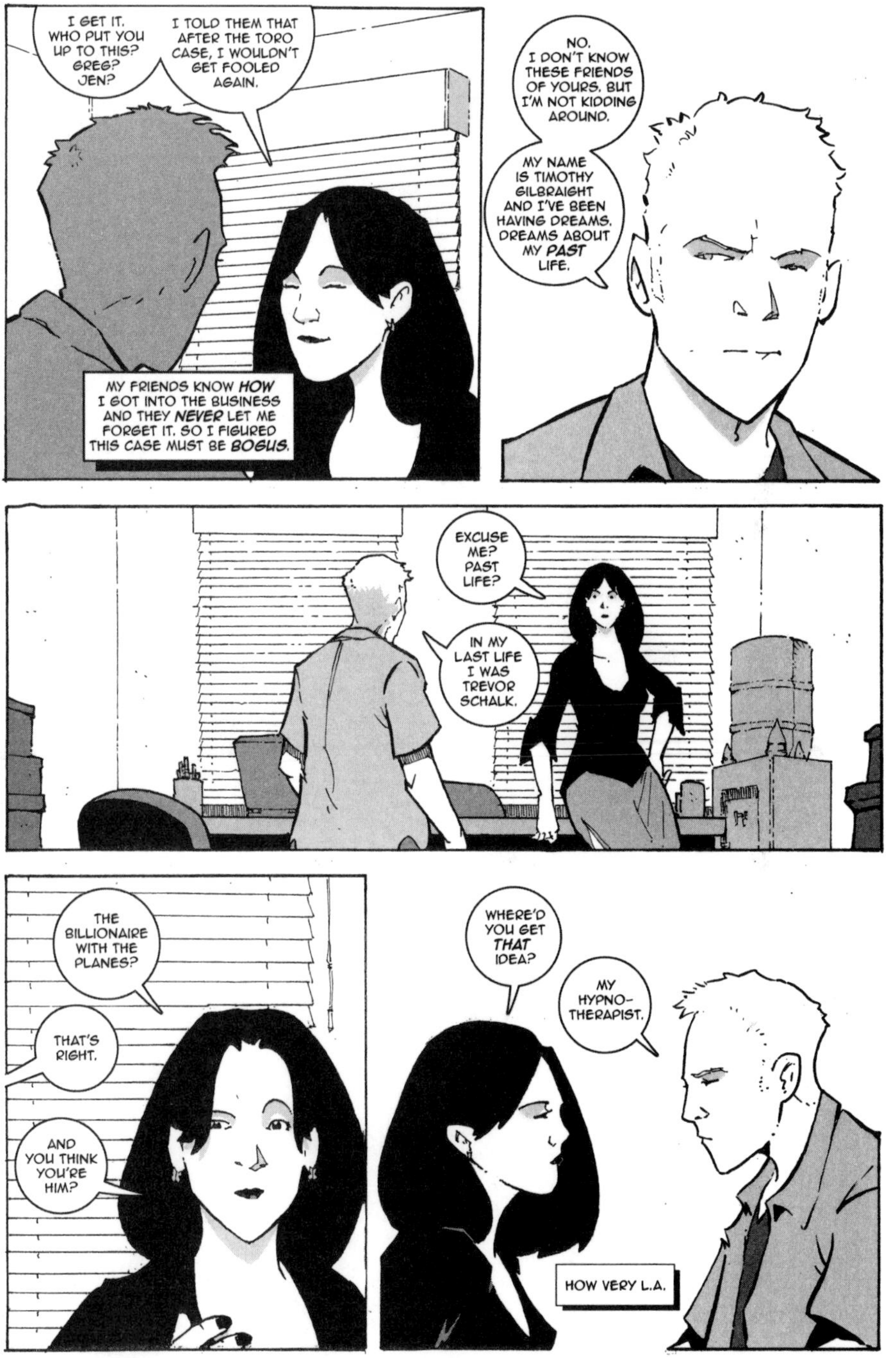
I GET IT. WHO PUT YOU UP TO THIS? GREG? JEN?
I TOLD THEM THAT AFTER THE TORO CASE, I WOULDN'T GET FOOLED AGAIN.
MY FRIENDS KNOW HOW I GOT INTO THE BUSINESS AND THEY NEVER LET ME FORGET IT. SO I FIGURED THIS CASE MUST BE BOGUS.
NO. I DON'T KNOW THESE FRIENDS OF YOURS. BUT I'M NOT KIDDING AROUND.
MY NAME IS TIMOTHY GILBRAIGHT AND I'VE BEEN HAVING DREAMS. DREAMS ABOUT MY PAST LIFE.
EXCUSE ME? PAST LIFE?
IN MY LAST LIFE I WAS TREVOR SCHALK.
THE BILLIONAIRE WITH THE PLANES?
THAT'S RIGHT.
AND YOU THINK YOU'RE HIM?
WHERE'D YOU GET THAT IDEA?
MY HYPNO-THERAPIST.
HOW VERY L.A.

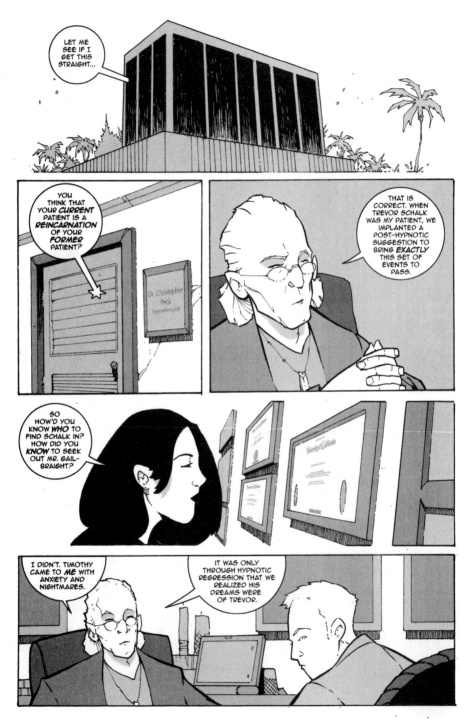

LET ME SEE IF I GET THIS STRAIGHT...

YOU THINK THAT YOUR *CURRENT* PATIENT IS A *REINCARNATION* OF YOUR *FORMER* PATIENT?

Dr. Christopher Peck
hypnotherapist

THAT IS CORRECT. WHEN TREVOR SCHALK WAS MY PATIENT, WE IMPLANTED A POST-HYPNOTIC SUGGESTION TO BRING *EXACTLY* THIS SET OF EVENTS TO PASS.

SO HOW'D YOU KNOW *WHO* TO FIND SCHALK IN? HOW DID YOU *KNOW* TO SEEK OUT MR. GAIL-BRAIGHT?

I DIDN'T. TIMOTHY CAME TO *ME* WITH ANXIETY AND NIGHTMARES.

IT WAS ONLY THROUGH HYPNOTIC REGRESSION THAT WE REALIZED HIS DREAMS WERE OF TREVOR.

24

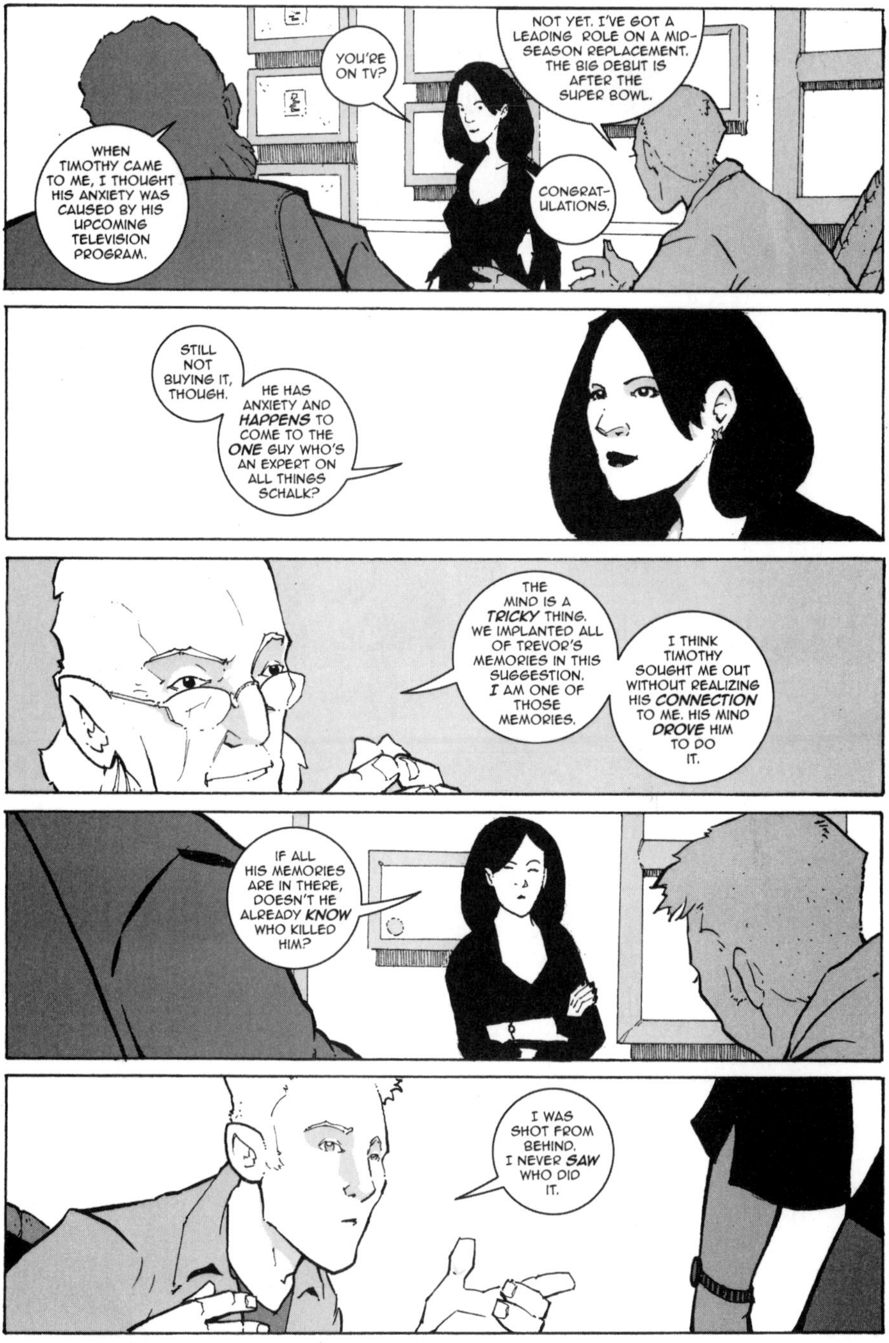
WHEN TIMOTHY CAME TO ME, I THOUGHT HIS ANXIETY WAS CAUSED BY HIS UPCOMING TELEVISION PROGRAM.
YOU'RE ON TV?
NOT YET. I'VE GOT A LEADING ROLE ON A MID-SEASON REPLACEMENT. THE BIG DEBUT IS AFTER THE SUPER BOWL.
CONGRAT-ULATIONS.
STILL NOT BUYING IT, THOUGH.
HE HAS ANXIETY AND HAPPENS TO COME TO THE ONE GUY WHO'S AN EXPERT ON ALL THINGS SCHALK?
THE MIND IS A TRICKY THING. WE IMPLANTED ALL OF TREVOR'S MEMORIES IN THIS SUGGESTION. I AM ONE OF THOSE MEMORIES.
I THINK TIMOTHY SOUGHT ME OUT WITHOUT REALIZING HIS CONNECTION TO ME. HIS MIND DROVE HIM TO DO IT.
IF ALL HIS MEMORIES ARE IN THERE, DOESN'T HE ALREADY KNOW WHO KILLED HIM?
I WAS SHOT FROM BEHIND. I NEVER SAW WHO DID IT.

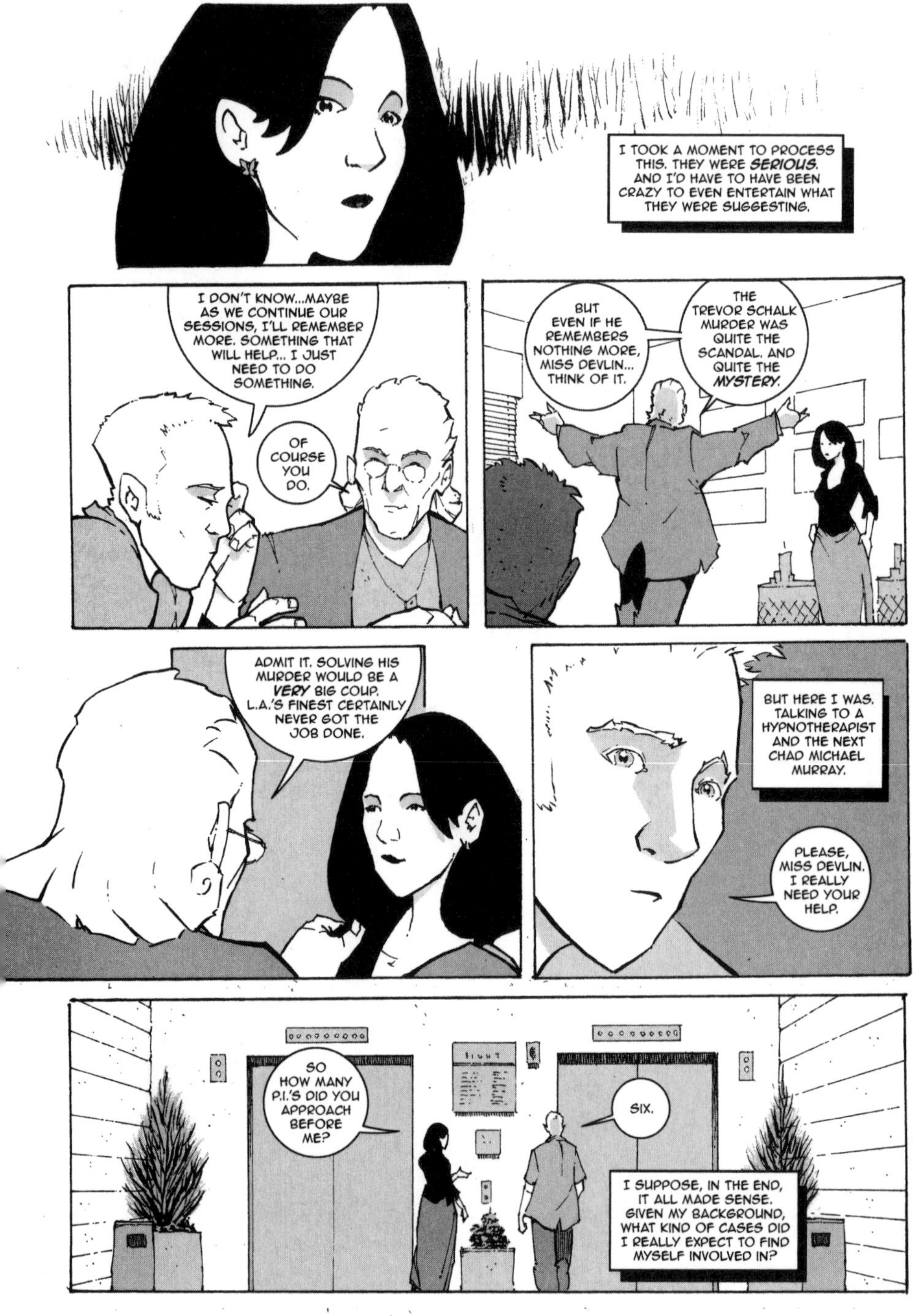
I TOOK A MOMENT TO PROCESS THIS. THEY WERE SERIOUS. AND I'D HAVE TO HAVE BEEN CRAZY TO EVEN ENTERTAIN WHAT THEY WERE SUGGESTING.
I DON'T KNOW...MAYBE AS WE CONTINUE OUR SESSIONS, I'LL REMEMBER MORE. SOMETHING THAT WILL HELP... I JUST NEED TO DO SOMETHING.
OF COURSE YOU DO.
THE TREVOR SCHALK MURDER WAS QUITE THE SCANDAL. AND QUITE THE MYSTERY.
BUT EVEN IF HE REMEMBERS NOTHING MORE, MISS DEVLIN... THINK OF IT.
ADMIT IT. SOLVING HIS MURDER WOULD BE A VERY BIG COUP. L.A.'S FINEST CERTAINLY NEVER GOT THE JOB DONE.
BUT HERE I WAS. TALKING TO A HYPNOTHERAPIST AND THE NEXT CHAD MICHAEL MURRAY.
PLEASE, MISS DEVLIN. I REALLY NEED YOUR HELP.
SO HOW MANY P.I.'S DID YOU APPROACH BEFORE ME?
SIX.
I SUPPOSE, IN THE END, IT ALL MADE SENSE. GIVEN MY BACKGROUND, WHAT KIND OF CASES DID I REALLY EXPECT TO FIND MYSELF INVOLVED IN?

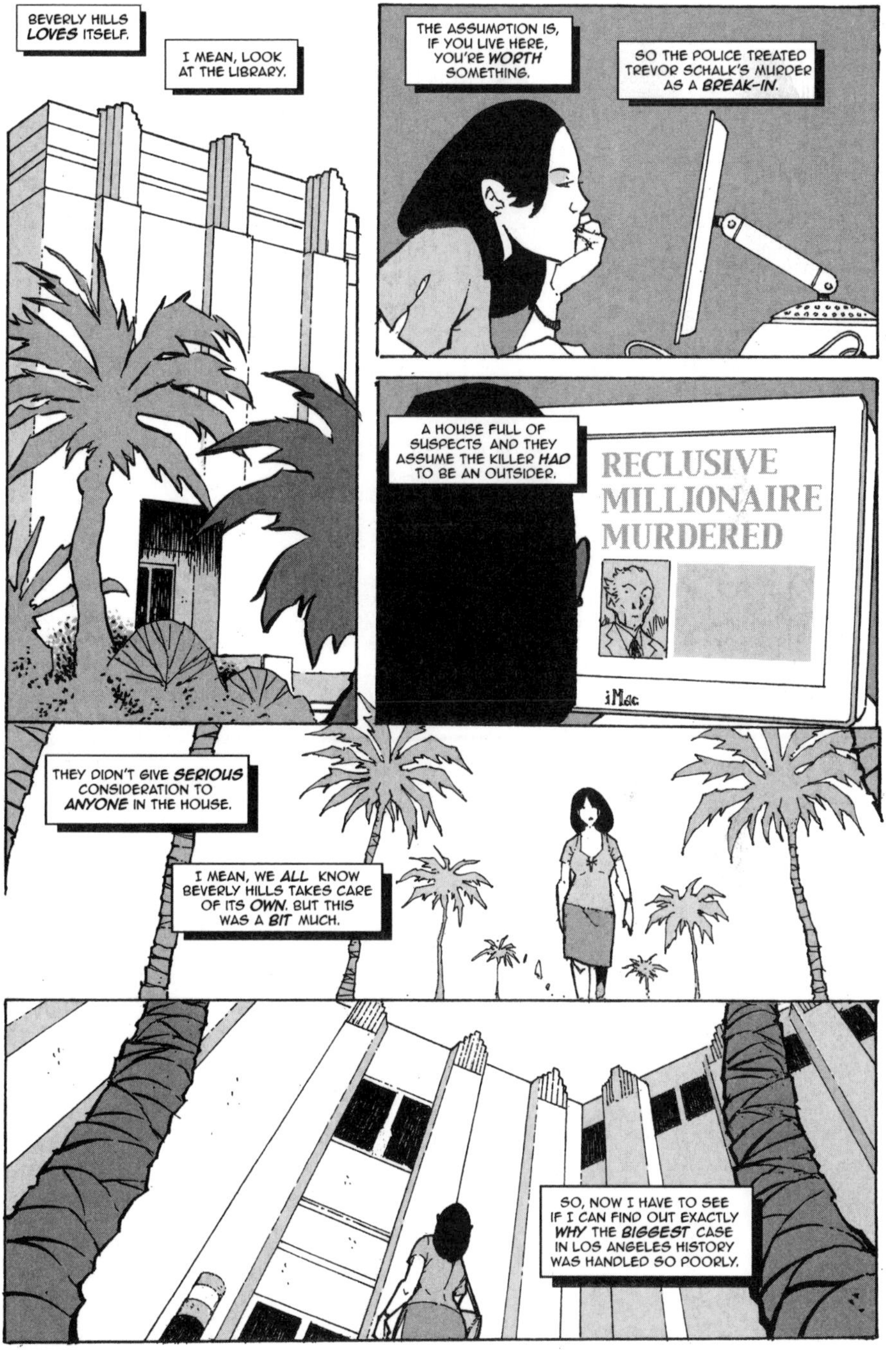
BEVERLY HILLS LOVES ITSELF.
I MEAN, LOOK AT THE LIBRARY.
THE ASSUMPTION IS, IF YOU LIVE HERE, YOU'RE WORTH SOMETHING.
SO THE POLICE TREATED TREVOR SCHALK'S MURDER AS A BREAK-IN.
A HOUSE FULL OF SUSPECTS AND THEY ASSUME THE KILLER HAD TO BE AN OUTSIDER.
RECLUSIVE MILLIONAIRE MURDERED
iMac
THEY DIDN'T GIVE SERIOUS CONSIDERATION TO ANYONE IN THE HOUSE.
I MEAN, WE ALL KNOW BEVERLY HILLS TAKES CARE OF ITS OWN. BUT THIS WAS A BIT MUCH.
SO, NOW I HAVE TO SEE IF I CAN FIND OUT EXACTLY WHY THE BIGGEST CASE IN LOS ANGELES HISTORY WAS HANDLED SO POORLY.

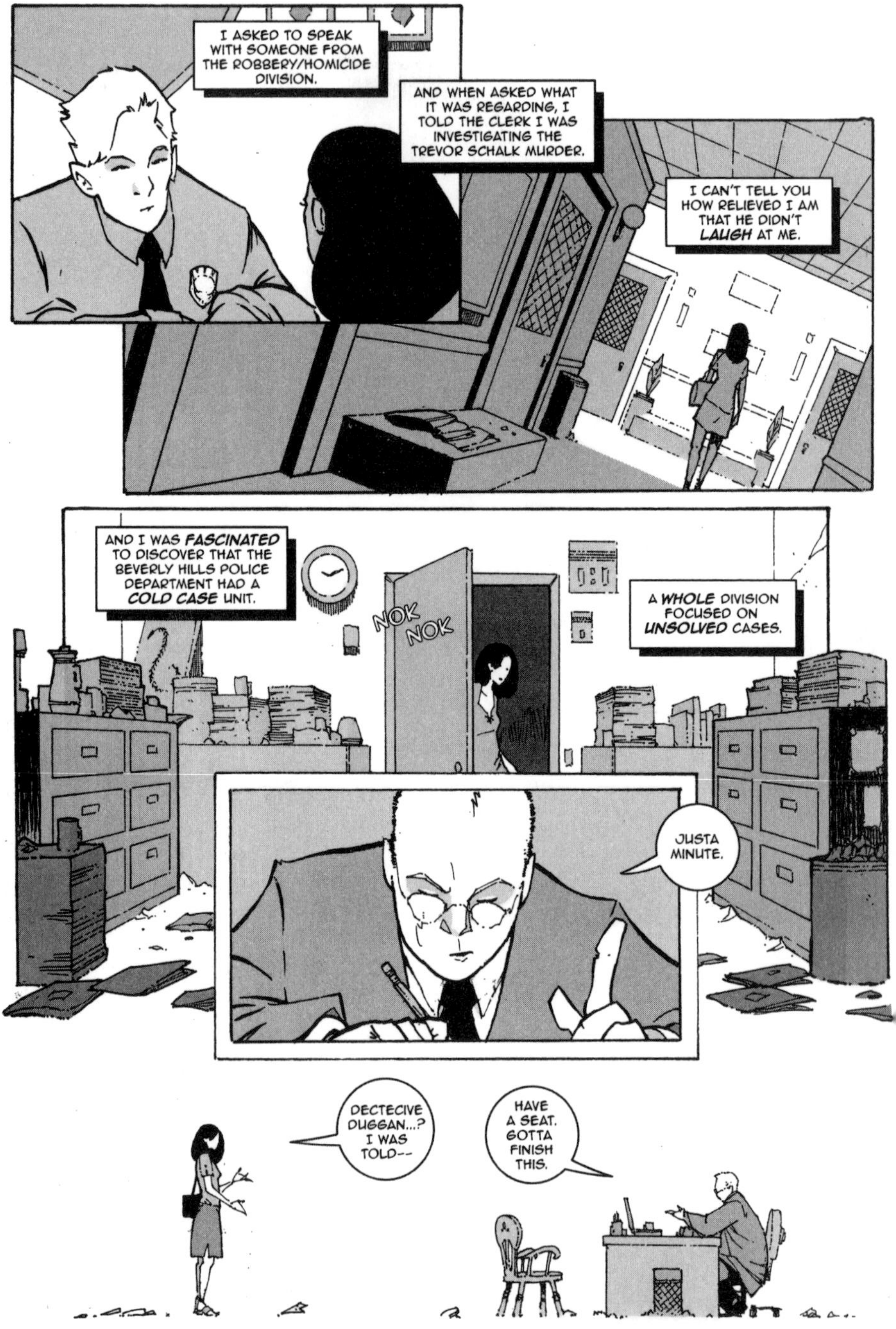
I ASKED TO SPEAK WITH SOMEONE FROM THE ROBBERY/HOMICIDE DIVISION.
AND WHEN ASKED WHAT IT WAS REGARDING, I TOLD THE CLERK I WAS INVESTIGATING THE TREVOR SCHALK MURDER.
I CAN'T TELL YOU HOW RELIEVED I AM THAT HE DIDN'T LAUGH AT ME.
AND I WAS FASCINATED TO DISCOVER THAT THE BEVERLY HILLS POLICE DEPARTMENT HAD A COLD CASE UNIT.
NOK NOK
A WHOLE DIVISION FOCUSED ON UNSOLVED CASES.
JUSTA MINUTE.
DECTECIVE DUGGAN...? I WAS TOLD--
HAVE A SEAT. GOTTA FINISH THIS.

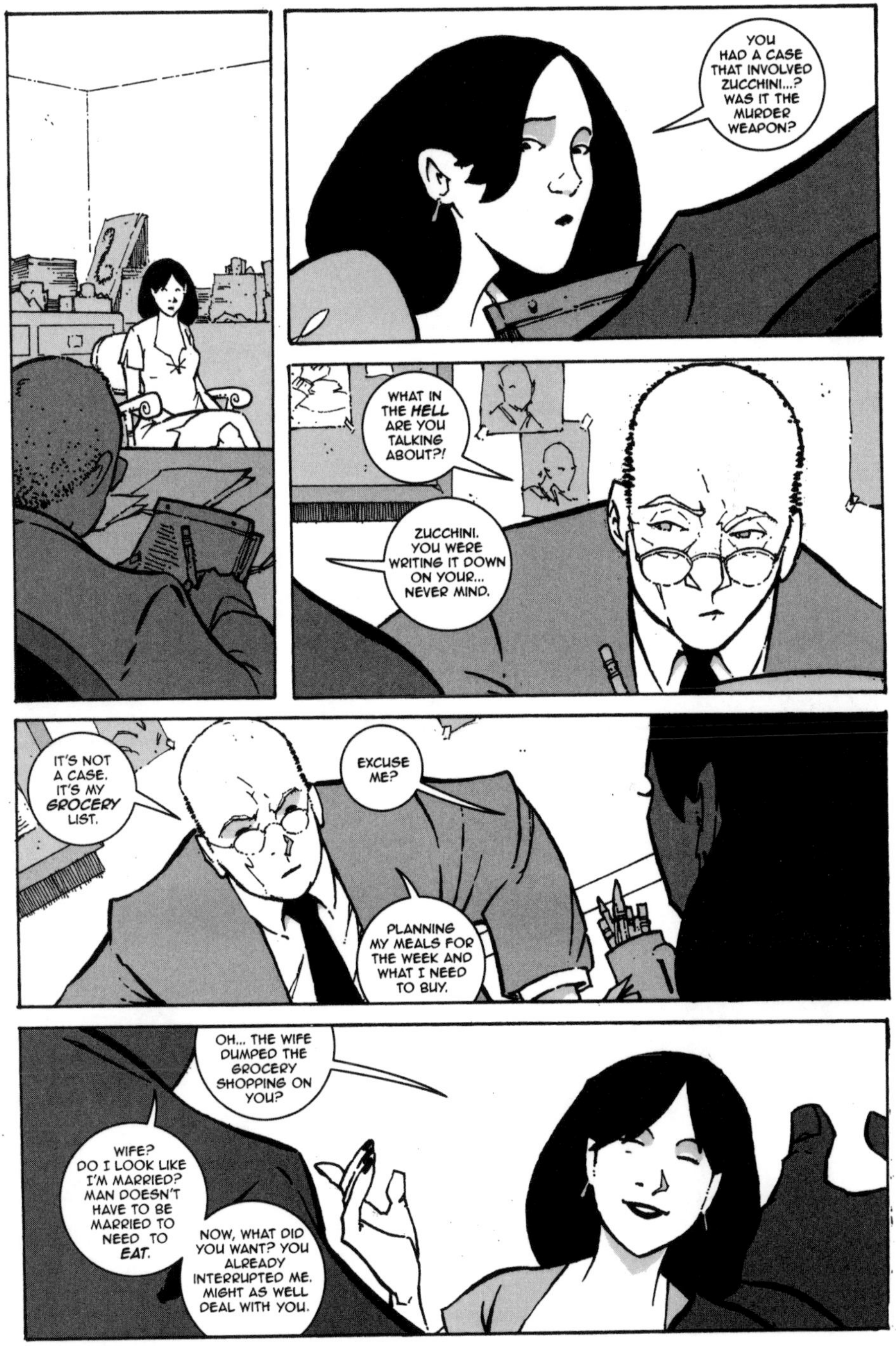
YOU HAD A CASE THAT INVOLVED ZUCCHINI...? WAS IT THE MURDER WEAPON?
WHAT IN THE HELL ARE YOU TALKING ABOUT?!
ZUCCHINI. YOU WERE WRITING IT DOWN ON YOUR... NEVER MIND.
IT'S NOT A CASE. IT'S MY GROCERY LIST.
EXCUSE ME?
PLANNING MY MEALS FOR THE WEEK AND WHAT I NEED TO BUY.
OH... THE WIFE DUMPED THE GROCERY SHOPPING ON YOU?
WIFE? DO I LOOK LIKE I'M MARRIED? MAN DOESN'T HAVE TO BE MARRIED TO NEED TO EAT.
NOW, WHAT DID YOU WANT? YOU ALREADY INTERRUPTED ME. MIGHT AS WELL DEAL WITH YOU.

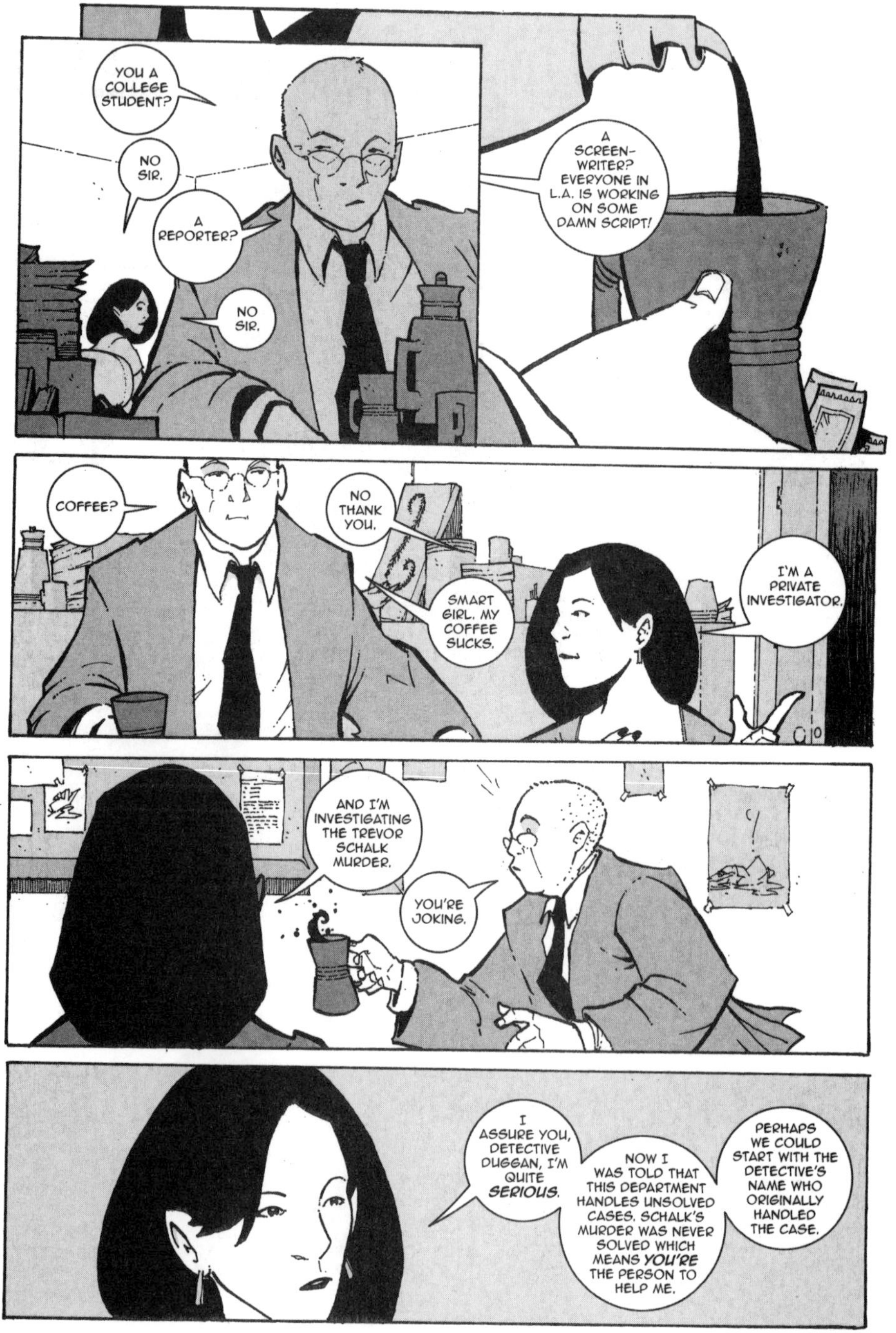
YOU A COLLEGE STUDENT?
NO SIR.
A REPORTER?
NO SIR.
A SCREEN-WRITER? EVERYONE IN L.A. IS WORKING ON SOME DAMN SCRIPT!
COFFEE?
NO THANK YOU.
SMART GIRL. MY COFFEE SUCKS.
I'M A PRIVATE INVESTIGATOR.
AND I'M INVESTIGATING THE TREVOR SCHALK MURDER.
YOU'RE JOKING.
I ASSURE YOU, DETECTIVE DUGGAN, I'M QUITE SERIOUS.
NOW I WAS TOLD THAT THIS DEPARTMENT HANDLES UNSOLVED CASES. SCHALK'S MURDER WAS NEVER SOLVED WHICH MEANS YOU'RE THE PERSON TO HELP ME.
PERHAPS WE COULD START WITH THE DETECTIVE'S NAME WHO ORIGINALLY HANDLED THE CASE.

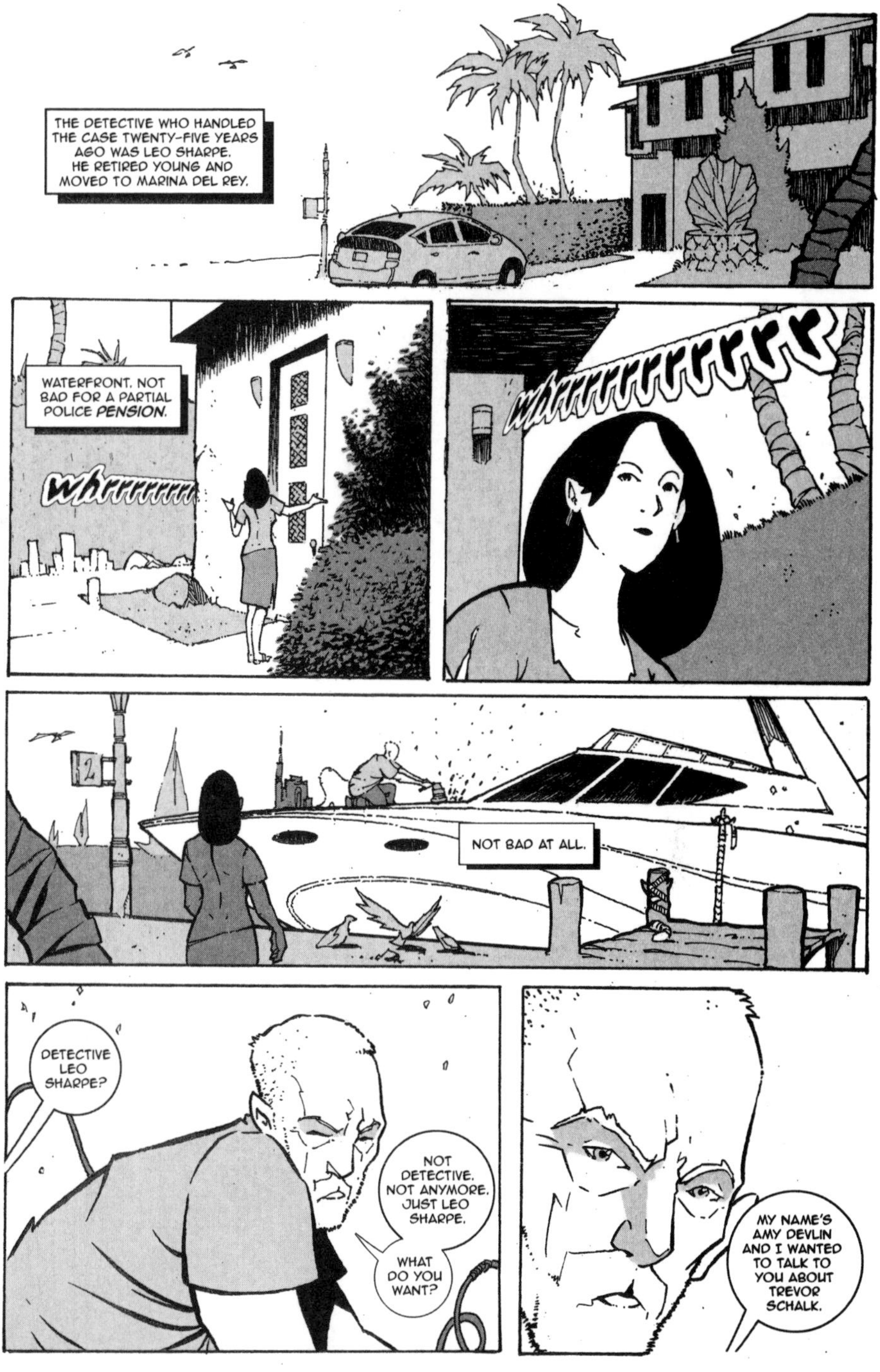
THE DETECTIVE WHO HANDLED THE CASE TWENTY-FIVE YEARS AGO WAS LEO SHARPE. HE RETIRED YOUNG AND MOVED TO MARINA DEL REY.
WATERFRONT. NOT BAD FOR A PARTIAL POLICE PENSION.
whrrrrrrrr
whrrrrrrrrrrrrr
NOT BAD AT ALL.
DETECTIVE LEO SHARPE?
NOT DETECTIVE. NOT ANYMORE. JUST LEO SHARPE.
WHAT DO YOU WANT?
MY NAME'S AMY DEVLIN AND I WANTED TO TALK TO YOU ABOUT TREVOR SCHALK.

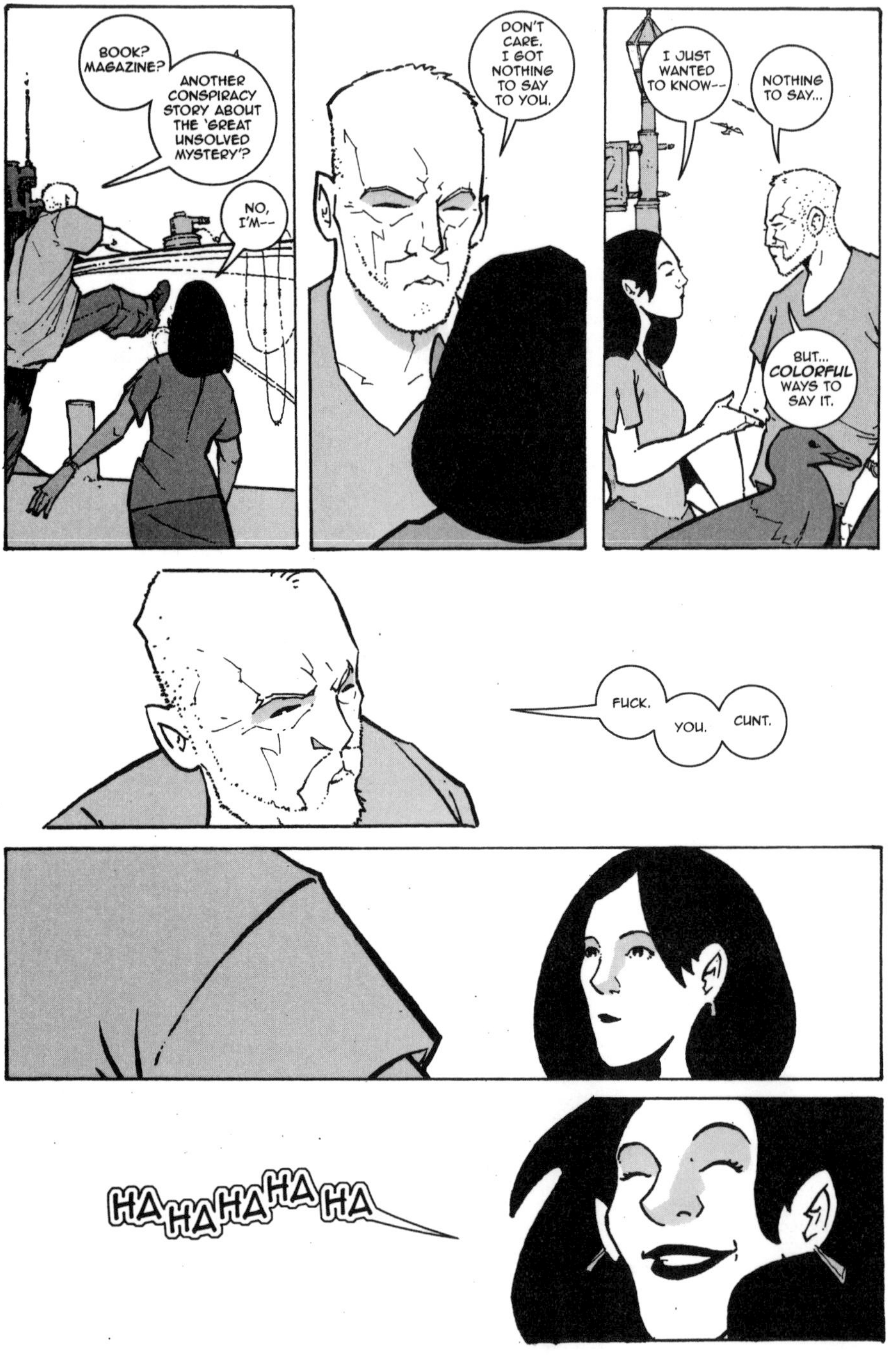
BOOK? MAGAZINE?
ANOTHER CONSPIRACY STORY ABOUT THE 'GREAT UNSOLVED MYSTERY'?
NO, I'M--
DON'T CARE. I GOT NOTHING TO SAY TO YOU.
I JUST WANTED TO KNOW--
NOTHING TO SAY...
BUT... COLORFUL WAYS TO SAY IT.
FUCK.
YOU.
CUNT.
HAHAHAHAHAHA

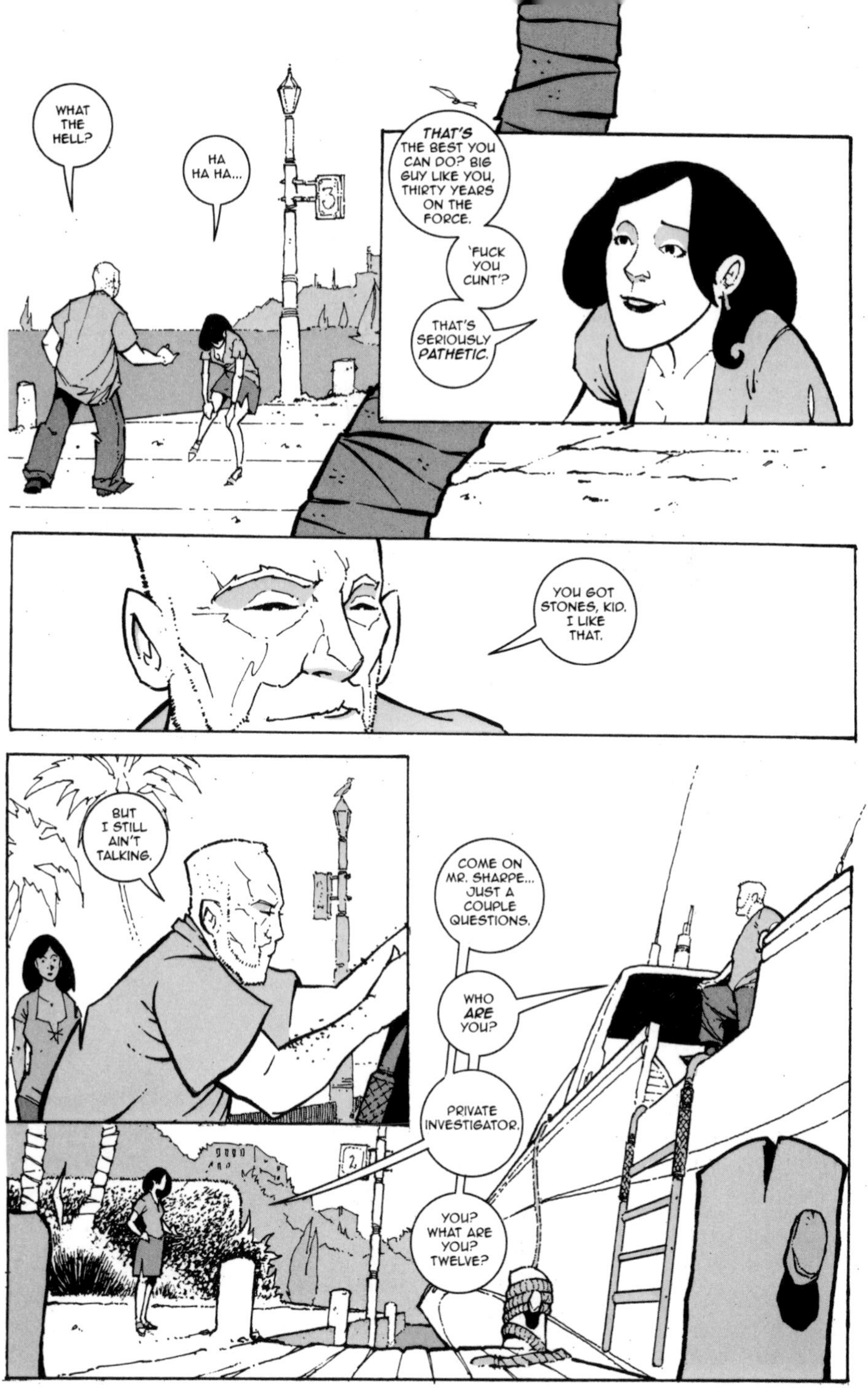
WHAT THE HELL?
HA HA HA...
THAT'S THE BEST YOU CAN DO? BIG GUY LIKE YOU, THIRTY YEARS ON THE FORCE.
'FUCK YOU CUNT'?
THAT'S SERIOUSLY PATHETIC.
YOU GOT STONES, KID. I LIKE THAT.
BUT I STILL AIN'T TALKING.
COME ON MR. SHARPE... JUST A COUPLE QUESTIONS.
WHO ARE YOU?
PRIVATE INVESTIGATOR.
YOU? WHAT ARE YOU? TWELVE?

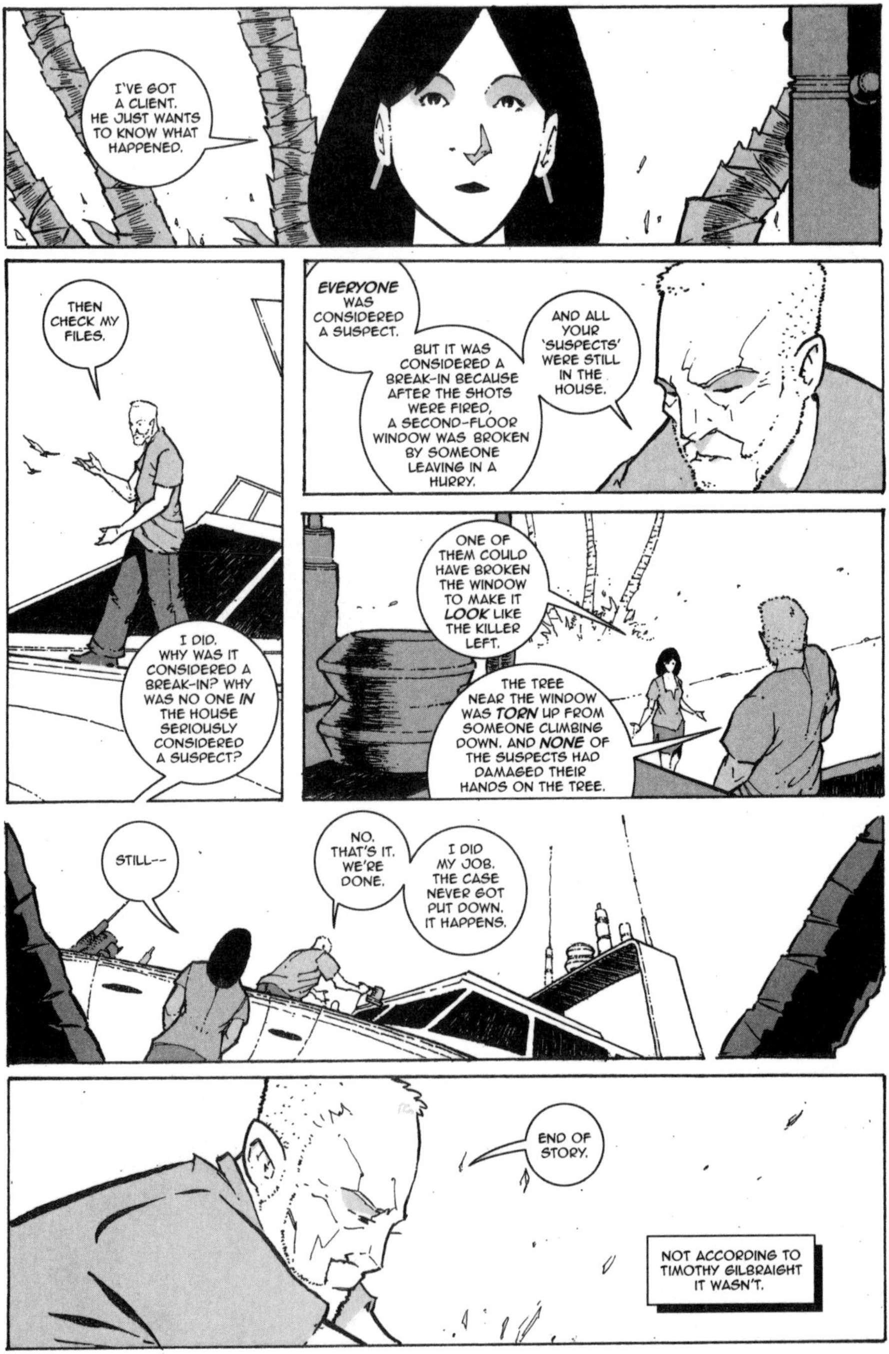

I'VE GOT A CLIENT. HE JUST WANTS TO KNOW WHAT HAPPENED.
THEN CHECK MY FILES.
I DID. WHY WAS IT CONSIDERED A BREAK-IN? WHY WAS NO ONE *IN* THE HOUSE SERIOUSLY CONSIDERED A SUSPECT?
EVERYONE WAS CONSIDERED A SUSPECT.
BUT IT WAS CONSIDERED A BREAK-IN BECAUSE AFTER THE SHOTS WERE FIRED, A SECOND-FLOOR WINDOW WAS BROKEN BY SOMEONE LEAVING IN A HURRY.
AND ALL YOUR 'SUSPECTS' WERE STILL IN THE HOUSE.
ONE OF THEM COULD HAVE BROKEN THE WINDOW TO MAKE IT *LOOK* LIKE THE KILLER LEFT.
THE TREE NEAR THE WINDOW WAS *TORN* UP FROM SOMEONE CLIMBING DOWN. AND *NONE* OF THE SUSPECTS HAD DAMAGED THEIR HANDS ON THE TREE.
STILL--
NO. THAT'S IT. WE'RE DONE.
I DID MY JOB. THE CASE NEVER GOT PUT DOWN. IT HAPPENS.
END OF STORY.
NOT ACCORDING TO TIMOTHY GILBRAIGHT IT WASN'T.

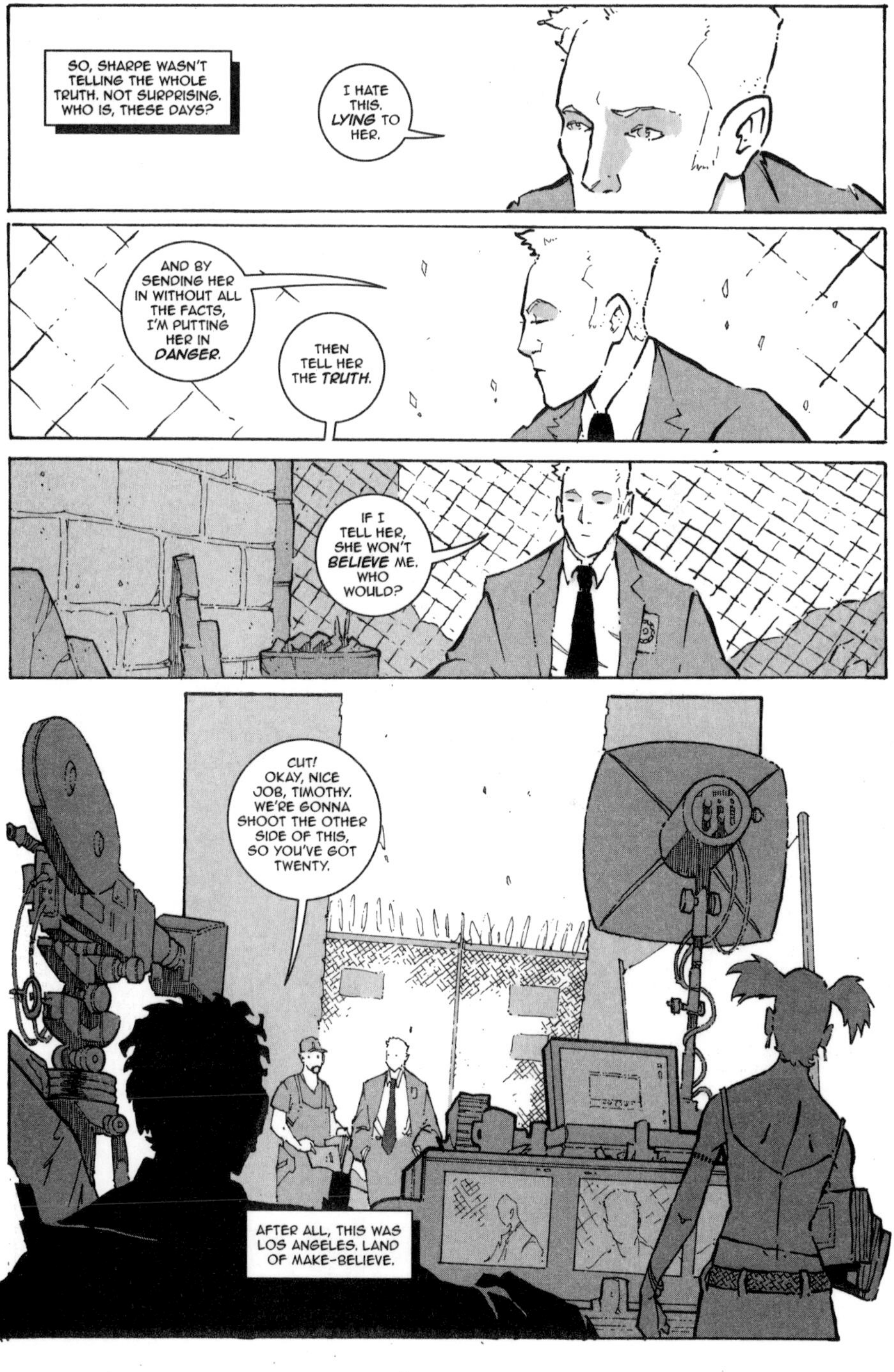

SO, SHARPE WASN'T TELLING THE WHOLE TRUTH. NOT SURPRISING. WHO IS, THESE DAYS?
I HATE THIS. LYING TO HER.
AND BY SENDING HER IN WITHOUT ALL THE FACTS, I'M PUTTING HER IN DANGER.
THEN TELL HER THE TRUTH.
IF I TELL HER, SHE WON'T BELIEVE ME. WHO WOULD?
CUT! OKAY, NICE JOB, TIMOTHY. WE'RE GONNA SHOOT THE OTHER SIDE OF THIS, SO YOU'VE GOT TWENTY.
AFTER ALL, THIS WAS LOS ANGELES. LAND OF MAKE-BELIEVE.

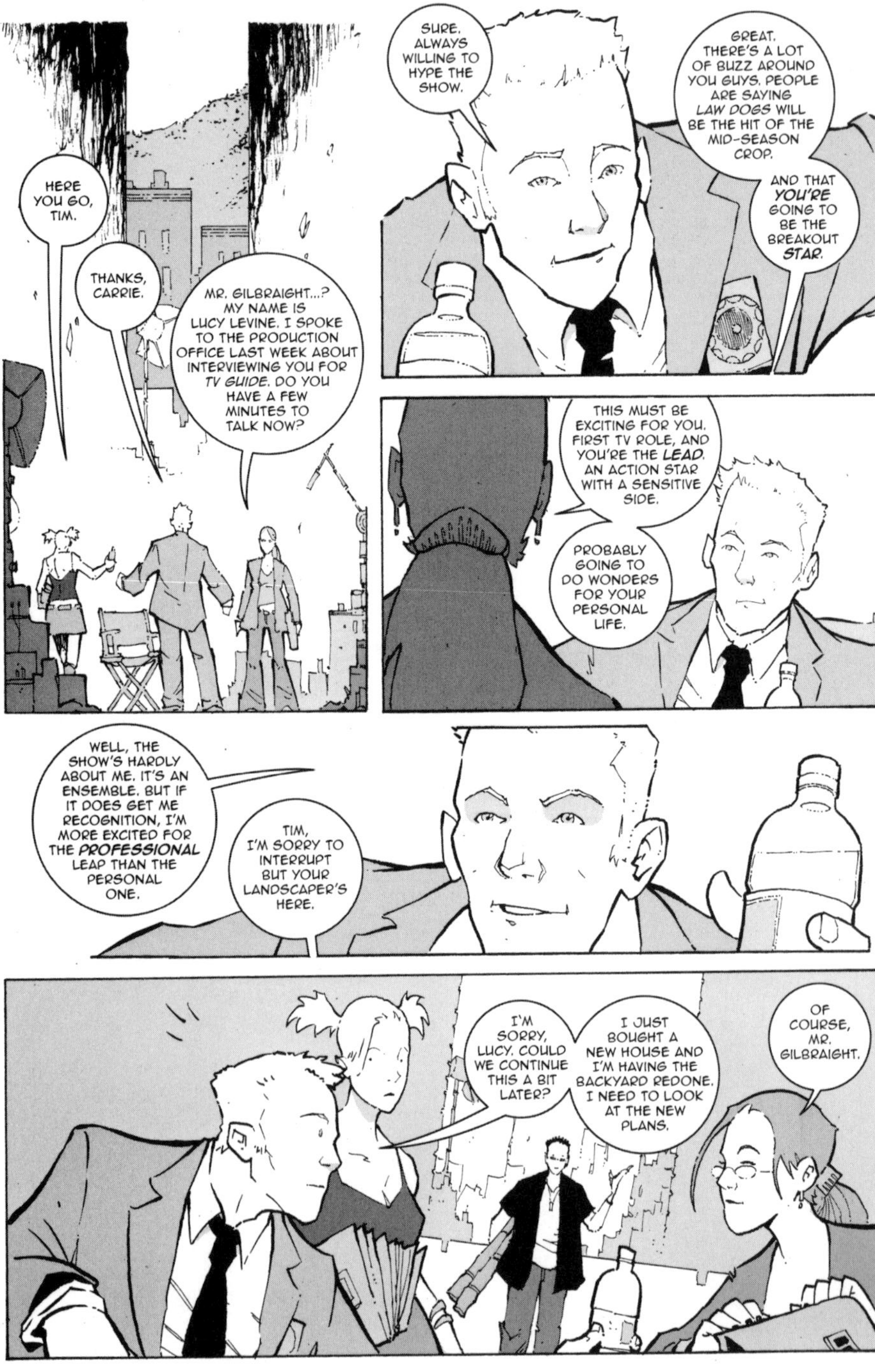
HERE YOU GO, TIM.
THANKS, CARRIE.
MR. GILBRAIGHT...? MY NAME IS LUCY LEVINE. I SPOKE TO THE PRODUCTION OFFICE LAST WEEK ABOUT INTERVIEWING YOU FOR TV GUIDE. DO YOU HAVE A FEW MINUTES TO TALK NOW?
SURE. ALWAYS WILLING TO HYPE THE SHOW.
GREAT. THERE'S A LOT OF BUZZ AROUND YOU GUYS. PEOPLE ARE SAYING LAW DOGS WILL BE THE HIT OF THE MID-SEASON CROP.
AND THAT YOU'RE GOING TO BE THE BREAKOUT STAR.
THIS MUST BE EXCITING FOR YOU. FIRST TV ROLE, AND YOU'RE THE LEAD. AN ACTION STAR WITH A SENSITIVE SIDE.
PROBABLY GOING TO DO WONDERS FOR YOUR PERSONAL LIFE.
WELL, THE SHOW'S HARDLY ABOUT ME. IT'S AN ENSEMBLE. BUT IF IT DOES GET ME RECOGNITION, I'M MORE EXCITED FOR THE PROFESSIONAL LEAP THAN THE PERSONAL ONE.
TIM, I'M SORRY TO INTERRUPT BUT YOUR LANDSCAPER'S HERE.
I'M SORRY, LUCY. COULD WE CONTINUE THIS A BIT LATER?
I JUST BOUGHT A NEW HOUSE AND I'M HAVING THE BACKYARD REDONE. I NEED TO LOOK AT THE NEW PLANS.
OF COURSE, MR. GILBRAIGHT.

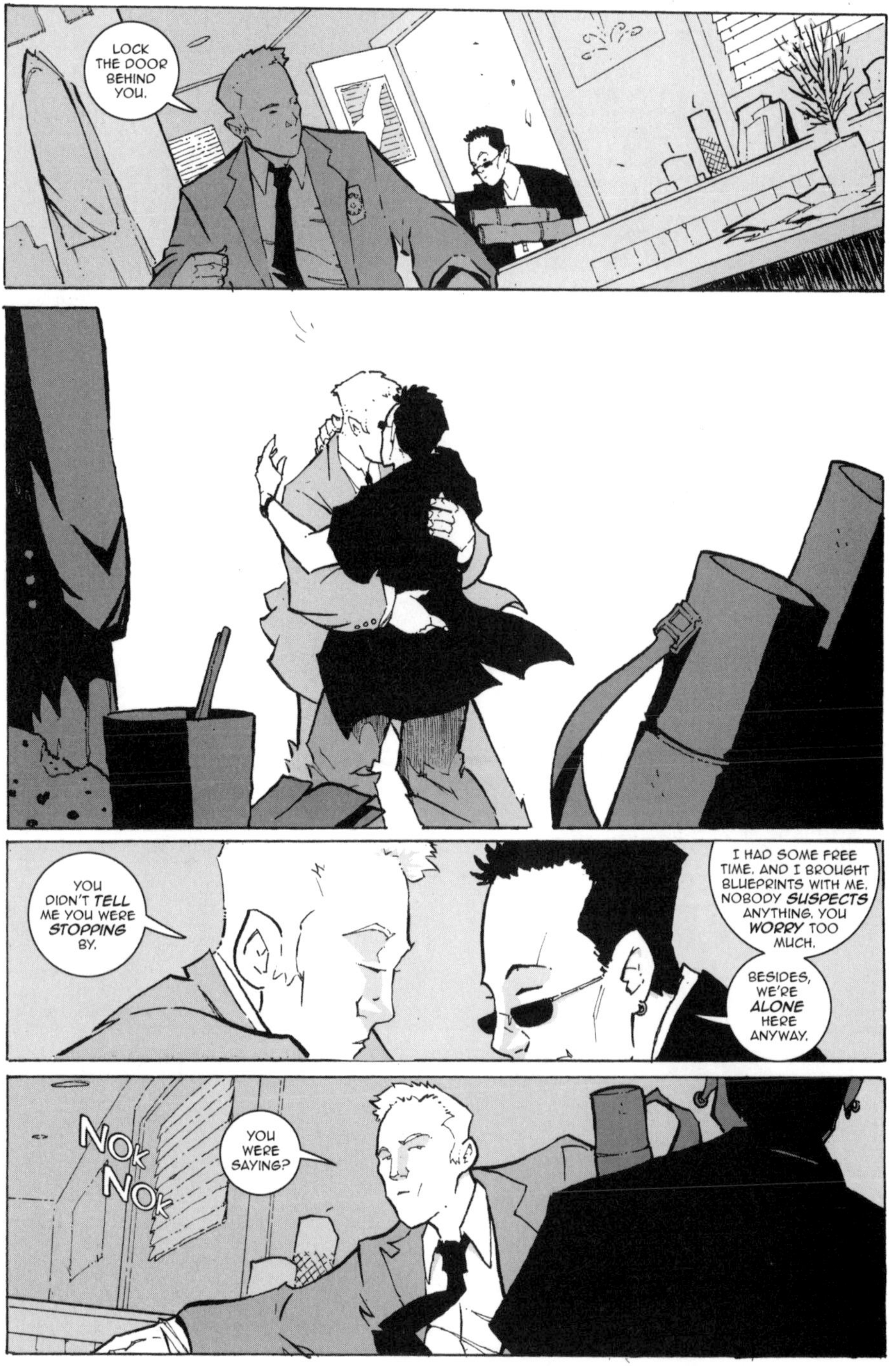
LOCK THE DOOR BEHIND YOU.
YOU DIDN'T TELL ME YOU WERE STOPPING BY.
I HAD SOME FREE TIME, AND I BROUGHT BLUEPRINTS WITH ME. NOBODY SUSPECTS ANYTHING. YOU WORRY TOO MUCH.
BESIDES, WE'RE ALONE HERE ANYWAY.
NOK NOK
YOU WERE SAYING?

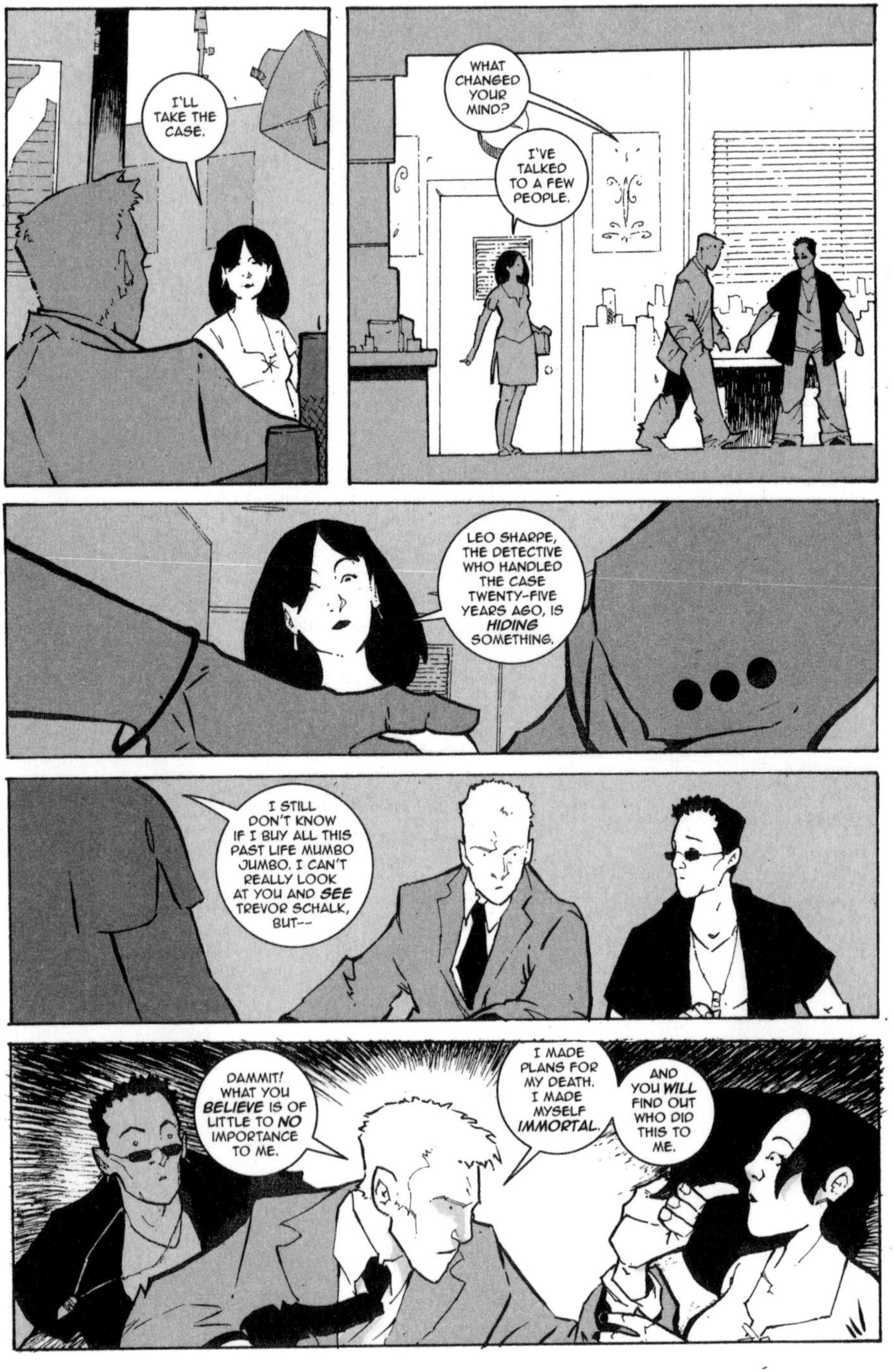
I'LL TAKE THE CASE.
WHAT CHANGED YOUR MIND?
I'VE TALKED TO A FEW PEOPLE.
LEO SHARPE, THE DETECTIVE WHO HANDLED THE CASE TWENTY-FIVE YEARS AGO, IS *HIDING* SOMETHING.
I STILL DON'T KNOW IF I BUY ALL THIS PAST LIFE MUMBO JUMBO. I CAN'T REALLY LOOK AT YOU AND *SEE* TREVOR SCHALK, BUT--
DAMMIT! WHAT YOU *BELIEVE* IS OF LITTLE TO *NO* IMPORTANCE TO ME.
I MADE PLANS FOR MY DEATH. I MADE MYSELF *IMMORTAL*.
AND YOU *WILL* FIND OUT WHO DID THIS TO ME.

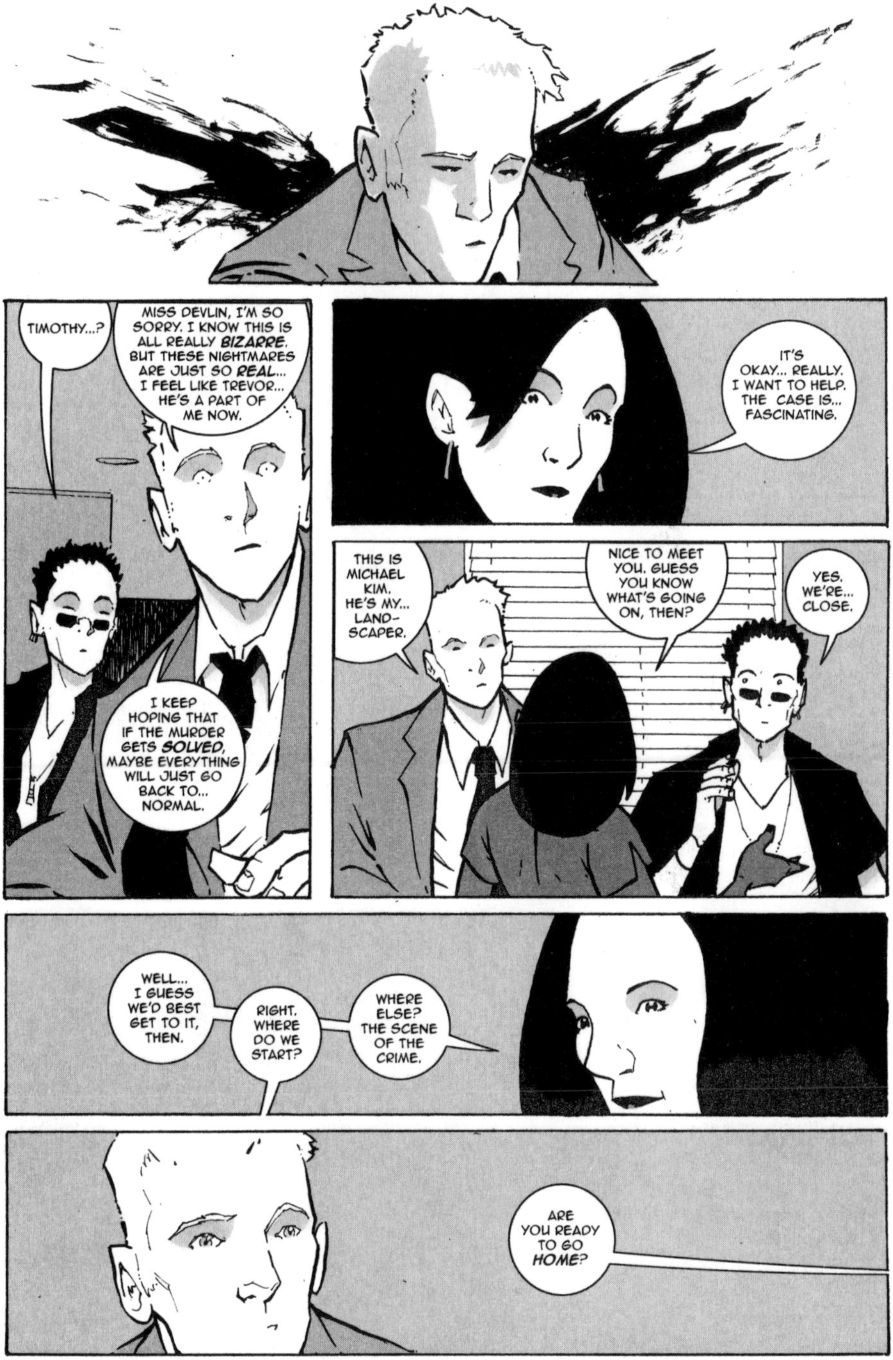
TIMOTHY...?
MISS DEVLIN, I'M SO SORRY. I KNOW THIS IS ALL REALLY BIZARRE. BUT THESE NIGHTMARES ARE JUST SO REAL... I FEEL LIKE TREVOR... HE'S A PART OF ME NOW.
I KEEP HOPING THAT IF THE MURDER GETS SOLVED, MAYBE EVERYTHING WILL JUST GO BACK TO... NORMAL.
IT'S OKAY... REALLY. I WANT TO HELP. THE CASE IS... FASCINATING.
THIS IS MICHAEL KIM. HE'S MY... LAND-SCAPER.
NICE TO MEET YOU. GUESS YOU KNOW WHAT'S GOING ON, THEN?
YES. WE'RE... CLOSE.
WELL... I GUESS WE'D BEST GET TO IT, THEN.
RIGHT. WHERE DO WE START?
WHERE ELSE? THE SCENE OF THE CRIME.
ARE YOU READY TO GO HOME?

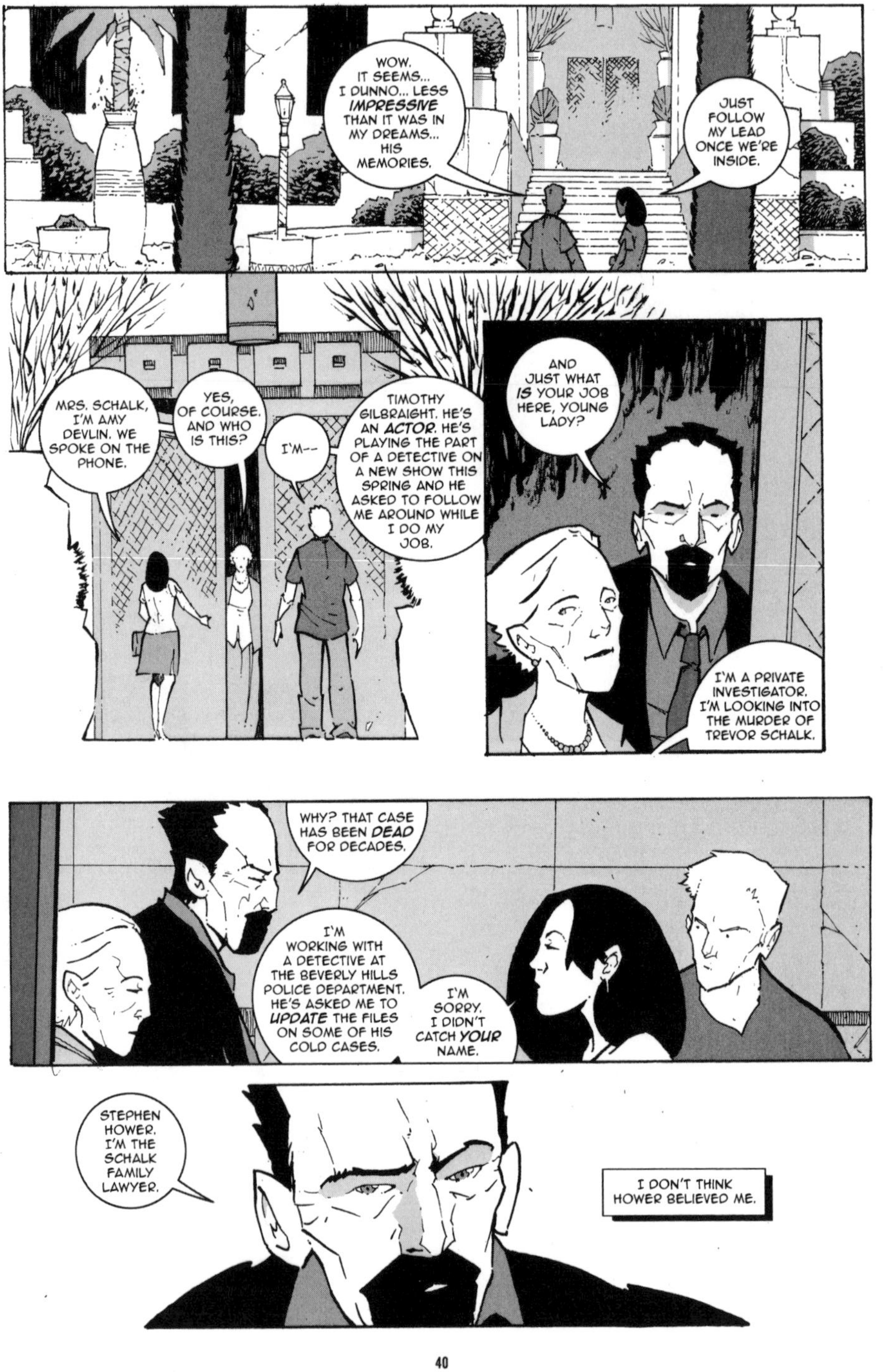
WOW. IT SEEMS... I DUNNO... LESS IMPRESSIVE THAN IT WAS IN MY DREAMS... HIS MEMORIES.
JUST FOLLOW MY LEAD ONCE WE'RE INSIDE.
MRS. SCHALK, I'M AMY DEVLIN. WE SPOKE ON THE PHONE.
YES, OF COURSE. AND WHO IS THIS?
I'M--
TIMOTHY GILBRAIGHT. HE'S AN ACTOR. HE'S PLAYING THE PART OF A DETECTIVE ON A NEW SHOW THIS SPRING AND HE ASKED TO FOLLOW ME AROUND WHILE I DO MY JOB.
AND JUST WHAT IS YOUR JOB HERE, YOUNG LADY?
I'M A PRIVATE INVESTIGATOR. I'M LOOKING INTO THE MURDER OF TREVOR SCHALK.
WHY? THAT CASE HAS BEEN DEAD FOR DECADES.
I'M WORKING WITH A DETECTIVE AT THE BEVERLY HILLS POLICE DEPARTMENT. HE'S ASKED ME TO UPDATE THE FILES ON SOME OF HIS COLD CASES.
I'M SORRY. I DIDN'T CATCH YOUR NAME.
STEPHEN HOWER. I'M THE SCHALK FAMILY LAWYER.
I DON'T THINK HOWER BELIEVED ME.

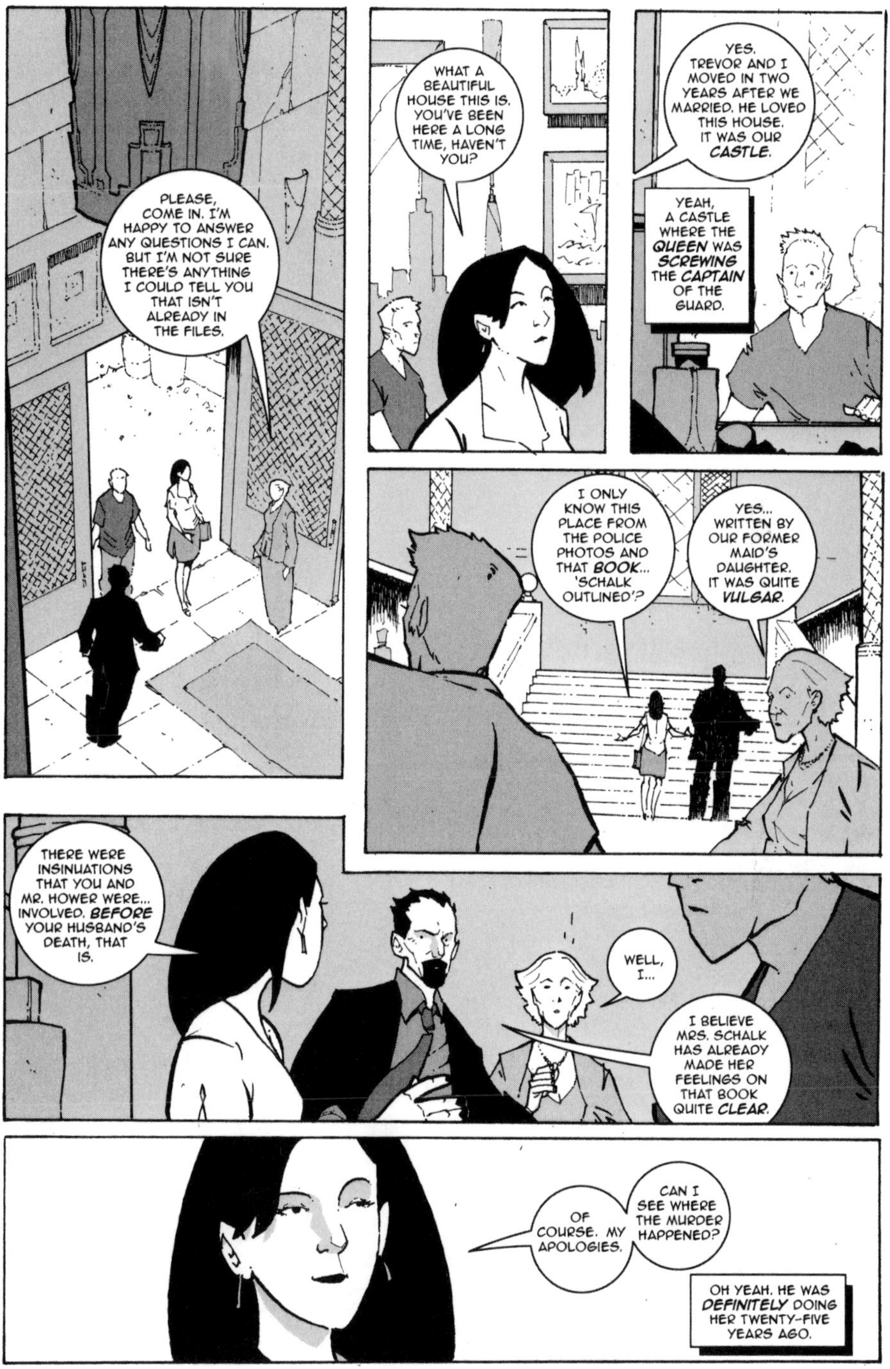
PLEASE, COME IN. I'M HAPPY TO ANSWER ANY QUESTIONS I CAN. BUT I'M NOT SURE THERE'S ANYTHING I COULD TELL YOU THAT ISN'T ALREADY IN THE FILES.
WHAT A BEAUTIFUL HOUSE THIS IS. YOU'VE BEEN HERE A LONG TIME, HAVEN'T YOU?
YES. TREVOR AND I MOVED IN TWO YEARS AFTER WE MARRIED. HE LOVED THIS HOUSE. IT WAS OUR CASTLE.
YEAH, A CASTLE WHERE THE QUEEN WAS SCREWING THE CAPTAIN OF THE GUARD.
I ONLY KNOW THIS PLACE FROM THE POLICE PHOTOS AND THAT BOOK... 'SCHALK OUTLINED'?
YES... WRITTEN BY OUR FORMER MAID'S DAUGHTER. IT WAS QUITE VULGAR.
THERE WERE INSINUATIONS THAT YOU AND MR. HOWER WERE... INVOLVED. BEFORE YOUR HUSBAND'S DEATH, THAT IS.
WELL, I...
I BELIEVE MRS. SCHALK HAS ALREADY MADE HER FEELINGS ON THAT BOOK QUITE CLEAR.
CAN I SEE WHERE THE MURDER HAPPENED?
OF COURSE. MY APOLOGIES.
OH YEAH. HE WAS DEFINITELY DOING HER TWENTY-FIVE YEARS AGO.

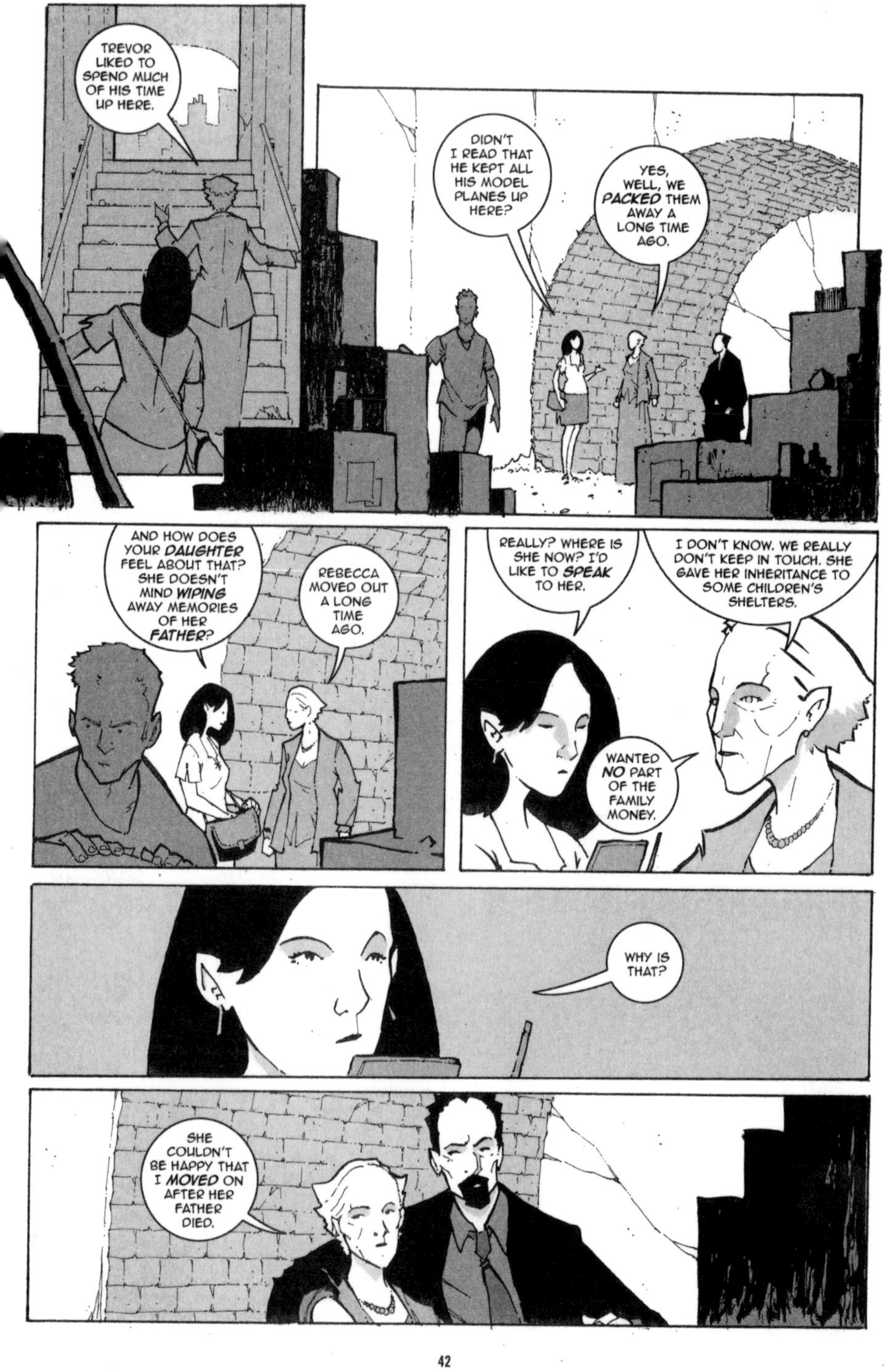
TREVOR LIKED TO SPEND MUCH OF HIS TIME UP HERE.
DIDN'T I READ THAT HE KEPT ALL HIS MODEL PLANES UP HERE?
YES, WELL, WE PACKED THEM AWAY A LONG TIME AGO.
AND HOW DOES YOUR DAUGHTER FEEL ABOUT THAT? SHE DOESN'T MIND WIPING AWAY MEMORIES OF HER FATHER?
REBECCA MOVED OUT A LONG TIME AGO.
REALLY? WHERE IS SHE NOW? I'D LIKE TO SPEAK TO HER.
I DON'T KNOW. WE REALLY DON'T KEEP IN TOUCH. SHE GAVE HER INHERITANCE TO SOME CHILDREN'S SHELTERS.
WANTED NO PART OF THE FAMILY MONEY.
WHY IS THAT?
SHE COULDN'T BE HAPPY THAT I MOVED ON AFTER HER FATHER DIED.

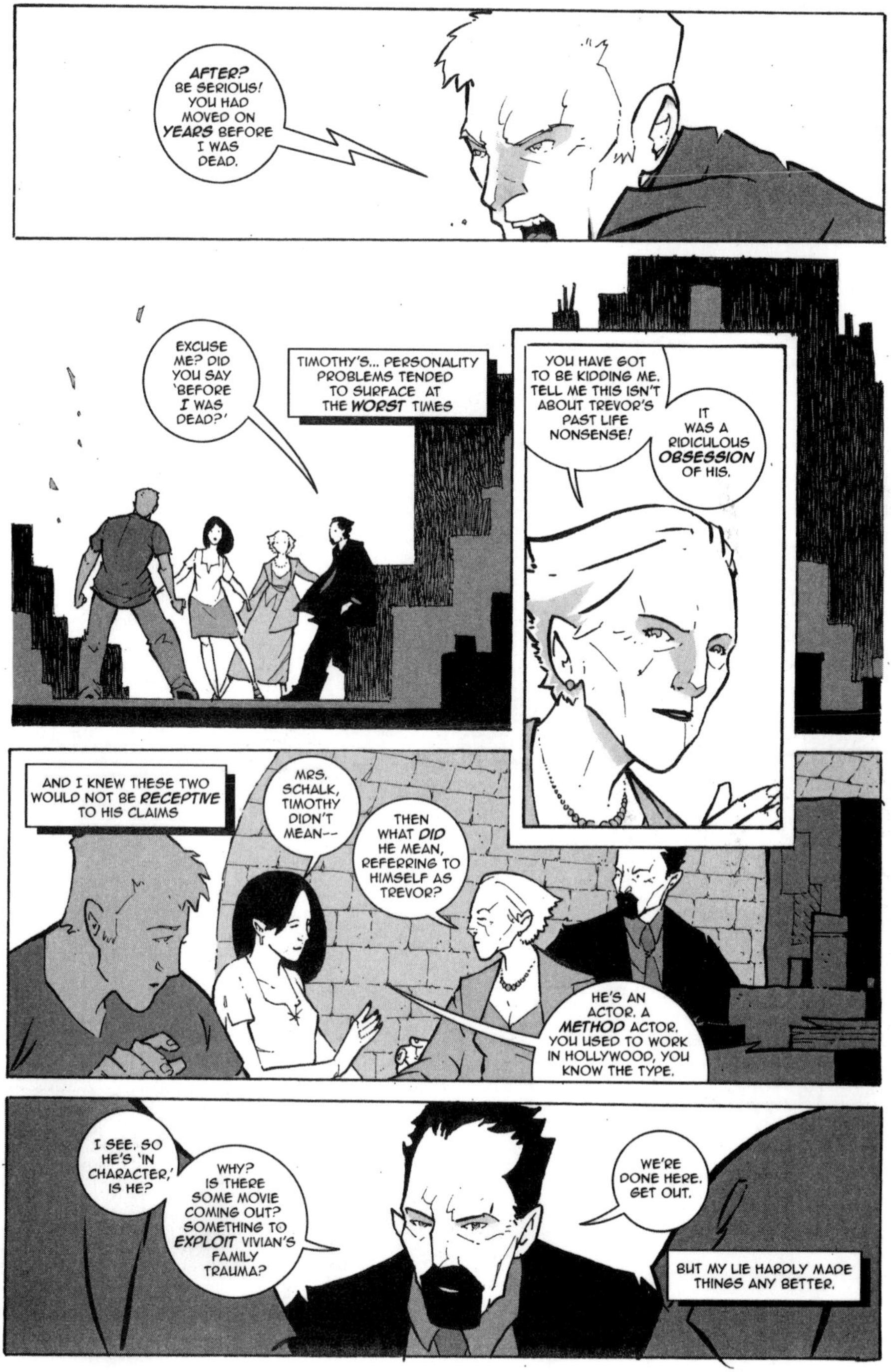
AFTER? BE SERIOUS! YOU HAD MOVED ON YEARS BEFORE I WAS DEAD.
EXCUSE ME? DID YOU SAY 'BEFORE I WAS DEAD?'
TIMOTHY'S... PERSONALITY PROBLEMS TENDED TO SURFACE AT THE WORST TIMES
YOU HAVE GOT TO BE KIDDING ME. TELL ME THIS ISN'T ABOUT TREVOR'S PAST LIFE NONSENSE!
IT WAS A RIDICULOUS OBSESSION OF HIS.
AND I KNEW THESE TWO WOULD NOT BE RECEPTIVE TO HIS CLAIMS
MRS. SCHALK, TIMOTHY DIDN'T MEAN--
THEN WHAT DID HE MEAN, REFERRING TO HIMSELF AS TREVOR?
HE'S AN ACTOR. A METHOD ACTOR. YOU USED TO WORK IN HOLLYWOOD, YOU KNOW THE TYPE.
I SEE. SO HE'S 'IN CHARACTER,' IS HE?
WHY? IS THERE SOME MOVIE COMING OUT? SOMETHING TO EXPLOIT VIVIAN'S FAMILY TRAUMA?
WE'RE DONE HERE. GET OUT.
BUT MY LIE HARDLY MADE THINGS ANY BETTER.

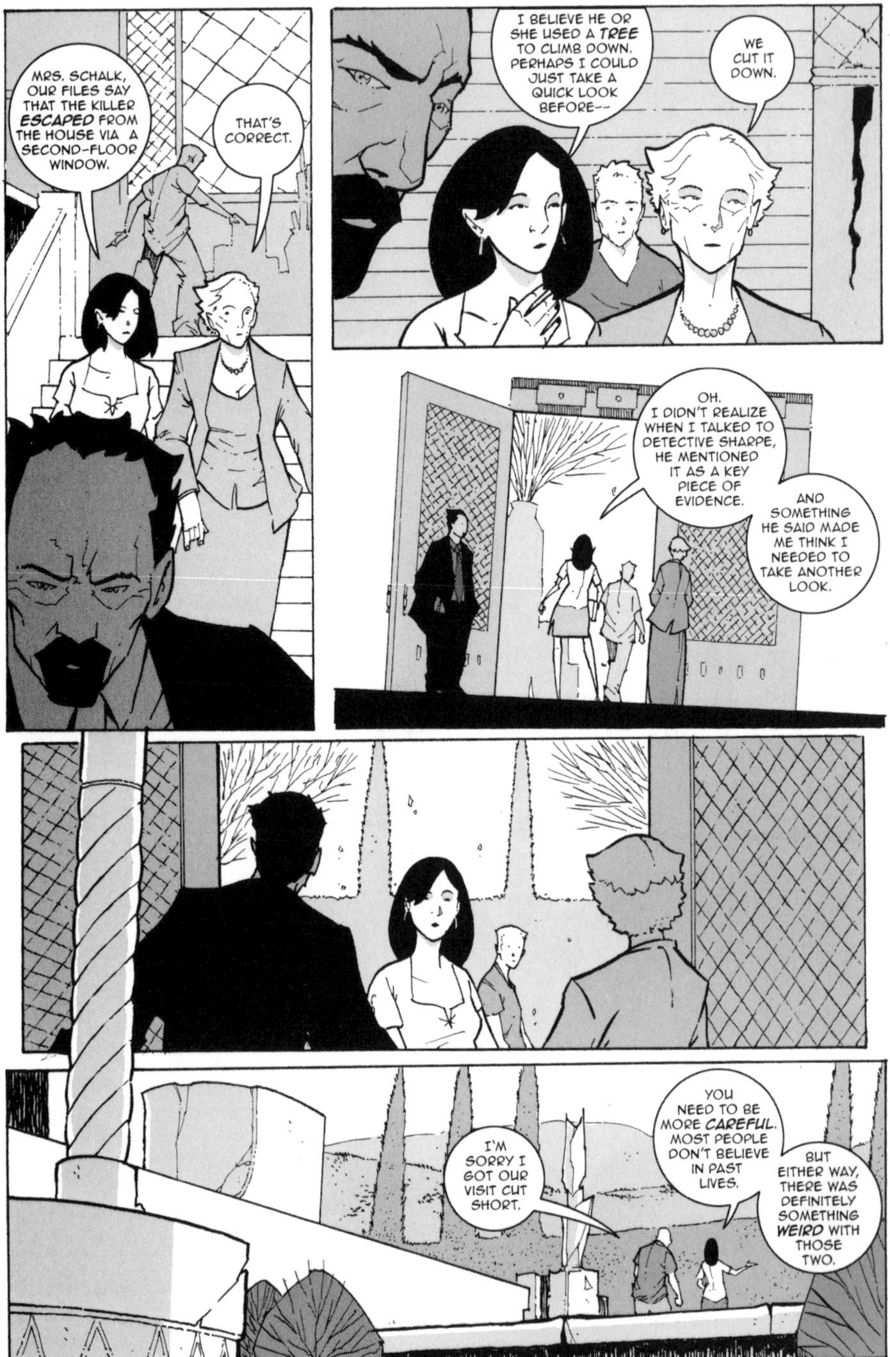
MRS. SCHALK, OUR FILES SAY THAT THE KILLER ESCAPED FROM THE HOUSE VIA A SECOND-FLOOR WINDOW.
THAT'S CORRECT.
I BELIEVE HE OR SHE USED A TREE TO CLIMB DOWN. PERHAPS I COULD JUST TAKE A QUICK LOOK BEFORE--
WE CUT IT DOWN.
OH. I DIDN'T REALIZE WHEN I TALKED TO DETECTIVE SHARPE, HE MENTIONED IT AS A KEY PIECE OF EVIDENCE.
AND SOMETHING HE SAID MADE ME THINK I NEEDED TO TAKE ANOTHER LOOK.
I'M SORRY I GOT OUR VISIT CUT SHORT.
YOU NEED TO BE MORE CAREFUL. MOST PEOPLE DON'T BELIEVE IN PAST LIVES.
BUT EITHER WAY, THERE WAS DEFINITELY SOMETHING WEIRD WITH THOSE TWO.

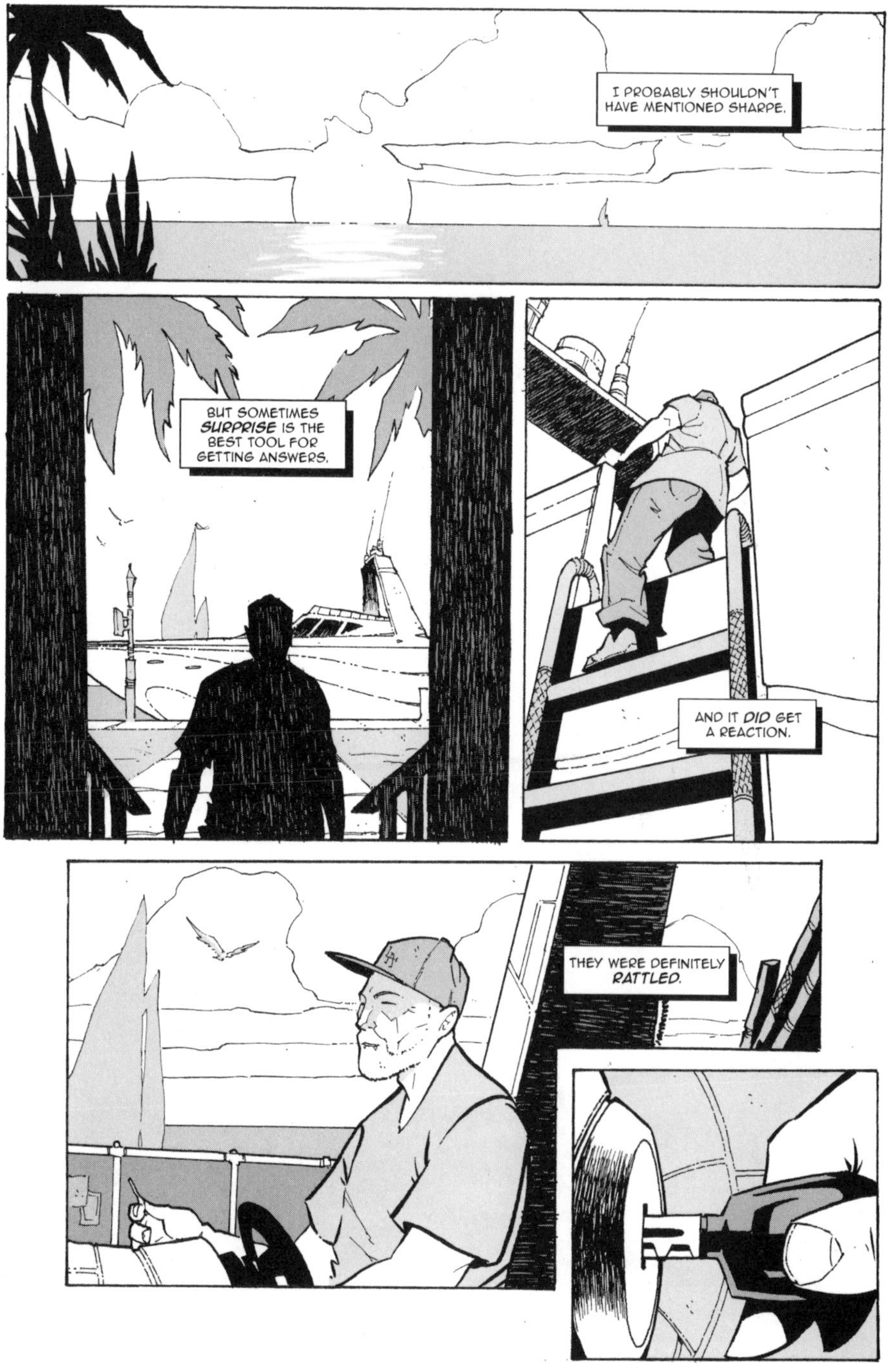
I PROBABLY SHOULDN'T HAVE MENTIONED SHARPE.
BUT SOMETIMES *SURPRISE* IS THE BEST TOOL FOR GETTING ANSWERS.
AND IT *DID* GET A REACTION.
THEY WERE DEFINITELY *RATTLED*.

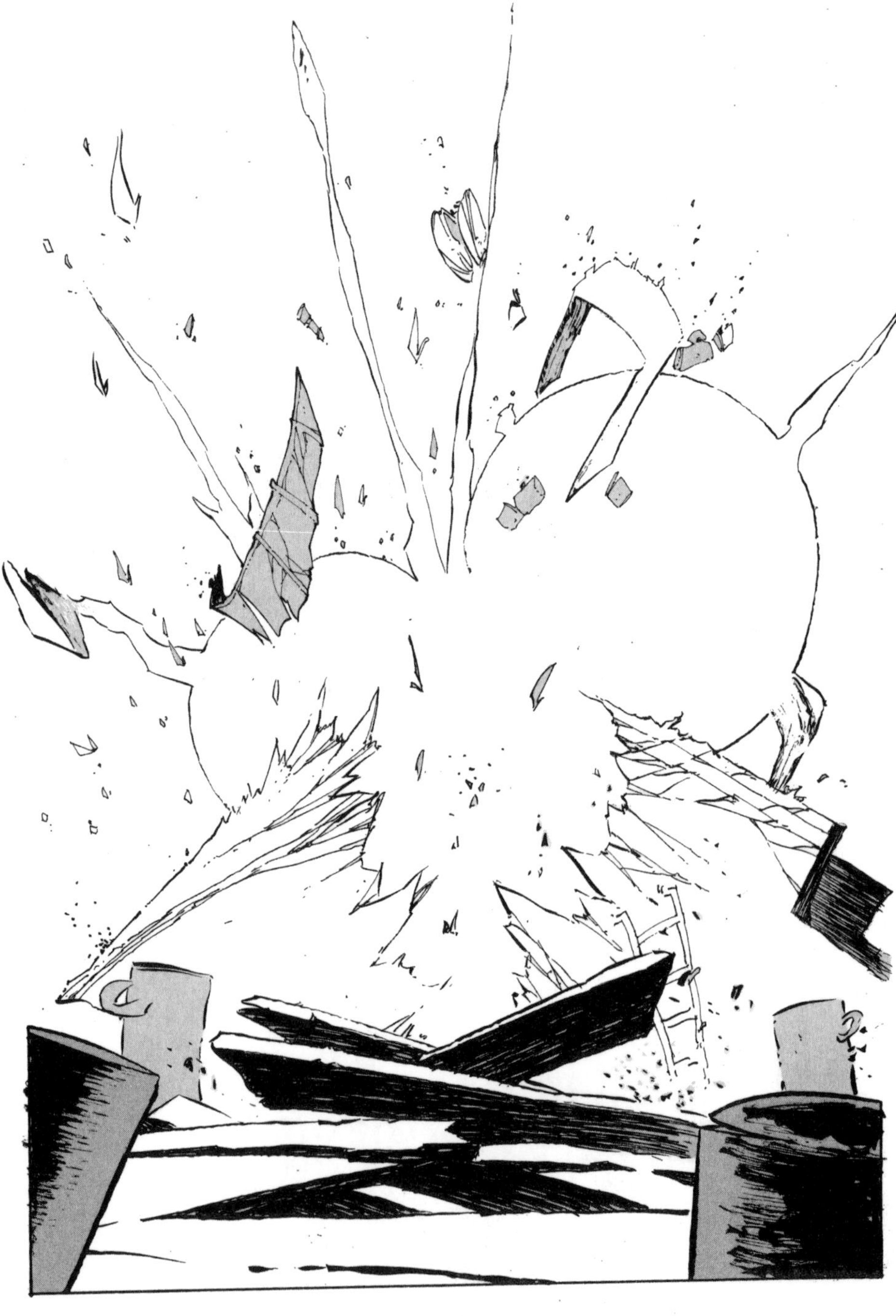

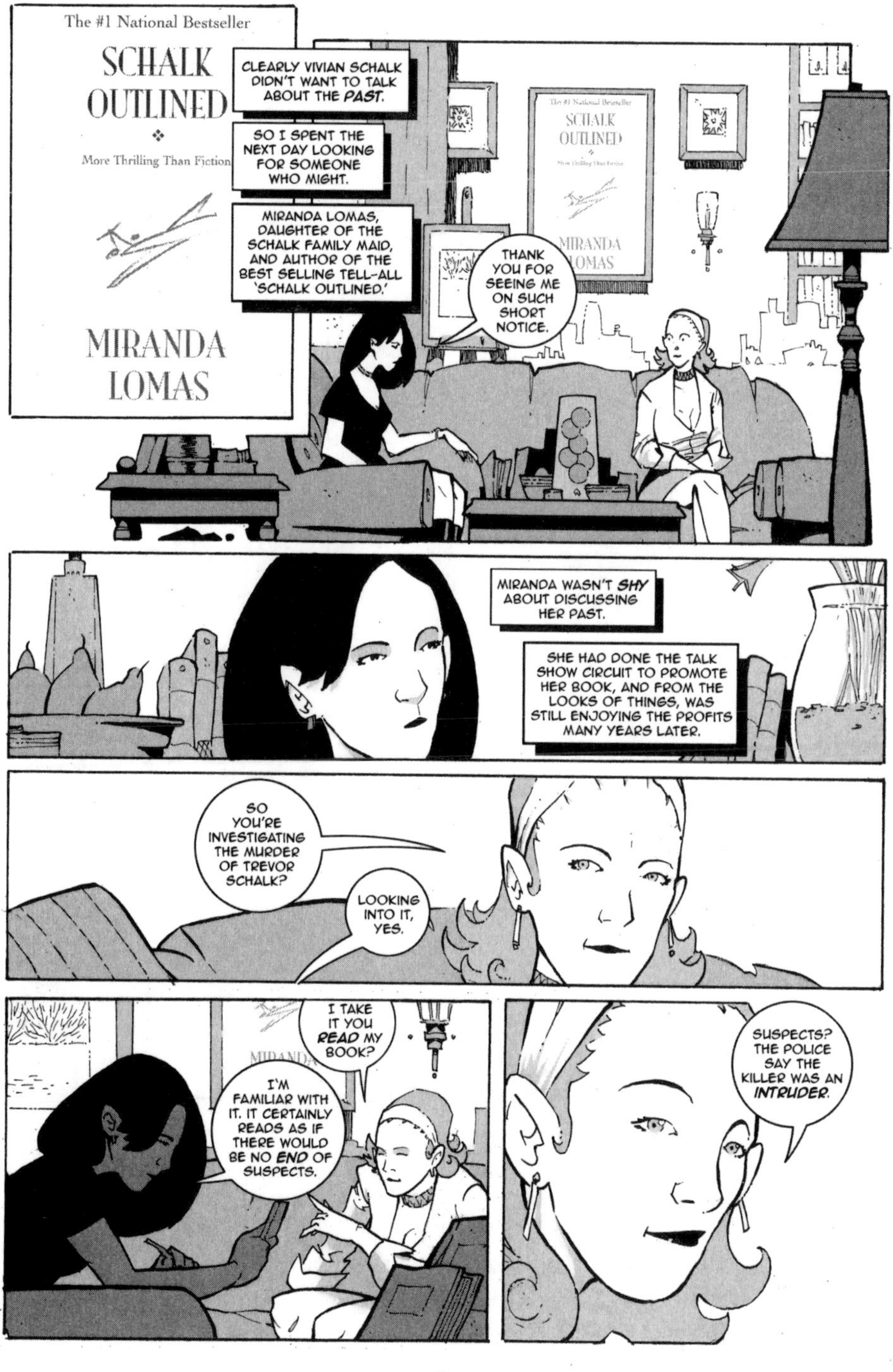
The #1 National Bestseller
SCHALK OUTLINED
More Thrilling Than Fiction
MIRANDA LOMAS
CLEARLY VIVIAN SCHALK DIDN'T WANT TO TALK ABOUT THE PAST.
SO I SPENT THE NEXT DAY LOOKING FOR SOMEONE WHO MIGHT.
MIRANDA LOMAS, DAUGHTER OF THE SCHALK FAMILY MAID, AND AUTHOR OF THE BEST SELLING TELL-ALL 'SCHALK OUTLINED.'
THANK YOU FOR SEEING ME ON SUCH SHORT NOTICE.
MIRANDA WASN'T SHY ABOUT DISCUSSING HER PAST.
SHE HAD DONE THE TALK SHOW CIRCUIT TO PROMOTE HER BOOK, AND FROM THE LOOKS OF THINGS, WAS STILL ENJOYING THE PROFITS MANY YEARS LATER.
SO YOU'RE INVESTIGATING THE MURDER OF TREVOR SCHALK?
LOOKING INTO IT, YES.
I TAKE IT YOU READ MY BOOK?
I'M FAMILIAR WITH IT. IT CERTAINLY READS AS IF THERE WOULD BE NO END OF SUSPECTS.
SUSPECTS? THE POLICE SAY THE KILLER WAS AN INTRUDER.

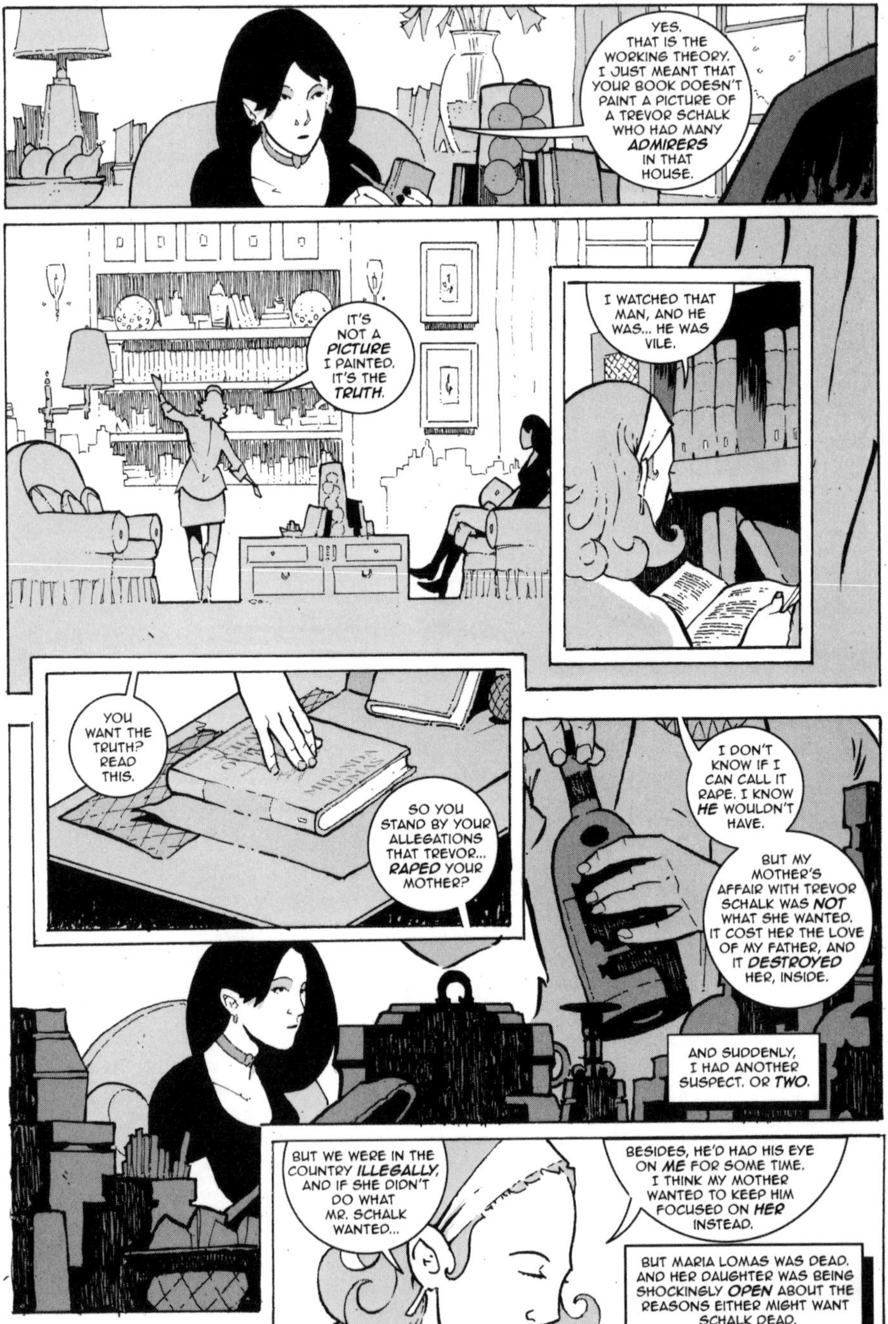
YES. THAT IS THE WORKING THEORY. I JUST MEANT THAT YOUR BOOK DOESN'T PAINT A PICTURE OF A TREVOR SCHALK WHO HAD MANY ADMIRERS IN THAT HOUSE.
IT'S NOT A PICTURE I PAINTED. IT'S THE TRUTH.
I WATCHED THAT MAN, AND HE WAS... HE WAS VILE.
YOU WANT THE TRUTH? READ THIS.
MIRANDA LOMAS
SO YOU STAND BY YOUR ALLEGATIONS THAT TREVOR... RAPED YOUR MOTHER?
I DON'T KNOW IF I CAN CALL IT RAPE. I KNOW HE WOULDN'T HAVE.
BUT MY MOTHER'S AFFAIR WITH TREVOR SCHALK WAS NOT WHAT SHE WANTED. IT COST HER THE LOVE OF MY FATHER, AND IT DESTROYED HER, INSIDE.
AND SUDDENLY, I HAD ANOTHER SUSPECT. OR TWO.
BUT WE WERE IN THE COUNTRY ILLEGALLY, AND IF SHE DIDN'T DO WHAT MR. SCHALK WANTED...
BESIDES, HE'D HAD HIS EYE ON ME FOR SOME TIME. I THINK MY MOTHER WANTED TO KEEP HIM FOCUSED ON HER INSTEAD.
BUT MARIA LOMAS WAS DEAD. AND HER DAUGHTER WAS BEING SHOCKINGLY OPEN ABOUT THE REASONS EITHER MIGHT WANT SCHALK DEAD.

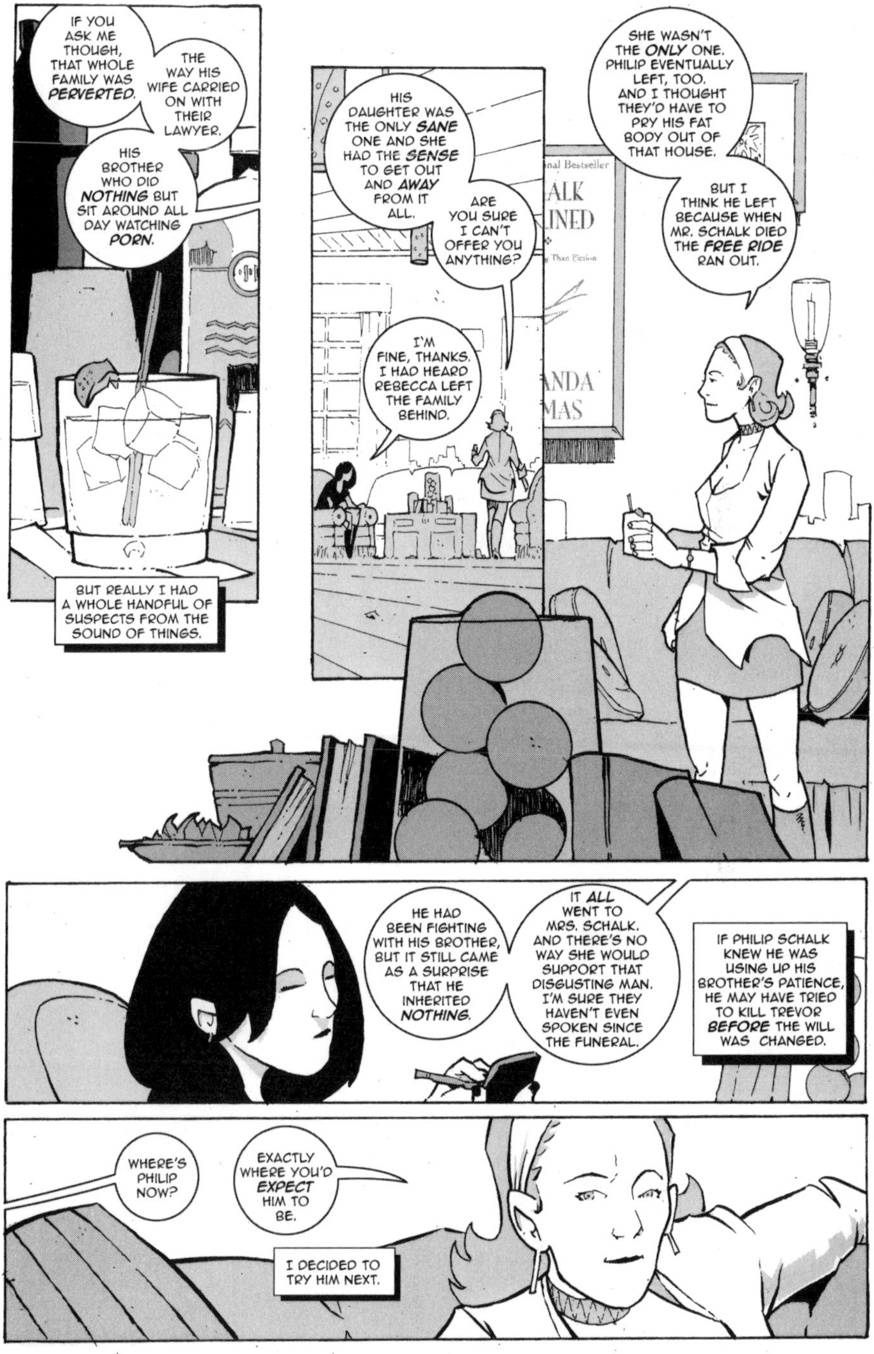
IF YOU ASK ME THOUGH, THAT WHOLE FAMILY WAS PERVERTED.
THE WAY HIS WIFE CARRIED ON WITH THEIR LAWYER.
HIS BROTHER WHO DID NOTHING BUT SIT AROUND ALL DAY WATCHING PORN.
BUT REALLY I HAD A WHOLE HANDFUL OF SUSPECTS FROM THE SOUND OF THINGS.
HIS DAUGHTER WAS THE ONLY SANE ONE AND SHE HAD THE SENSE TO GET OUT AND AWAY FROM IT ALL.
ARE YOU SURE I CAN'T OFFER YOU ANYTHING?
I'M FINE, THANKS. I HAD HEARD REBECCA LEFT THE FAMILY BEHIND.
SHE WASN'T THE ONLY ONE. PHILIP EVENTUALLY LEFT, TOO. AND I THOUGHT THEY'D HAVE TO PRY HIS FAT BODY OUT OF THAT HOUSE.
BUT I THINK HE LEFT BECAUSE WHEN MR. SCHALK DIED THE FREE RIDE RAN OUT.
HE HAD BEEN FIGHTING WITH HIS BROTHER, BUT IT STILL CAME AS A SURPRISE THAT HE INHERITED NOTHING.
IT ALL WENT TO MRS. SCHALK. AND THERE'S NO WAY SHE WOULD SUPPORT THAT DISGUSTING MAN. I'M SURE THEY HAVEN'T EVEN SPOKEN SINCE THE FUNERAL.
IF PHILIP SCHALK KNEW HE WAS USING UP HIS BROTHER'S PATIENCE, HE MAY HAVE TRIED TO KILL TREVOR BEFORE THE WILL WAS CHANGED.
WHERE'S PHILIP NOW?
EXACTLY WHERE YOU'D EXPECT HIM TO BE.
I DECIDED TO TRY HIM NEXT.

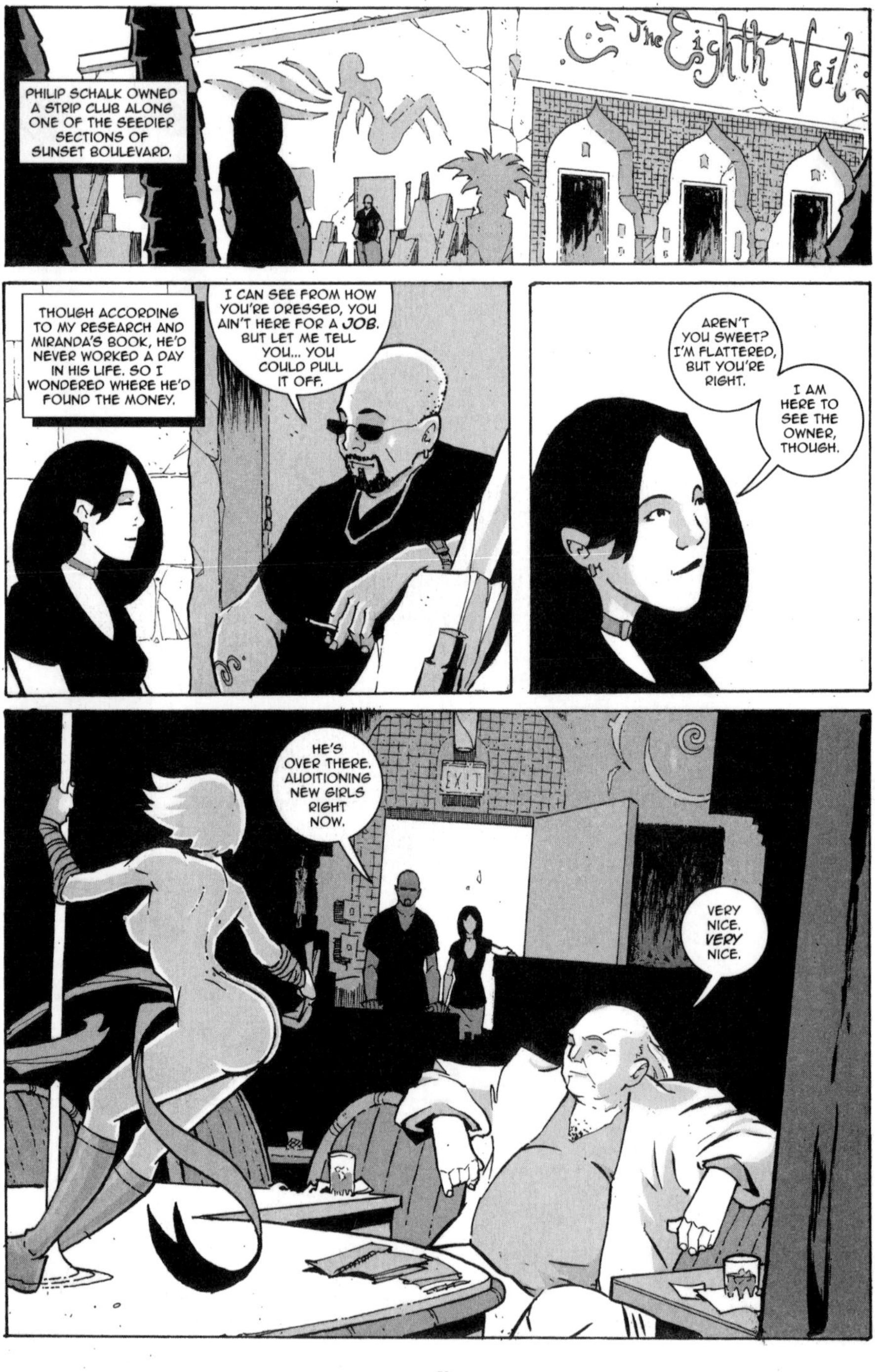
The Eighth Veil
PHILIP SCHALK OWNED A STRIP CLUB ALONG ONE OF THE SEEDIER SECTIONS OF SUNSET BOULEVARD.
THOUGH ACCORDING TO MY RESEARCH AND MIRANDA'S BOOK, HE'D NEVER WORKED A DAY IN HIS LIFE. SO I WONDERED WHERE HE'D FOUND THE MONEY.
I CAN SEE FROM HOW YOU'RE DRESSED, YOU AIN'T HERE FOR A *JOB*. BUT LET ME TELL YOU... YOU COULD PULL IT OFF.
AREN'T YOU SWEET? I'M FLATTERED, BUT YOU'RE RIGHT.
I AM HERE TO SEE THE OWNER, THOUGH.
EXIT
HE'S OVER THERE. AUDITIONING NEW GIRLS RIGHT NOW.
VERY NICE. *VERY* NICE.

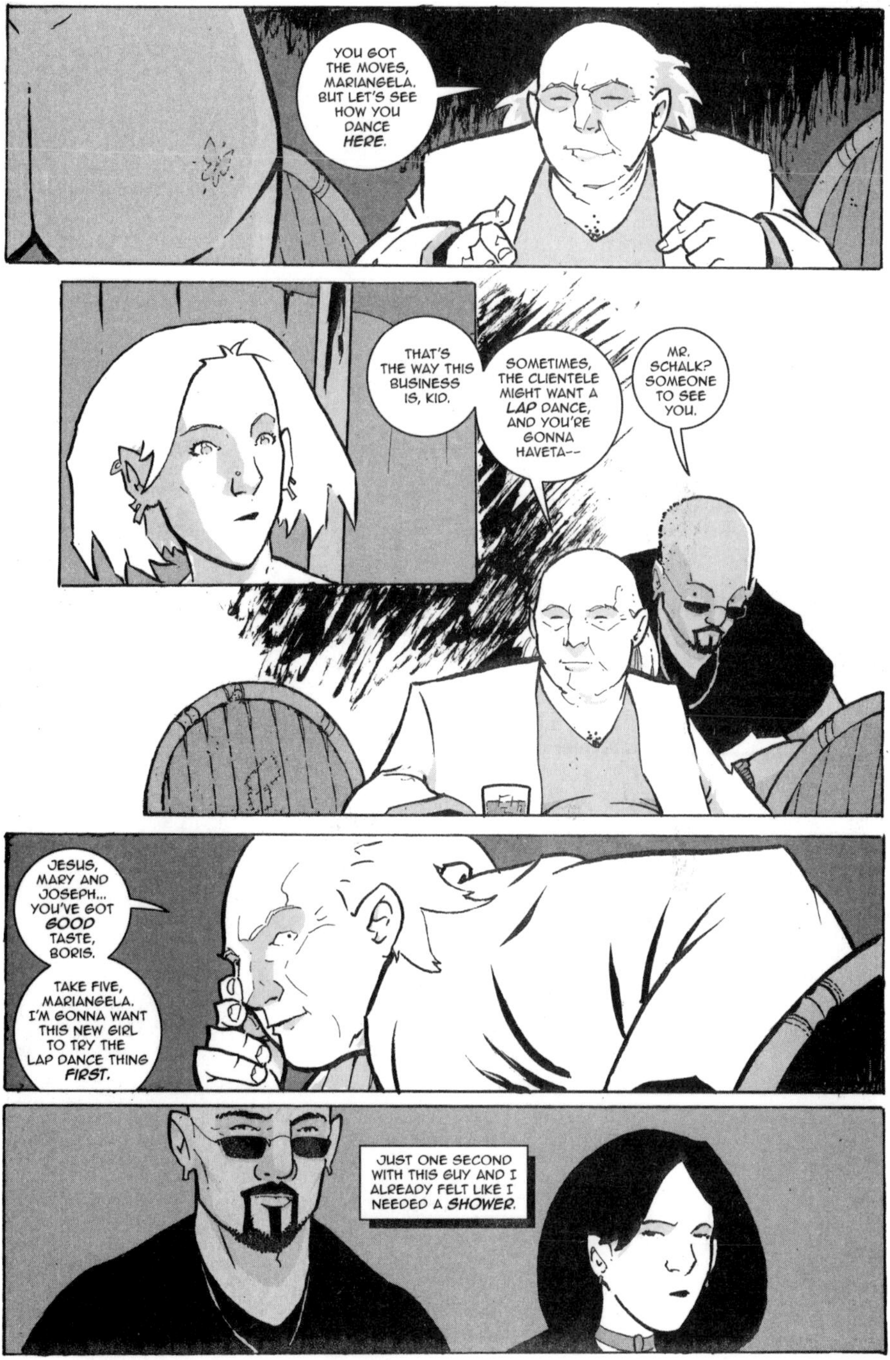
YOU GOT THE MOVES, MARIANGELA. BUT LET'S SEE HOW YOU DANCE *HERE*.
THAT'S THE WAY THIS BUSINESS IS, KID.
SOMETIMES, THE CLIENTELE MIGHT WANT A *LAP* DANCE, AND YOU'RE GONNA HAVETA--
MR. SCHALK? SOMEONE TO SEE YOU.
JESUS, MARY AND JOSEPH... YOU'VE GOT *GOOD* TASTE, BORIS.
TAKE FIVE, MARIANGELA. I'M GONNA WANT THIS NEW GIRL TO TRY THE LAP DANCE THING *FIRST*.
JUST ONE SECOND WITH THIS GUY AND I ALREADY FELT LIKE I NEEDED A *SHOWER*.

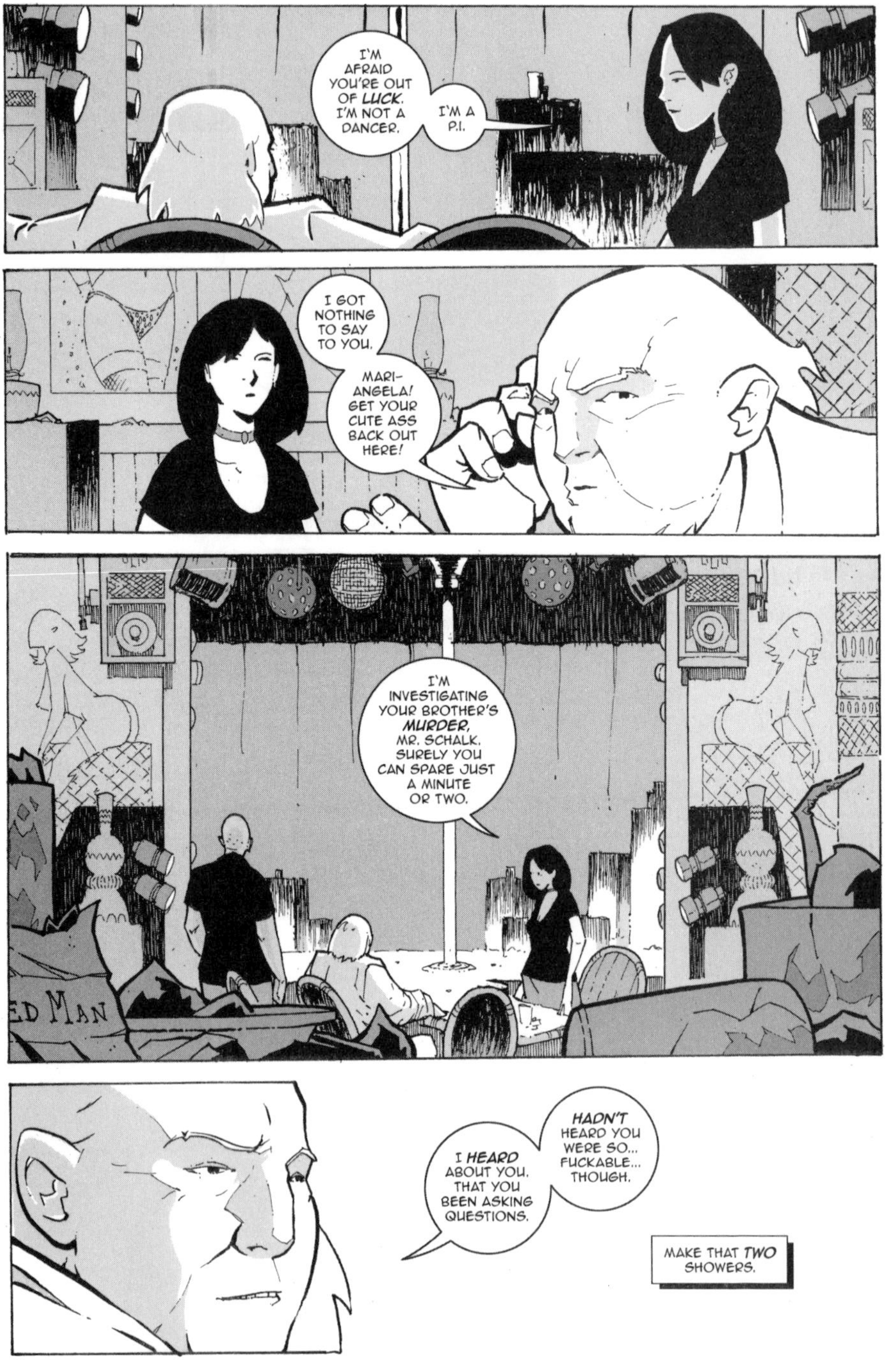
I'M AFRAID YOU'RE OUT OF LUCK. I'M NOT A DANCER.
I'M A P.I.
I GOT NOTHING TO SAY TO YOU.
MARI-ANGELA! GET YOUR CUTE ASS BACK OUT HERE!
I'M INVESTIGATING YOUR BROTHER'S MURDER, MR. SCHALK. SURELY YOU CAN SPARE JUST A MINUTE OR TWO.
ED MAN
I HEARD ABOUT YOU. THAT YOU BEEN ASKING QUESTIONS.
HADN'T HEARD YOU WERE SO... FUCKABLE... THOUGH.
MAKE THAT TWO SHOWERS.

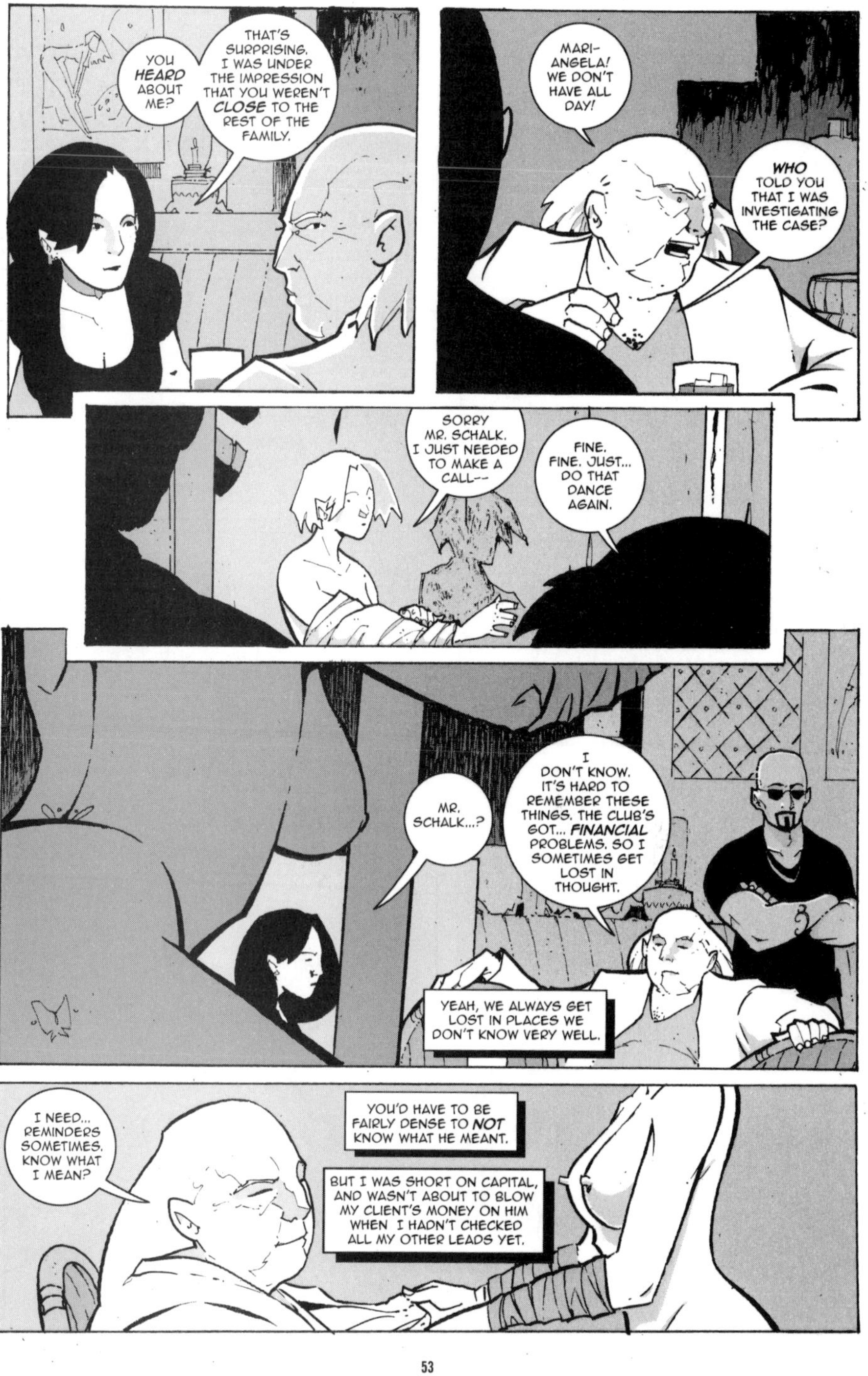
YOU HEARD ABOUT ME?
THAT'S SURPRISING. I WAS UNDER THE IMPRESSION THAT YOU WEREN'T CLOSE TO THE REST OF THE FAMILY.
MARI-ANGELA! WE DON'T HAVE ALL DAY!
WHO TOLD YOU THAT I WAS INVESTIGATING THE CASE?
SORRY MR. SCHALK. I JUST NEEDED TO MAKE A CALL--
FINE. FINE. JUST... DO THAT DANCE AGAIN.
MR. SCHALK...?
I DON'T KNOW. IT'S HARD TO REMEMBER THESE THINGS. THE CLUB'S GOT... FINANCIAL PROBLEMS. SO I SOMETIMES GET LOST IN THOUGHT.
YEAH, WE ALWAYS GET LOST IN PLACES WE DON'T KNOW VERY WELL.
I NEED... REMINDERS SOMETIMES. KNOW WHAT I MEAN?
YOU'D HAVE TO BE FAIRLY DENSE TO NOT KNOW WHAT HE MEANT.
BUT I WAS SHORT ON CAPITAL, AND WASN'T ABOUT TO BLOW MY CLIENT'S MONEY ON HIM WHEN I HADN'T CHECKED ALL MY OTHER LEADS YET.

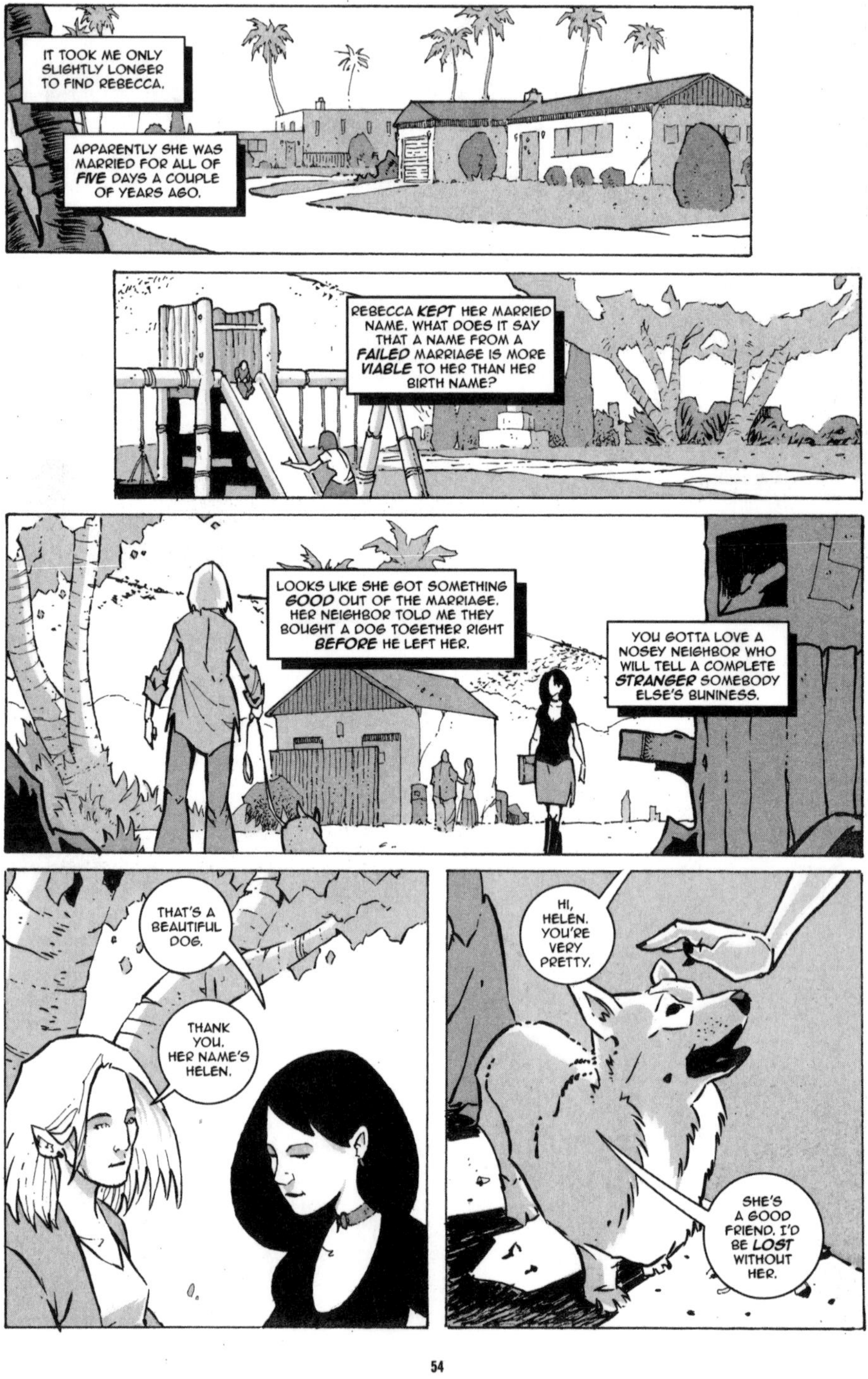

IT TOOK ME ONLY SLIGHTLY LONGER TO FIND REBECCA.
APPARENTLY SHE WAS MARRIED FOR ALL OF *FIVE* DAYS A COUPLE OF YEARS AGO.
REBECCA *KEPT* HER MARRIED NAME. WHAT DOES IT SAY THAT A NAME FROM A *FAILED* MARRIAGE IS MORE *VIABLE* TO HER THAN HER BIRTH NAME?
LOOKS LIKE SHE GOT SOMETHING *GOOD* OUT OF THE MARRIAGE. HER NEIGHBOR TOLD ME THEY BOUGHT A DOG TOGETHER RIGHT *BEFORE* HE LEFT HER.
YOU GOTTA LOVE A NOSEY NEIGHBOR WHO WILL TELL A COMPLETE *STRANGER* SOMEBODY ELSE'S BUNINESS.
THAT'S A BEAUTIFUL DOG.
THANK YOU. HER NAME'S HELEN.
HI, HELEN. YOU'RE VERY PRETTY.
SHE'S A GOOD FRIEND. I'D BE *LOST* WITHOUT HER.

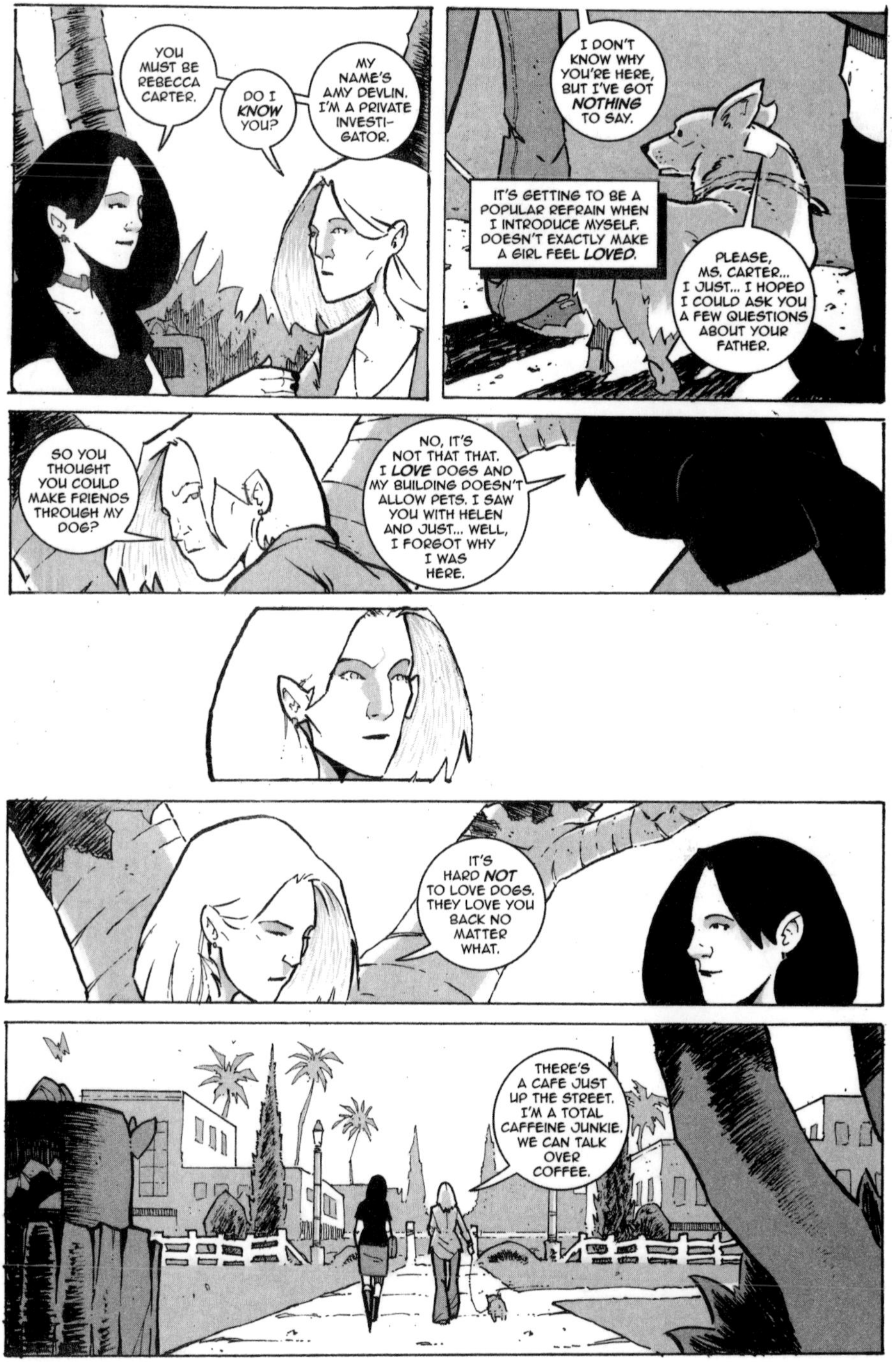
YOU MUST BE REBECCA CARTER.
DO I KNOW YOU?
MY NAME'S AMY DEVLIN. I'M A PRIVATE INVESTI-GATOR.
I DON'T KNOW WHY YOU'RE HERE, BUT I'VE GOT NOTHING TO SAY.
IT'S GETTING TO BE A POPULAR REFRAIN WHEN I INTRODUCE MYSELF. DOESN'T EXACTLY MAKE A GIRL FEEL LOVED.
PLEASE, MS. CARTER... I JUST... I HOPED I COULD ASK YOU A FEW QUESTIONS ABOUT YOUR FATHER.
SO YOU THOUGHT YOU COULD MAKE FRIENDS THROUGH MY DOG?
NO, IT'S NOT THAT THAT. I LOVE DOGS AND MY BUILDING DOESN'T ALLOW PETS. I SAW YOU WITH HELEN AND JUST... WELL, I FORGOT WHY I WAS HERE.
IT'S HARD NOT TO LOVE DOGS. THEY LOVE YOU BACK NO MATTER WHAT.
THERE'S A CAFE JUST UP THE STREET. I'M A TOTAL CAFFEINE JUNKIE. WE CAN TALK OVER COFFEE.

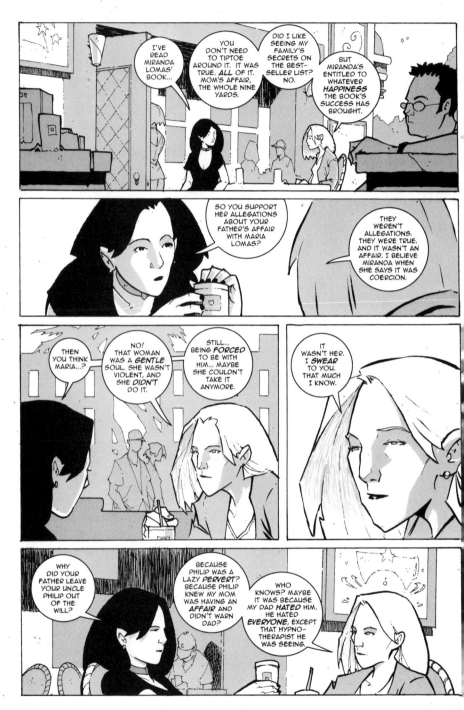

I'VE READ MIRANDA LOMAS' BOOK...

YOU DON'T NEED TO TIPTOE AROUND IT. IT WAS TRUE. *ALL* OF IT. MOM'S AFFAIR, THE WHOLE NINE YARDS.

DID I LIKE SEEING MY FAMILY'S SECRETS ON THE BEST-SELLER LIST? NO.

BUT MIRANDA'S ENTITLED TO WHATEVER *HAPPINESS* THE BOOK'S SUCCESS HAS BROUGHT.

SO YOU SUPPORT HER ALLEGATIONS ABOUT YOUR FATHER'S AFFAIR WITH MARIA LOMAS?

THEY WEREN'T ALLEGATIONS. THEY WERE TRUE. AND IT WASN'T AN AFFAIR. I BELIEVE MIRANDA WHEN SHE SAYS IT WAS COERCION.

THEN YOU THINK MARIA...?

NO! THAT WOMAN WAS A *GENTLE* SOUL. SHE WASN'T VIOLENT, AND SHE *DIDN'T* DO IT.

STILL... BEING *FORCED* TO BE WITH HIM... MAYBE SHE COULDN'T TAKE IT ANYMORE.

IT WASN'T HER. I *SWEAR* TO YOU. THAT MUCH I KNOW.

WHY DID YOUR FATHER LEAVE YOUR UNCLE PHILIP OUT OF THE WILL?

BECAUSE PHILIP WAS A LAZY *PERVERT*? BECAUSE PHILIP KNEW MY MOM WAS HAVING AN *AFFAIR* AND DIDN'T WARN DAD?

WHO KNOWS? MAYBE IT WAS BECAUSE MY DAD *HATED* HIM. HE HATED *EVERYONE*, EXCEPT THAT HYPNO-THERAPIST HE WAS SEEING.

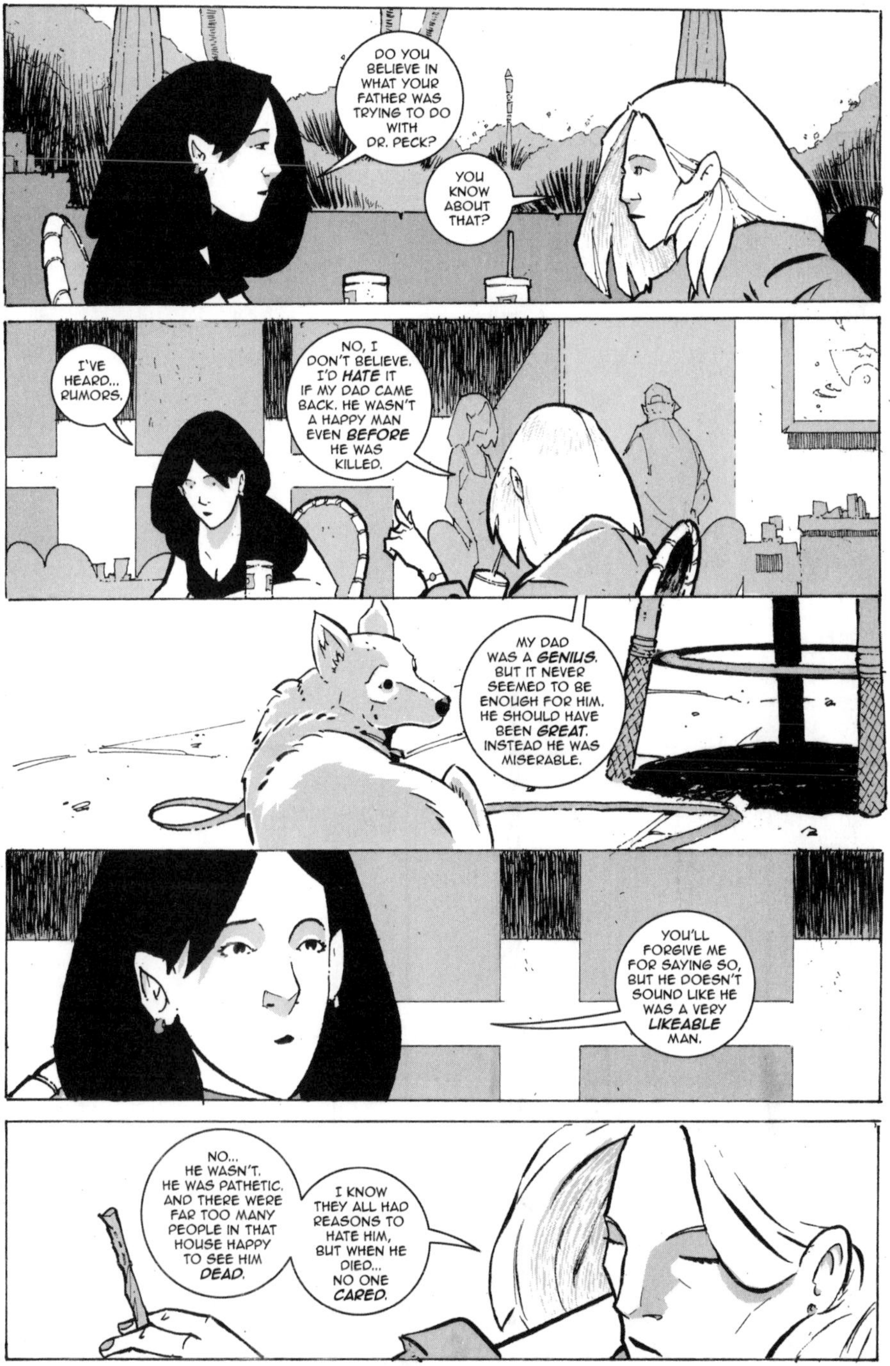
DO YOU BELIEVE IN WHAT YOUR FATHER WAS TRYING TO DO WITH DR. PECK?
YOU KNOW ABOUT THAT?
I'VE HEARD... RUMORS.
NO, I DON'T BELIEVE. I'D HATE IT IF MY DAD CAME BACK. HE WASN'T A HAPPY MAN EVEN BEFORE HE WAS KILLED.
MY DAD WAS A GENIUS. BUT IT NEVER SEEMED TO BE ENOUGH FOR HIM. HE SHOULD HAVE BEEN GREAT. INSTEAD HE WAS MISERABLE.
YOU'LL FORGIVE ME FOR SAYING SO, BUT HE DOESN'T SOUND LIKE HE WAS A VERY LIKEABLE MAN.
NO... HE WASN'T. HE WAS PATHETIC. AND THERE WERE FAR TOO MANY PEOPLE IN THAT HOUSE HAPPY TO SEE HIM DEAD.
I KNOW THEY ALL HAD REASONS TO HATE HIM, BUT WHEN HE DIED... NO ONE CARED.

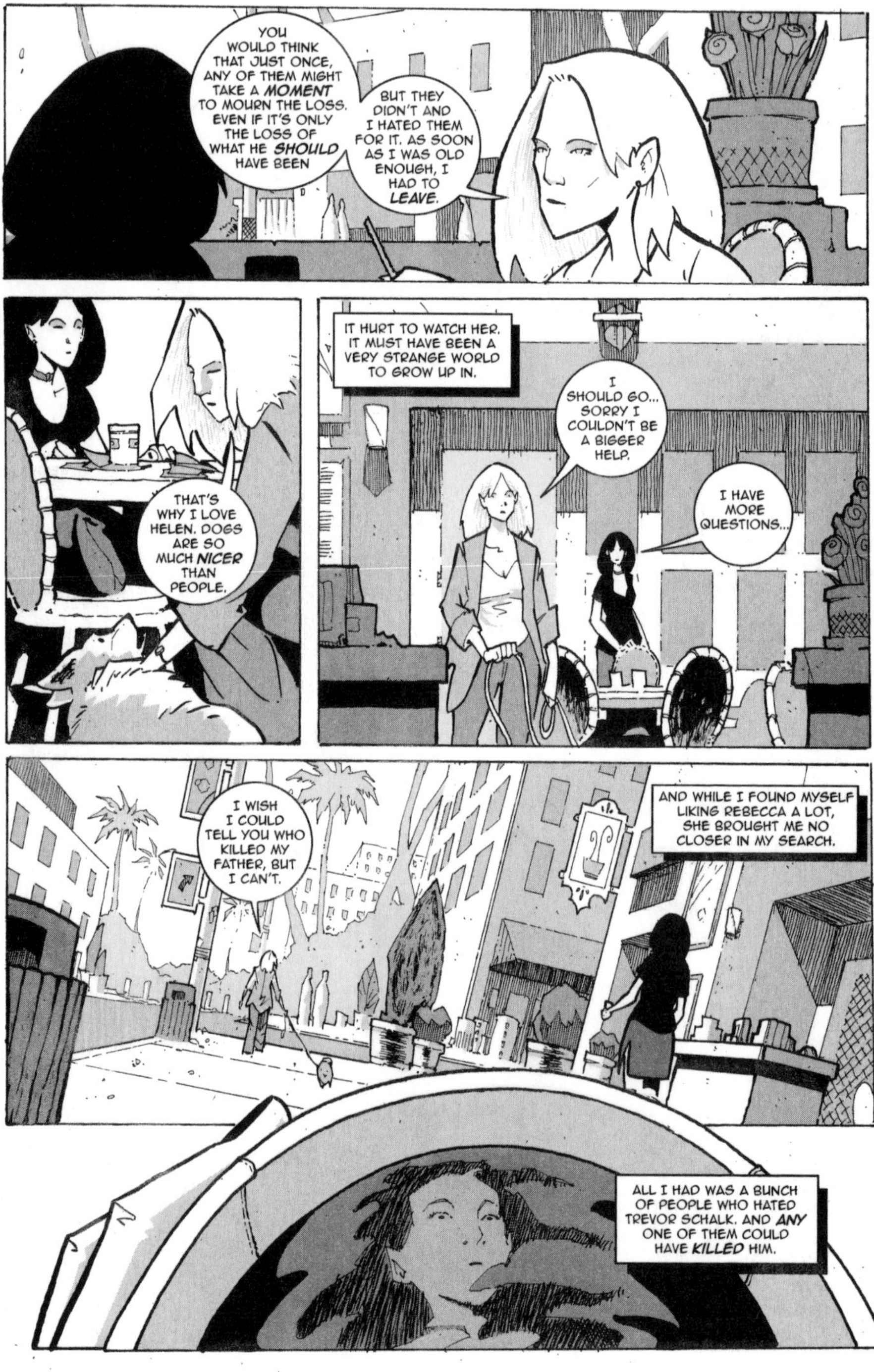
YOU WOULD THINK THAT JUST ONCE, ANY OF THEM MIGHT TAKE A MOMENT TO MOURN THE LOSS. EVEN IF IT'S ONLY THE LOSS OF WHAT HE SHOULD HAVE BEEN
BUT THEY DIDN'T AND I HATED THEM FOR IT. AS SOON AS I WAS OLD ENOUGH, I HAD TO LEAVE.
THAT'S WHY I LOVE HELEN. DOGS ARE SO MUCH NICER THAN PEOPLE.
IT HURT TO WATCH HER. IT MUST HAVE BEEN A VERY STRANGE WORLD TO GROW UP IN.
I SHOULD GO... SORRY I COULDN'T BE A BIGGER HELP.
I HAVE MORE QUESTIONS...
I WISH I COULD TELL YOU WHO KILLED MY FATHER, BUT I CAN'T.
AND WHILE I FOUND MYSELF LIKING REBECCA A LOT, SHE BROUGHT ME NO CLOSER IN MY SEARCH.
ALL I HAD WAS A BUNCH OF PEOPLE WHO HATED TREVOR SCHALK. AND ANY ONE OF THEM COULD HAVE KILLED HIM.

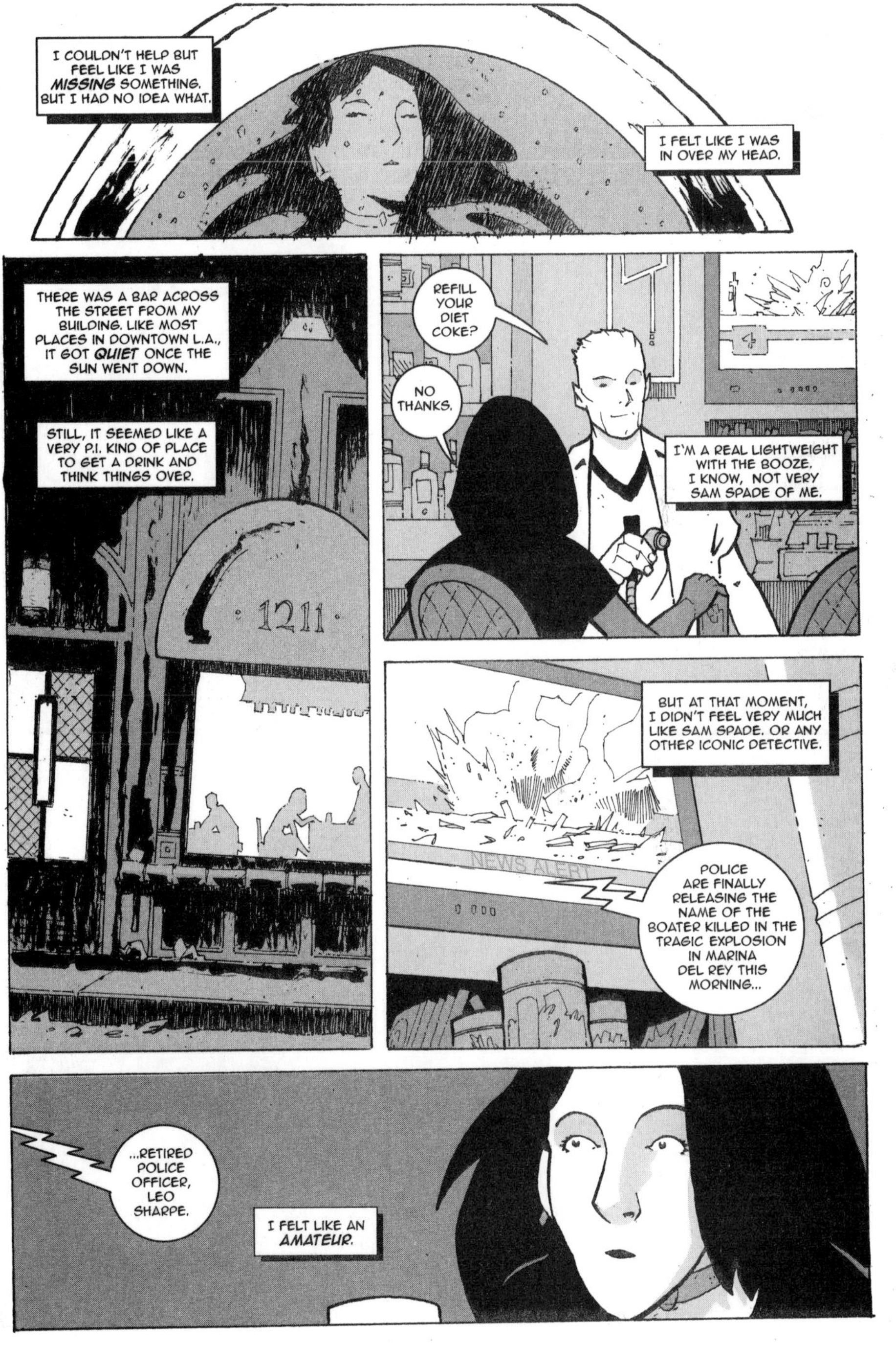
I COULDN'T HELP BUT FEEL LIKE I WAS MISSING SOMETHING. BUT I HAD NO IDEA WHAT.
I FELT LIKE I WAS IN OVER MY HEAD.
THERE WAS A BAR ACROSS THE STREET FROM MY BUILDING. LIKE MOST PLACES IN DOWNTOWN L.A., IT GOT QUIET ONCE THE SUN WENT DOWN.
STILL, IT SEEMED LIKE A VERY P.I. KIND OF PLACE TO GET A DRINK AND THINK THINGS OVER.
1211
REFILL YOUR DIET COKE?
NO THANKS.
I'M A REAL LIGHTWEIGHT WITH THE BOOZE. I KNOW, NOT VERY SAM SPADE OF ME.
BUT AT THAT MOMENT, I DIDN'T FEEL VERY MUCH LIKE SAM SPADE. OR ANY OTHER ICONIC DETECTIVE.
NEWS ALERT
POLICE ARE FINALLY RELEASING THE NAME OF THE BOATER KILLED IN THE TRAGIC EXPLOSION IN MARINA DEL REY THIS MORNING...
...RETIRED POLICE OFFICER, LEO SHARPE.
I FELT LIKE AN AMATEUR.

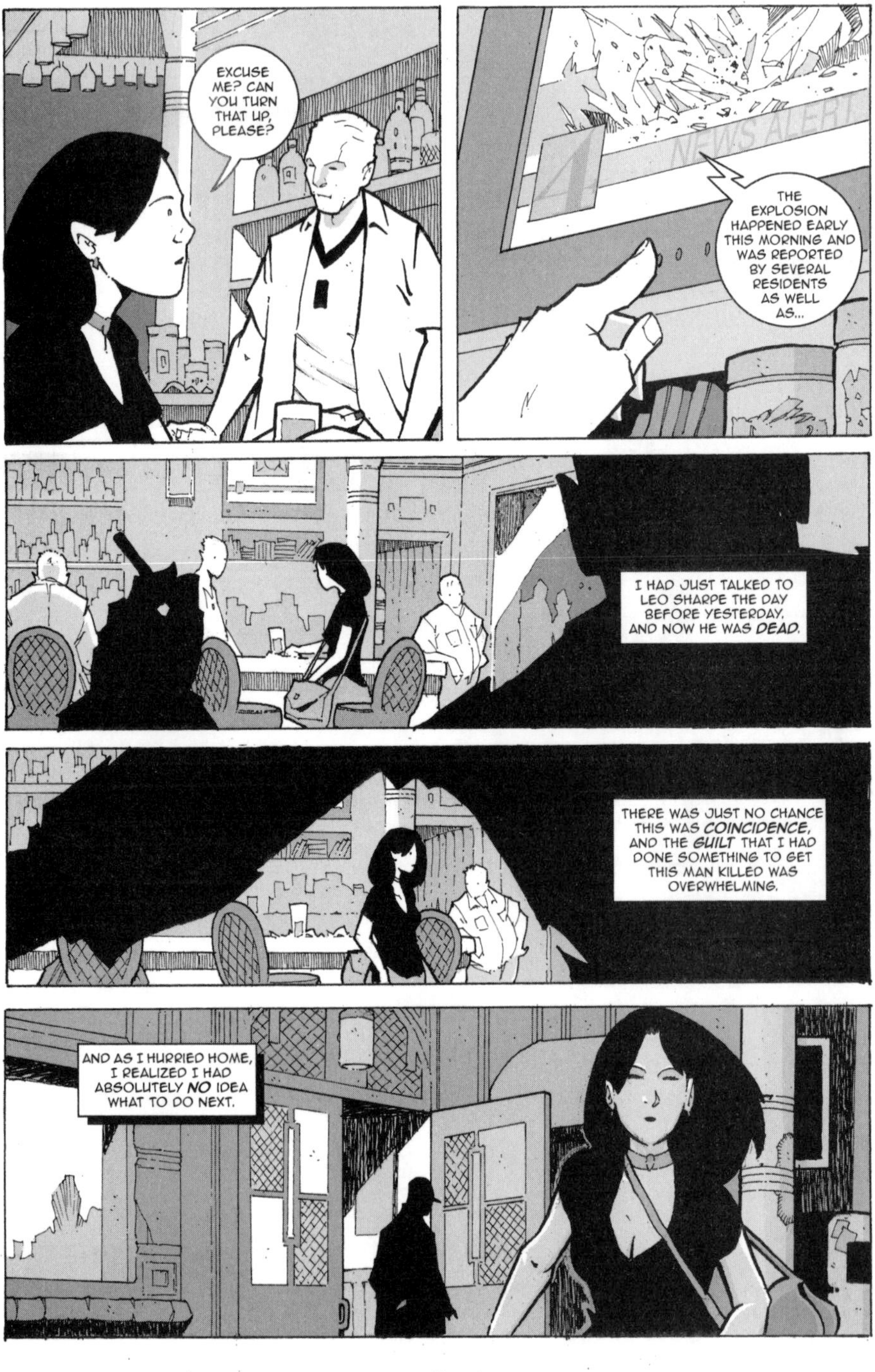
EXCUSE ME? CAN YOU TURN THAT UP, PLEASE?
NEWS ALERT
THE EXPLOSION HAPPENED EARLY THIS MORNING AND WAS REPORTED BY SEVERAL RESIDENTS AS WELL AS...
I HAD JUST TALKED TO LEO SHARPE THE DAY BEFORE YESTERDAY. AND NOW HE WAS *DEAD*.
THERE WAS JUST NO CHANCE THIS WAS *COINCIDENCE*, AND THE *GUILT* THAT I HAD DONE SOMETHING TO GET THIS MAN KILLED WAS OVERWHELMING.
AND AS I HURRIED HOME, I REALIZED I HAD ABSOLUTELY *NO* IDEA WHAT TO DO NEXT.

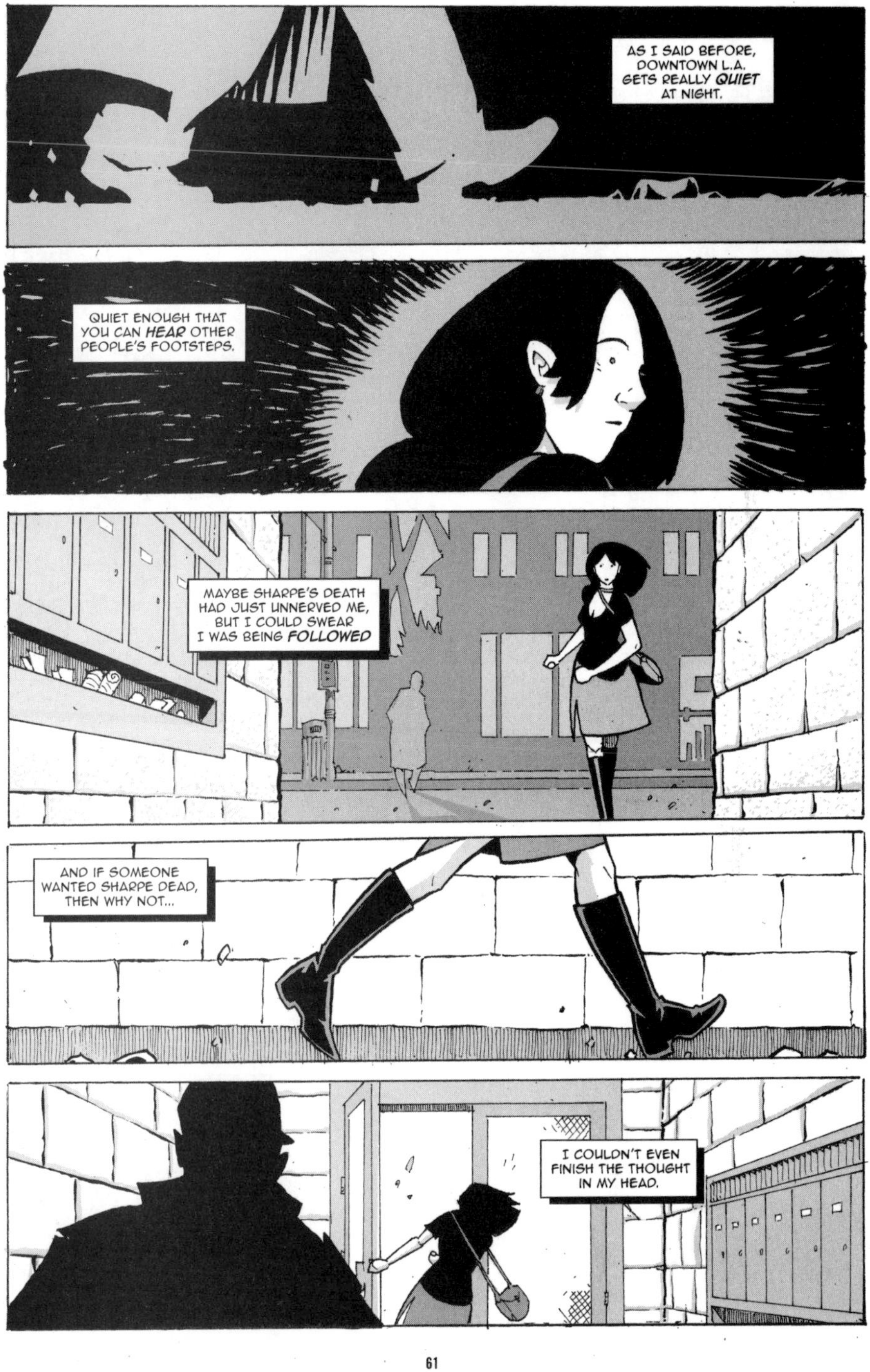

AS I SAID BEFORE, DOWNTOWN L.A. GETS REALLY QUIET AT NIGHT.
QUIET ENOUGH THAT YOU CAN HEAR OTHER PEOPLE'S FOOTSTEPS.
MAYBE SHARPE'S DEATH HAD JUST UNNERVED ME, BUT I COULD SWEAR I WAS BEING FOLLOWED
AND IF SOMEONE WANTED SHARPE DEAD, THEN WHY NOT...
I COULDN'T EVEN FINISH THE THOUGHT IN MY HEAD.

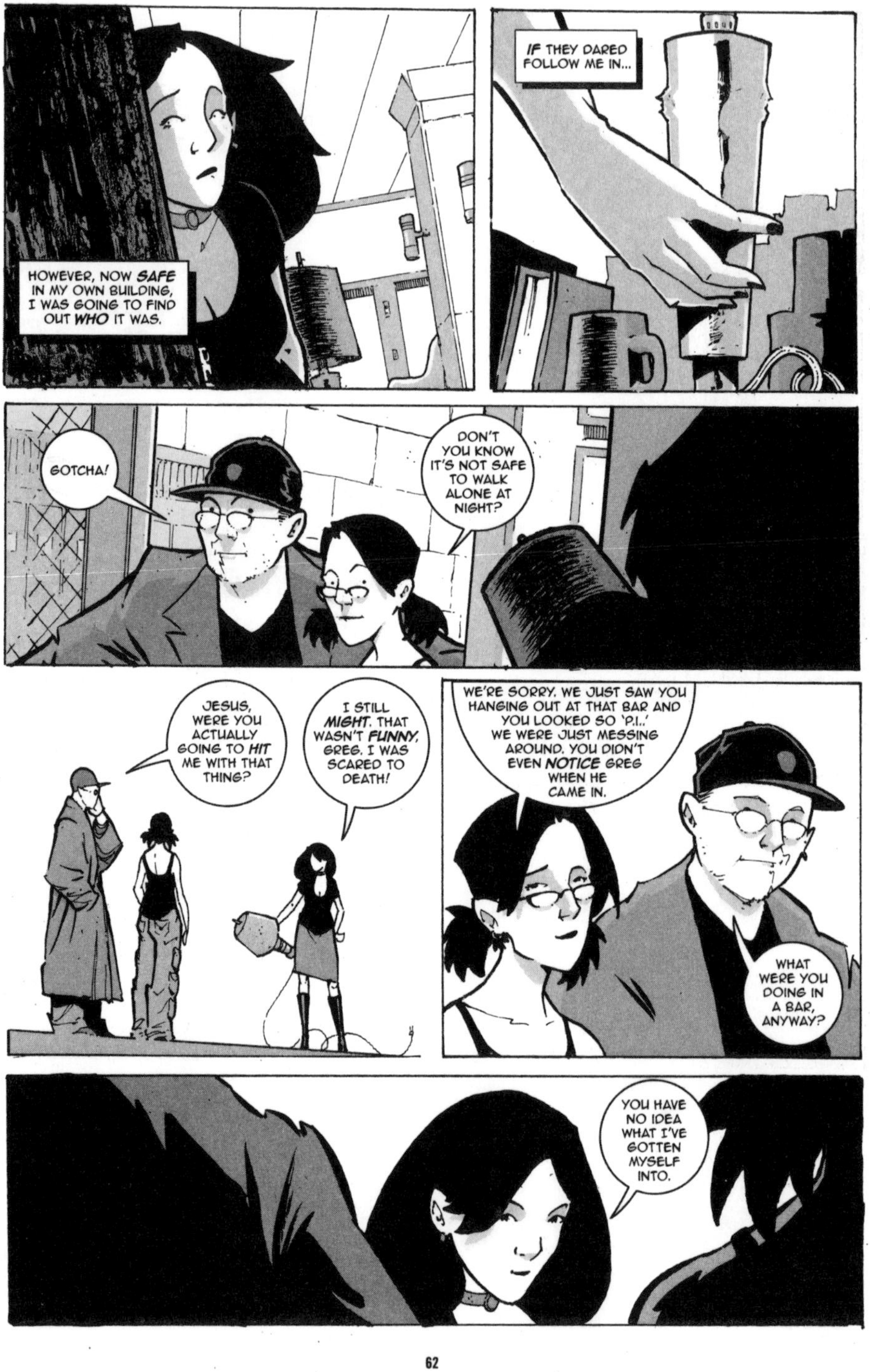
HOWEVER, NOW SAFE IN MY OWN BUILDING, I WAS GOING TO FIND OUT WHO IT WAS.
IF THEY DARED FOLLOW ME IN...
GOTCHA!
DON'T YOU KNOW IT'S NOT SAFE TO WALK ALONE AT NIGHT?
JESUS, WERE YOU ACTUALLY GOING TO HIT ME WITH THAT THING?
I STILL MIGHT. THAT WASN'T FUNNY, GREG. I WAS SCARED TO DEATH!
WE'RE SORRY. WE JUST SAW YOU HANGING OUT AT THAT BAR AND YOU LOOKED SO 'P.I..' WE WERE JUST MESSING AROUND. YOU DIDN'T EVEN NOTICE GREG WHEN HE CAME IN.
WHAT WERE YOU DOING IN A BAR, ANYWAY?
YOU HAVE NO IDEA WHAT I'VE GOTTEN MYSELF INTO.

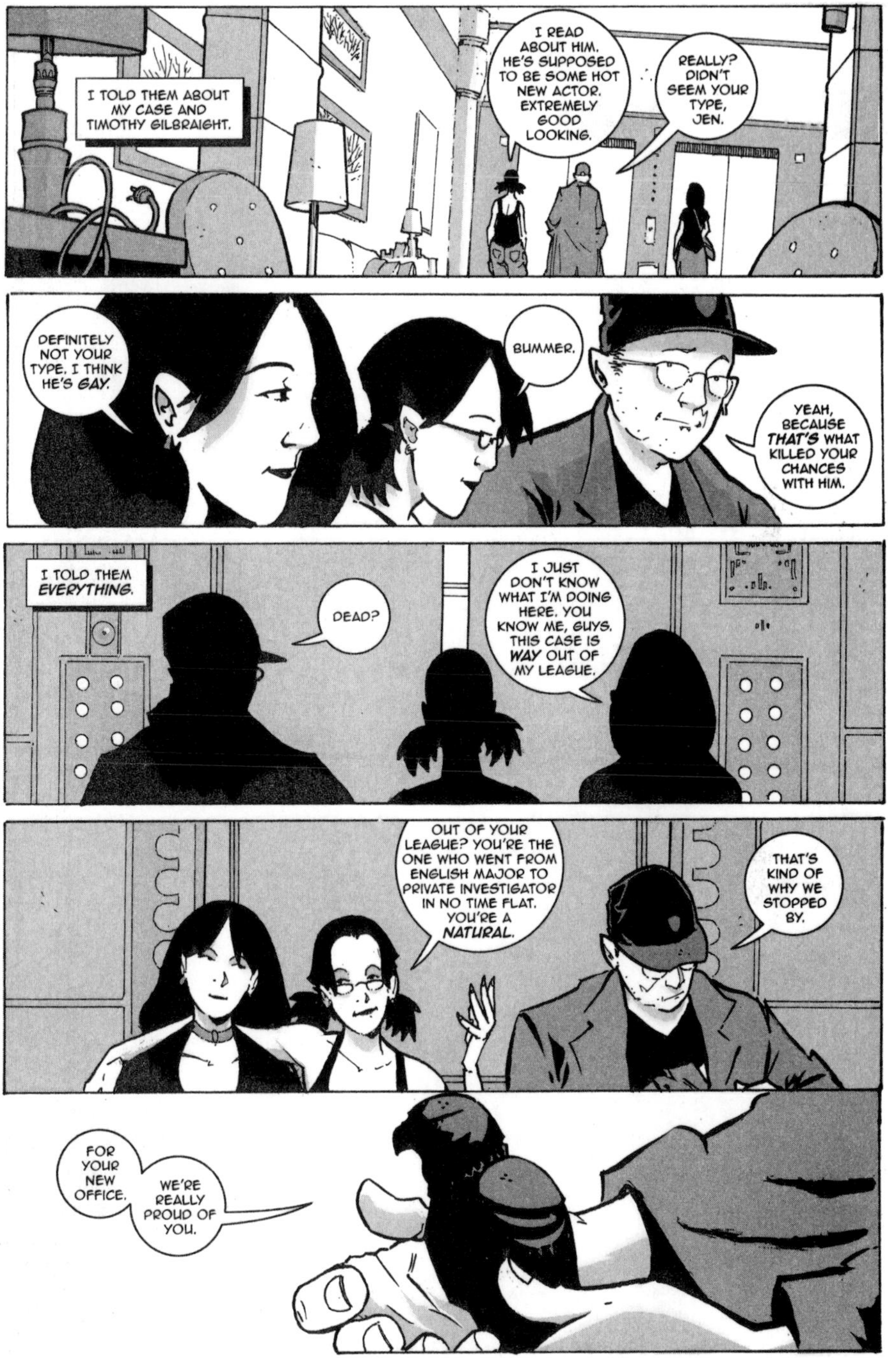
I TOLD THEM ABOUT MY CASE AND TIMOTHY GILBRAIGHT.
I READ ABOUT HIM. HE'S SUPPOSED TO BE SOME HOT NEW ACTOR. EXTREMELY GOOD LOOKING.
REALLY? DIDN'T SEEM YOUR TYPE, JEN.
DEFINITELY NOT YOUR TYPE. I THINK HE'S GAY.
BUMMER.
YEAH, BECAUSE THAT'S WHAT KILLED YOUR CHANCES WITH HIM.
I TOLD THEM EVERYTHING.
DEAD?
I JUST DON'T KNOW WHAT I'M DOING HERE. YOU KNOW ME, GUYS. THIS CASE IS WAY OUT OF MY LEAGUE.
OUT OF YOUR LEAGUE? YOU'RE THE ONE WHO WENT FROM ENGLISH MAJOR TO PRIVATE INVESTIGATOR IN NO TIME FLAT. YOU'RE A NATURAL.
THAT'S KIND OF WHY WE STOPPED BY.
FOR YOUR NEW OFFICE.
WE'RE REALLY PROUD OF YOU.

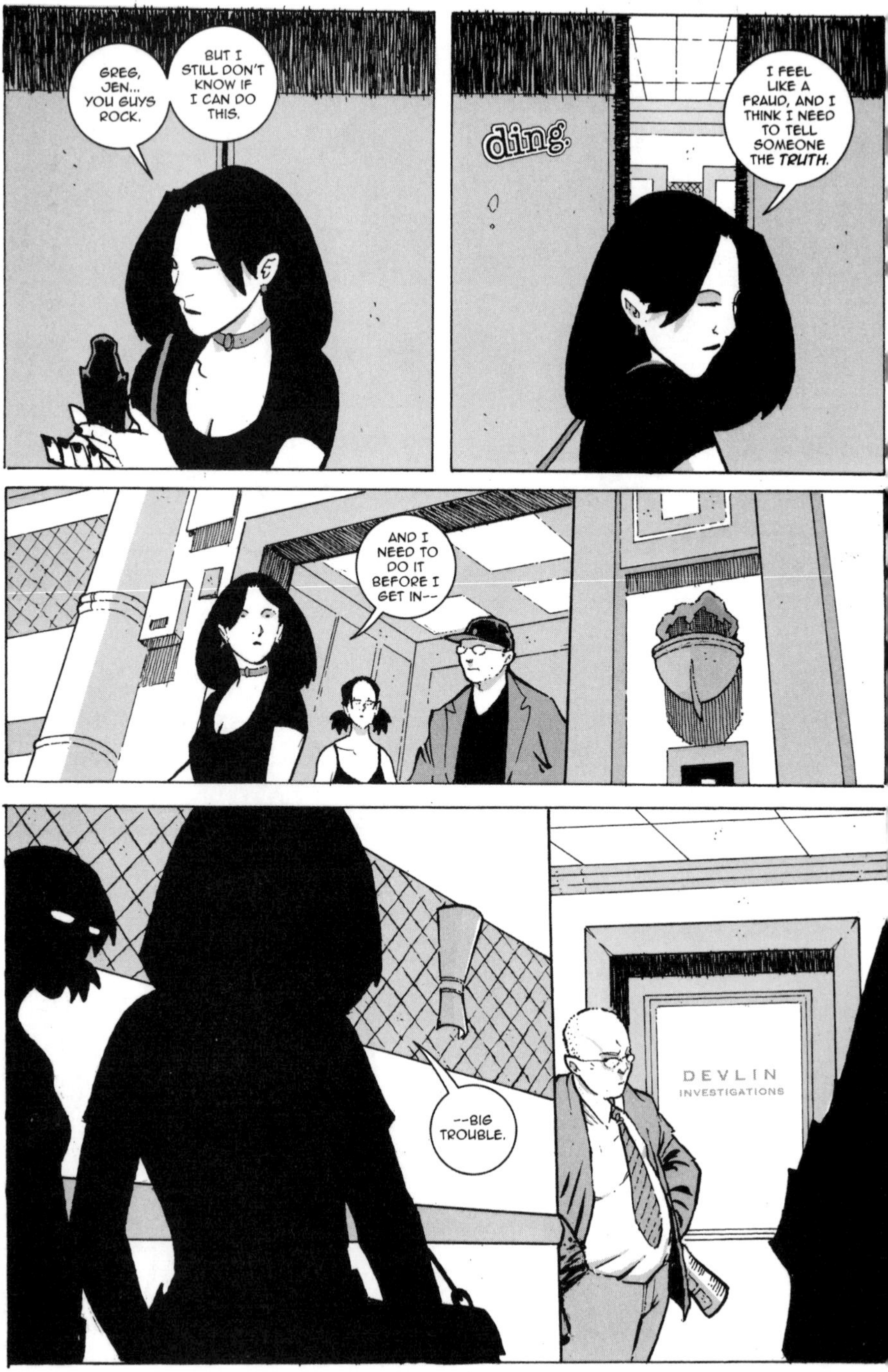
GREG, JEN... YOU GUYS ROCK.
BUT I STILL DON'T KNOW IF I CAN DO THIS.
ding.
I FEEL LIKE A FRAUD, AND I THINK I NEED TO TELL SOMEONE THE TRUTH.
AND I NEED TO DO IT BEFORE I GET IN--
DEVLIN INVESTIGATIONS
--BIG TROUBLE.

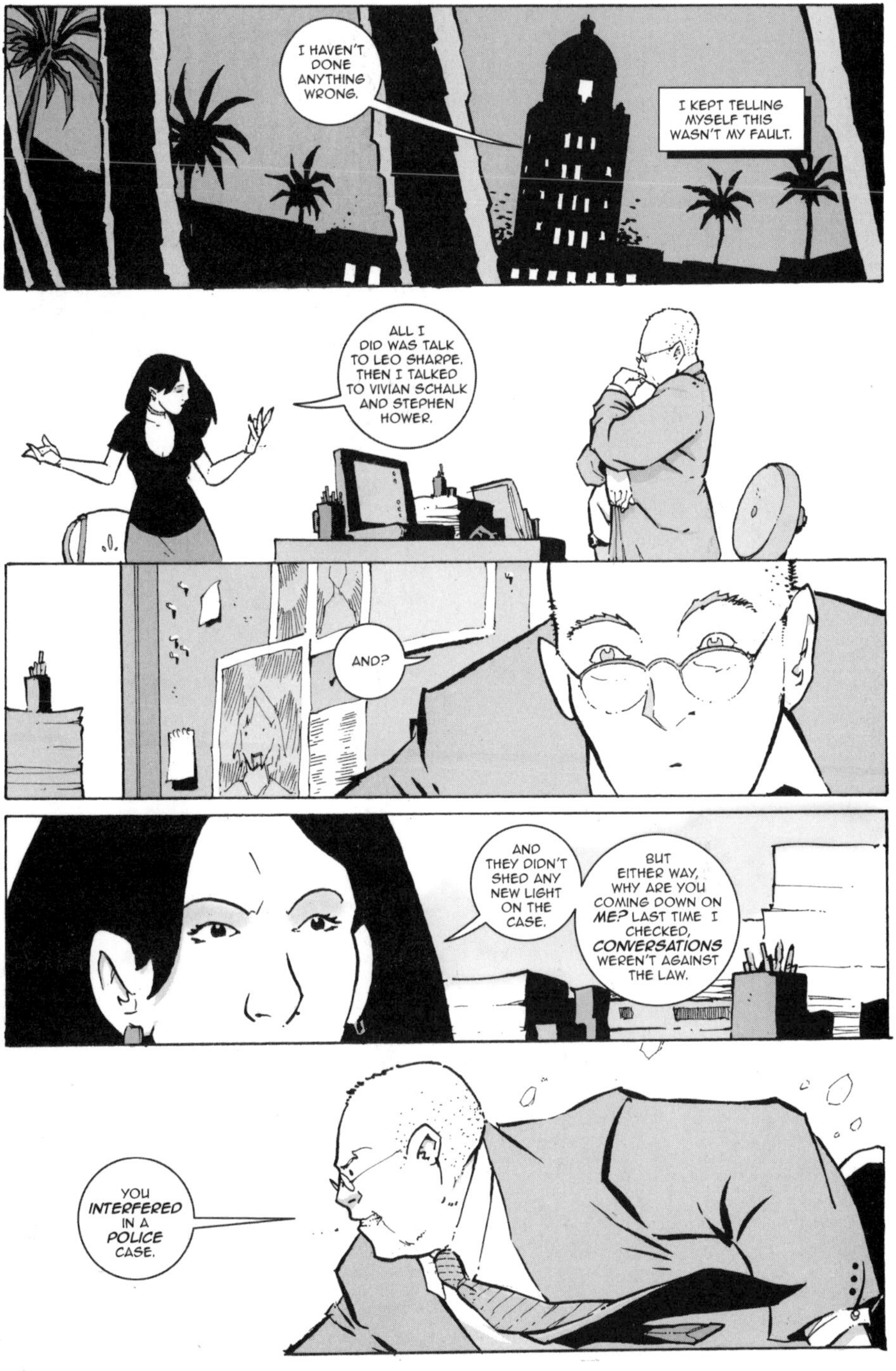
I HAVEN'T DONE ANYTHING WRONG.
I KEPT TELLING MYSELF THIS WASN'T MY FAULT.
ALL I DID WAS TALK TO LEO SHARPE. THEN I TALKED TO VIVIAN SCHALK AND STEPHEN HOWER.
AND?
AND THEY DIDN'T SHED ANY NEW LIGHT ON THE CASE.
BUT EITHER WAY, WHY ARE YOU COMING DOWN ON ME? LAST TIME I CHECKED, CONVERSATIONS WEREN'T AGAINST THE LAW.
YOU INTERFERED IN A POLICE CASE.

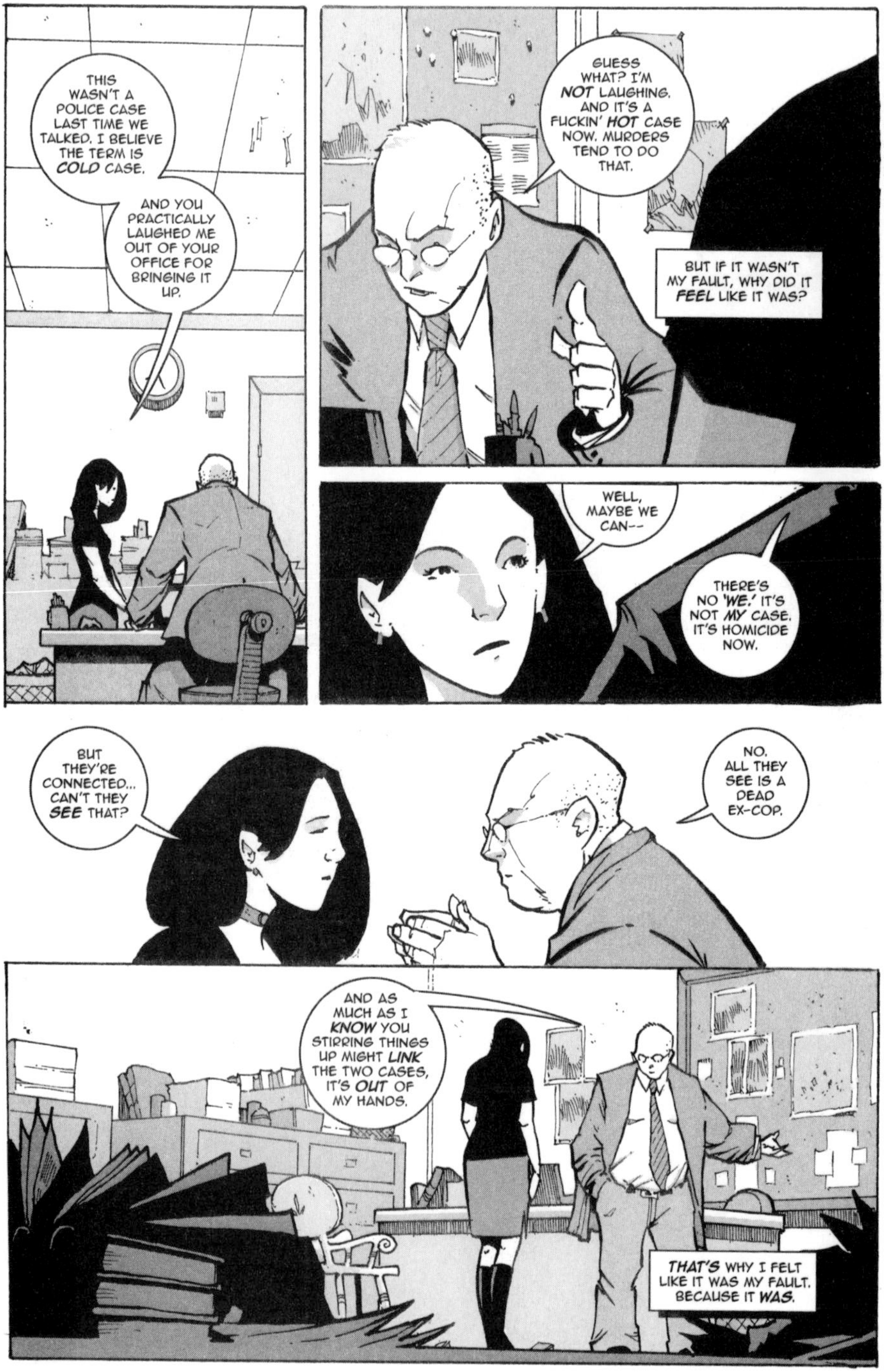
THIS WASN'T A POLICE CASE LAST TIME WE TALKED. I BELIEVE THE TERM IS COLD CASE.
AND YOU PRACTICALLY LAUGHED ME OUT OF YOUR OFFICE FOR BRINGING IT UP.
GUESS WHAT? I'M NOT LAUGHING. AND IT'S A FUCKIN' HOT CASE NOW. MURDERS TEND TO DO THAT.
BUT IF IT WASN'T MY FAULT, WHY DID IT FEEL LIKE IT WAS?
WELL, MAYBE WE CAN--
THERE'S NO 'WE.' IT'S NOT MY CASE. IT'S HOMICIDE NOW.
BUT THEY'RE CONNECTED... CAN'T THEY SEE THAT?
NO. ALL THEY SEE IS A DEAD EX-COP.
AND AS MUCH AS I KNOW YOU STIRRING THINGS UP MIGHT LINK THE TWO CASES, IT'S OUT OF MY HANDS.
THAT'S WHY I FELT LIKE IT WAS MY FAULT. BECAUSE IT WAS.

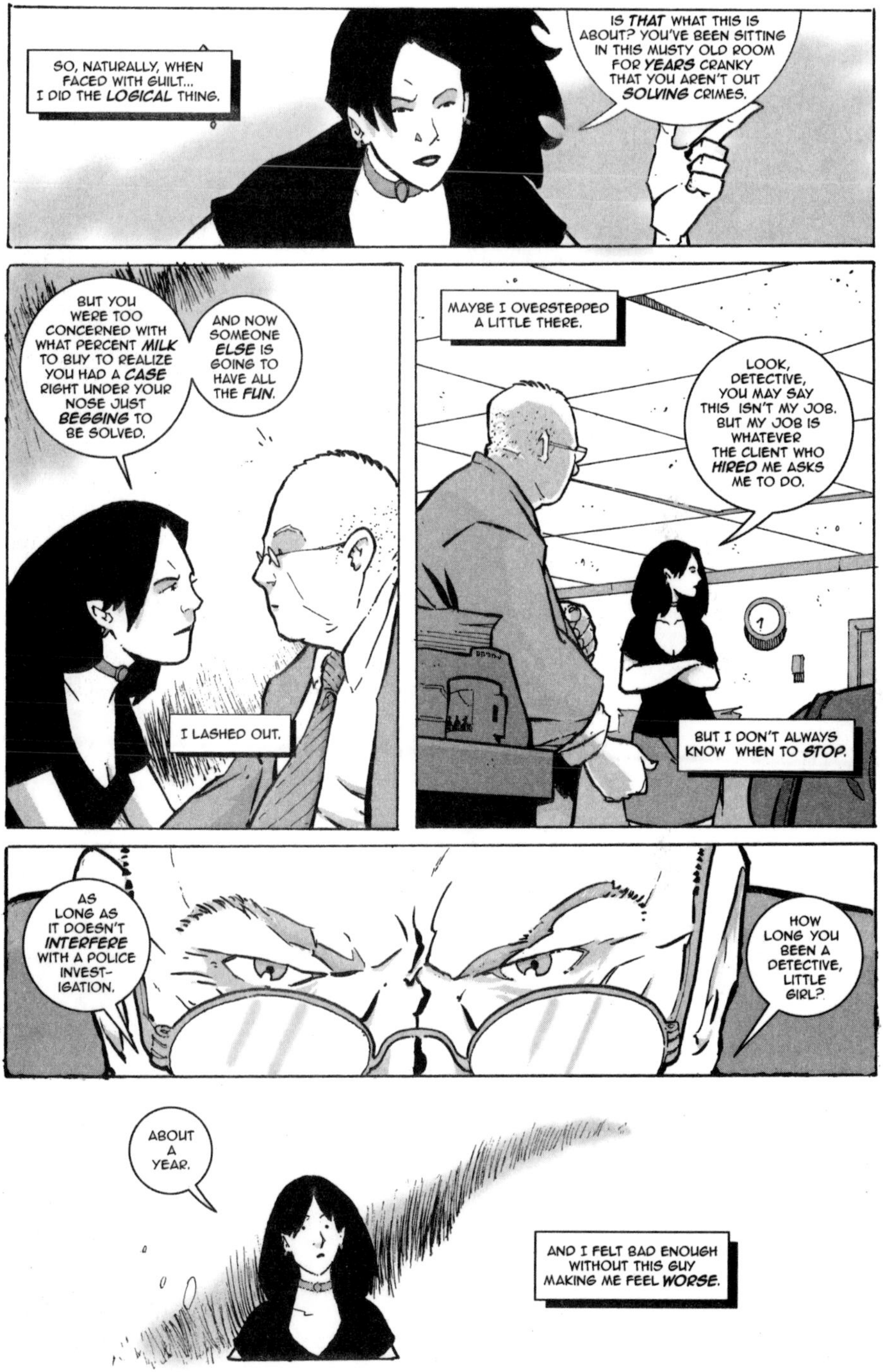
SO, NATURALLY, WHEN FACED WITH GUILT... I DID THE LOGICAL THING.
IS THAT WHAT THIS IS ABOUT? YOU'VE BEEN SITTING IN THIS MUSTY OLD ROOM FOR YEARS CRANKY THAT YOU AREN'T OUT SOLVING CRIMES.
BUT YOU WERE TOO CONCERNED WITH WHAT PERCENT MILK TO BUY TO REALIZE YOU HAD A CASE RIGHT UNDER YOUR NOSE JUST BEGGING TO BE SOLVED.
AND NOW SOMEONE ELSE IS GOING TO HAVE ALL THE FUN.
I LASHED OUT.
MAYBE I OVERSTEPPED A LITTLE THERE.
LOOK, DETECTIVE, YOU MAY SAY THIS ISN'T MY JOB. BUT MY JOB IS WHATEVER THE CLIENT WHO HIRED ME ASKS ME TO DO.
BUT I DON'T ALWAYS KNOW WHEN TO STOP.
AS LONG AS IT DOESN'T INTERFERE WITH A POLICE INVEST-IGATION.
HOW LONG YOU BEEN A DETECTIVE, LITTLE GIRL?
ABOUT A YEAR.
AND I FELT BAD ENOUGH WITHOUT THIS GUY MAKING ME FEEL WORSE.

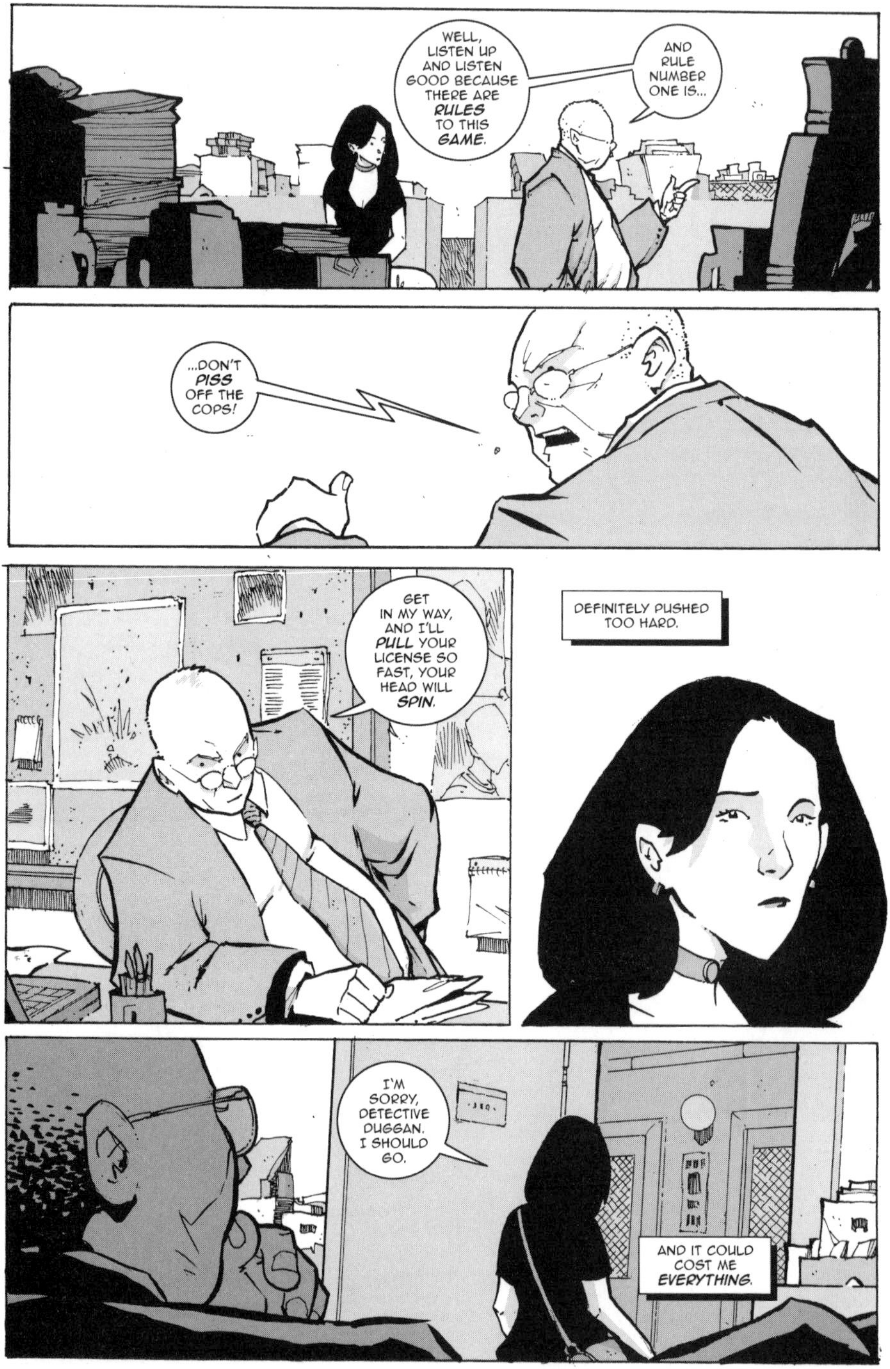
WELL, LISTEN UP AND LISTEN GOOD BECAUSE THERE ARE RULES TO THIS GAME.
AND RULE NUMBER ONE IS...
...DON'T PISS OFF THE COPS!
GET IN MY WAY, AND I'LL PULL YOUR LICENSE SO FAST, YOUR HEAD WILL SPIN.
DEFINITELY PUSHED TOO HARD.
I'M SORRY, DETECTIVE DUGGAN. I SHOULD GO.
AND IT COULD COST ME EVERYTHING.

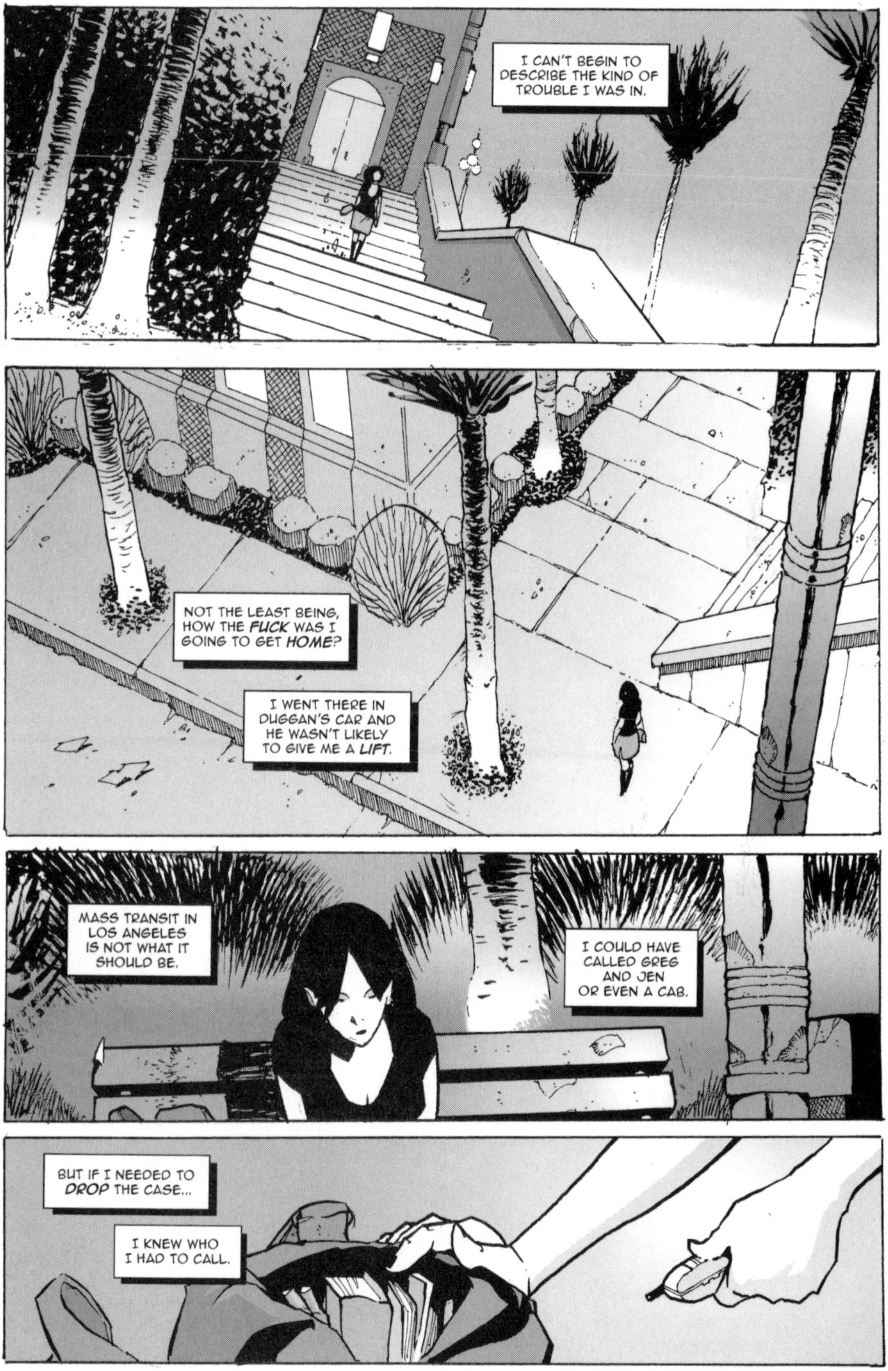
I CAN'T BEGIN TO DESCRIBE THE KIND OF TROUBLE I WAS IN.
NOT THE LEAST BEING, HOW THE FUCK WAS I GOING TO GET HOME?
I WENT THERE IN DUGGAN'S CAR AND HE WASN'T LIKELY TO GIVE ME A LIFT.
MASS TRANSIT IN LOS ANGELES IS NOT WHAT IT SHOULD BE.
I COULD HAVE CALLED GREG AND JEN OR EVEN A CAB.
BUT IF I NEEDED TO DROP THE CASE...
I KNEW WHO I HAD TO CALL.

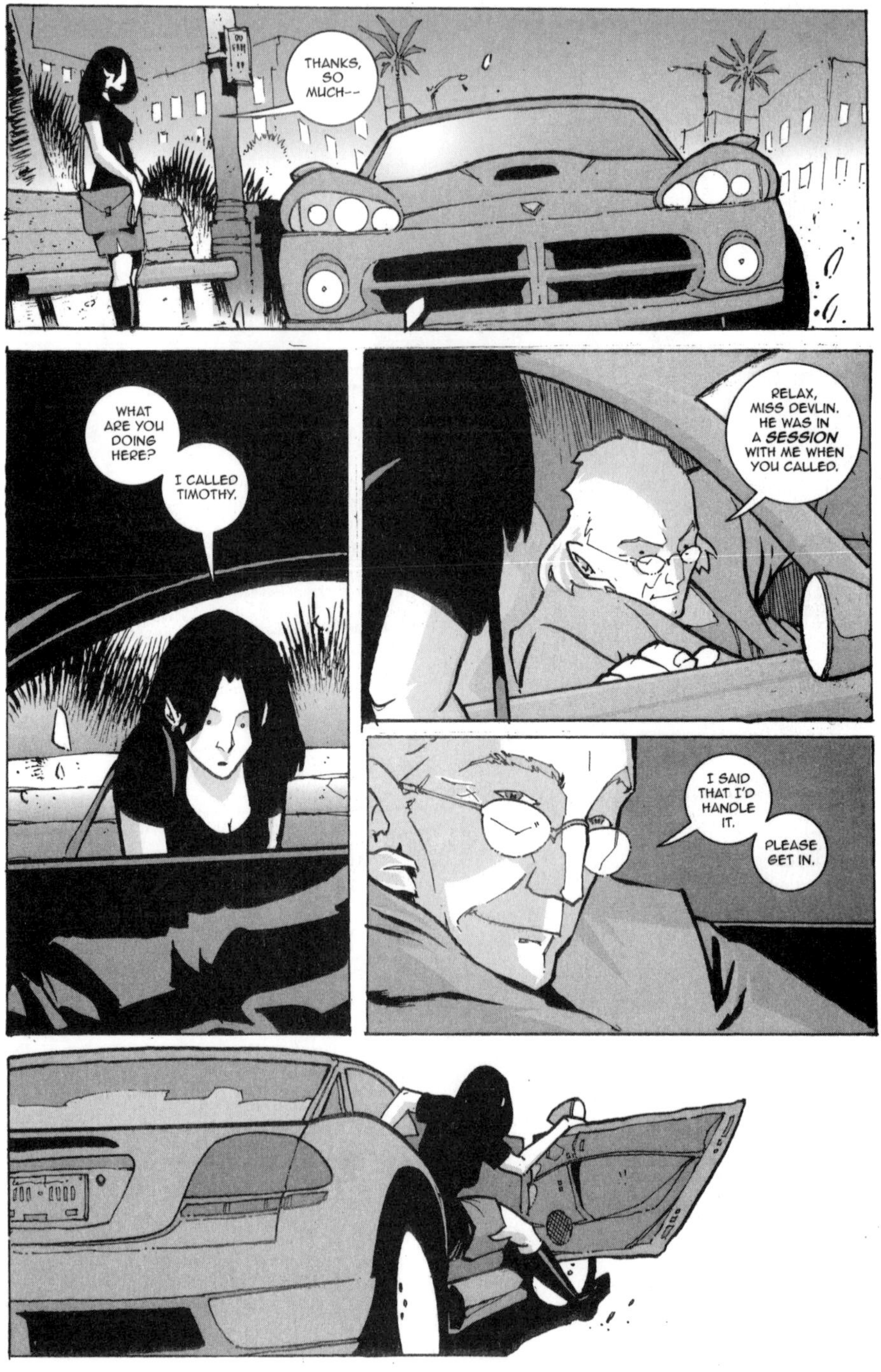

THANKS, SO MUCH--
WHAT ARE YOU DOING HERE?
I CALLED TIMOTHY.
RELAX, MISS DEVLIN. HE WAS IN A ***SESSION*** WITH ME WHEN YOU CALLED.
I SAID THAT I'D HANDLE IT.
PLEASE GET IN.

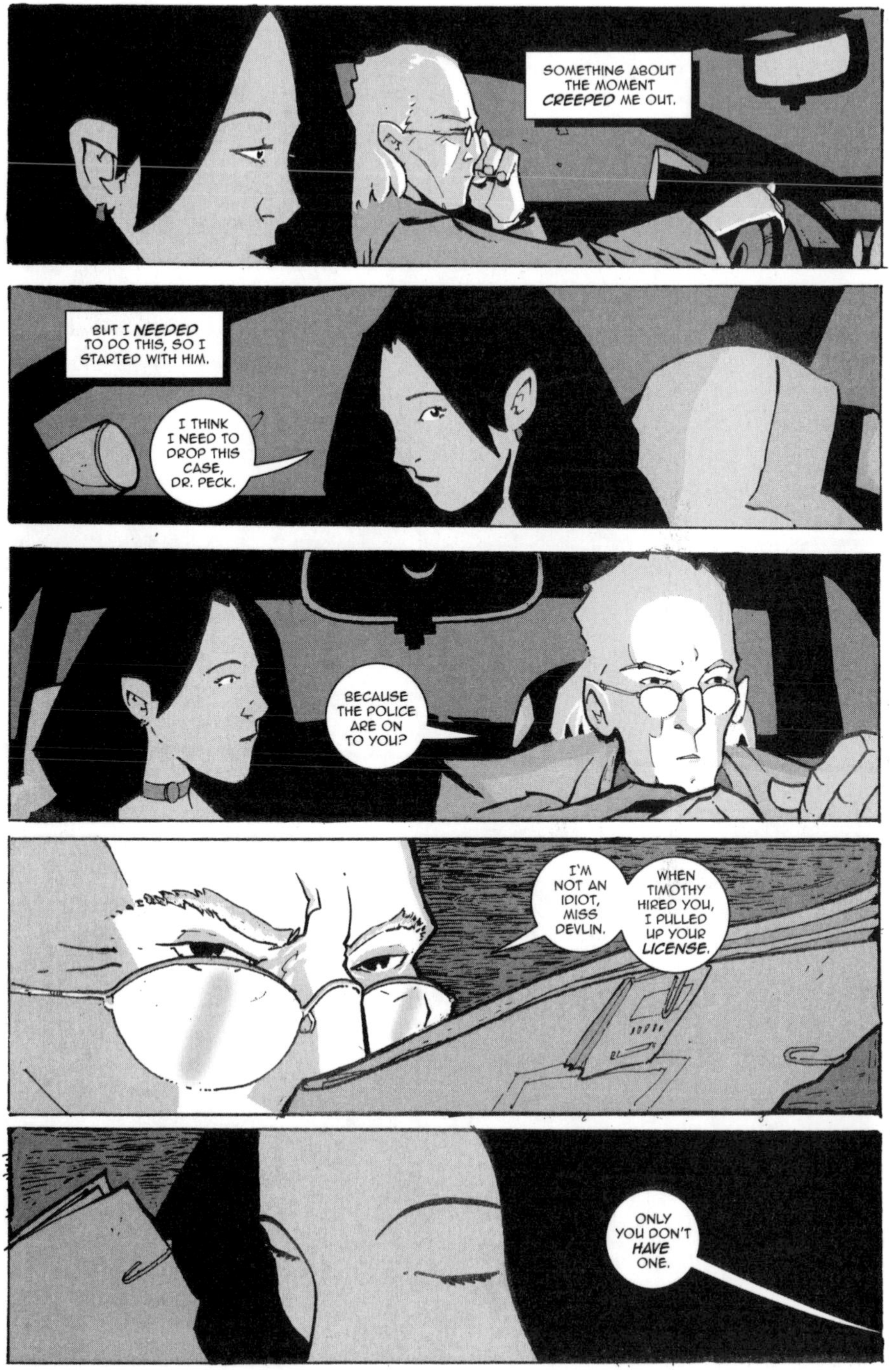
SOMETHING ABOUT THE MOMENT CREEPED ME OUT.
BUT I NEEDED TO DO THIS, SO I STARTED WITH HIM.
I THINK I NEED TO DROP THIS CASE, DR. PECK.
BECAUSE THE POLICE ARE ON TO YOU?
I'M NOT AN IDIOT, MISS DEVLIN.
WHEN TIMOTHY HIRED YOU, I PULLED UP YOUR LICENSE.
ONLY YOU DON'T HAVE ONE.

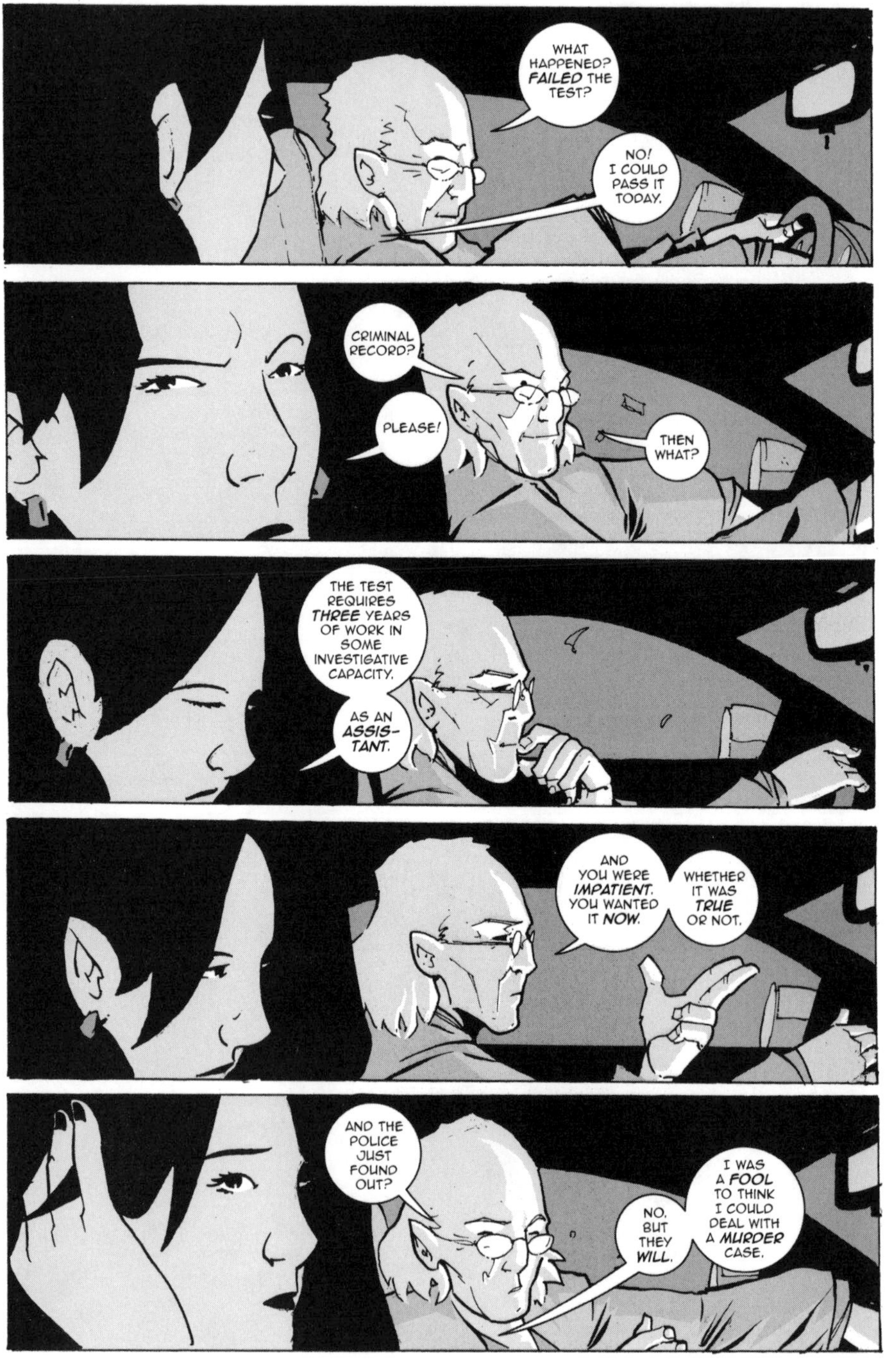
WHAT HAPPENED? FAILED THE TEST?
NO! I COULD PASS IT TODAY.
CRIMINAL RECORD?
PLEASE!
THEN WHAT?
THE TEST REQUIRES THREE YEARS OF WORK IN SOME INVESTIGATIVE CAPACITY.
AS AN ASSIS-TANT.
AND YOU WERE IMPATIENT. YOU WANTED IT NOW.
WHETHER IT WAS TRUE OR NOT.
AND THE POLICE JUST FOUND OUT?
NO, BUT THEY WILL.
I WAS A FOOL TO THINK I COULD DEAL WITH A MURDER CASE.

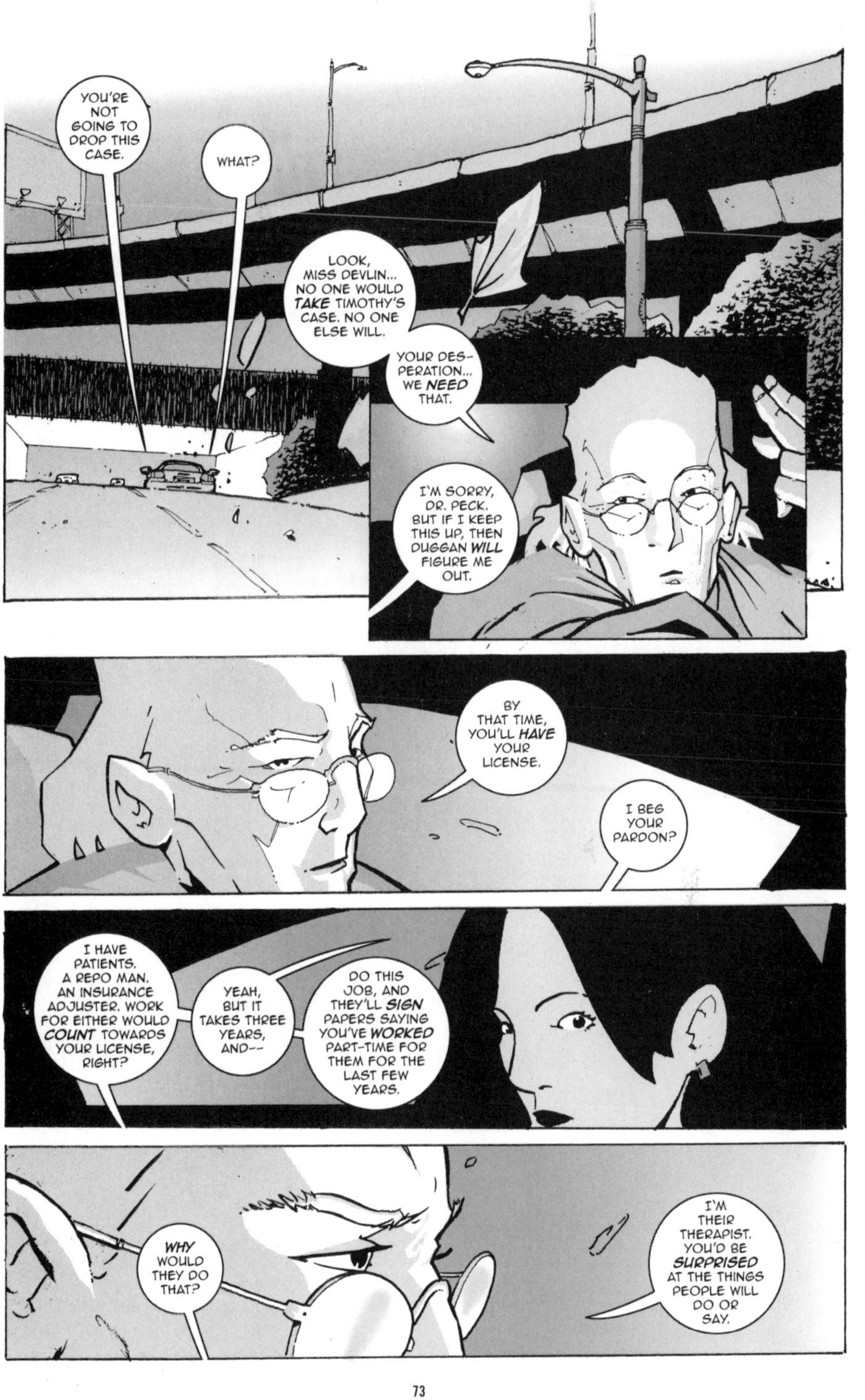

YOU'RE NOT GOING TO DROP THIS CASE.
WHAT?
LOOK, MISS DEVLIN... NO ONE WOULD TAKE TIMOTHY'S CASE. NO ONE ELSE WILL.
YOUR DESPERATION... WE NEED THAT.
I'M SORRY, DR. PECK. BUT IF I KEEP THIS UP, THEN DUGGAN WILL FIGURE ME OUT.
BY THAT TIME, YOU'LL HAVE YOUR LICENSE.
I BEG YOUR PARDON?
I HAVE PATIENTS. A REPO MAN. AN INSURANCE ADJUSTER. WORK FOR EITHER WOULD COUNT TOWARDS YOUR LICENSE, RIGHT?
YEAH, BUT IT TAKES THREE YEARS, AND--
DO THIS JOB, AND THEY'LL SIGN PAPERS SAYING YOU'VE WORKED PART-TIME FOR THEM FOR THE LAST FEW YEARS.
WHY WOULD THEY DO THAT?
I'M THEIR THERAPIST. YOU'D BE SURPRISED AT THE THINGS PEOPLE WILL DO OR SAY.

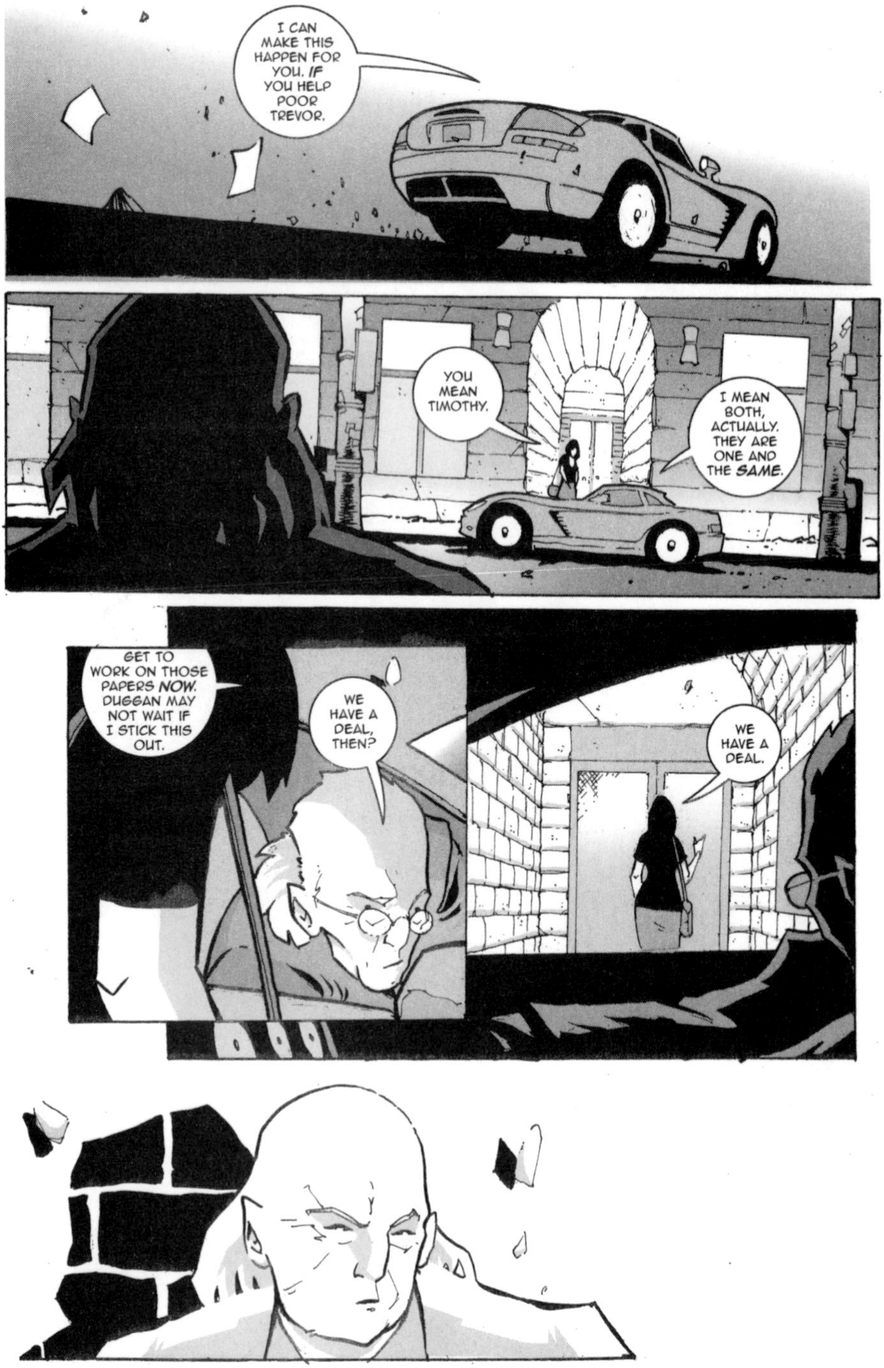
I CAN MAKE THIS HAPPEN FOR YOU. IF YOU HELP POOR TREVOR.
YOU MEAN TIMOTHY.
I MEAN BOTH, ACTUALLY. THEY ARE ONE AND THE SAME.
GET TO WORK ON THOSE PAPERS NOW. DUGGAN MAY NOT WAIT IF I STICK THIS OUT.
WE HAVE A DEAL, THEN?
WE HAVE A DEAL.

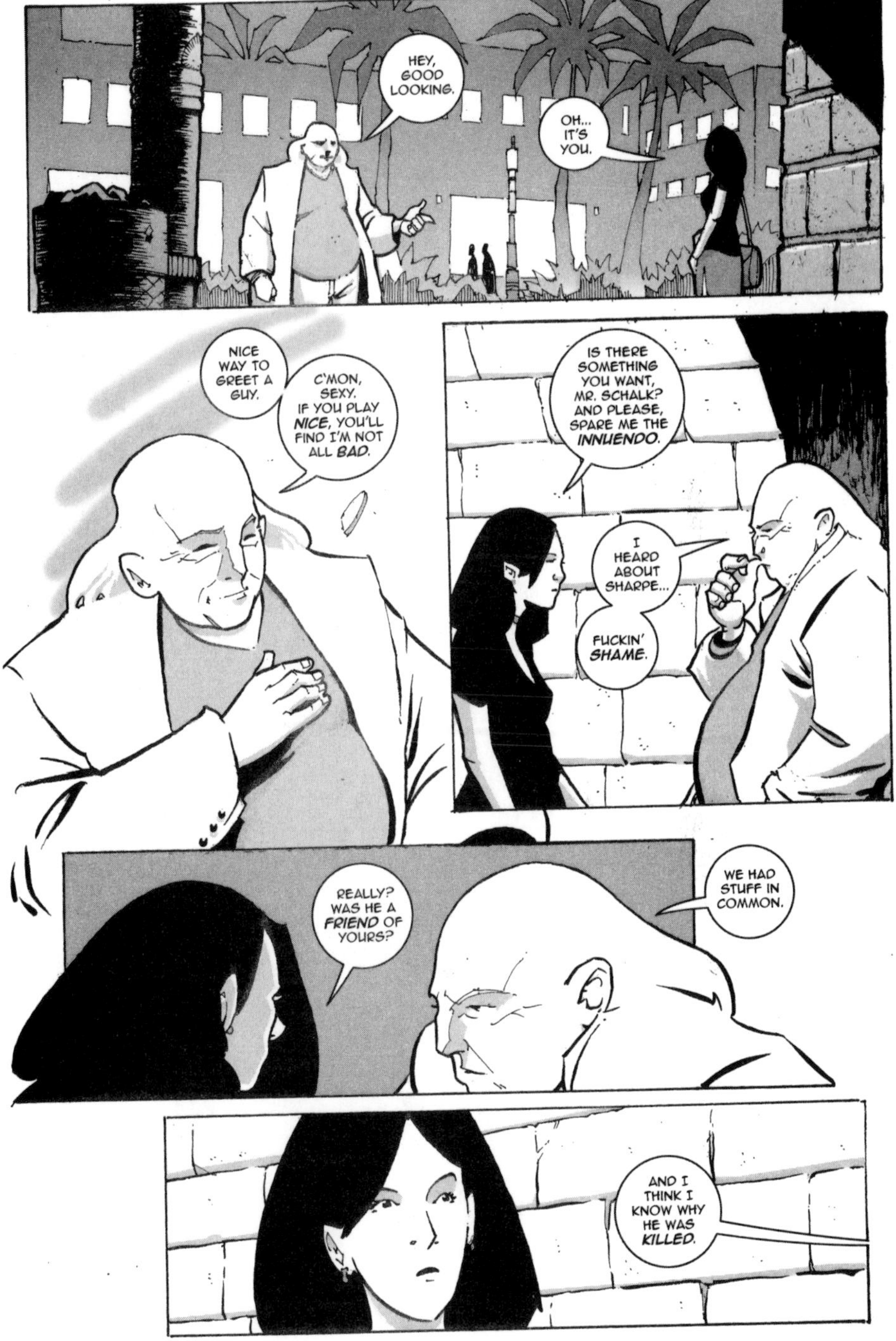
HEY, GOOD LOOKING.
OH... IT'S YOU.
NICE WAY TO GREET A GUY.
C'MON, SEXY. IF YOU PLAY NICE, YOU'LL FIND I'M NOT ALL BAD.
IS THERE SOMETHING YOU WANT, MR. SCHALK? AND PLEASE, SPARE ME THE INNUENDO.
I HEARD ABOUT SHARPE...
FUCKIN' SHAME.
REALLY? WAS HE A FRIEND OF YOURS?
WE HAD STUFF IN COMMON.
AND I THINK I KNOW WHY HE WAS KILLED.

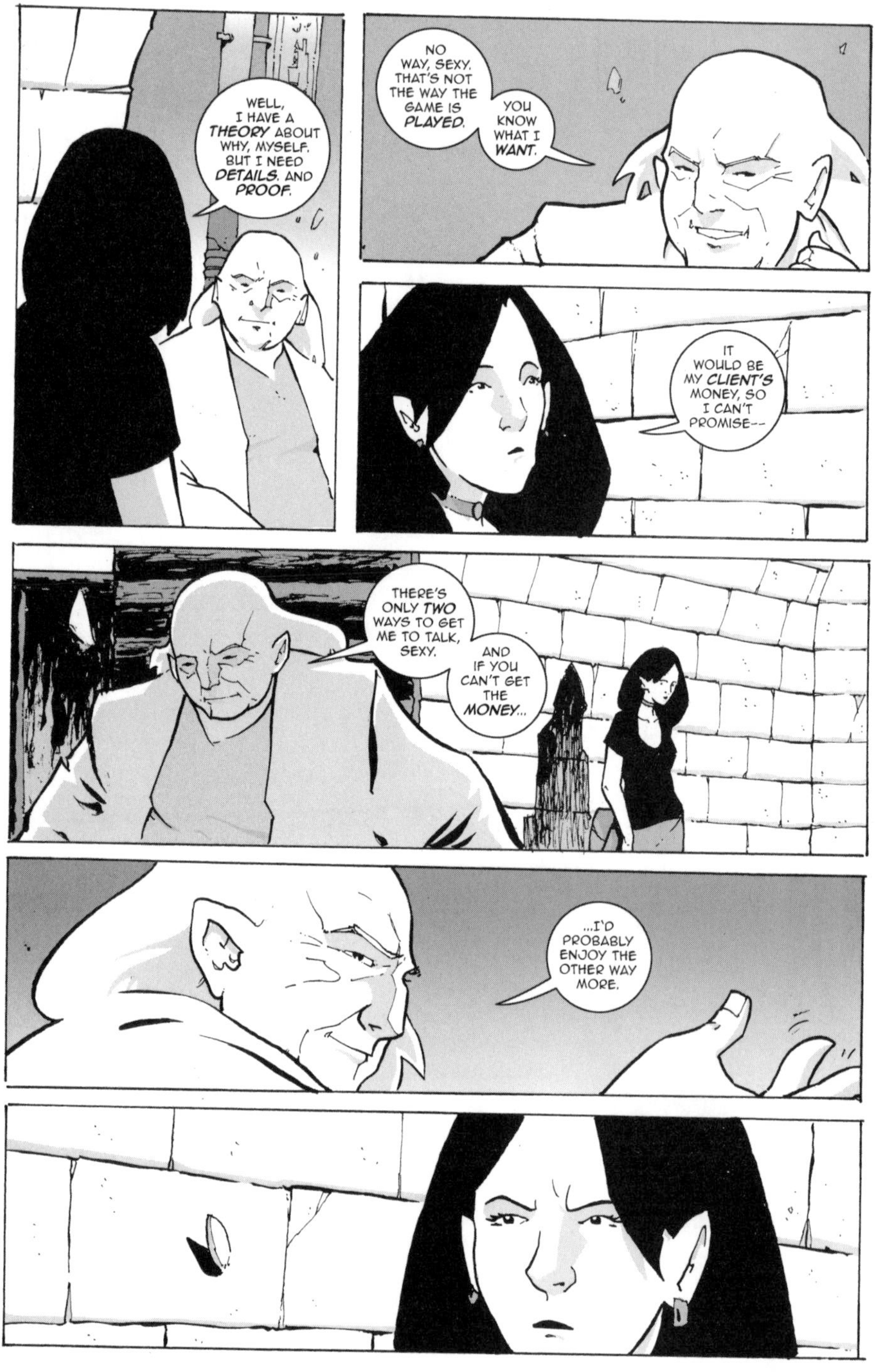
WELL, I HAVE A THEORY ABOUT WHY, MYSELF. BUT I NEED DETAILS. AND PROOF.
NO WAY, SEXY. THAT'S NOT THE WAY THE GAME IS PLAYED.
YOU KNOW WHAT I WANT.
IT WOULD BE MY CLIENT'S MONEY, SO I CAN'T PROMISE--
THERE'S ONLY TWO WAYS TO GET ME TO TALK, SEXY.
AND IF YOU CAN'T GET THE MONEY...
...I'D PROBABLY ENJOY THE OTHER WAY MORE.

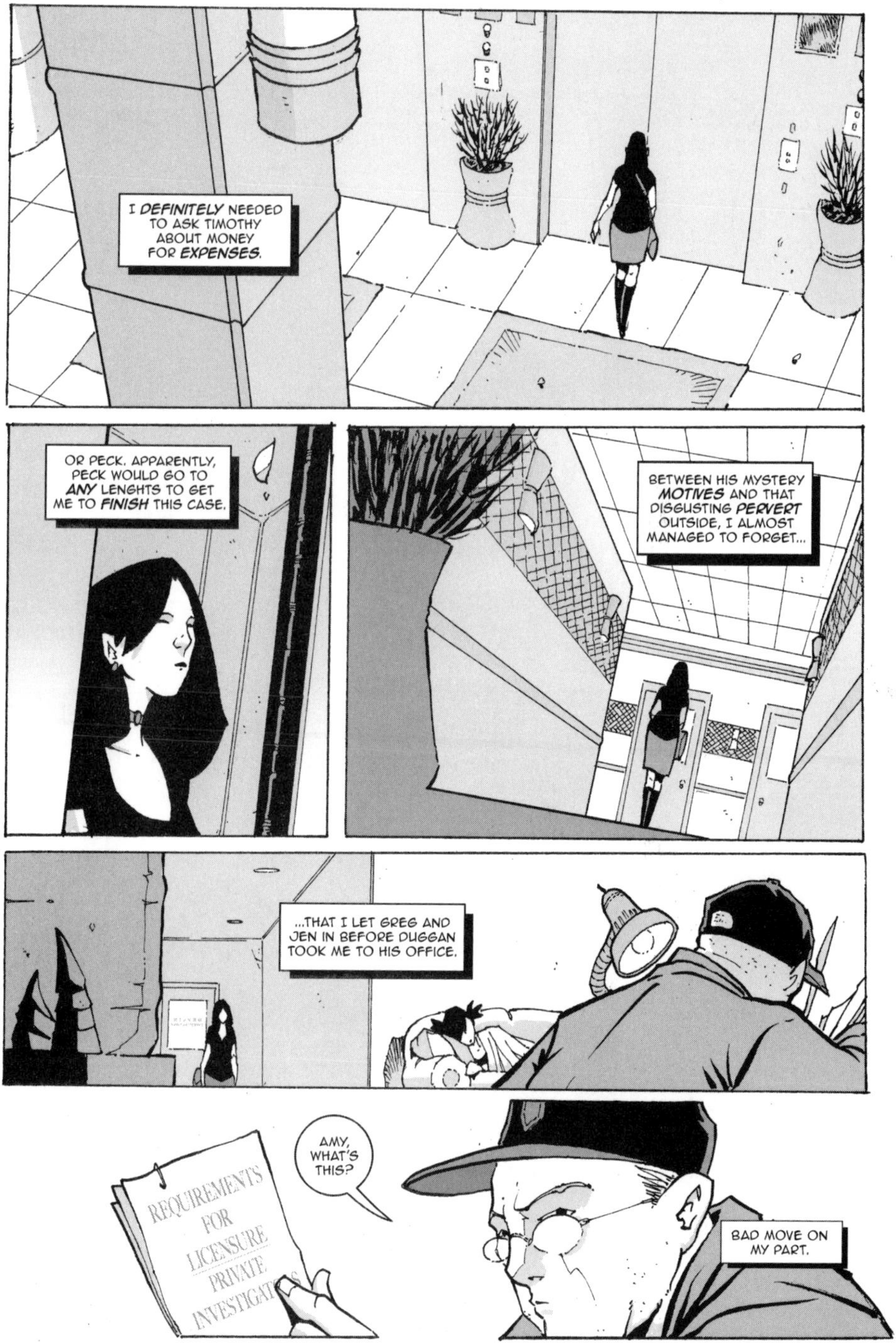
I DEFINITELY NEEDED TO ASK TIMOTHY ABOUT MONEY FOR EXPENSES.
OR PECK. APPARENTLY, PECK WOULD GO TO ANY LENGHTS TO GET ME TO FINISH THIS CASE.
BETWEEN HIS MYSTERY MOTIVES AND THAT DISGUSTING PERVERT OUTSIDE, I ALMOST MANAGED TO FORGET...
...THAT I LET GREG AND JEN IN BEFORE DUGGAN TOOK ME TO HIS OFFICE.
AMY, WHAT'S THIS?
REQUIREMENTS FOR LICENSURE PRIVATE INVESTIGAT
BAD MOVE ON MY PART.

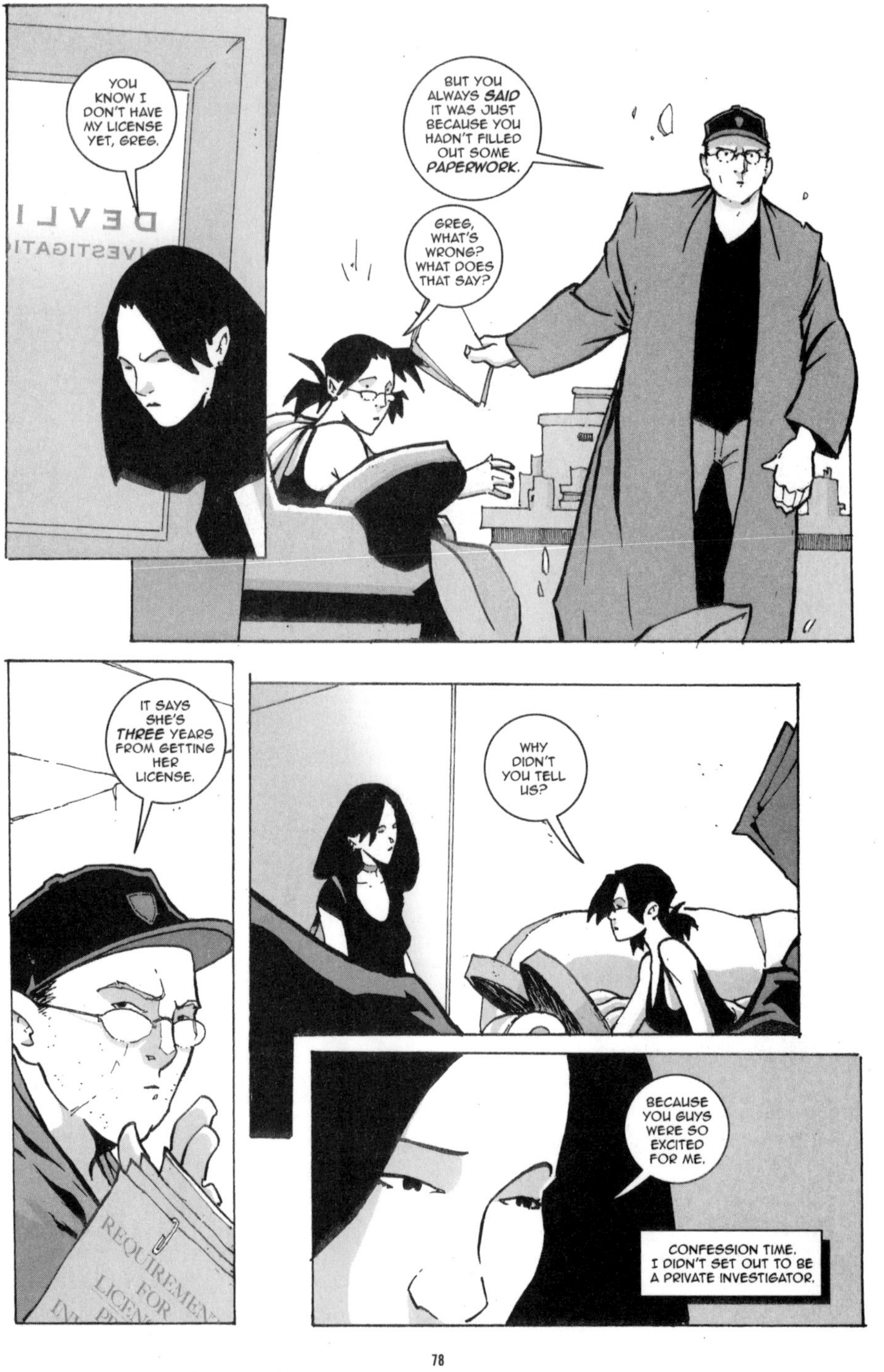
YOU KNOW I DON'T HAVE MY LICENSE YET, GREG.
BUT YOU ALWAYS *SAID* IT WAS JUST BECAUSE YOU HADN'T FILLED OUT SOME *PAPERWORK*.
GREG, WHAT'S WRONG? WHAT DOES THAT SAY?
IT SAYS SHE'S *THREE* YEARS FROM GETTING HER LICENSE.
WHY DIDN'T YOU TELL US?
BECAUSE YOU GUYS WERE SO EXCITED FOR ME.
CONFESSION TIME. I DIDN'T SET OUT TO BE A PRIVATE INVESTIGATOR.

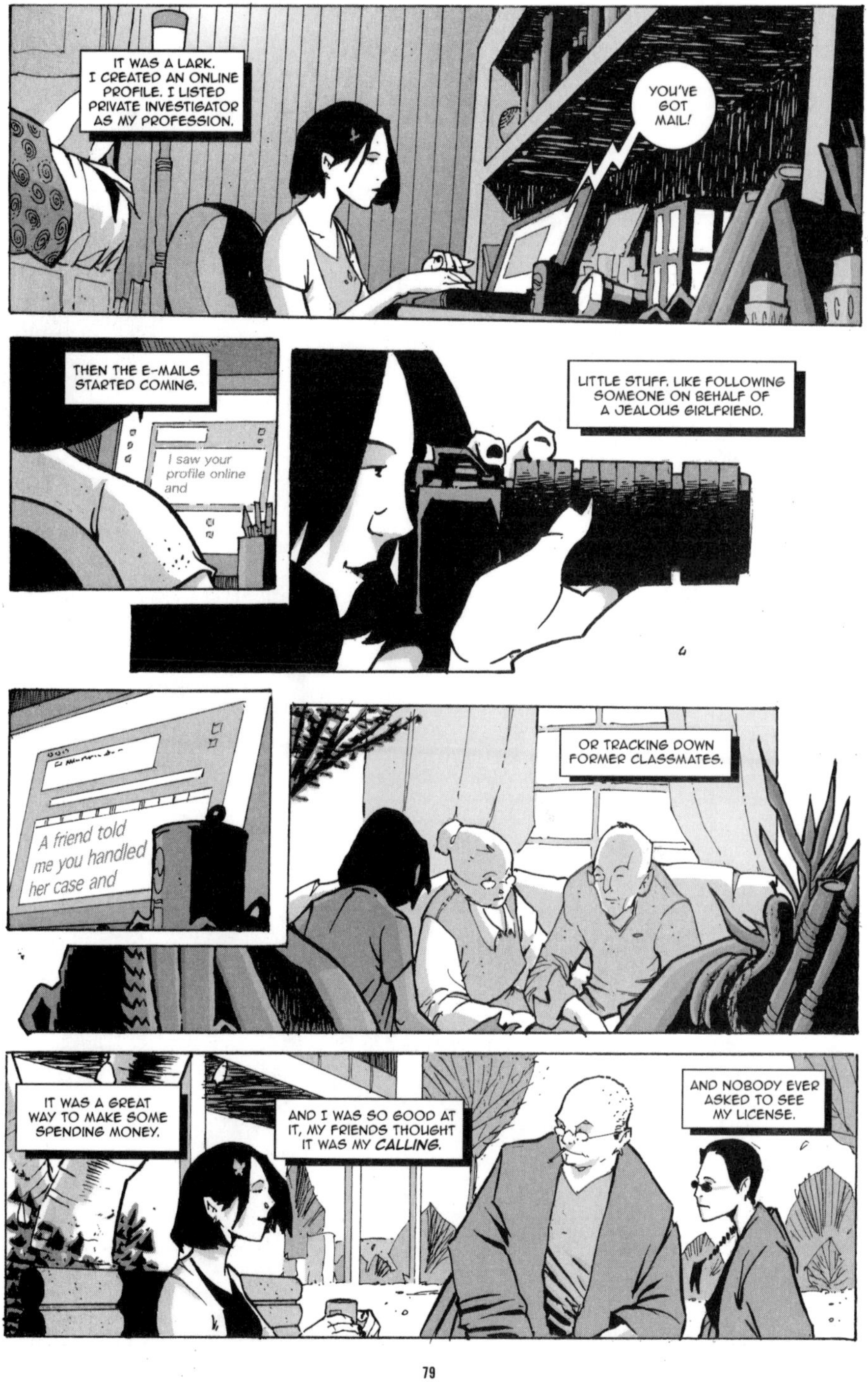
IT WAS A LARK. I CREATED AN ONLINE PROFILE. I LISTED PRIVATE INVESTIGATOR AS MY PROFESSION.
YOU'VE GOT MAIL!
THEN THE E-MAILS STARTED COMING.
I saw your profile online and
LITTLE STUFF. LIKE FOLLOWING SOMEONE ON BEHALF OF A JEALOUS GIRLFRIEND.
A friend told me you handled her case and
OR TRACKING DOWN FORMER CLASSMATES.
IT WAS A GREAT WAY TO MAKE SOME SPENDING MONEY.
AND I WAS SO GOOD AT IT, MY FRIENDS THOUGHT IT WAS MY *CALLING*.
AND NOBODY EVER ASKED TO SEE MY LICENSE.

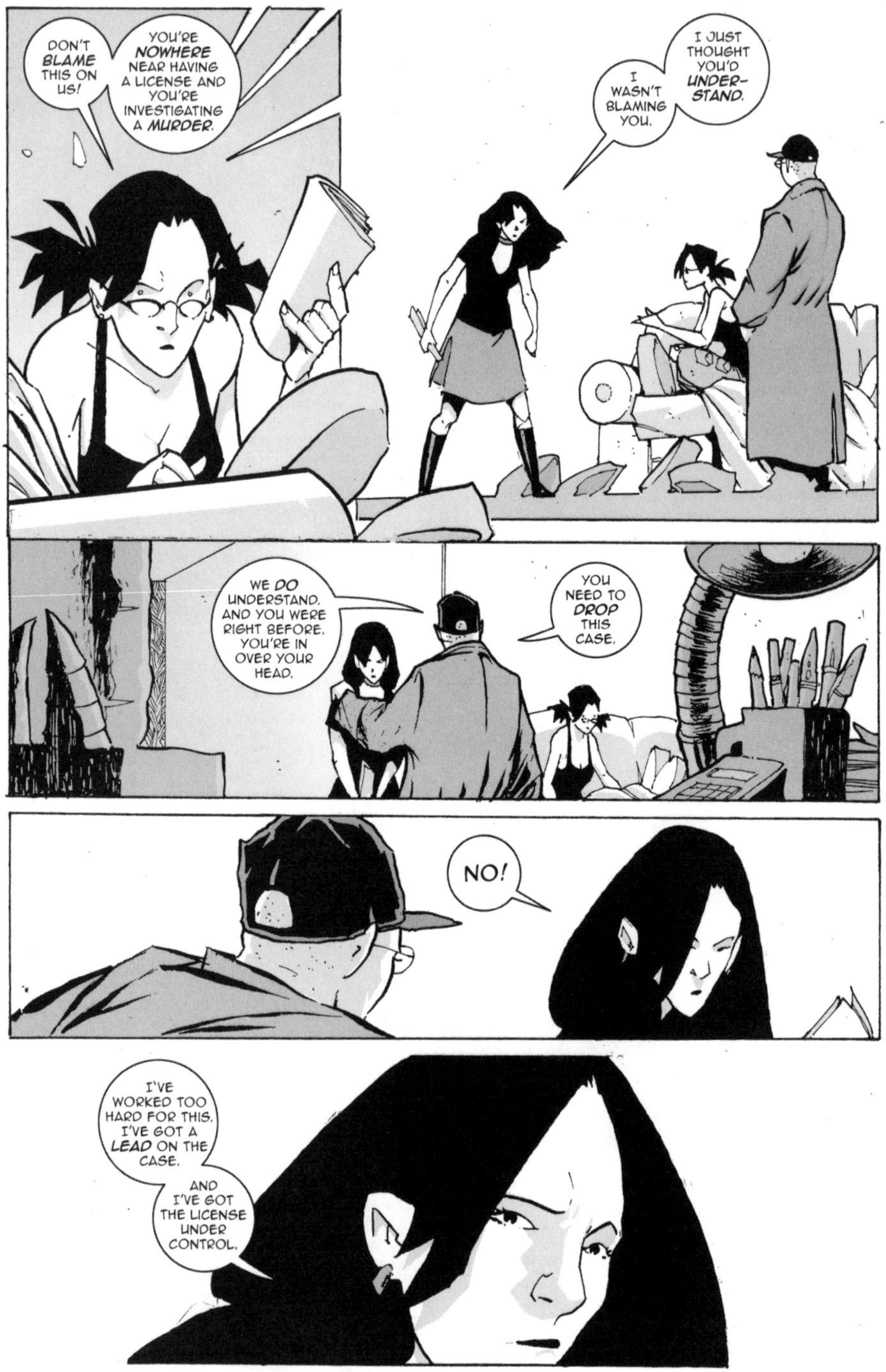
DON'T BLAME THIS ON US!
YOU'RE NOWHERE NEAR HAVING A LICENSE AND YOU'RE INVESTIGATING A MURDER.
I WASN'T BLAMING YOU.
I JUST THOUGHT YOU'D UNDER-STAND.
WE DO UNDERSTAND, AND YOU WERE RIGHT BEFORE. YOU'RE IN OVER YOUR HEAD.
YOU NEED TO DROP THIS CASE.
NO!
I'VE WORKED TOO HARD FOR THIS. I'VE GOT A LEAD ON THE CASE.
AND I'VE GOT THE LICENSE UNDER CONTROL.

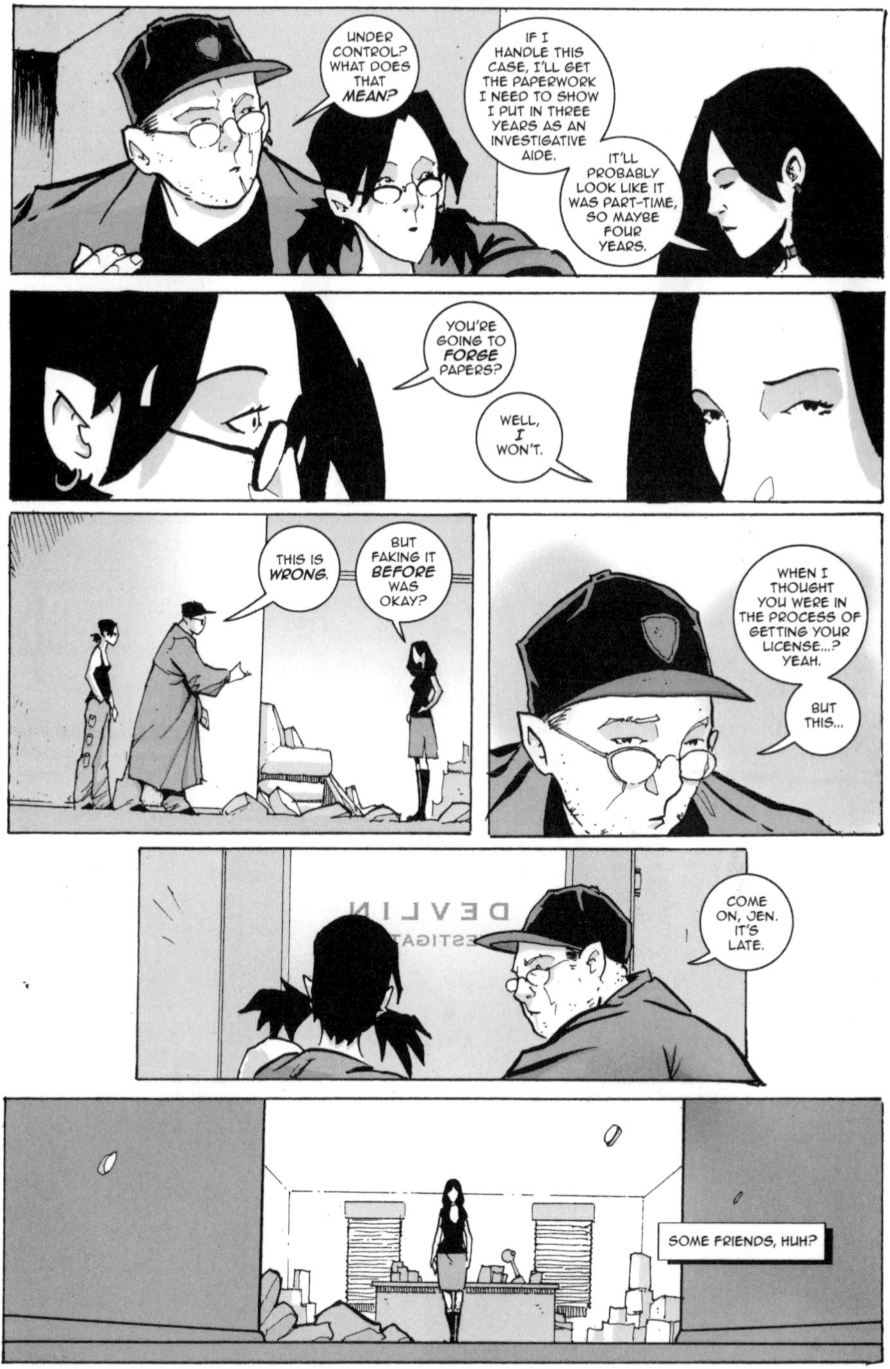
UNDER CONTROL? WHAT DOES THAT MEAN?
IF I HANDLE THIS CASE, I'LL GET THE PAPERWORK I NEED TO SHOW I PUT IN THREE YEARS AS AN INVESTIGATIVE AIDE.
IT'LL PROBABLY LOOK LIKE IT WAS PART-TIME, SO MAYBE FOUR YEARS.
YOU'RE GOING TO FORGE PAPERS?
WELL, I WON'T.
THIS IS WRONG.
BUT FAKING IT BEFORE WAS OKAY?
WHEN I THOUGHT YOU WERE IN THE PROCESS OF GETTING YOUR LICENSE...? YEAH.
BUT THIS...
COME ON, JEN. IT'S LATE.
SOME FRIENDS, HUH?

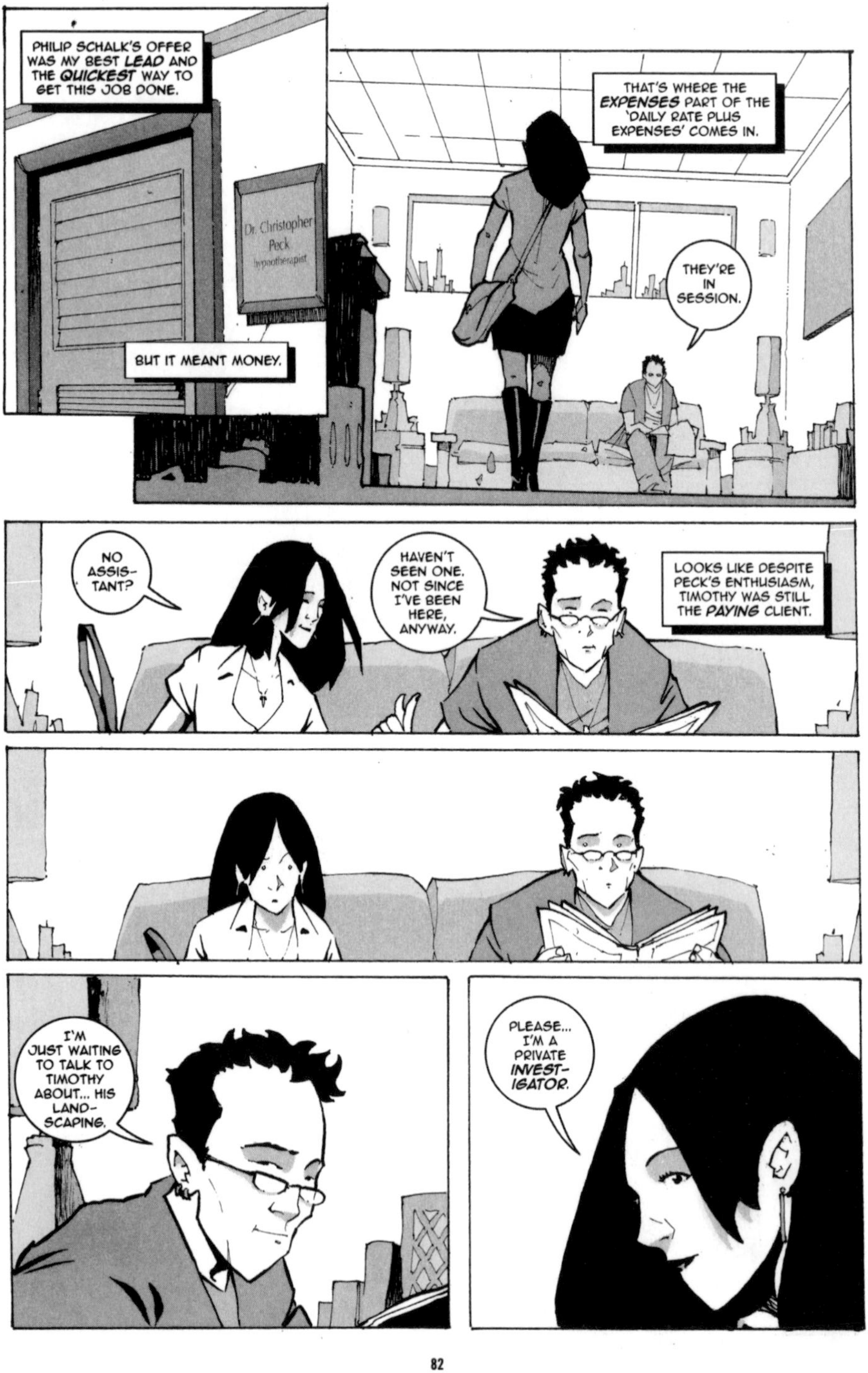
PHILIP SCHALK'S OFFER WAS MY BEST LEAD AND THE QUICKEST WAY TO GET THIS JOB DONE.
Dr. Christopher Peck hypnotherapist
BUT IT MEANT MONEY.
THAT'S WHERE THE EXPENSES PART OF THE 'DAILY RATE PLUS EXPENSES' COMES IN.
THEY'RE IN SESSION.
NO ASSIS-TANT?
HAVEN'T SEEN ONE. NOT SINCE I'VE BEEN HERE, ANYWAY.
LOOKS LIKE DESPITE PECK'S ENTHUSIASM, TIMOTHY WAS STILL THE PAYING CLIENT.
I'M JUST WAITING TO TALK TO TIMOTHY ABOUT... HIS LAND-SCAPING.
PLEASE... I'M A PRIVATE INVEST-IGATOR.

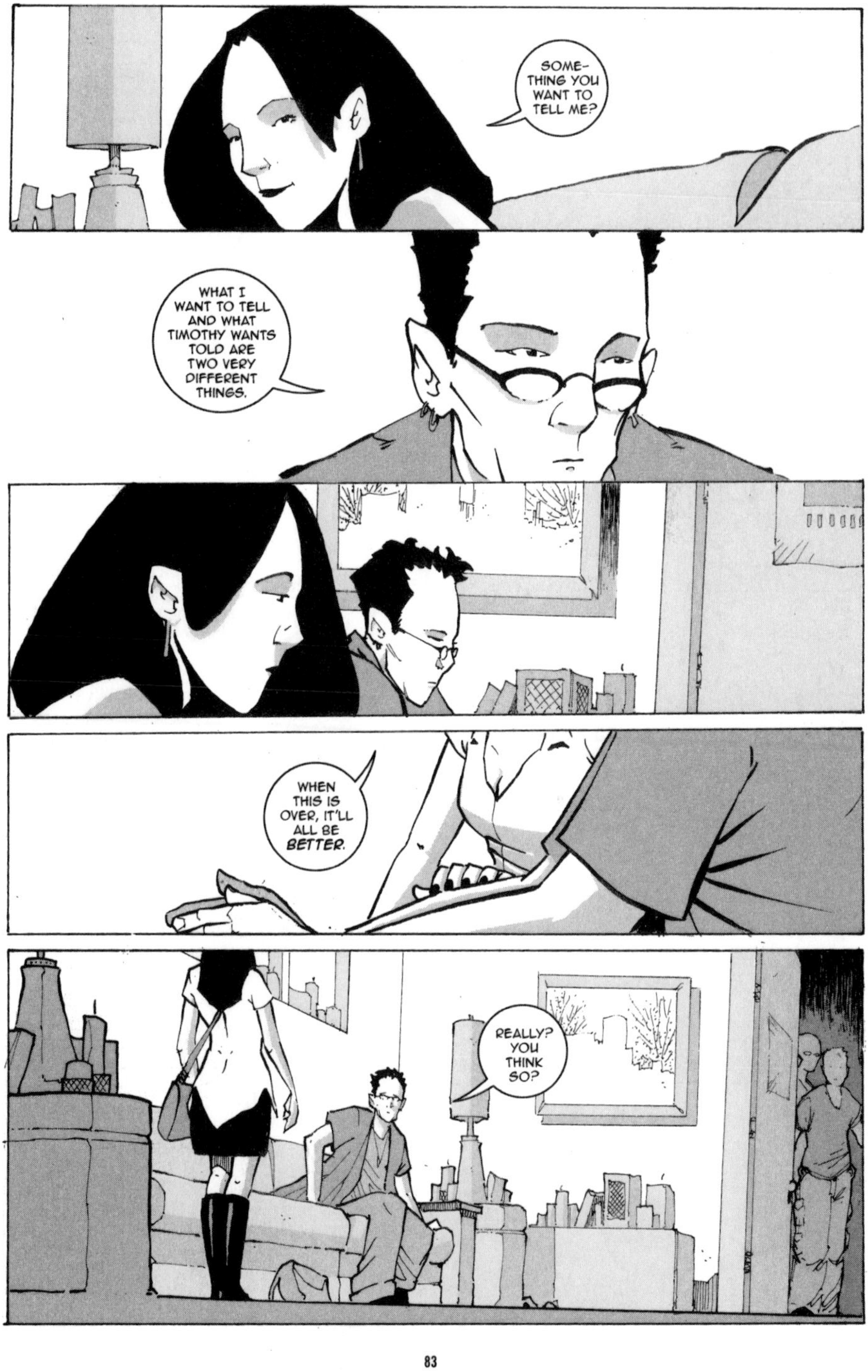
SOME-THING YOU WANT TO TELL ME?
WHAT I WANT TO TELL AND WHAT TIMOTHY WANTS TOLD ARE TWO VERY DIFFERENT THINGS.
WHEN THIS IS OVER, IT'LL ALL BE *BETTER*.
REALLY? YOU THINK SO?

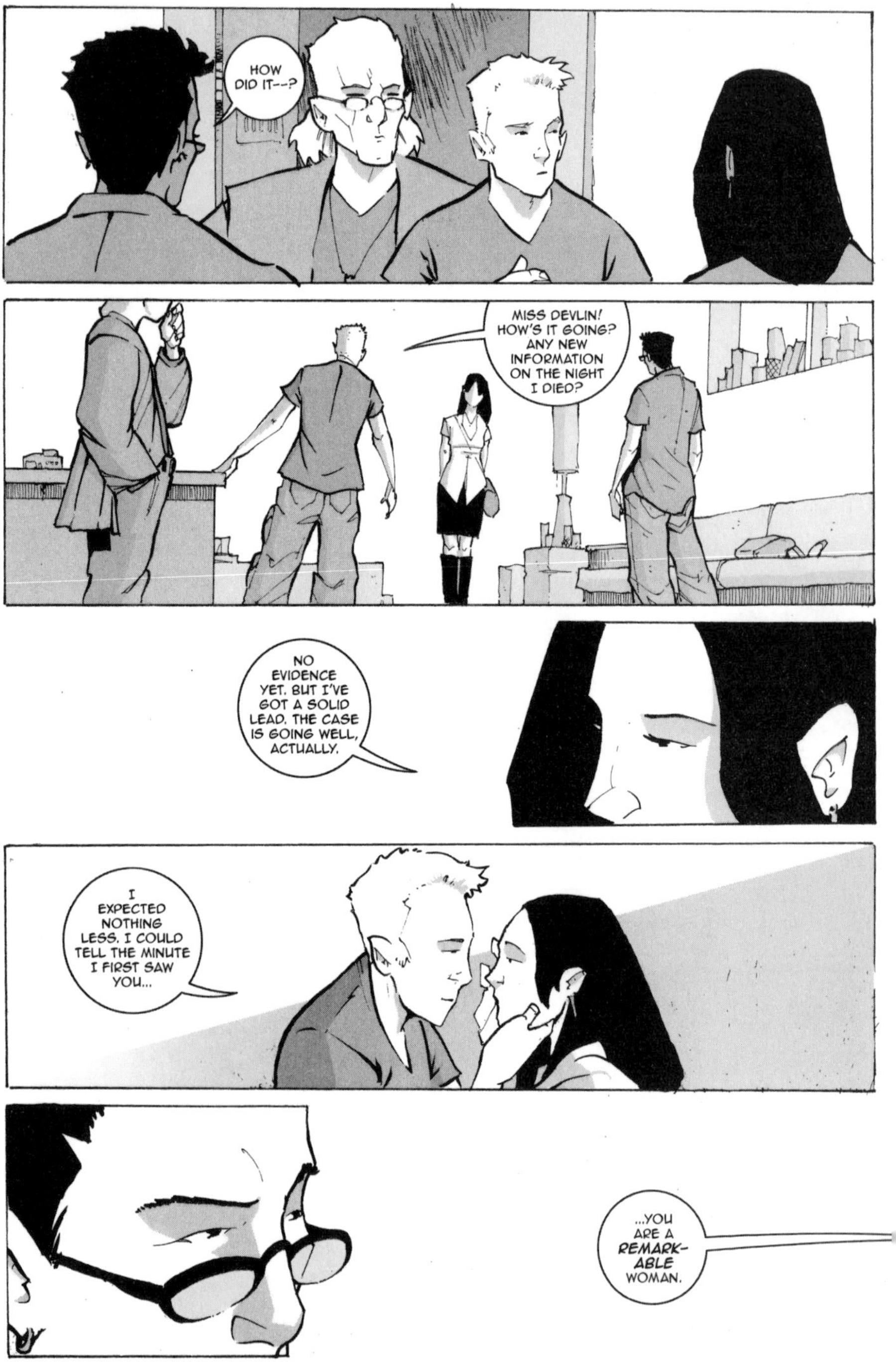
HOW DID IT--?
MISS DEVLIN! HOW'S IT GOING? ANY NEW INFORMATION ON THE NIGHT I DIED?
NO EVIDENCE YET. BUT I'VE GOT A SOLID LEAD. THE CASE IS GOING WELL, ACTUALLY.
I EXPECTED NOTHING LESS. I COULD TELL THE MINUTE I FIRST SAW YOU...
...YOU ARE A ***REMARK-ABLE*** WOMAN.

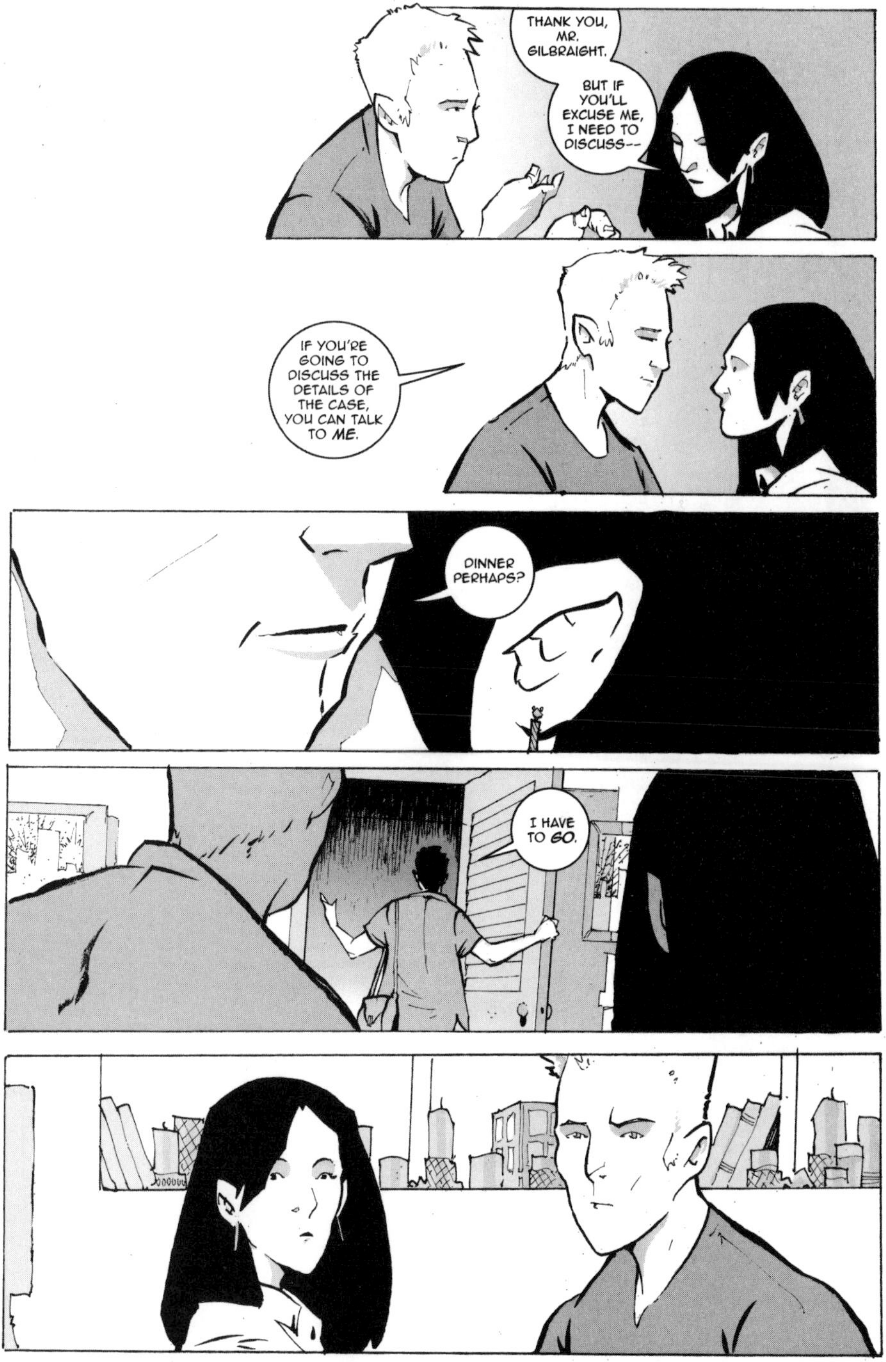
THANK YOU, MR. GILBRAIGHT.
BUT IF YOU'LL EXCUSE ME, I NEED TO DISCUSS--
IF YOU'RE GOING TO DISCUSS THE DETAILS OF THE CASE, YOU CAN TALK TO *ME*.
DINNER PERHAPS?
I HAVE TO *GO*.

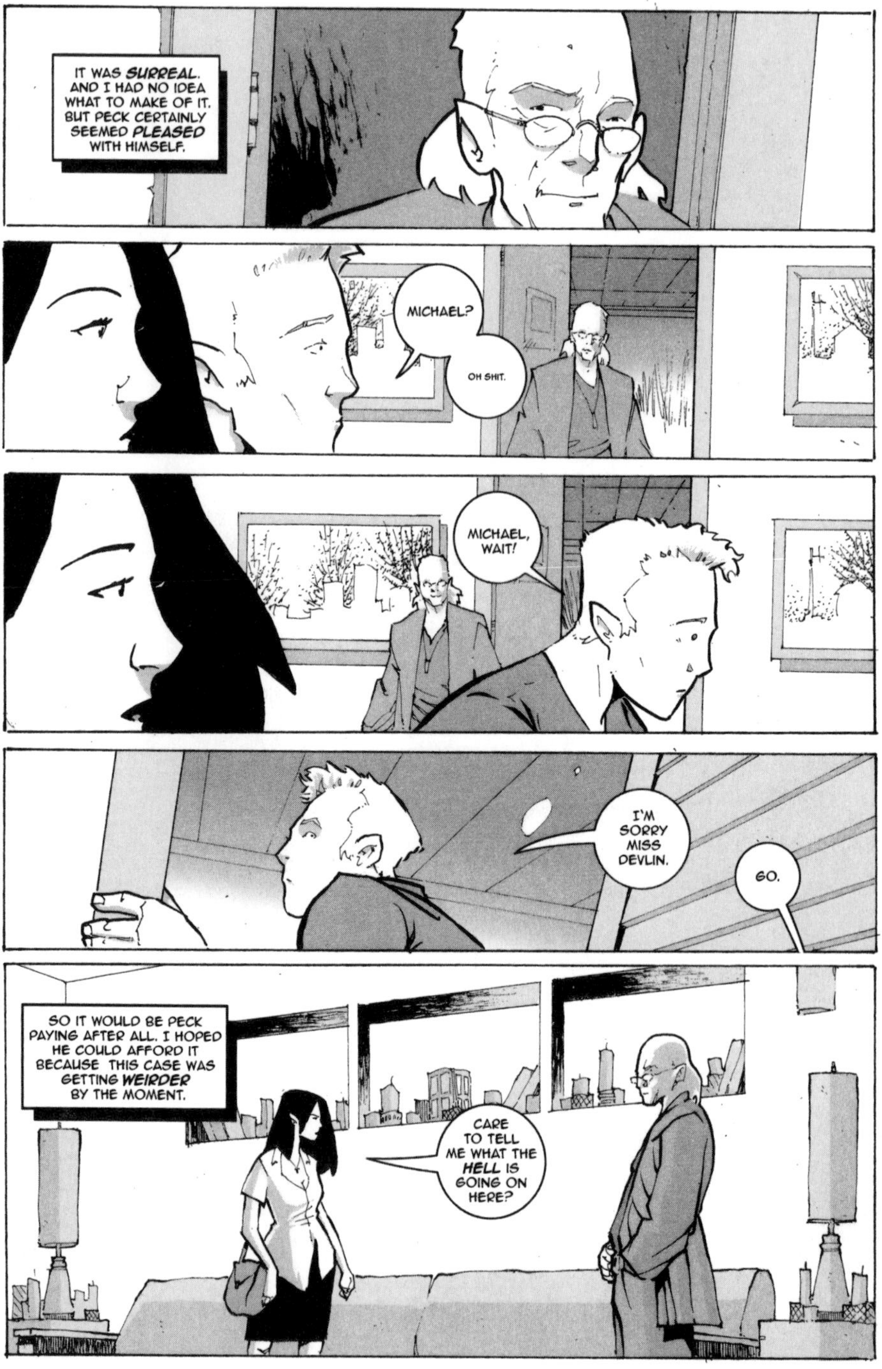

IT WAS SURREAL. AND I HAD NO IDEA WHAT TO MAKE OF IT. BUT PECK CERTAINLY SEEMED PLEASED WITH HIMSELF.
MICHAEL?
OH SHIT.
MICHAEL, WAIT!
I'M SORRY MISS DEVLIN.
GO.
SO IT WOULD BE PECK PAYING AFTER ALL. I HOPED HE COULD AFFORD IT BECAUSE THIS CASE WAS GETTING WEIRDER BY THE MOMENT.
CARE TO TELL ME WHAT THE HELL IS GOING ON HERE?

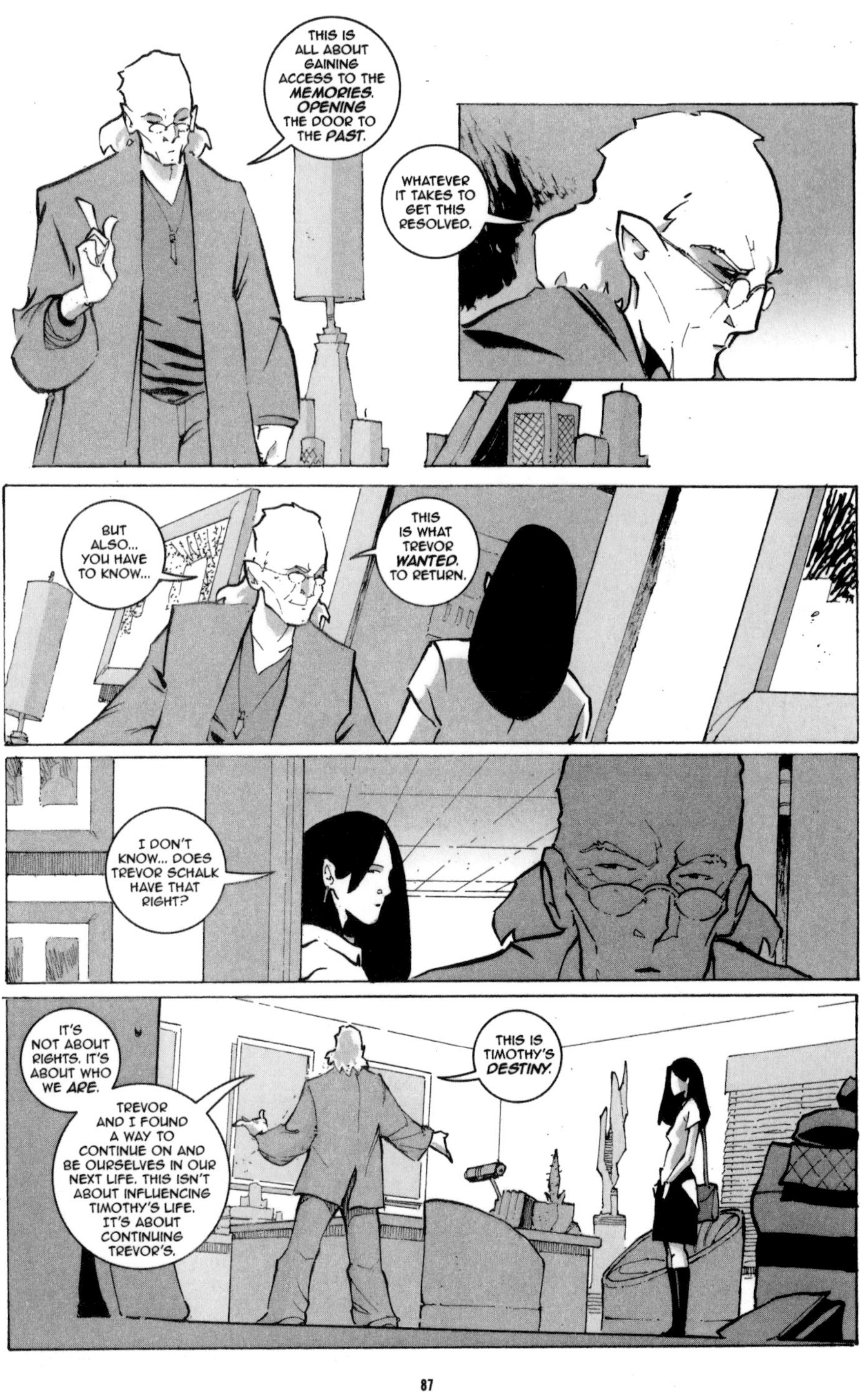

THIS IS ALL ABOUT GAINING ACCESS TO THE MEMORIES. OPENING THE DOOR TO THE PAST.
WHATEVER IT TAKES TO GET THIS RESOLVED.
BUT ALSO... YOU HAVE TO KNOW...
THIS IS WHAT TREVOR WANTED. TO RETURN.
I DON'T KNOW... DOES TREVOR SCHALK HAVE THAT RIGHT?
IT'S NOT ABOUT RIGHTS. IT'S ABOUT WHO WE ARE.
TREVOR AND I FOUND A WAY TO CONTINUE ON AND BE OURSELVES IN OUR NEXT LIFE. THIS ISN'T ABOUT INFLUENCING TIMOTHY'S LIFE. IT'S ABOUT CONTINUING TREVOR'S.
THIS IS TIMOTHY'S DESTINY.

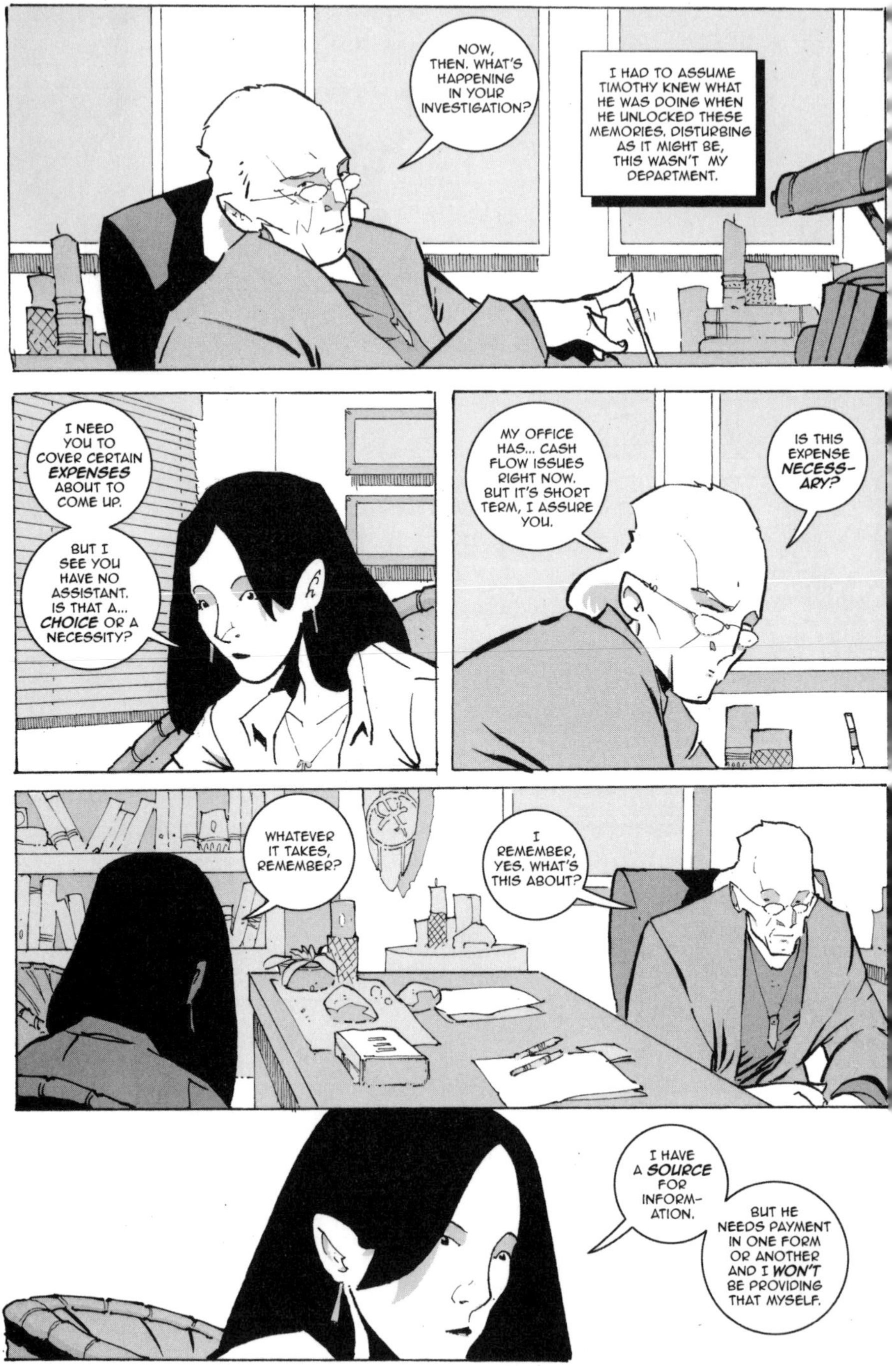
NOW, THEN. WHAT'S HAPPENING IN YOUR INVESTIGATION?
I HAD TO ASSUME TIMOTHY KNEW WHAT HE WAS DOING WHEN HE UNLOCKED THESE MEMORIES. DISTURBING AS IT MIGHT BE, THIS WASN'T MY DEPARTMENT.
I NEED YOU TO COVER CERTAIN *EXPENSES* ABOUT TO COME UP.
BUT I SEE YOU HAVE NO ASSISTANT. IS THAT A... *CHOICE* OR A NECESSITY?
MY OFFICE HAS... CASH FLOW ISSUES RIGHT NOW. BUT IT'S SHORT TERM, I ASSURE YOU.
IS THIS EXPENSE *NECESSARY?*
WHATEVER IT TAKES, REMEMBER?
I REMEMBER, YES. WHAT'S THIS ABOUT?
I HAVE A *SOURCE* FOR INFORMATION.
BUT HE NEEDS PAYMENT IN ONE FORM OR ANOTHER AND I *WON'T* BE PROVIDING THAT MYSELF.

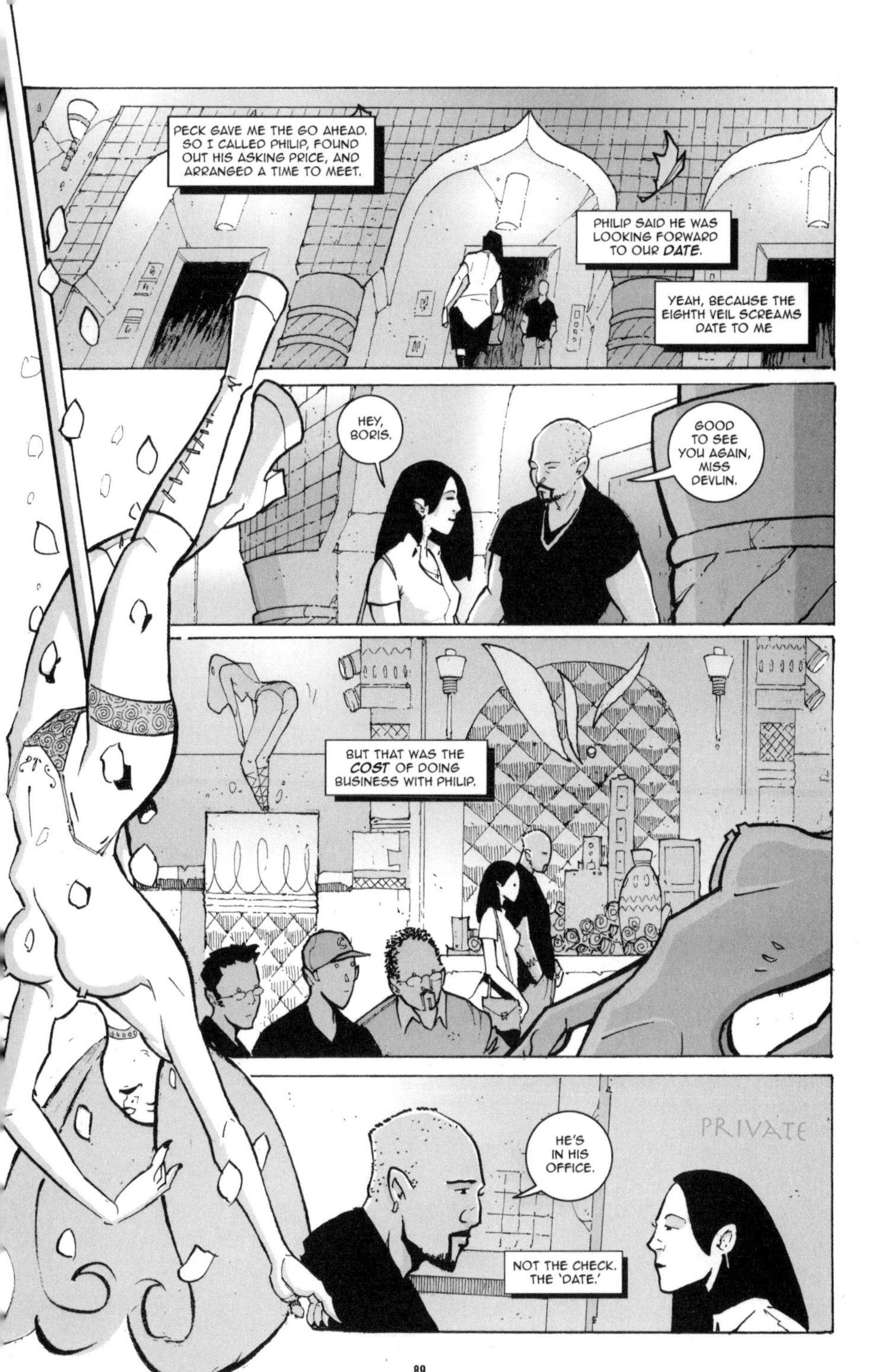

PECK GAVE ME THE GO AHEAD, SO I CALLED PHILIP, FOUND OUT HIS ASKING PRICE, AND ARRANGED A TIME TO MEET.
PHILIP SAID HE WAS LOOKING FORWARD TO OUR DATE.
YEAH, BECAUSE THE EIGHTH VEIL SCREAMS DATE TO ME
HEY, BORIS.
GOOD TO SEE YOU AGAIN, MISS DEVLIN.
BUT THAT WAS THE COST OF DOING BUSINESS WITH PHILIP.
PRIVATE
HE'S IN HIS OFFICE.
NOT THE CHECK. THE 'DATE.'

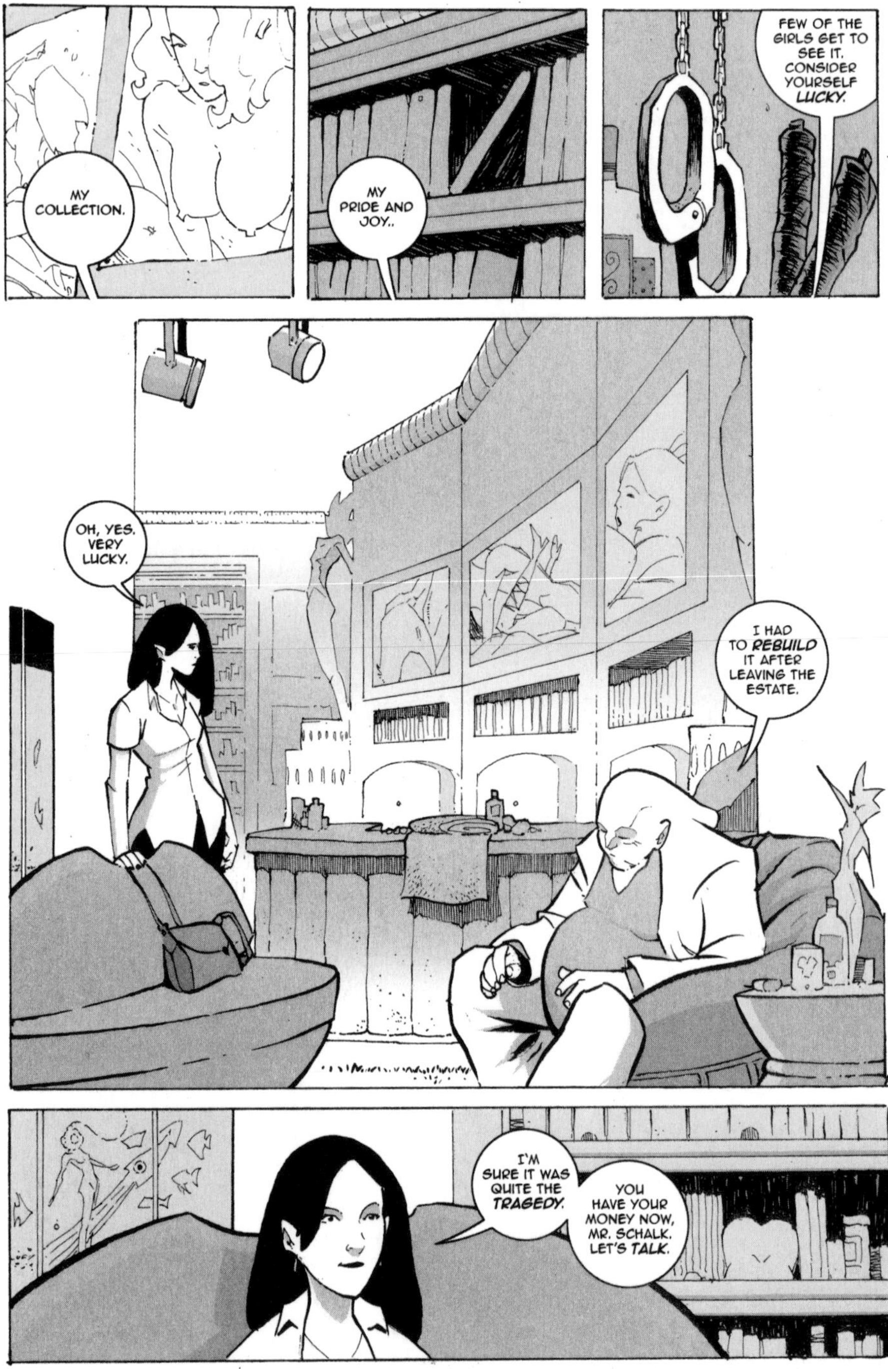

MY COLLECTION.
MY PRIDE AND JOY..
FEW OF THE GIRLS GET TO SEE IT. CONSIDER YOURSELF LUCKY.
OH, YES. VERY LUCKY.
I HAD TO REBUILD IT AFTER LEAVING THE ESTATE.
I'M SURE IT WAS QUITE THE TRAGEDY.
YOU HAVE YOUR MONEY NOW, MR. SCHALK. LET'S TALK.

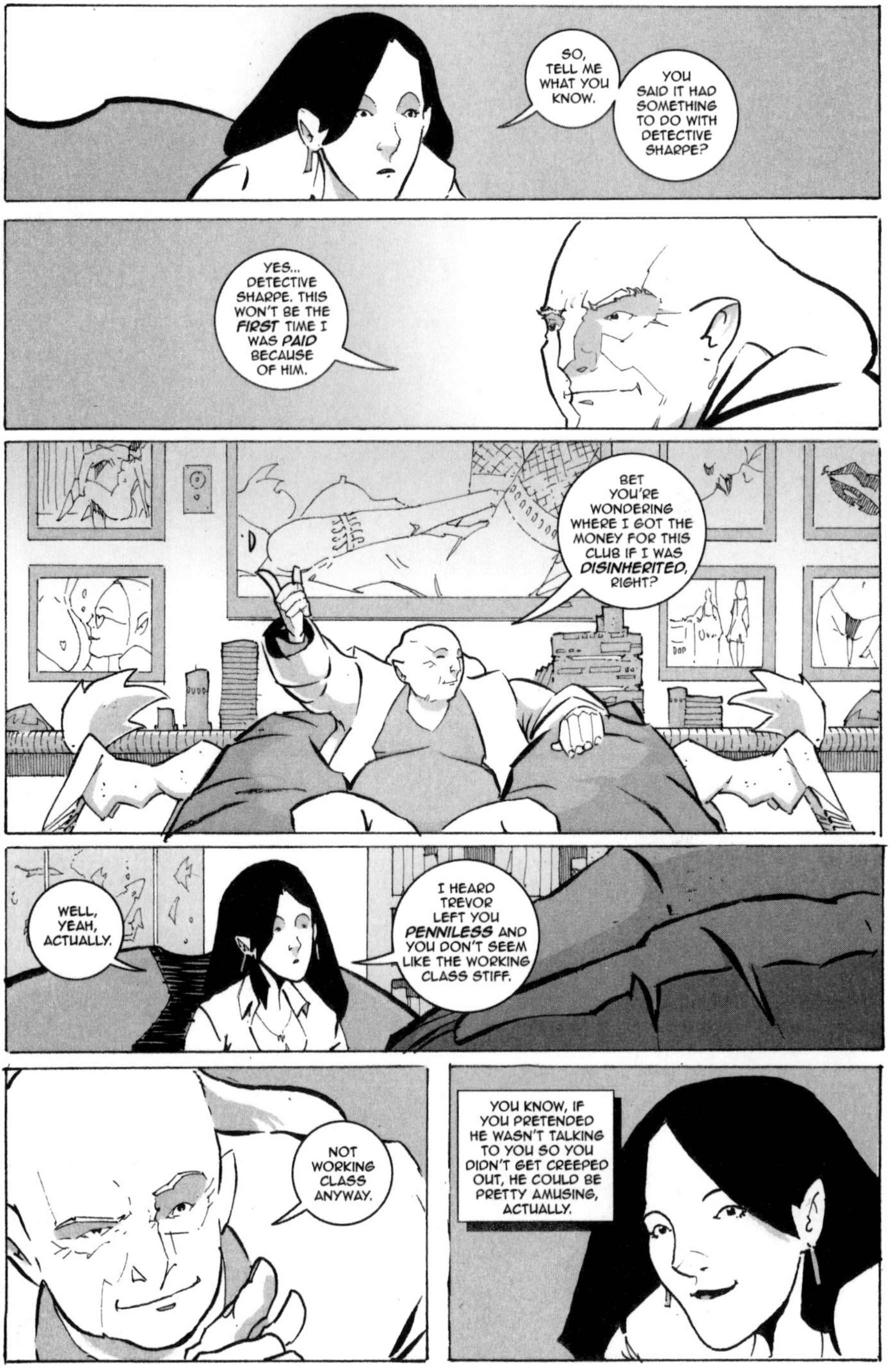
SO, TELL ME WHAT YOU KNOW.
YOU SAID IT HAD SOMETHING TO DO WITH DETECTIVE SHARPE?
YES... DETECTIVE SHARPE. THIS WON'T BE THE *FIRST* TIME I WAS *PAID* BECAUSE OF HIM.
BET YOU'RE WONDERING WHERE I GOT THE MONEY FOR THIS CLUB IF I WAS *DISINHERITED*, RIGHT?
WELL, YEAH, ACTUALLY.
I HEARD TREVOR LEFT YOU *PENNILESS* AND YOU DON'T SEEM LIKE THE WORKING CLASS STIFF.
NOT WORKING CLASS ANYWAY.
YOU KNOW, IF YOU PRETENDED HE WASN'T TALKING TO YOU SO YOU DIDN'T GET CREEPED OUT, HE COULD BE PRETTY AMUSING, ACTUALLY.

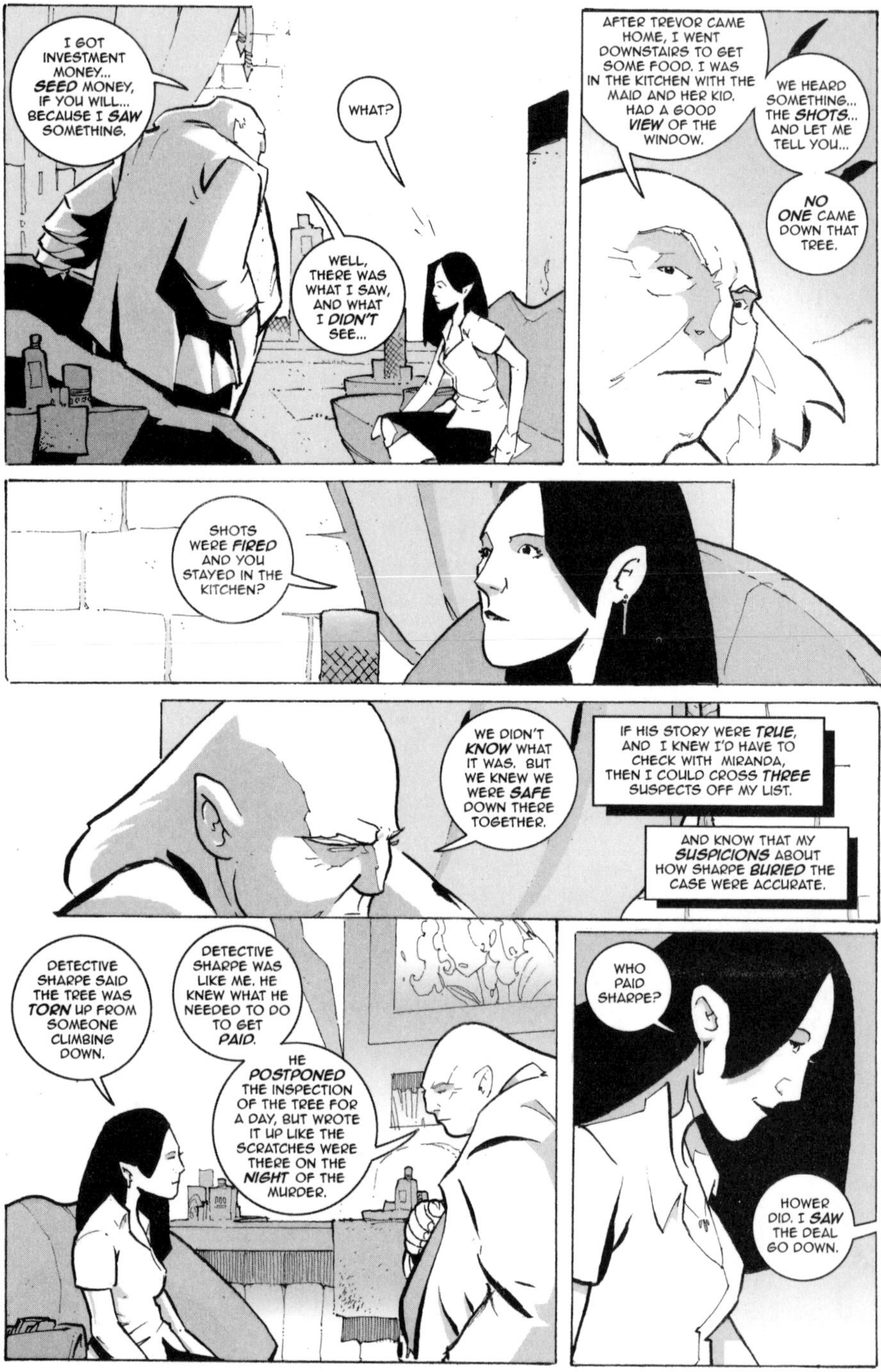
I GOT INVESTMENT MONEY... SEED MONEY, IF YOU WILL... BECAUSE I SAW SOMETHING.
WHAT?
WELL, THERE WAS WHAT I SAW, AND WHAT I DIDN'T SEE...
AFTER TREVOR CAME HOME, I WENT DOWNSTAIRS TO GET SOME FOOD. I WAS IN THE KITCHEN WITH THE MAID AND HER KID. HAD A GOOD VIEW OF THE WINDOW.
WE HEARD SOMETHING... THE SHOTS... AND LET ME TELL YOU...
NO ONE CAME DOWN THAT TREE.
SHOTS WERE FIRED AND YOU STAYED IN THE KITCHEN?
WE DIDN'T KNOW WHAT IT WAS. BUT WE KNEW WE WERE SAFE DOWN THERE TOGETHER.
IF HIS STORY WERE TRUE, AND I KNEW I'D HAVE TO CHECK WITH MIRANDA, THEN I COULD CROSS THREE SUSPECTS OFF MY LIST.
AND KNOW THAT MY SUSPICIONS ABOUT HOW SHARPE BURIED THE CASE WERE ACCURATE.
DETECTIVE SHARPE SAID THE TREE WAS TORN UP FROM SOMEONE CLIMBING DOWN.
DETECTIVE SHARPE WAS LIKE ME. HE KNEW WHAT HE NEEDED TO DO TO GET PAID.
HE POSTPONED THE INSPECTION OF THE TREE FOR A DAY, BUT WROTE IT UP LIKE THE SCRATCHES WERE THERE ON THE NIGHT OF THE MURDER.
WHO PAID SHARPE?
HOWER DID. I SAW THE DEAL GO DOWN.

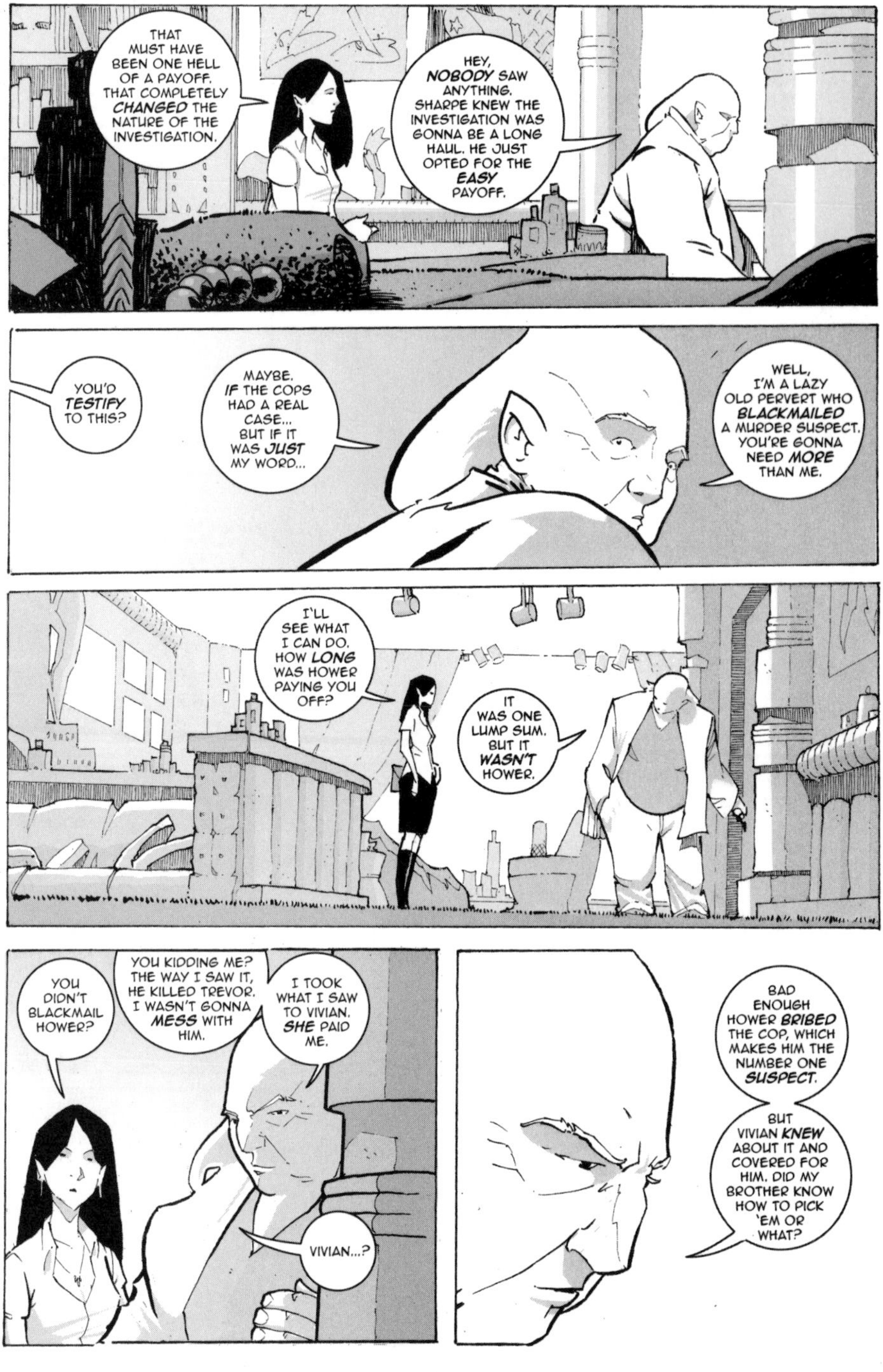
THAT MUST HAVE BEEN ONE HELL OF A PAYOFF. THAT COMPLETELY CHANGED THE NATURE OF THE INVESTIGATION.
HEY, NOBODY SAW ANYTHING. SHARPE KNEW THE INVESTIGATION WAS GONNA BE A LONG HAUL. HE JUST OPTED FOR THE EASY PAYOFF.
YOU'D TESTIFY TO THIS?
MAYBE. IF THE COPS HAD A REAL CASE... BUT IF IT WAS JUST MY WORD...
WELL, I'M A LAZY OLD PERVERT WHO BLACKMAILED A MURDER SUSPECT. YOU'RE GONNA NEED MORE THAN ME.
I'LL SEE WHAT I CAN DO. HOW LONG WAS HOWER PAYING YOU OFF?
IT WAS ONE LUMP SUM. BUT IT WASN'T HOWER.
YOU DIDN'T BLACKMAIL HOWER?
YOU KIDDING ME? THE WAY I SAW IT, HE KILLED TREVOR. I WASN'T GONNA MESS WITH HIM.
I TOOK WHAT I SAW TO VIVIAN. SHE PAID ME.
VIVIAN...?
BAD ENOUGH HOWER BRIBED THE COP, WHICH MAKES HIM THE NUMBER ONE SUSPECT.
BUT VIVIAN KNEW ABOUT IT AND COVERED FOR HIM. DID MY BROTHER KNOW HOW TO PICK 'EM OR WHAT?

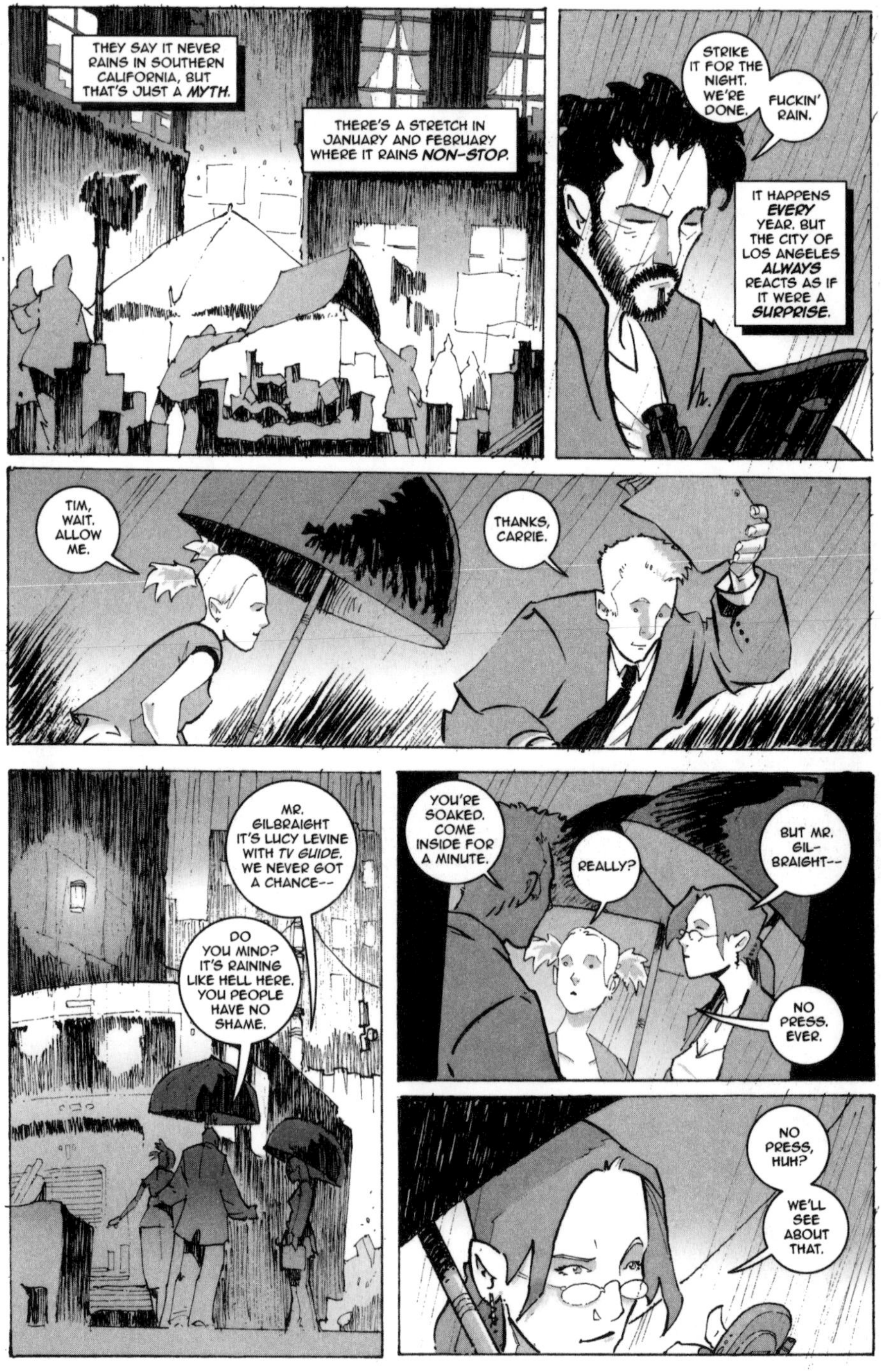
THEY SAY IT NEVER RAINS IN SOUTHERN CALIFORNIA, BUT THAT'S JUST A *MYTH*.
THERE'S A STRETCH IN JANUARY AND FEBRUARY WHERE IT RAINS *NON-STOP*.
STRIKE IT FOR THE NIGHT. WE'RE DONE.
FUCKIN' RAIN.
IT HAPPENS *EVERY* YEAR. BUT THE CITY OF LOS ANGELES *ALWAYS* REACTS AS IF IT WERE A *SURPRISE*.
TIM, WAIT. ALLOW ME.
THANKS, CARRIE.
MR. GILBRAIGHT IT'S LUCY LEVINE WITH *TV GUIDE*. WE NEVER GOT A CHANCE--
DO YOU MIND? IT'S RAINING LIKE HELL HERE. YOU PEOPLE HAVE NO SHAME.
YOU'RE SOAKED. COME INSIDE FOR A MINUTE.
REALLY?
BUT MR. GIL-BRAIGHT--
NO PRESS. EVER.
NO PRESS, HUH?
WE'LL SEE ABOUT THAT.

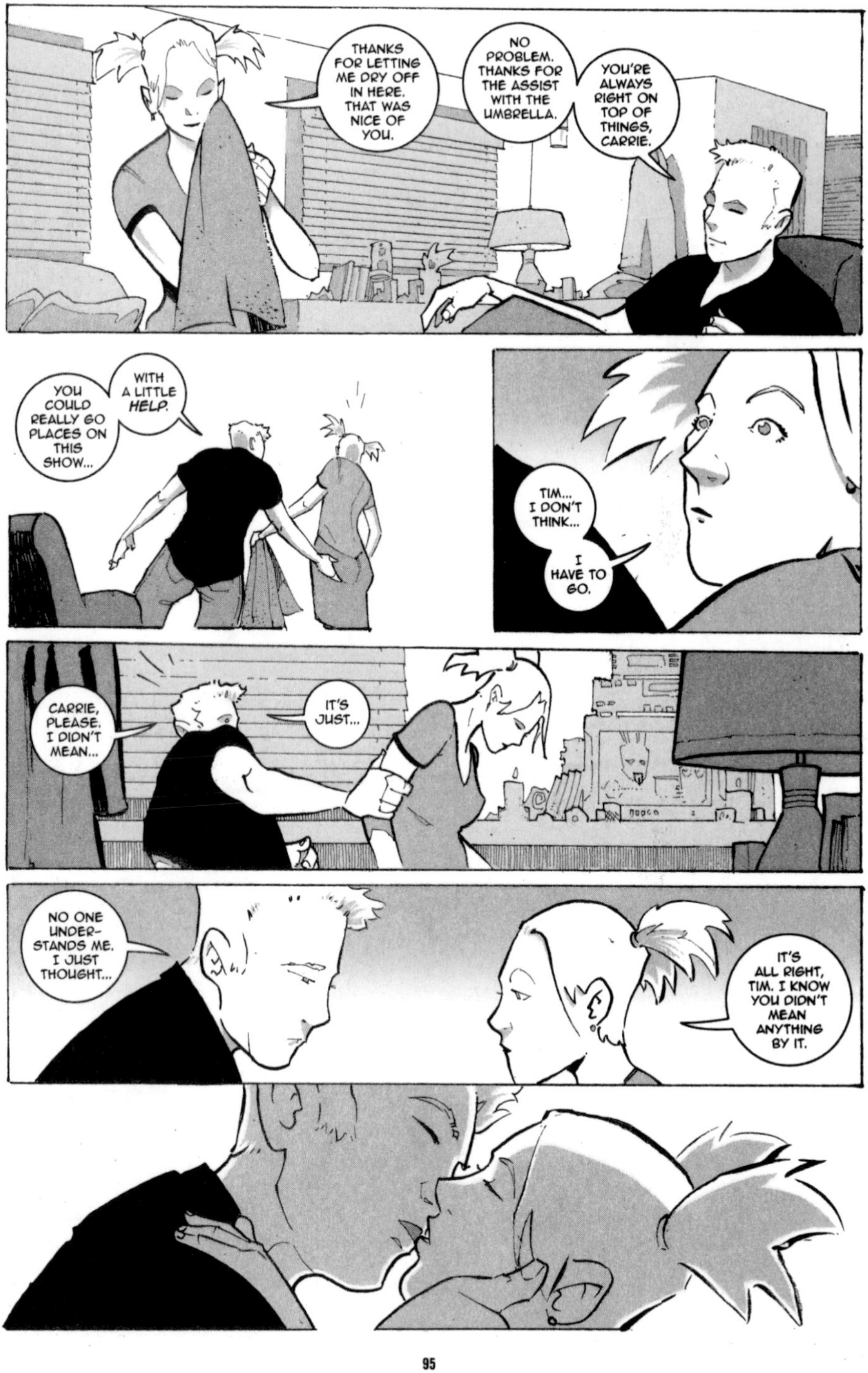
THANKS FOR LETTING ME DRY OFF IN HERE. THAT WAS NICE OF YOU.
NO PROBLEM. THANKS FOR THE ASSIST WITH THE UMBRELLA.
YOU'RE ALWAYS RIGHT ON TOP OF THINGS, CARRIE.
YOU COULD REALLY GO PLACES ON THIS SHOW...
WITH A LITTLE *HELP*.
TIM... I DON'T THINK...
I HAVE TO GO.
CARRIE, PLEASE. I DIDN'T MEAN...
IT'S JUST...
NO ONE UNDER-STANDS ME. I JUST THOUGHT...
IT'S ALL RIGHT, TIM. I KNOW YOU DIDN'T MEAN ANYTHING BY IT.

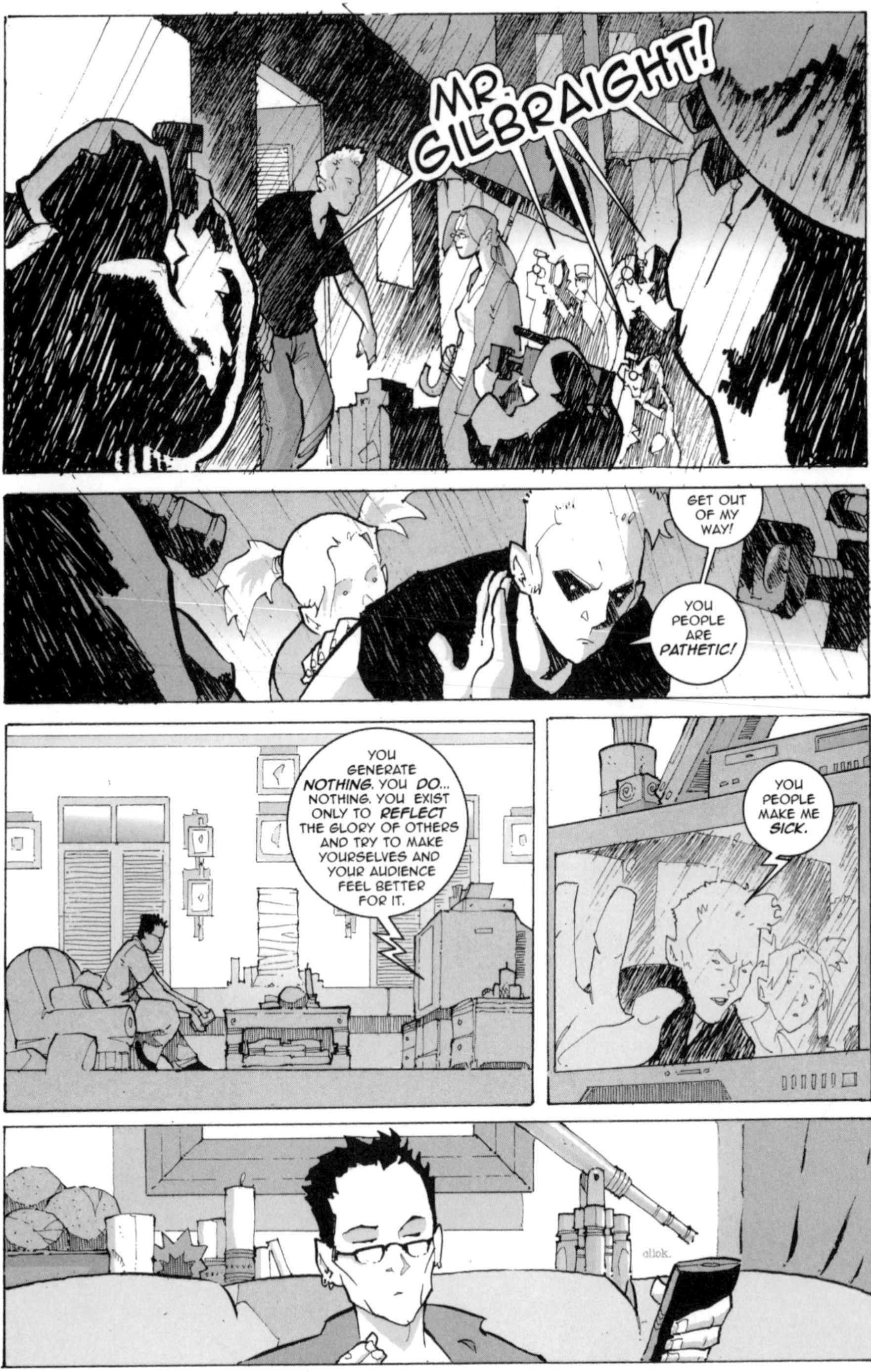
MR. GILBRAIGHT!
GET OUT OF MY WAY!
YOU PEOPLE ARE PATHETIC!
YOU GENERATE NOTHING. YOU DO... NOTHING. YOU EXIST ONLY TO REFLECT THE GLORY OF OTHERS AND TRY TO MAKE YOURSELVES AND YOUR AUDIENCE FEEL BETTER FOR IT.
YOU PEOPLE MAKE ME SICK.
click.

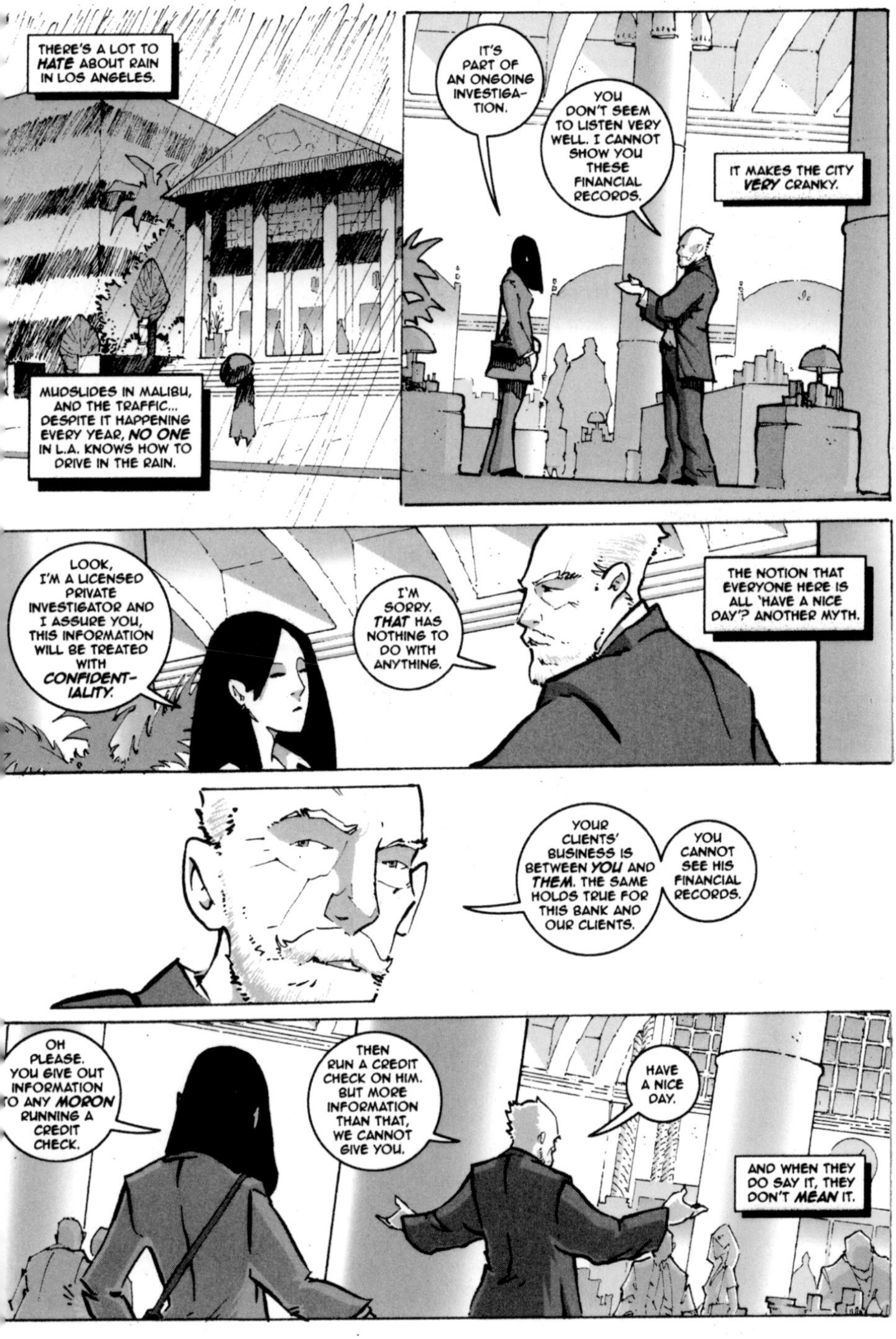

THERE'S A LOT TO HATE ABOUT RAIN IN LOS ANGELES.
MUDSLIDES IN MALIBU, AND THE TRAFFIC... DESPITE IT HAPPENING EVERY YEAR, NO ONE IN L.A. KNOWS HOW TO DRIVE IN THE RAIN.
IT'S PART OF AN ONGOING INVESTIGA-TION.
YOU DON'T SEEM TO LISTEN VERY WELL. I CANNOT SHOW YOU THESE FINANCIAL RECORDS.
IT MAKES THE CITY VERY CRANKY.
LOOK, I'M A LICENSED PRIVATE INVESTIGATOR AND I ASSURE YOU, THIS INFORMATION WILL BE TREATED WITH CONFIDENT-IALITY.
I'M SORRY. THAT HAS NOTHING TO DO WITH ANYTHING.
THE NOTION THAT EVERYONE HERE IS ALL 'HAVE A NICE DAY'? ANOTHER MYTH.
YOUR CLIENTS' BUSINESS IS BETWEEN YOU AND THEM. THE SAME HOLDS TRUE FOR THIS BANK AND OUR CLIENTS.
YOU CANNOT SEE HIS FINANCIAL RECORDS.
OH PLEASE. YOU GIVE OUT INFORMATION TO ANY MORON RUNNING A CREDIT CHECK.
THEN RUN A CREDIT CHECK ON HIM. BUT MORE INFORMATION THAN THAT, WE CANNOT GIVE YOU.
HAVE A NICE DAY.
AND WHEN THEY DO SAY IT, THEY DON'T MEAN IT.

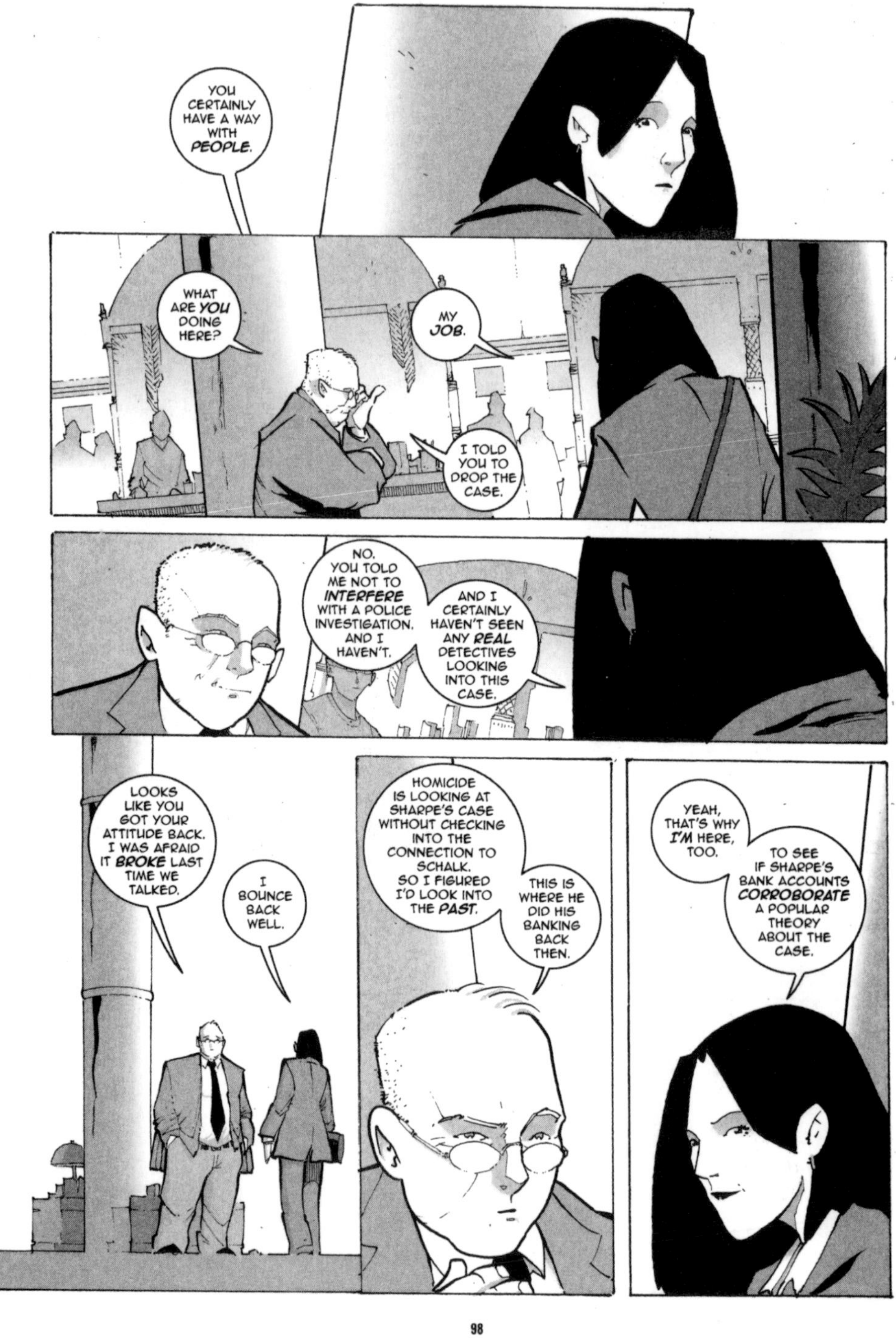
YOU CERTAINLY HAVE A WAY WITH PEOPLE.
WHAT ARE YOU DOING HERE?
MY JOB.
I TOLD YOU TO DROP THE CASE.
NO. YOU TOLD ME NOT TO INTERFERE WITH A POLICE INVESTIGATION. AND I HAVEN'T.
AND I CERTAINLY HAVEN'T SEEN ANY REAL DETECTIVES LOOKING INTO THIS CASE.
LOOKS LIKE YOU GOT YOUR ATTITUDE BACK. I WAS AFRAID IT BROKE LAST TIME WE TALKED.
I BOUNCE BACK WELL.
HOMICIDE IS LOOKING AT SHARPE'S CASE WITHOUT CHECKING INTO THE CONNECTION TO SCHALK. SO I FIGURED I'D LOOK INTO THE PAST.
THIS IS WHERE HE DID HIS BANKING BACK THEN.
YEAH, THAT'S WHY I'M HERE, TOO.
TO SEE IF SHARPE'S BANK ACCOUNTS CORROBORATE A POPULAR THEORY ABOUT THE CASE.

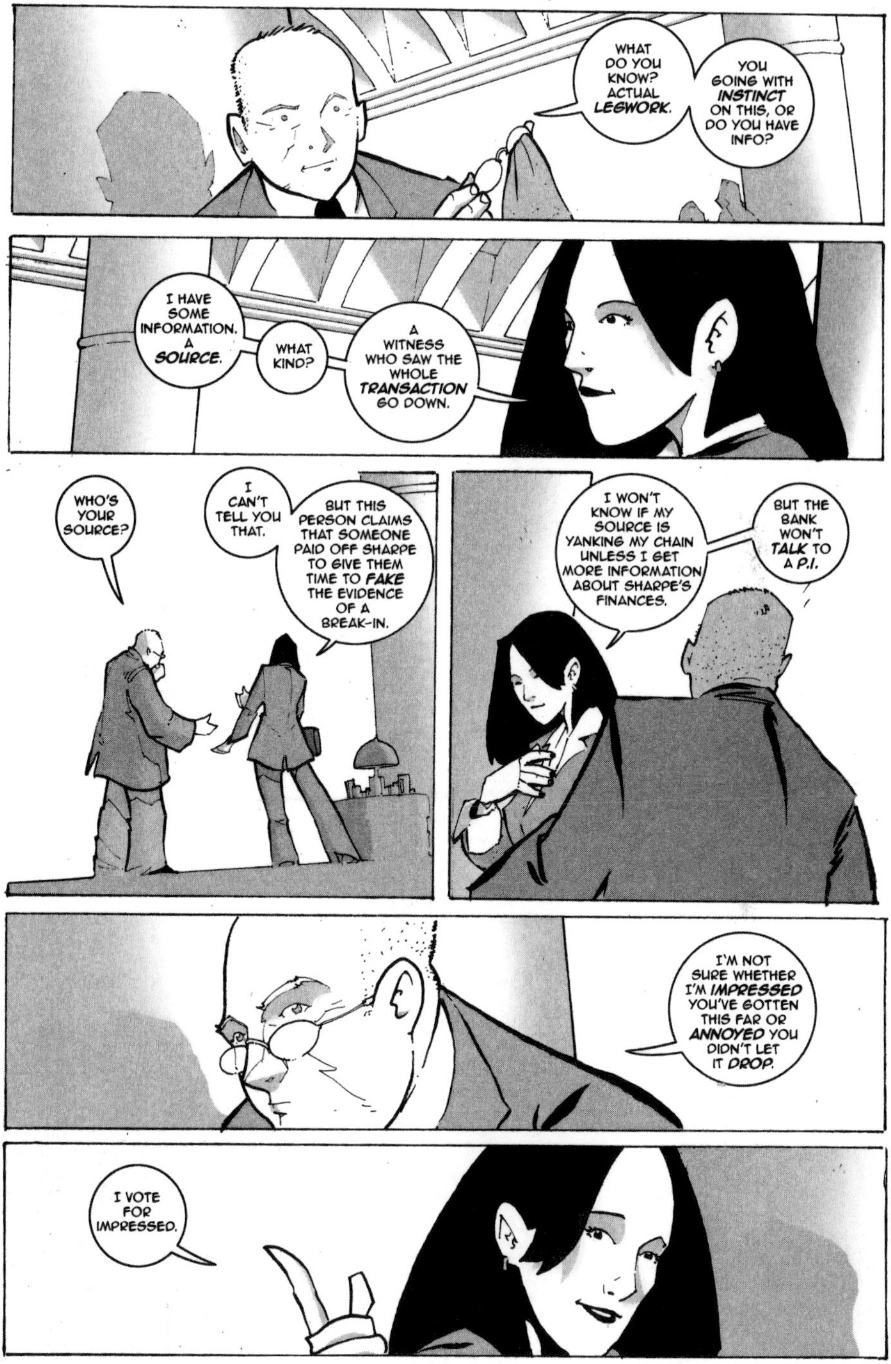
WHAT DO YOU KNOW? ACTUAL LEGWORK.
YOU GOING WITH INSTINCT ON THIS, OR DO YOU HAVE INFO?
I HAVE SOME INFORMATION. A SOURCE.
WHAT KIND?
A WITNESS WHO SAW THE WHOLE TRANSACTION GO DOWN.
WHO'S YOUR SOURCE?
I CAN'T TELL YOU THAT.
BUT THIS PERSON CLAIMS THAT SOMEONE PAID OFF SHARPE TO GIVE THEM TIME TO FAKE THE EVIDENCE OF A BREAK-IN.
I WON'T KNOW IF MY SOURCE IS YANKING MY CHAIN UNLESS I GET MORE INFORMATION ABOUT SHARPE'S FINANCES.
BUT THE BANK WON'T TALK TO A P.I.
I'M NOT SURE WHETHER I'M IMPRESSED YOU'VE GOTTEN THIS FAR OR ANNOYED YOU DIDN'T LET IT DROP.
I VOTE FOR IMPRESSED.

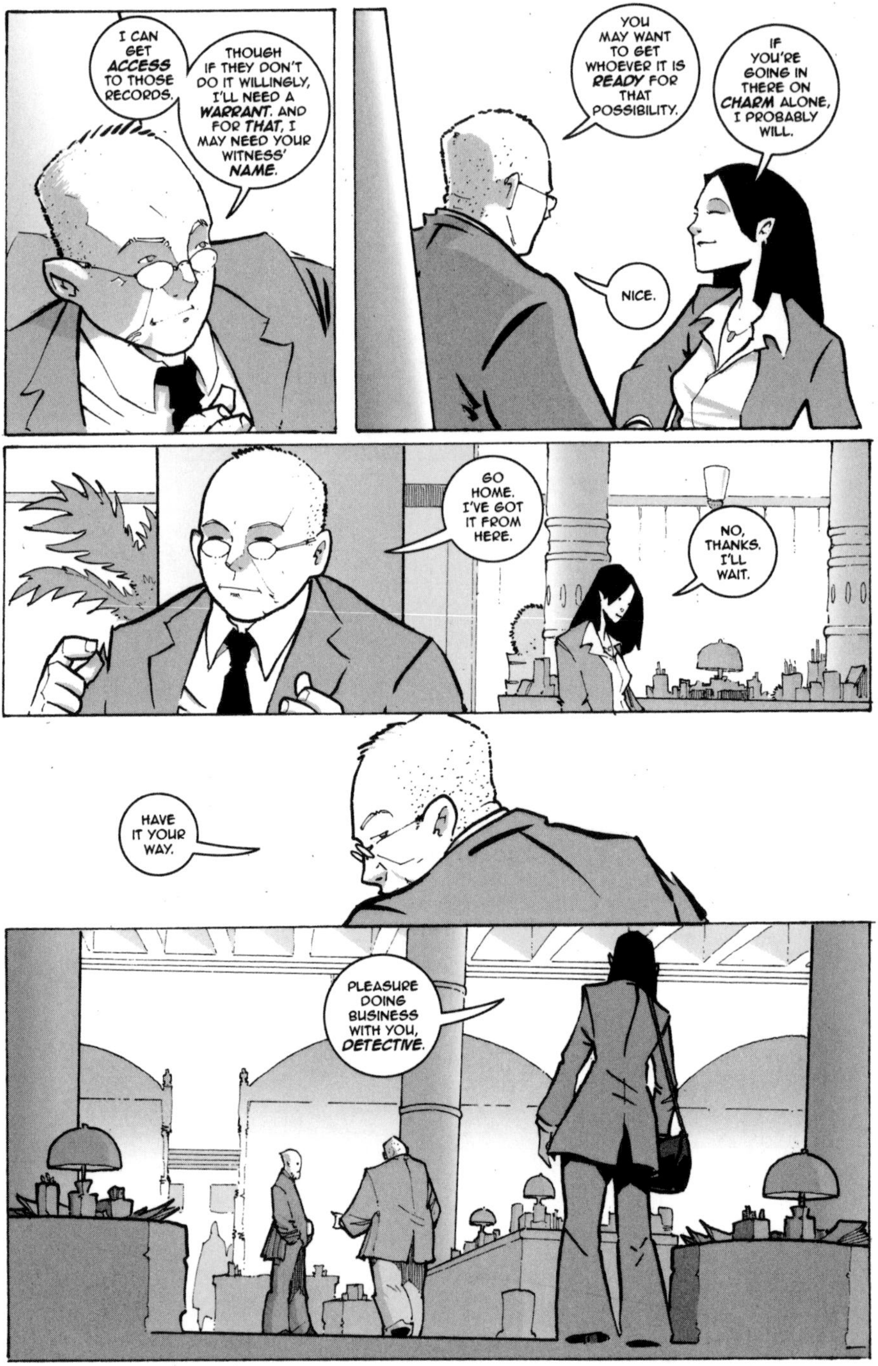
I CAN GET ACCESS TO THOSE RECORDS.
THOUGH IF THEY DON'T DO IT WILLINGLY, I'LL NEED A WARRANT. AND FOR THAT, I MAY NEED YOUR WITNESS' NAME.
YOU MAY WANT TO GET WHOEVER IT IS READY FOR THAT POSSIBILITY.
IF YOU'RE GOING IN THERE ON CHARM ALONE, I PROBABLY WILL.
NICE.
GO HOME. I'VE GOT IT FROM HERE.
NO, THANKS. I'LL WAIT.
HAVE IT YOUR WAY.
PLEASURE DOING BUSINESS WITH YOU, DETECTIVE.

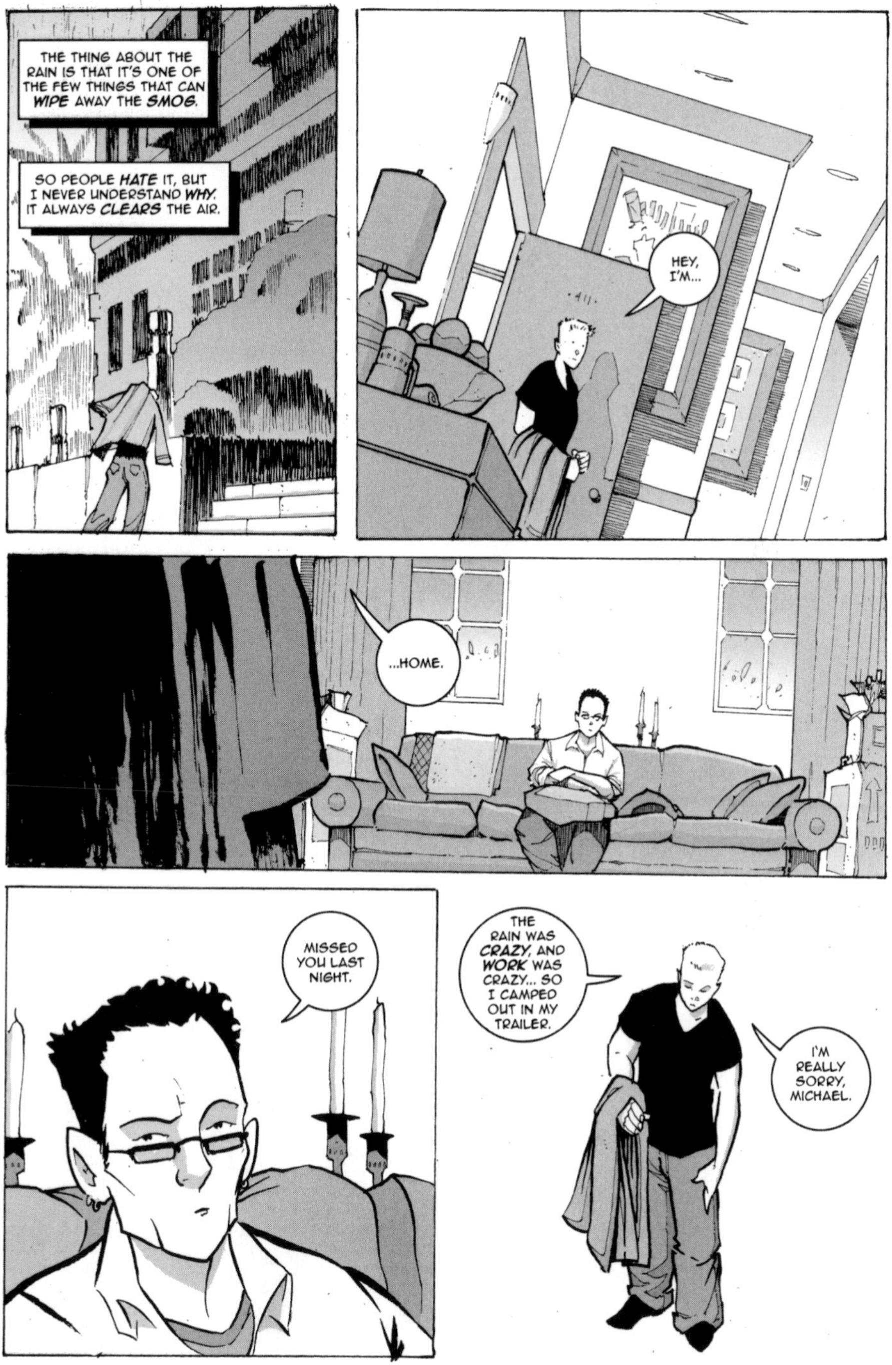
THE THING ABOUT THE RAIN IS THAT IT'S ONE OF THE FEW THINGS THAT CAN WIPE AWAY THE SMOG.
SO PEOPLE HATE IT, BUT I NEVER UNDERSTAND WHY. IT ALWAYS CLEARS THE AIR.
HEY, I'M...
...HOME.
MISSED YOU LAST NIGHT.
THE RAIN WAS CRAZY, AND WORK WAS CRAZY... SO I CAMPED OUT IN MY TRAILER.
I'M REALLY SORRY, MICHAEL.

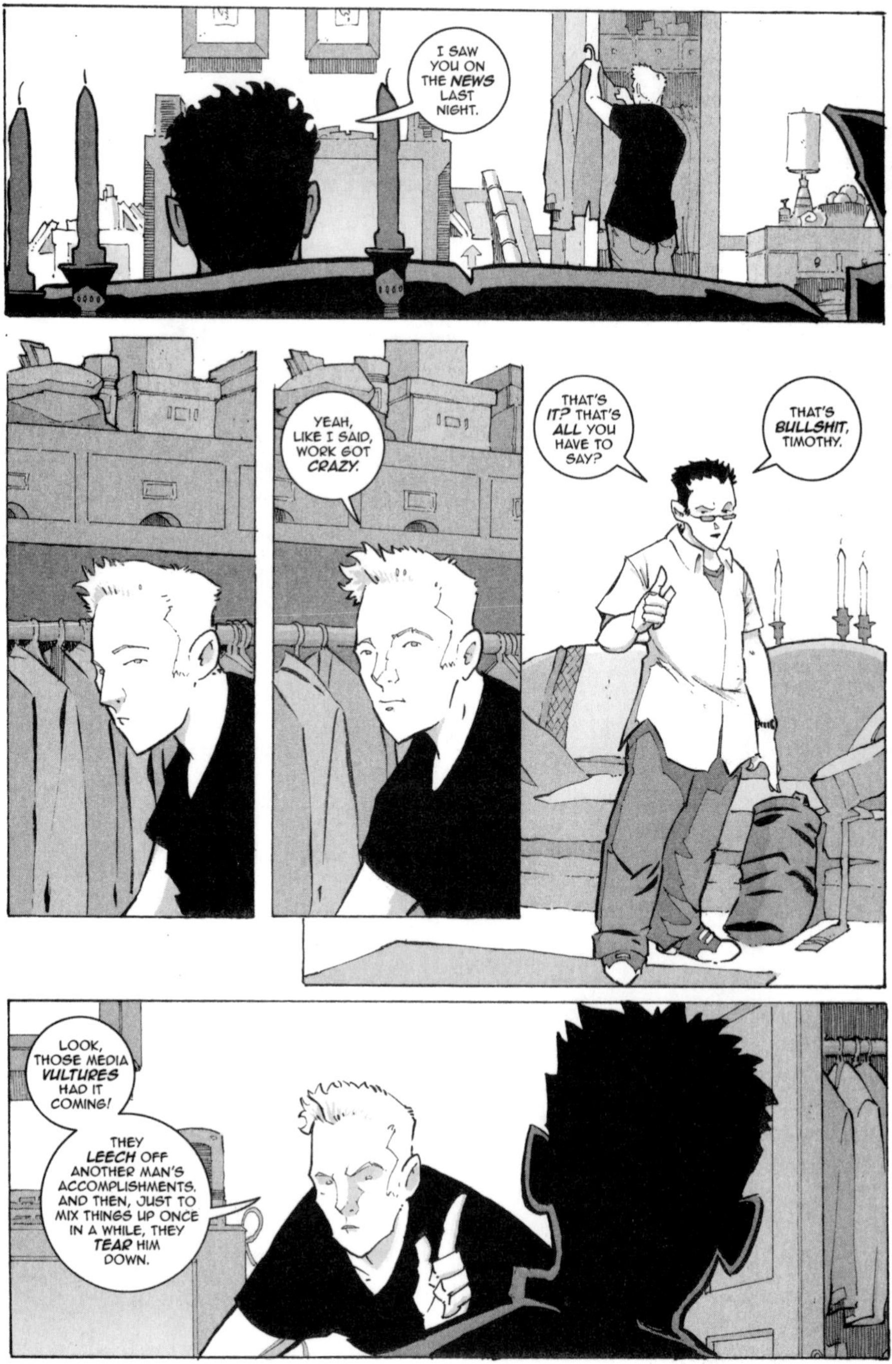
I SAW YOU ON THE NEWS LAST NIGHT.
YEAH, LIKE I SAID, WORK GOT CRAZY.
THAT'S IT? THAT'S ALL YOU HAVE TO SAY?
THAT'S BULLSHIT, TIMOTHY.
LOOK, THOSE MEDIA VULTURES HAD IT COMING!
THEY LEECH OFF ANOTHER MAN'S ACCOMPLISHMENTS. AND THEN, JUST TO MIX THINGS UP ONCE IN A WHILE, THEY TEAR HIM DOWN.

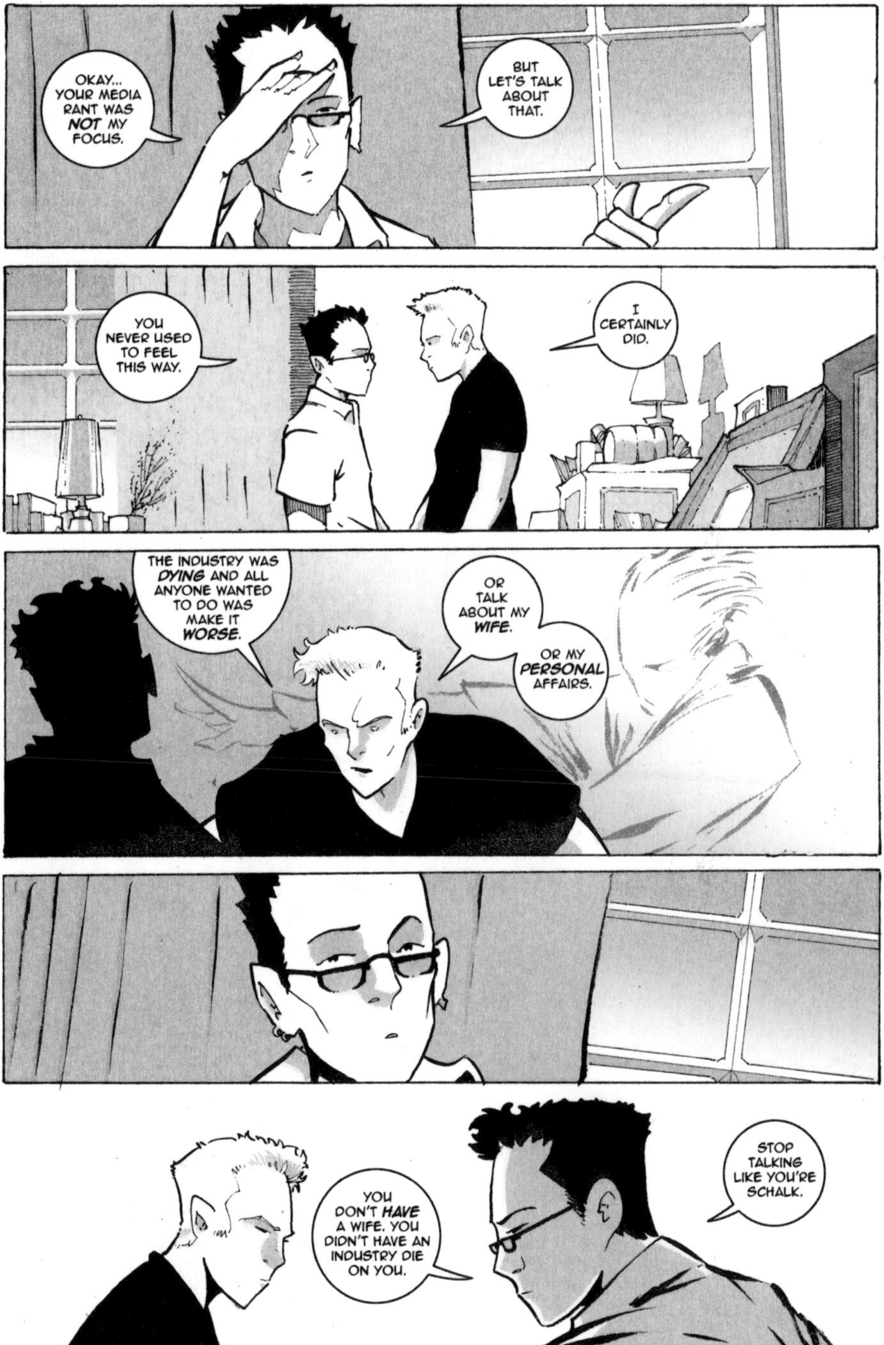
OKAY... YOUR MEDIA RANT WAS NOT MY FOCUS.
BUT LET'S TALK ABOUT THAT.
YOU NEVER USED TO FEEL THIS WAY.
I CERTAINLY DID.
THE INDUSTRY WAS DYING AND ALL ANYONE WANTED TO DO WAS MAKE IT WORSE.
OR TALK ABOUT MY WIFE.
OR MY PERSONAL AFFAIRS.
YOU DON'T HAVE A WIFE. YOU DIDN'T HAVE AN INDUSTRY DIE ON YOU.
STOP TALKING LIKE YOU'RE SCHALK.

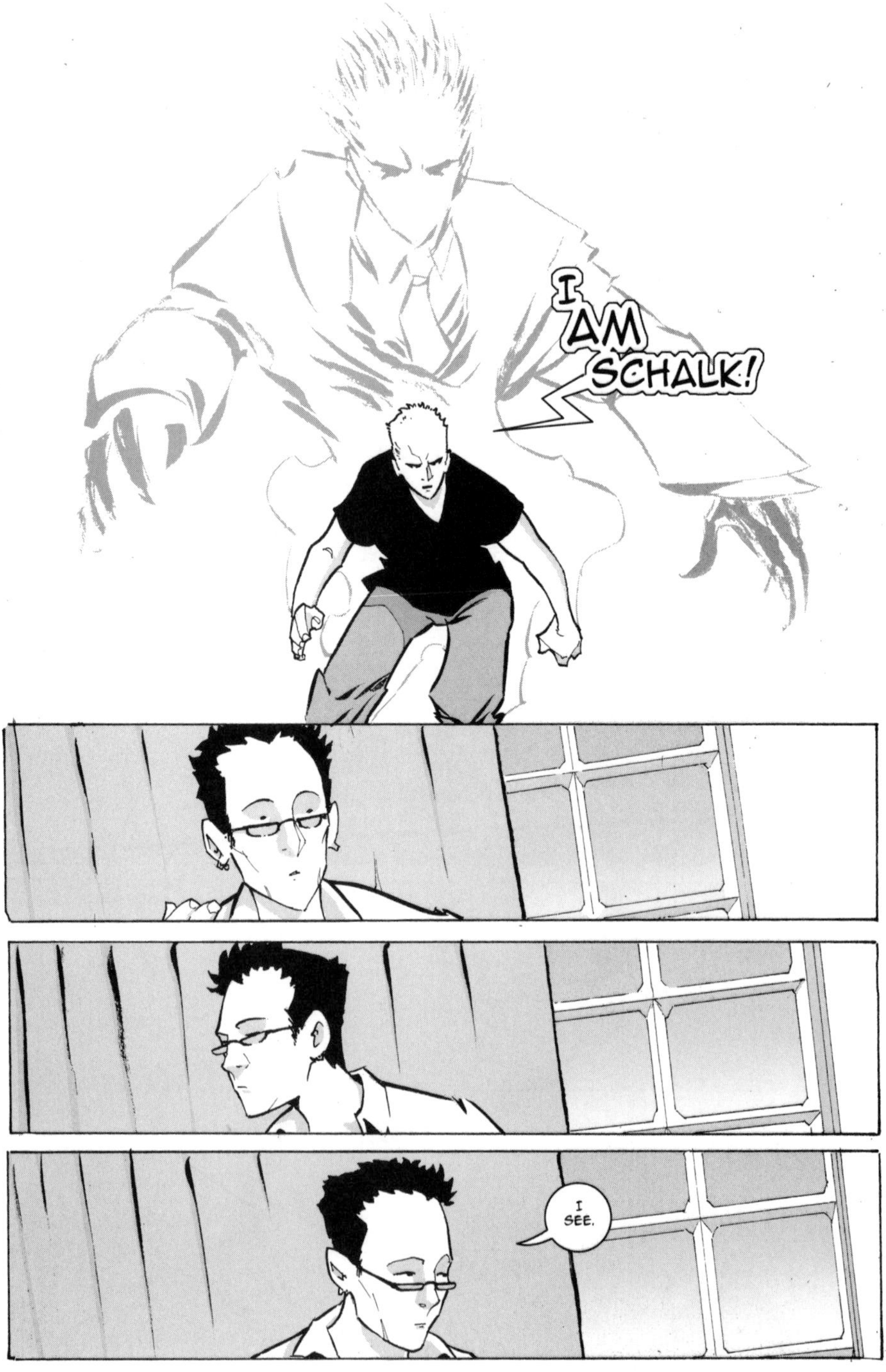
I AM SCHALK!
I SEE.

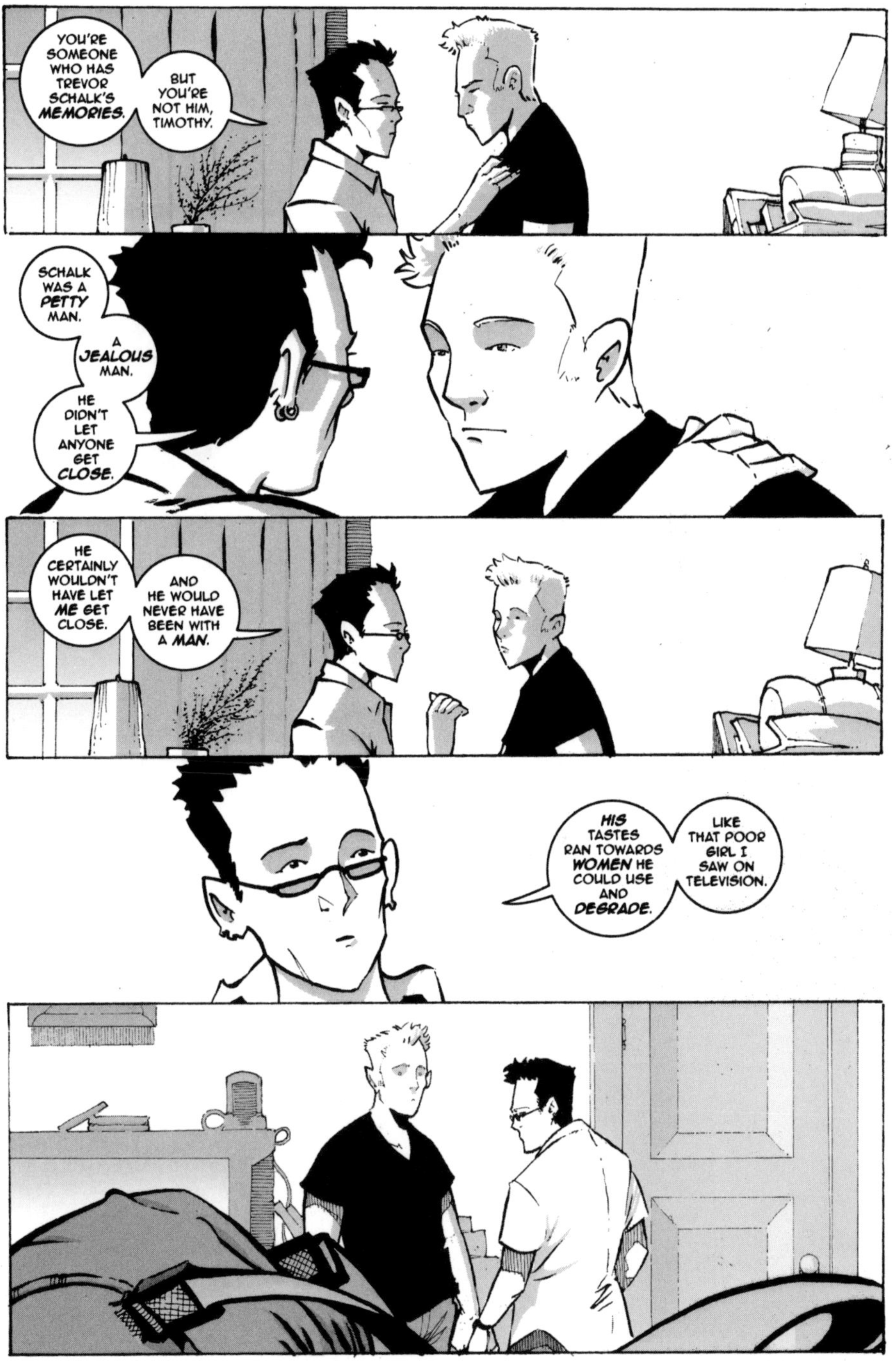
YOU'RE SOMEONE WHO HAS TREVOR SCHALK'S MEMORIES.
BUT YOU'RE NOT HIM, TIMOTHY.
SCHALK WAS A PETTY MAN.
A JEALOUS MAN.
HE DIDN'T LET ANYONE GET CLOSE.
HE CERTAINLY WOULDN'T HAVE LET ME GET CLOSE.
AND HE WOULD NEVER HAVE BEEN WITH A MAN.
HIS TASTES RAN TOWARDS WOMEN HE COULD USE AND DEGRADE.
LIKE THAT POOR GIRL I SAW ON TELEVISION.

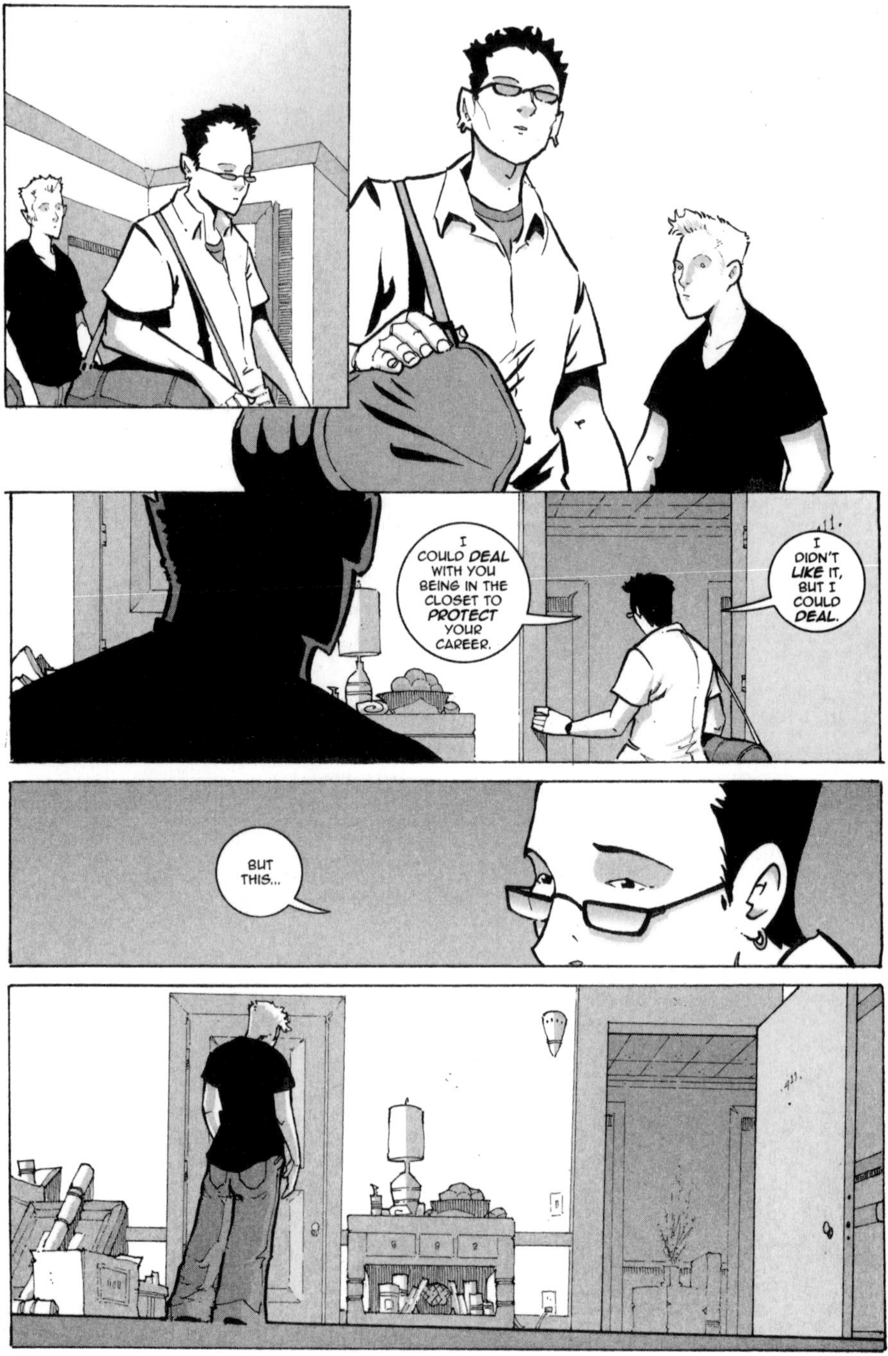
I COULD DEAL WITH YOU BEING IN THE CLOSET TO PROTECT YOUR CAREER.
I DIDN'T LIKE IT, BUT I COULD DEAL.
BUT THIS...

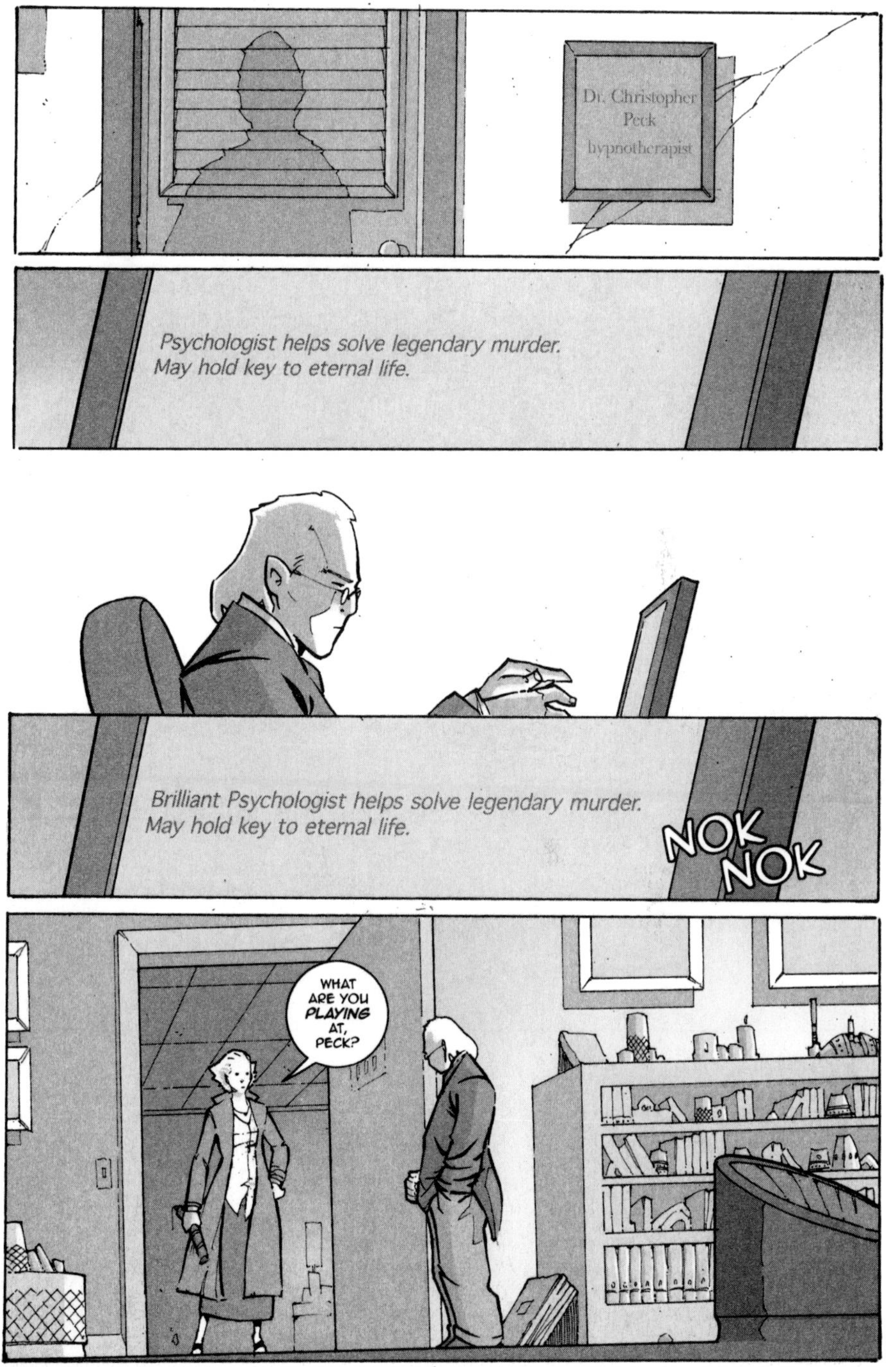
Dr. Christopher Peck hypnotherapist
Psychologist helps solve legendary murder. May hold key to eternal life.
Brilliant Psychologist helps solve legendary murder. May hold key to eternal life.
NOK NOK
WHAT ARE YOU PLAYING AT, PECK?

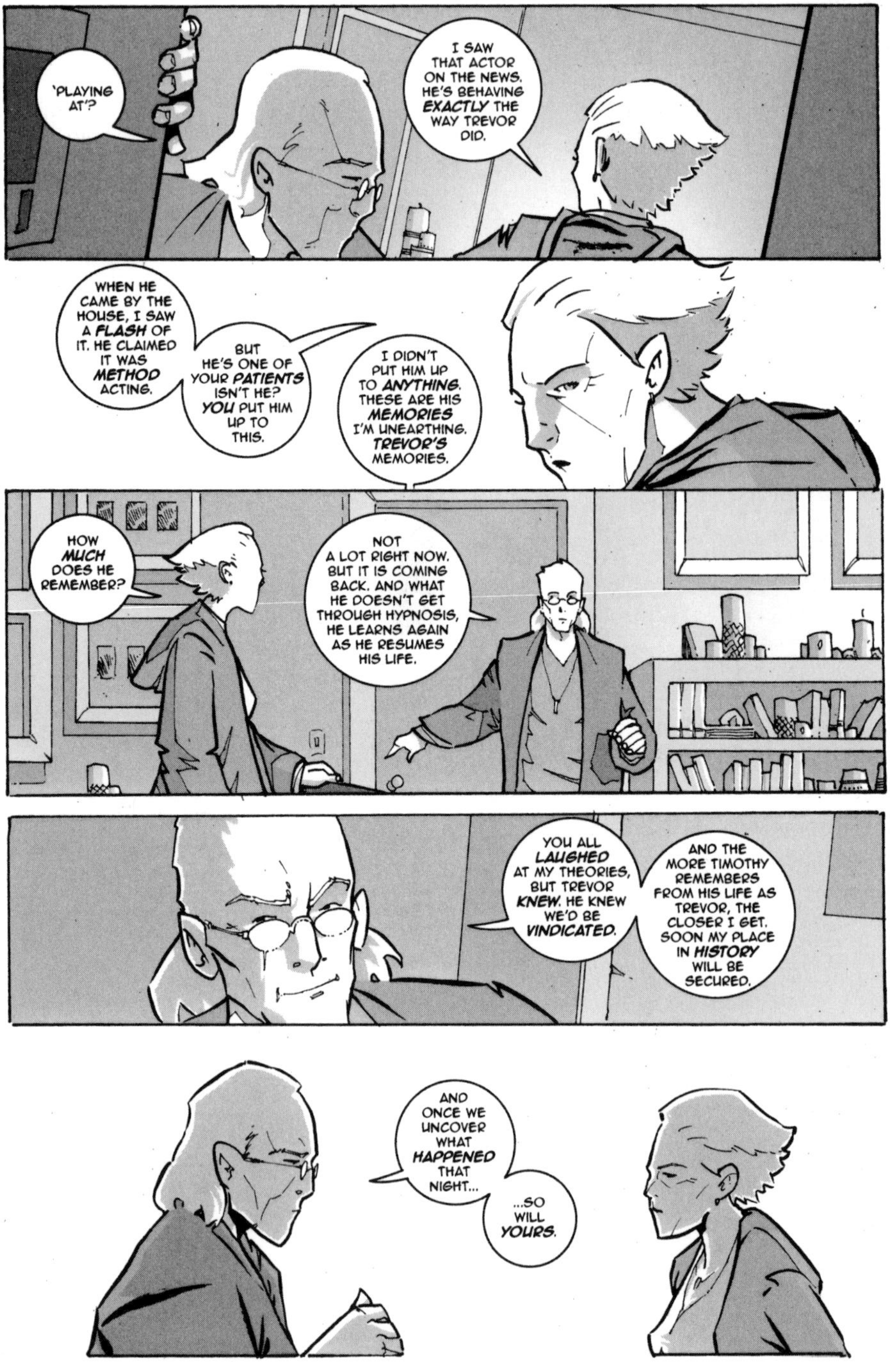
'PLAYING AT'?
I SAW THAT ACTOR ON THE NEWS. HE'S BEHAVING EXACTLY THE WAY TREVOR DID.
WHEN HE CAME BY THE HOUSE, I SAW A FLASH OF IT. HE CLAIMED IT WAS METHOD ACTING.
BUT HE'S ONE OF YOUR PATIENTS ISN'T HE? YOU PUT HIM UP TO THIS.
I DIDN'T PUT HIM UP TO ANYTHING. THESE ARE HIS MEMORIES I'M UNEARTHING. TREVOR'S MEMORIES.
HOW MUCH DOES HE REMEMBER?
NOT A LOT RIGHT NOW. BUT IT IS COMING BACK. AND WHAT HE DOESN'T GET THROUGH HYPNOSIS, HE LEARNS AGAIN AS HE RESUMES HIS LIFE.
YOU ALL LAUGHED AT MY THEORIES, BUT TREVOR KNEW. HE KNEW WE'D BE VINDICATED.
AND THE MORE TIMOTHY REMEMBERS FROM HIS LIFE AS TREVOR, THE CLOSER I GET. SOON MY PLACE IN HISTORY WILL BE SECURED.
AND ONCE WE UNCOVER WHAT HAPPENED THAT NIGHT...
...SO WILL YOURS.

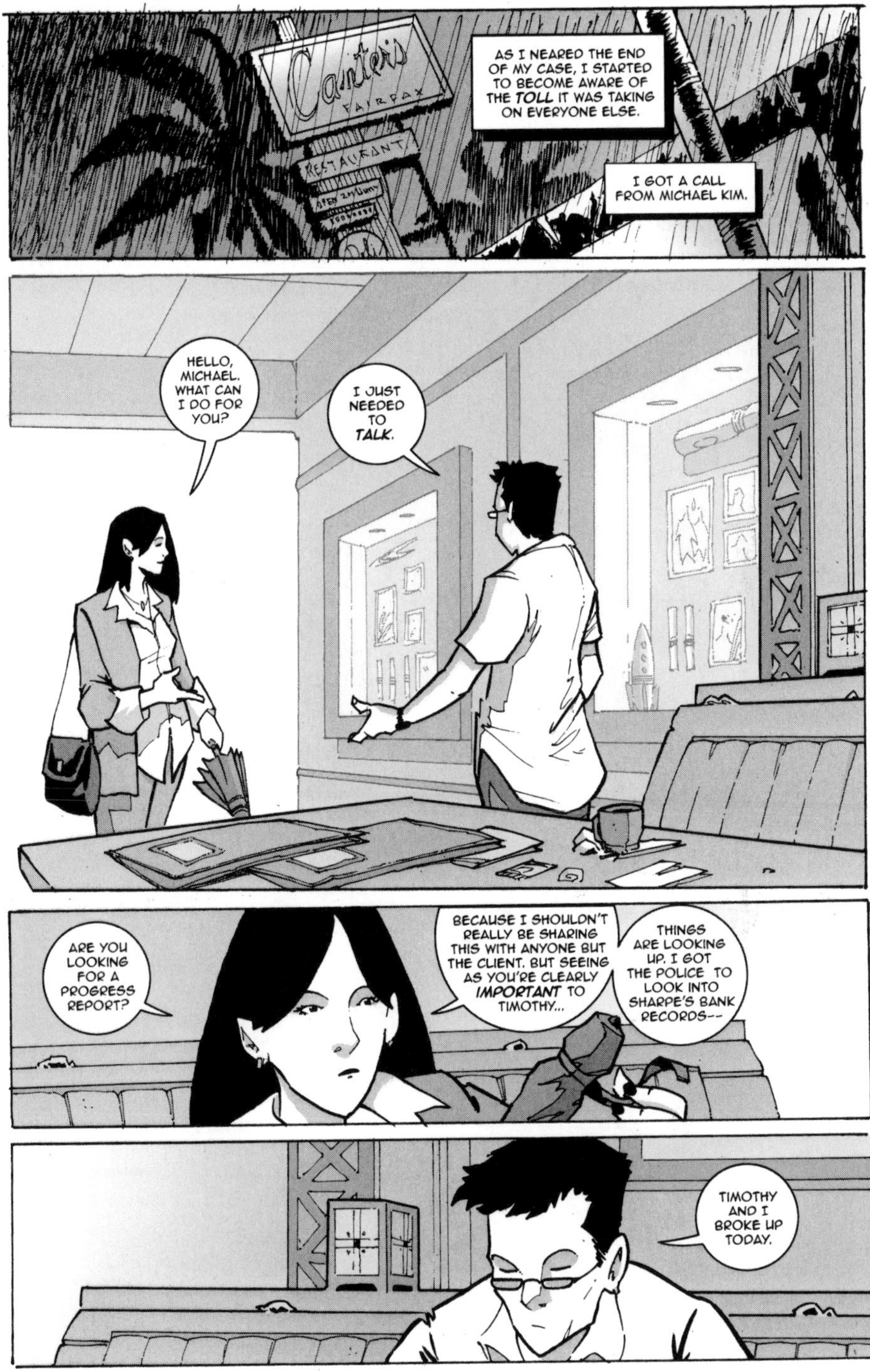
Canter's
FAIRFAX
RESTAURANT
AS I NEARED THE END OF MY CASE, I STARTED TO BECOME AWARE OF THE *TOLL* IT WAS TAKING ON EVERYONE ELSE.
I GOT A CALL FROM MICHAEL KIM.
HELLO, MICHAEL. WHAT CAN I DO FOR YOU?
I JUST NEEDED TO *TALK*.
ARE YOU LOOKING FOR A PROGRESS REPORT?
BECAUSE I SHOULDN'T REALLY BE SHARING THIS WITH ANYONE BUT THE CLIENT. BUT SEEING AS YOU'RE CLEARLY *IMPORTANT* TO TIMOTHY...
THINGS ARE LOOKING UP. I GOT THE POLICE TO LOOK INTO SHARPE'S BANK RECORDS--
TIMOTHY AND I BROKE UP TODAY.

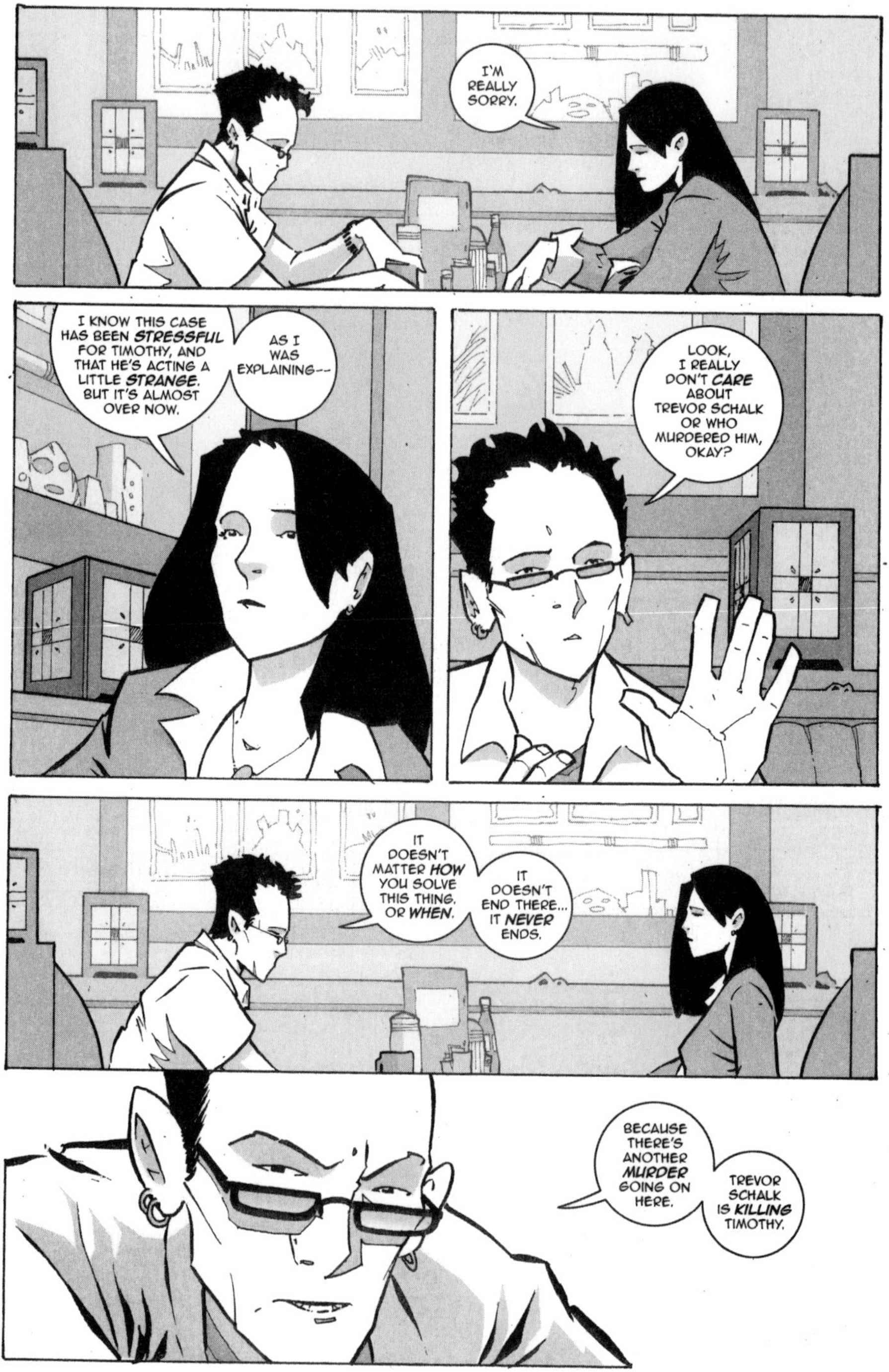
I'M REALLY SORRY.
I KNOW THIS CASE HAS BEEN STRESSFUL FOR TIMOTHY, AND THAT HE'S ACTING A LITTLE STRANGE. BUT IT'S ALMOST OVER NOW.
AS I WAS EXPLAINING--
LOOK, I REALLY DON'T CARE ABOUT TREVOR SCHALK OR WHO MURDERED HIM, OKAY?
IT DOESN'T MATTER HOW YOU SOLVE THIS THING, OR WHEN.
IT DOESN'T END THERE... IT NEVER ENDS.
BECAUSE THERE'S ANOTHER MURDER GOING ON HERE.
TREVOR SCHALK IS KILLING TIMOTHY.

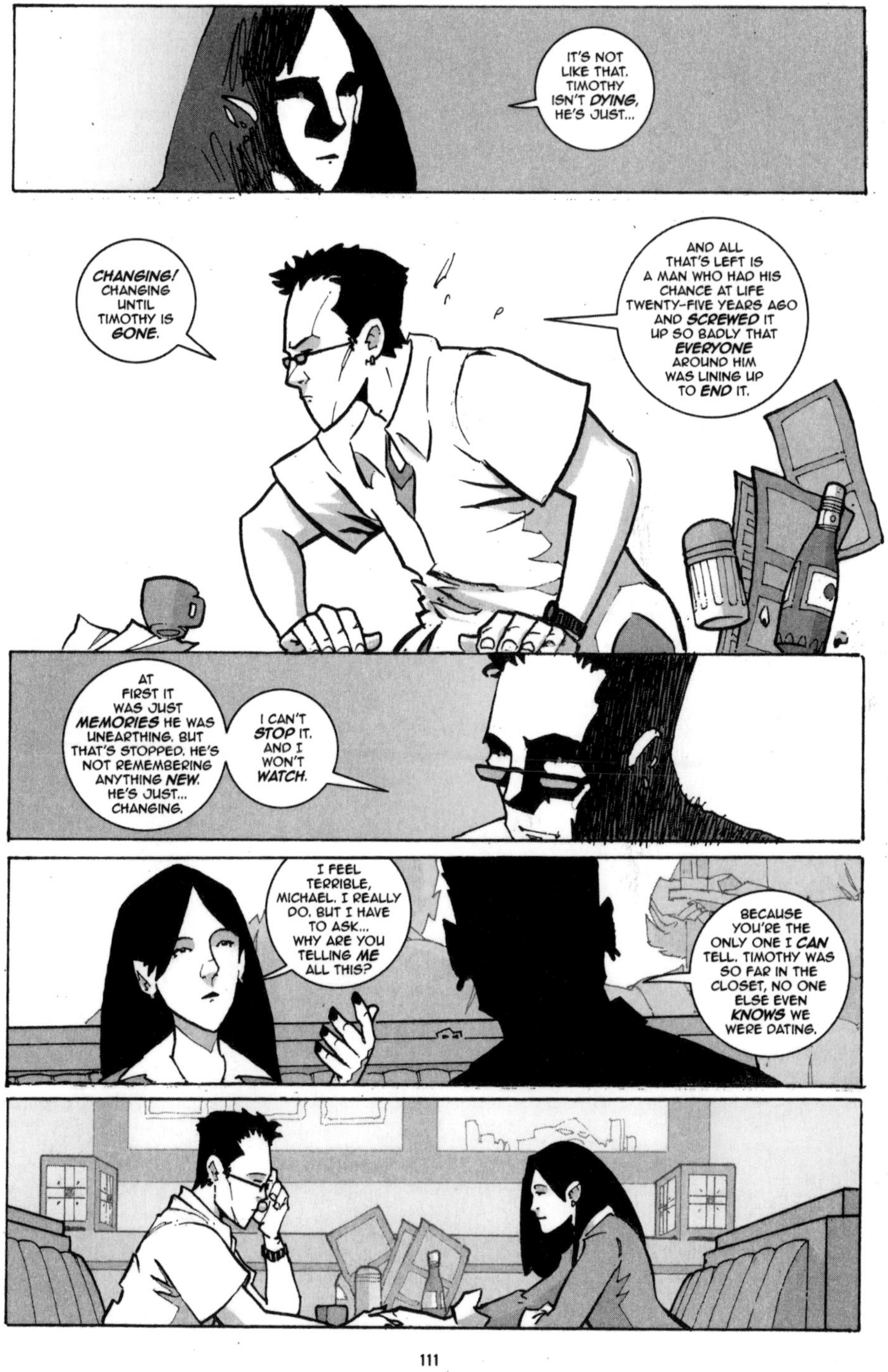
IT'S NOT LIKE THAT. TIMOTHY ISN'T *DYING*, HE'S JUST...
CHANGING! CHANGING UNTIL TIMOTHY IS *GONE*.
AND ALL THAT'S LEFT IS A MAN WHO HAD HIS CHANCE AT LIFE TWENTY-FIVE YEARS AGO AND *SCREWED* IT UP SO BADLY THAT *EVERYONE* AROUND HIM WAS LINING UP TO *END* IT.
AT FIRST IT WAS JUST *MEMORIES* HE WAS UNEARTHING, BUT THAT'S STOPPED. HE'S NOT REMEMBERING ANYTHING *NEW*. HE'S JUST... CHANGING.
I CAN'T *STOP* IT. AND I WON'T *WATCH*.
I FEEL TERRIBLE, MICHAEL. I REALLY DO. BUT I HAVE TO ASK... WHY ARE YOU TELLING *ME* ALL THIS?
BECAUSE YOU'RE THE ONLY ONE I *CAN* TELL. TIMOTHY WAS SO FAR IN THE CLOSET, NO ONE ELSE EVEN *KNOWS* WE WERE DATING.

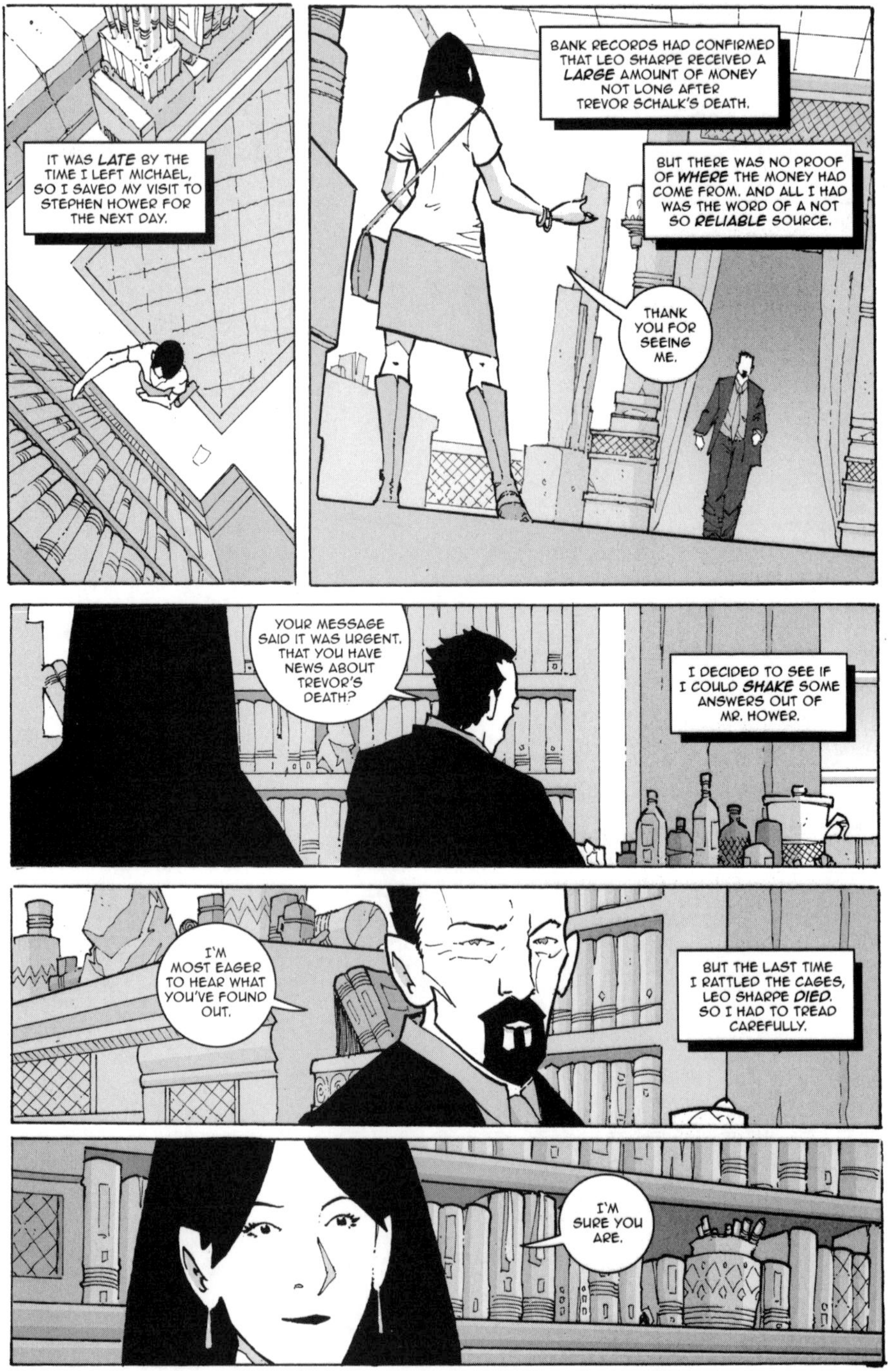
IT WAS LATE BY THE TIME I LEFT MICHAEL, SO I SAVED MY VISIT TO STEPHEN HOWER FOR THE NEXT DAY.
BANK RECORDS HAD CONFIRMED THAT LEO SHARPE RECEIVED A LARGE AMOUNT OF MONEY NOT LONG AFTER TREVOR SCHALK'S DEATH.
BUT THERE WAS NO PROOF OF WHERE THE MONEY HAD COME FROM. AND ALL I HAD WAS THE WORD OF A NOT SO RELIABLE SOURCE.
THANK YOU FOR SEEING ME.
YOUR MESSAGE SAID IT WAS URGENT. THAT YOU HAVE NEWS ABOUT TREVOR'S DEATH?
I DECIDED TO SEE IF I COULD SHAKE SOME ANSWERS OUT OF MR. HOWER.
I'M MOST EAGER TO HEAR WHAT YOU'VE FOUND OUT.
BUT THE LAST TIME I RATTLED THE CAGES, LEO SHARPE DIED. SO I HAD TO TREAD CAREFULLY.
I'M SURE YOU ARE.

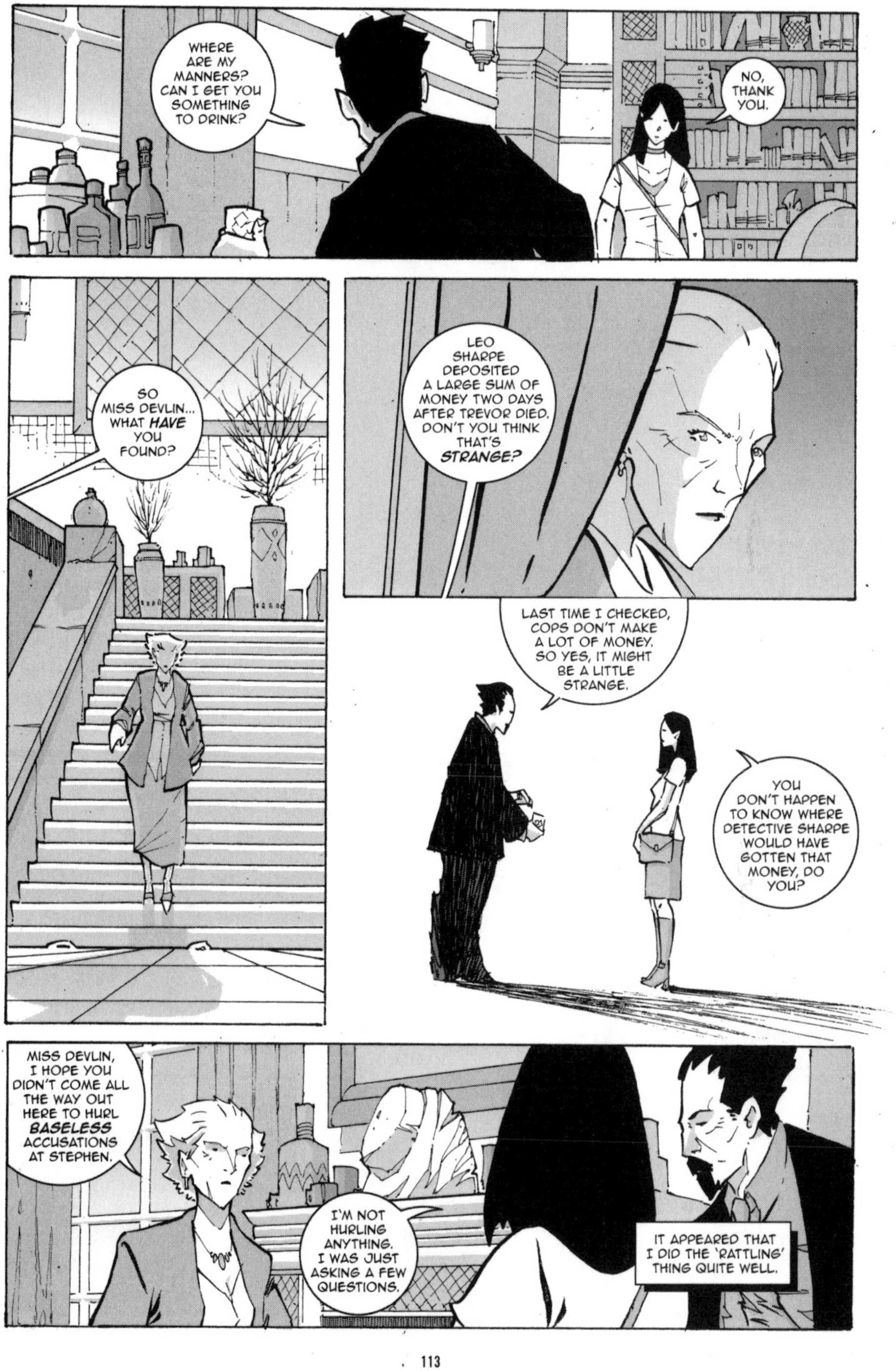
WHERE ARE MY MANNERS? CAN I GET YOU SOMETHING TO DRINK?
NO, THANK YOU.
SO MISS DEVLIN... WHAT **HAVE** YOU FOUND?
LEO SHARPE DEPOSITED A LARGE SUM OF MONEY TWO DAYS AFTER TREVOR DIED. DON'T YOU THINK THAT'S **STRANGE?**
LAST TIME I CHECKED, COPS DON'T MAKE A LOT OF MONEY. SO YES, IT MIGHT BE A LITTLE STRANGE.
YOU DON'T HAPPEN TO KNOW WHERE DETECTIVE SHARPE WOULD HAVE GOTTEN THAT MONEY, DO YOU?
MISS DEVLIN, I HOPE YOU DIDN'T COME ALL THE WAY OUT HERE TO HURL **BASELESS** ACCUSATIONS AT STEPHEN.
I'M NOT HURLING ANYTHING. I WAS JUST ASKING A FEW QUESTIONS.
IT APPEARED THAT I DID THE 'RATTLING' THING QUITE WELL.

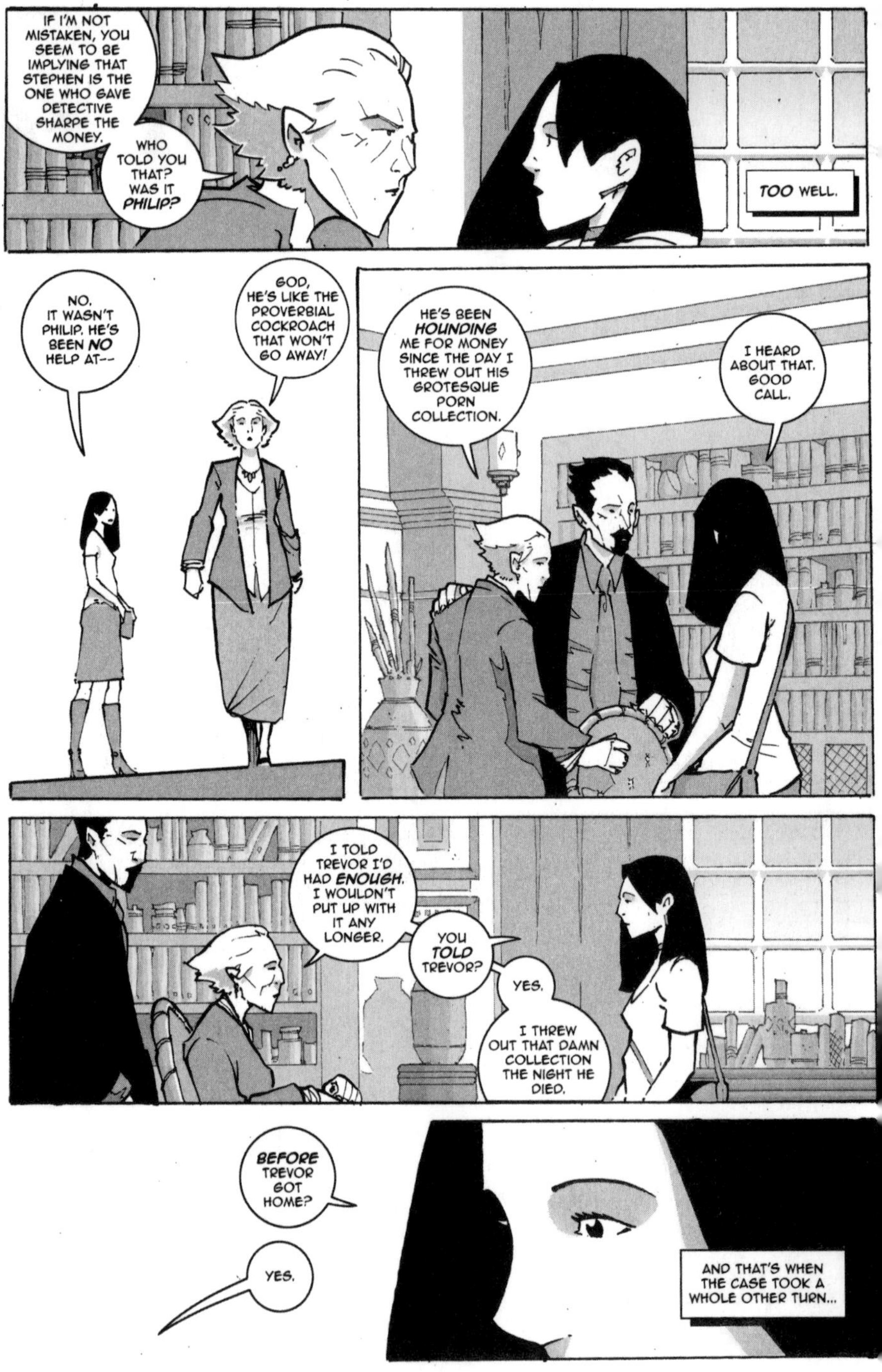
IF I'M NOT MISTAKEN, YOU SEEM TO BE IMPLYING THAT STEPHEN IS THE ONE WHO GAVE DETECTIVE SHARPE THE MONEY.
WHO TOLD YOU THAT? WAS IT PHILIP?
TOO WELL.
NO. IT WASN'T PHILIP. HE'S BEEN NO HELP AT--
GOD, HE'S LIKE THE PROVERBIAL COCKROACH THAT WON'T GO AWAY!
HE'S BEEN HOUNDING ME FOR MONEY SINCE THE DAY I THREW OUT HIS GROTESQUE PORN COLLECTION.
I HEARD ABOUT THAT. GOOD CALL.
I TOLD TREVOR I'D HAD ENOUGH. I WOULDN'T PUT UP WITH IT ANY LONGER.
YOU TOLD TREVOR?
YES.
I THREW OUT THAT DAMN COLLECTION THE NIGHT HE DIED.
BEFORE TREVOR GOT HOME?
YES.
AND THAT'S WHEN THE CASE TOOK A WHOLE OTHER TURN...

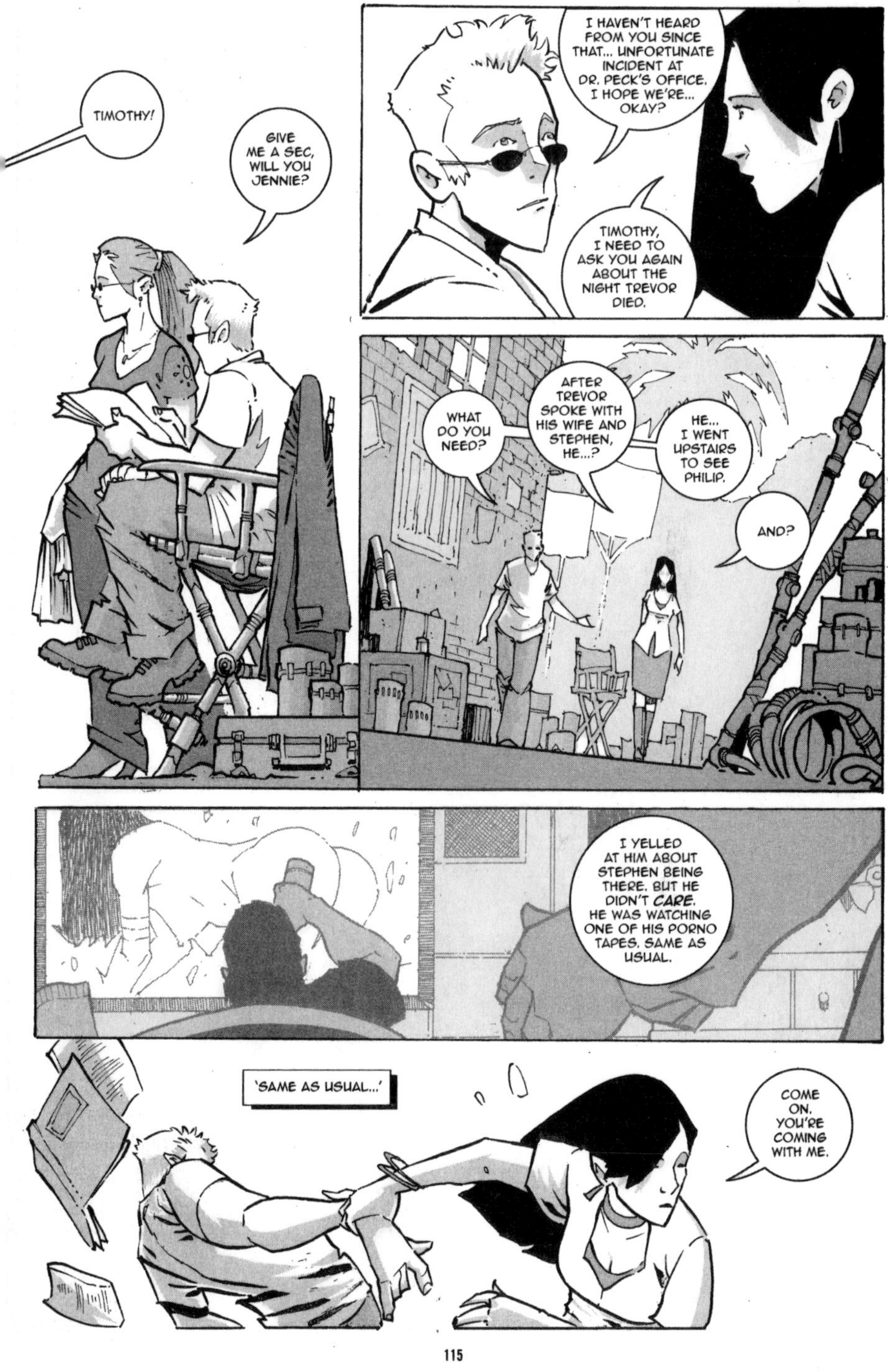

TIMOTHY!
GIVE ME A SEC, WILL YOU JENNIE?
I HAVEN'T HEARD FROM YOU SINCE THAT... UNFORTUNATE INCIDENT AT DR. PECK'S OFFICE. I HOPE WE'RE... OKAY?
TIMOTHY, I NEED TO ASK YOU AGAIN ABOUT THE NIGHT TREVOR DIED.
WHAT DO YOU NEED?
AFTER TREVOR SPOKE WITH HIS WIFE AND STEPHEN, HE...?
HE... I WENT UPSTAIRS TO SEE PHILIP.
AND?
I YELLED AT HIM ABOUT STEPHEN BEING THERE. BUT HE DIDN'T CARE. HE WAS WATCHING ONE OF HIS PORNO TAPES. SAME AS USUAL.
'SAME AS USUAL...'
COME ON. YOU'RE COMING WITH ME.

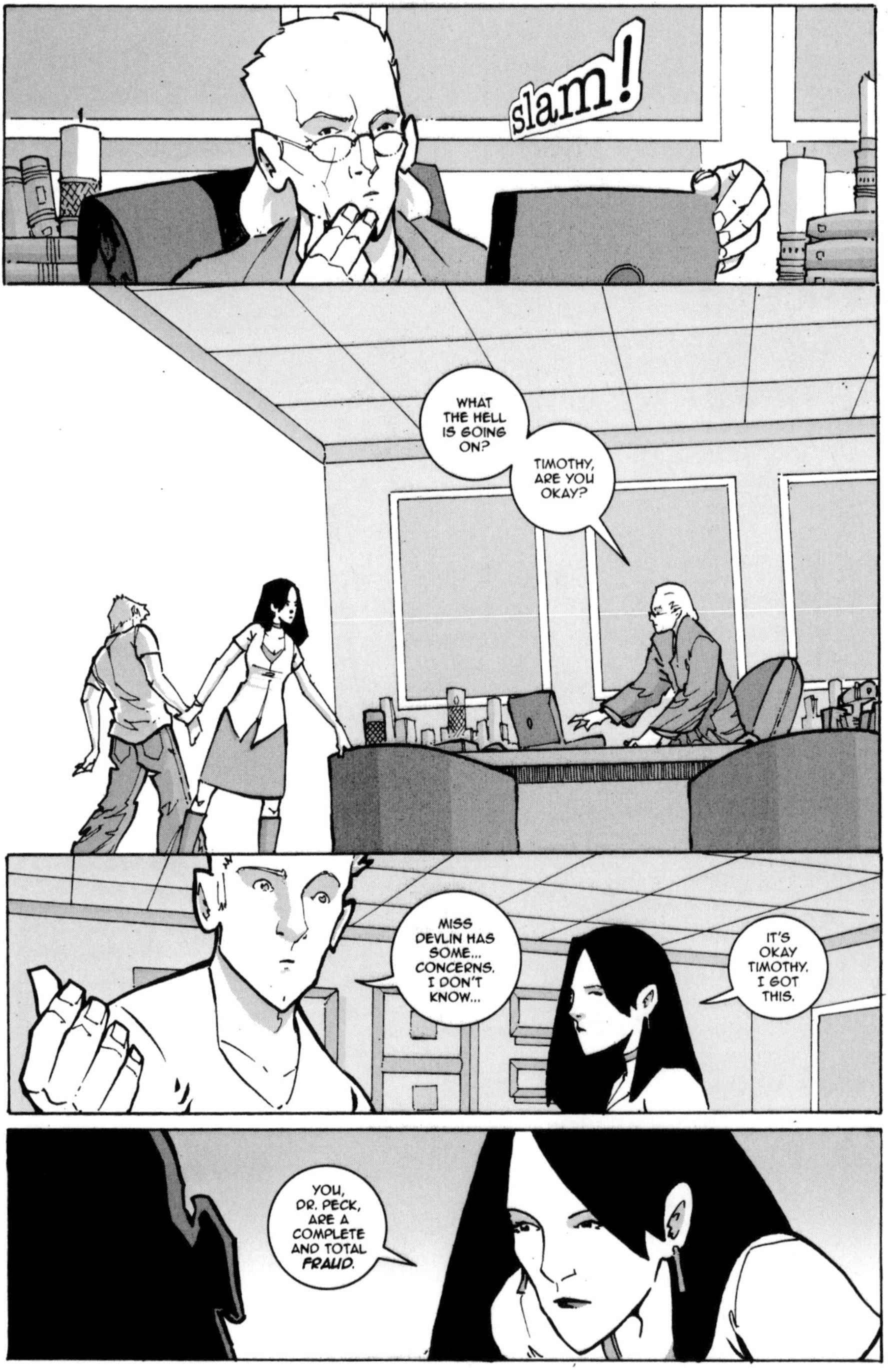
slam!
WHAT THE HELL IS GOING ON?
TIMOTHY, ARE YOU OKAY?
MISS DEVLIN HAS SOME... CONCERNS. I DON'T KNOW...
IT'S OKAY TIMOTHY. I GOT THIS.
YOU, DR. PECK, ARE A COMPLETE AND TOTAL *FRAUD*.

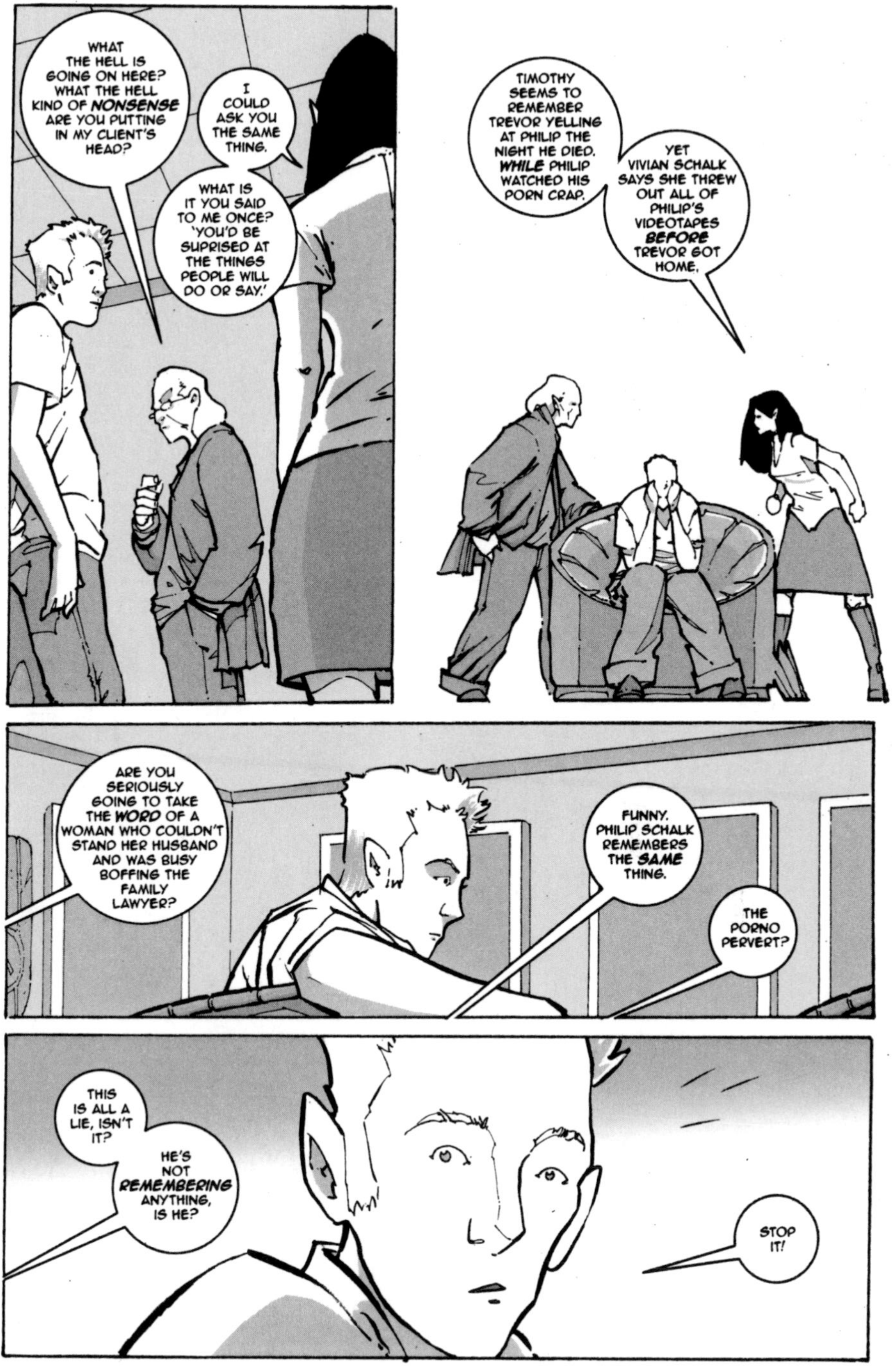

WHAT THE HELL IS GOING ON HERE? WHAT THE HELL KIND OF NONSENSE ARE YOU PUTTING IN MY CLIENT'S HEAD?
I COULD ASK YOU THE SAME THING.
WHAT IS IT YOU SAID TO ME ONCE? 'YOU'D BE SUPRISED AT THE THINGS PEOPLE WILL DO OR SAY.'
TIMOTHY SEEMS TO REMEMBER TREVOR YELLING AT PHILIP THE NIGHT HE DIED. WHILE PHILIP WATCHED HIS PORN CRAP.
YET VIVIAN SCHALK SAYS SHE THREW OUT ALL OF PHILIP'S VIDEOTAPES BEFORE TREVOR GOT HOME.
ARE YOU SERIOUSLY GOING TO TAKE THE WORD OF A WOMAN WHO COULDN'T STAND HER HUSBAND AND WAS BUSY BOFFING THE FAMILY LAWYER?
FUNNY. PHILIP SCHALK REMEMBERS THE SAME THING.
THE PORNO PERVERT?
THIS IS ALL A LIE, ISN'T IT?
HE'S NOT REMEMBERING ANYTHING, IS HE?
STOP IT!

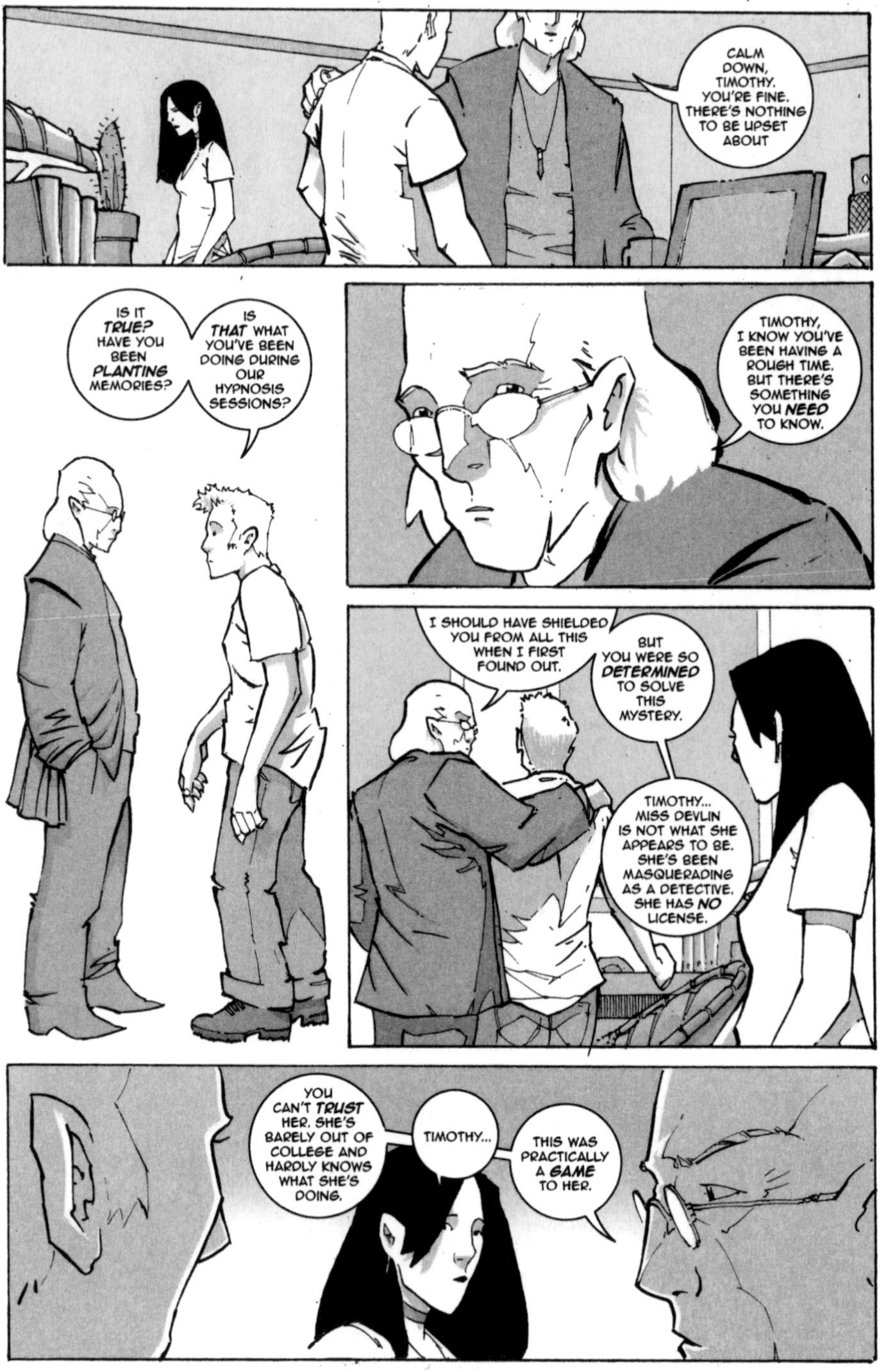
CALM DOWN, TIMOTHY. YOU'RE FINE. THERE'S NOTHING TO BE UPSET ABOUT
IS IT TRUE? HAVE YOU BEEN PLANTING MEMORIES?
IS THAT WHAT YOU'VE BEEN DOING DURING OUR HYPNOSIS SESSIONS?
TIMOTHY, I KNOW YOU'VE BEEN HAVING A ROUGH TIME. BUT THERE'S SOMETHING YOU NEED TO KNOW.
I SHOULD HAVE SHIELDED YOU FROM ALL THIS WHEN I FIRST FOUND OUT.
BUT YOU WERE SO DETERMINED TO SOLVE THIS MYSTERY.
TIMOTHY... MISS DEVLIN IS NOT WHAT SHE APPEARS TO BE. SHE'S BEEN MASQUERADING AS A DETECTIVE. SHE HAS NO LICENSE.
YOU CAN'T TRUST HER. SHE'S BARELY OUT OF COLLEGE AND HARDLY KNOWS WHAT SHE'S DOING.
TIMOTHY...
THIS WAS PRACTICALLY A GAME TO HER.

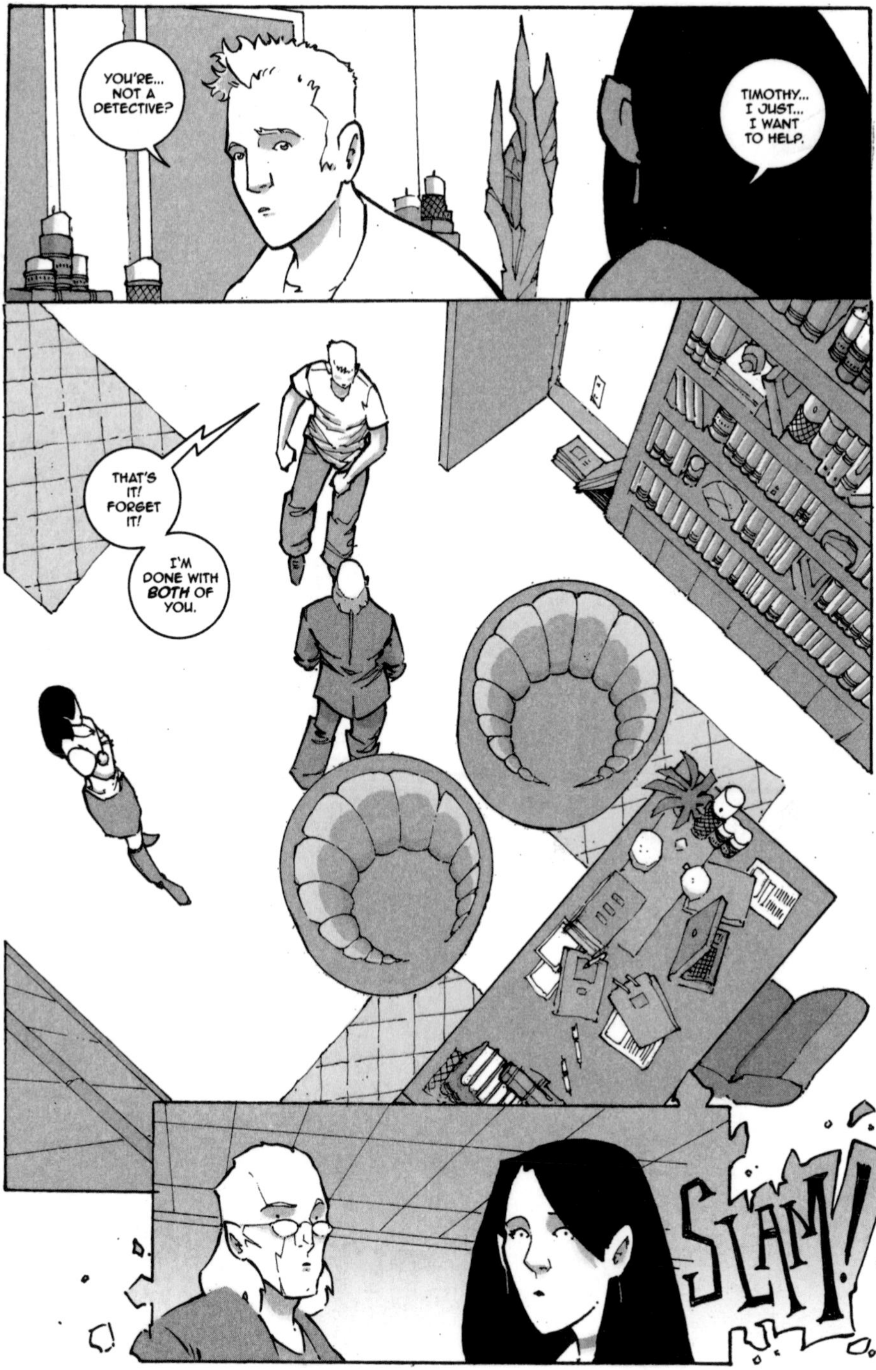
YOU'RE... NOT A DETECTIVE?
TIMOTHY... I JUST... I WANT TO HELP.
THAT'S IT! FORGET IT!
I'M DONE WITH *BOTH* OF YOU.
SLAM!

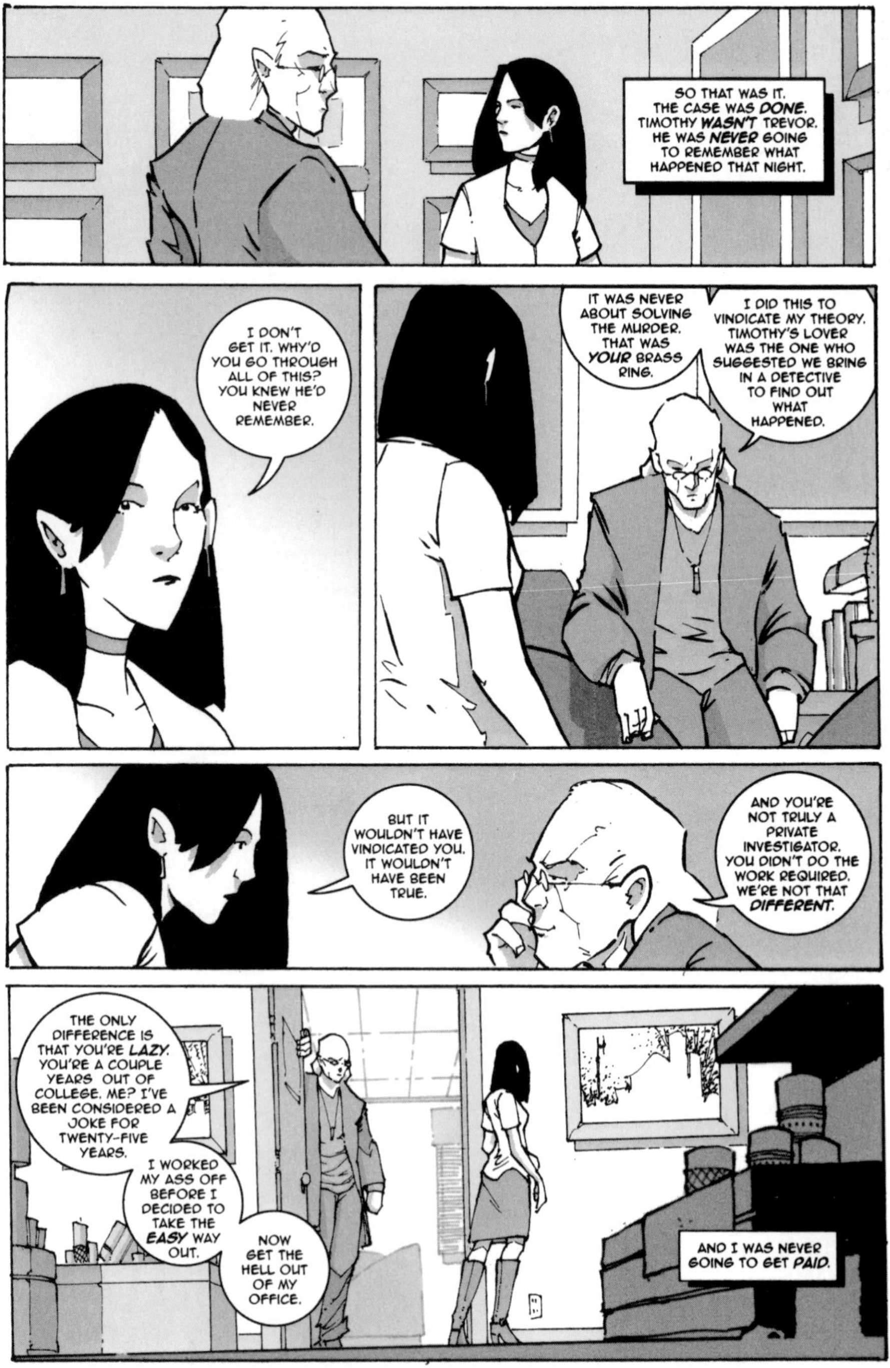
SO THAT WAS IT. THE CASE WAS DONE. TIMOTHY WASN'T TREVOR. HE WAS NEVER GOING TO REMEMBER WHAT HAPPENED THAT NIGHT.
I DON'T GET IT. WHY'D YOU GO THROUGH ALL OF THIS? YOU KNEW HE'D NEVER REMEMBER.
IT WAS NEVER ABOUT SOLVING THE MURDER. THAT WAS YOUR BRASS RING.
I DID THIS TO VINDICATE MY THEORY. TIMOTHY'S LOVER WAS THE ONE WHO SUGGESTED WE BRING IN A DETECTIVE TO FIND OUT WHAT HAPPENED.
BUT IT WOULDN'T HAVE VINDICATED YOU. IT WOULDN'T HAVE BEEN TRUE.
AND YOU'RE NOT TRULY A PRIVATE INVESTIGATOR. YOU DIDN'T DO THE WORK REQUIRED. WE'RE NOT THAT DIFFERENT.
THE ONLY DIFFERENCE IS THAT YOU'RE LAZY. YOU'RE A COUPLE YEARS OUT OF COLLEGE. ME? I'VE BEEN CONSIDERED A JOKE FOR TWENTY-FIVE YEARS.
I WORKED MY ASS OFF BEFORE I DECIDED TO TAKE THE EASY WAY OUT.
NOW GET THE HELL OUT OF MY OFFICE.
AND I WAS NEVER GOING TO GET PAID.

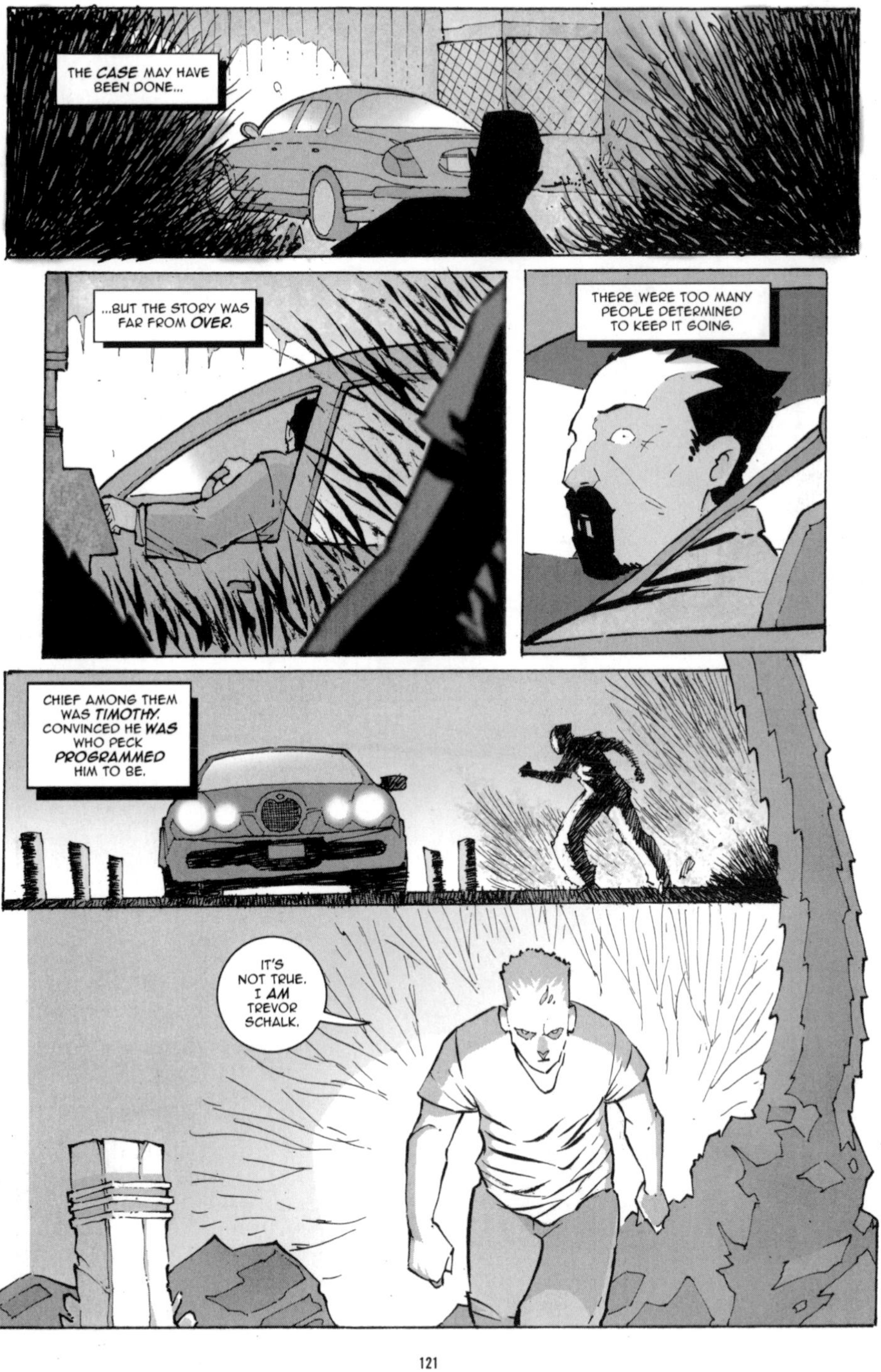
THE CASE MAY HAVE BEEN DONE...
...BUT THE STORY WAS FAR FROM OVER.
THERE WERE TOO MANY PEOPLE DETERMINED TO KEEP IT GOING.
CHIEF AMONG THEM WAS TIMOTHY. CONVINCED HE WAS WHO PECK PROGRAMMED HIM TO BE.
IT'S NOT TRUE. I AM TREVOR SCHALK.

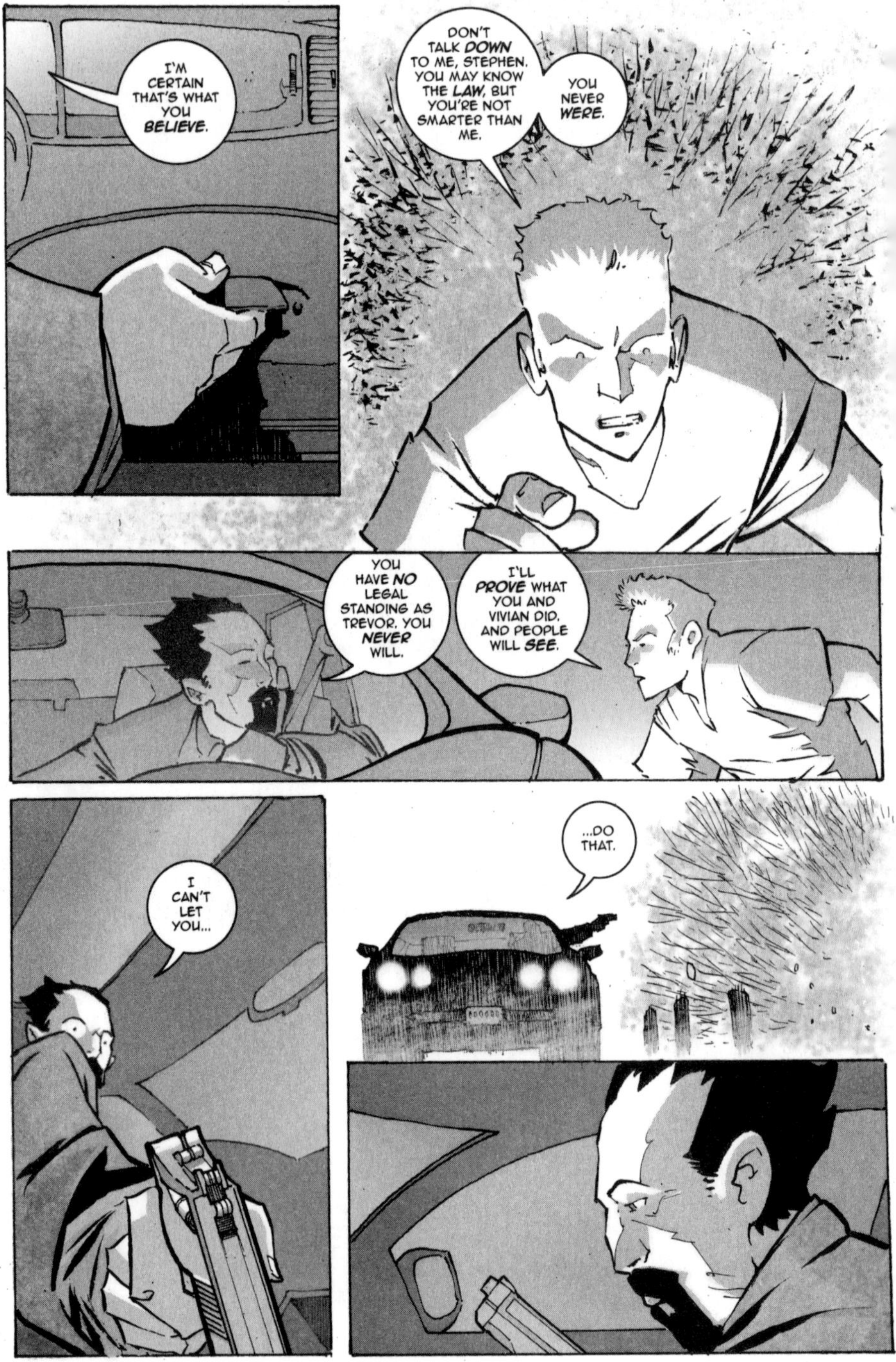
I'M CERTAIN THAT'S WHAT YOU BELIEVE.
DON'T TALK DOWN TO ME, STEPHEN. YOU MAY KNOW THE LAW, BUT YOU'RE NOT SMARTER THAN ME.
YOU NEVER WERE.
YOU HAVE NO LEGAL STANDING AS TREVOR. YOU NEVER WILL.
I'LL PROVE WHAT YOU AND VIVIAN DID, AND PEOPLE WILL SEE.
I CAN'T LET YOU...
...DO THAT.

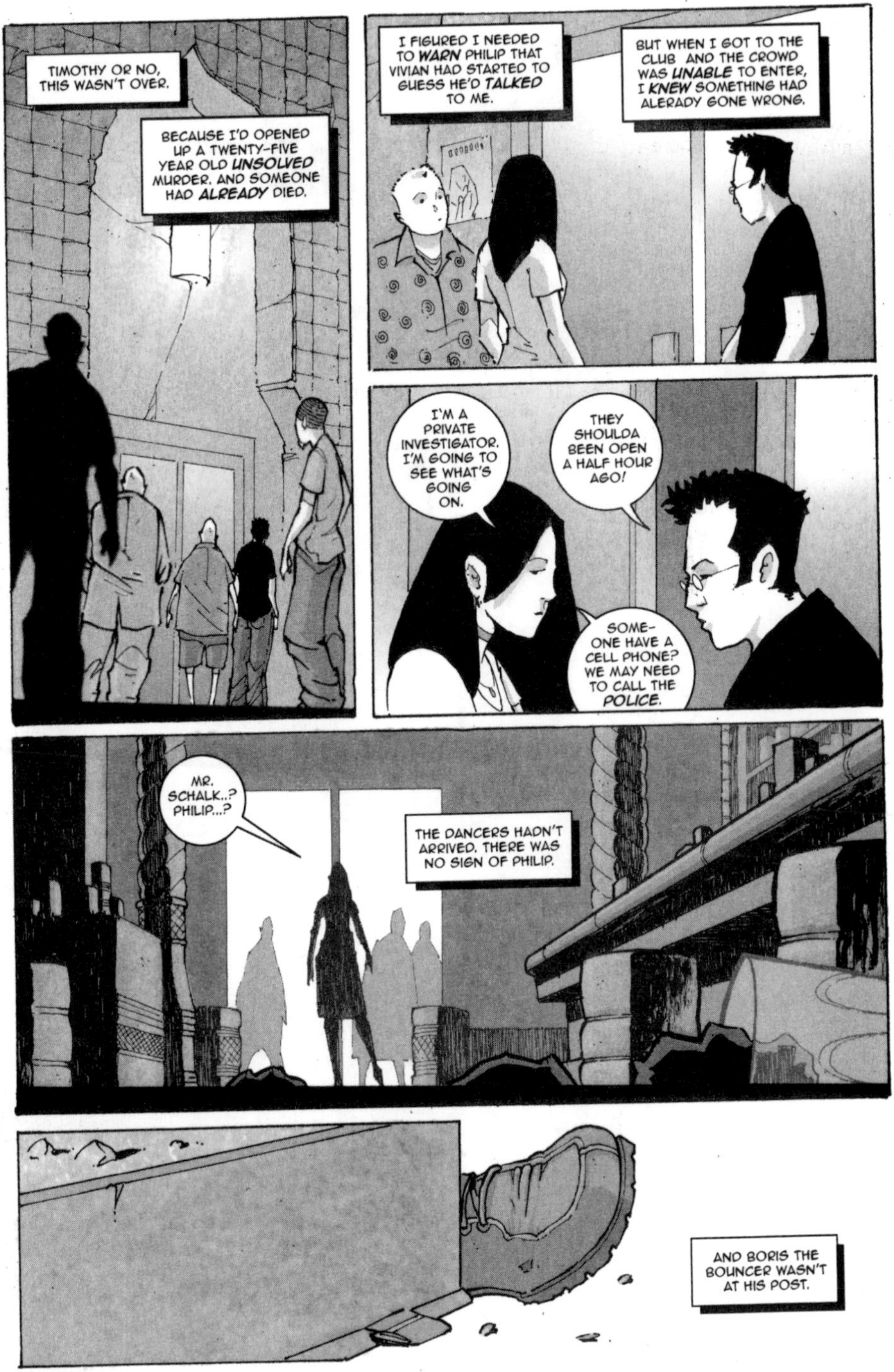
TIMOTHY OR NO, THIS WASN'T OVER.
BECAUSE I'D OPENED UP A TWENTY-FIVE YEAR OLD UNSOLVED MURDER, AND SOMEONE HAD ALREADY DIED.
I FIGURED I NEEDED TO WARN PHILIP THAT VIVIAN HAD STARTED TO GUESS HE'D TALKED TO ME.
BUT WHEN I GOT TO THE CLUB AND THE CROWD WAS UNABLE TO ENTER, I KNEW SOMETHING HAD ALERADY GONE WRONG.
I'M A PRIVATE INVESTIGATOR. I'M GOING TO SEE WHAT'S GOING ON.
THEY SHOULDA BEEN OPEN A HALF HOUR AGO!
SOME-ONE HAVE A CELL PHONE? WE MAY NEED TO CALL THE POLICE.
MR. SCHALK..? PHILIP...?
THE DANCERS HADN'T ARRIVED. THERE WAS NO SIGN OF PHILIP.
AND BORIS THE BOUNCER WASN'T AT HIS POST.

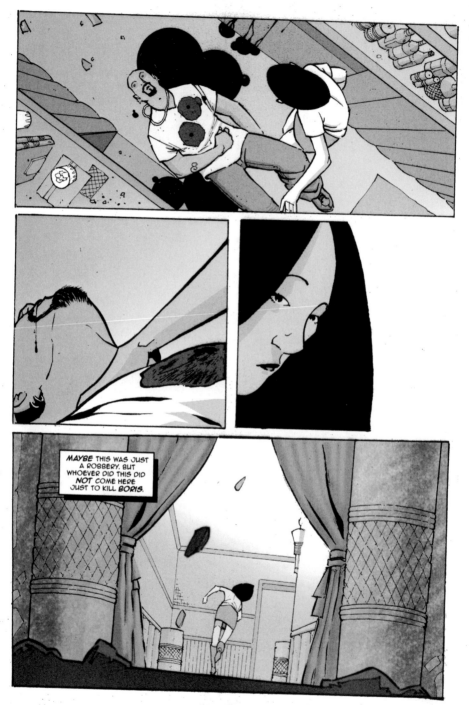

MAYBE THIS WAS JUST A ROBBERY, BUT WHOEVER DID THIS DID *NOT* COME HERE JUST TO KILL *BORIS*.

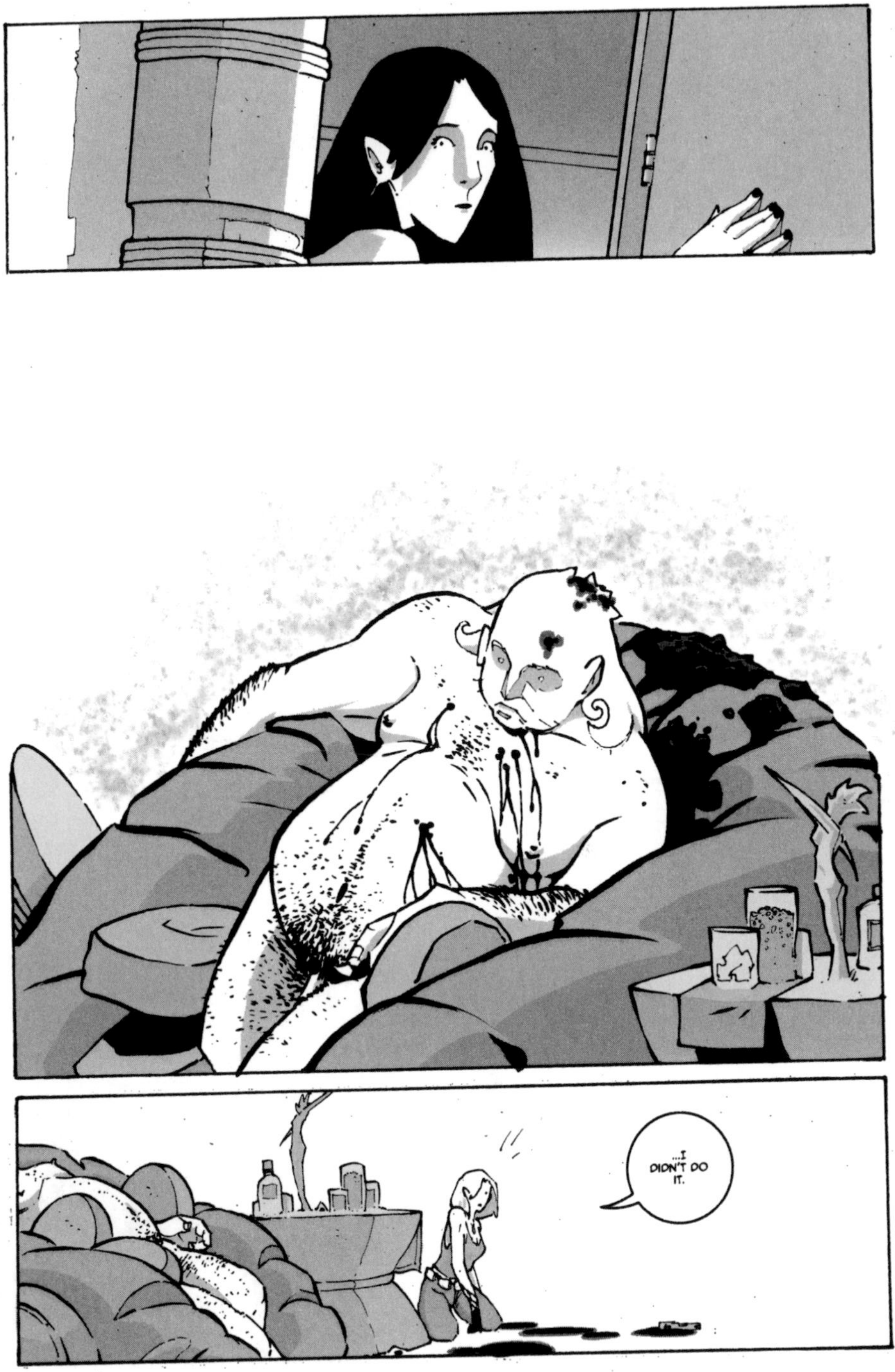
...I DIDN'T DO IT.

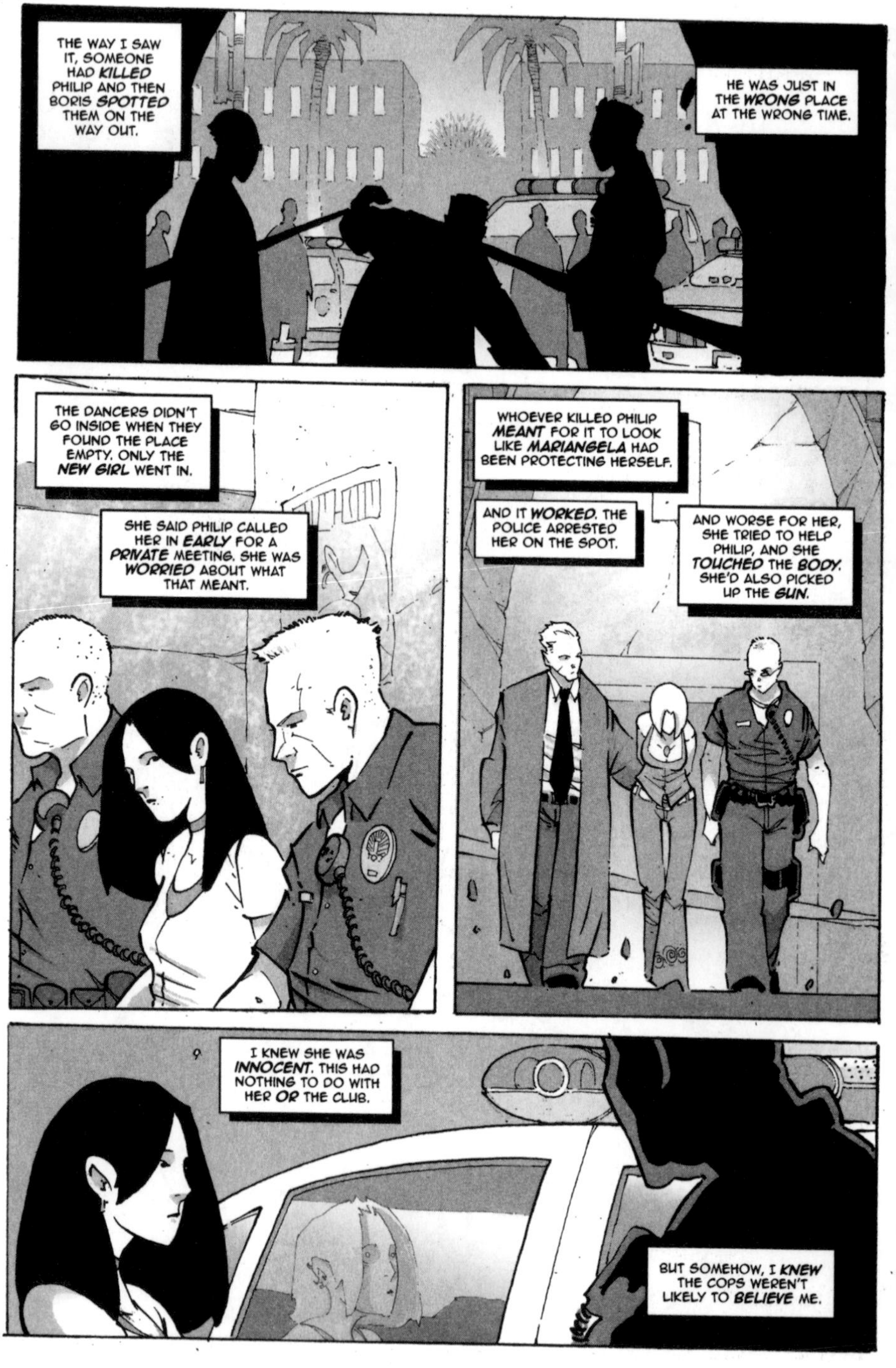
THE WAY I SAW IT, SOMEONE HAD KILLED PHILIP AND THEN BORIS SPOTTED THEM ON THE WAY OUT.
HE WAS JUST IN THE WRONG PLACE AT THE WRONG TIME.
THE DANCERS DIDN'T GO INSIDE WHEN THEY FOUND THE PLACE EMPTY. ONLY THE NEW GIRL WENT IN.
SHE SAID PHILIP CALLED HER IN EARLY FOR A PRIVATE MEETING. SHE WAS WORRIED ABOUT WHAT THAT MEANT.
WHOEVER KILLED PHILIP MEANT FOR IT TO LOOK LIKE MARIANGELA HAD BEEN PROTECTING HERSELF.
AND IT WORKED. THE POLICE ARRESTED HER ON THE SPOT.
AND WORSE FOR HER, SHE TRIED TO HELP PHILIP, AND SHE TOUCHED THE BODY. SHE'D ALSO PICKED UP THE GUN.
I KNEW SHE WAS INNOCENT. THIS HAD NOTHING TO DO WITH HER OR THE CLUB.
BUT SOMEHOW, I KNEW THE COPS WEREN'T LIKELY TO BELIEVE ME.

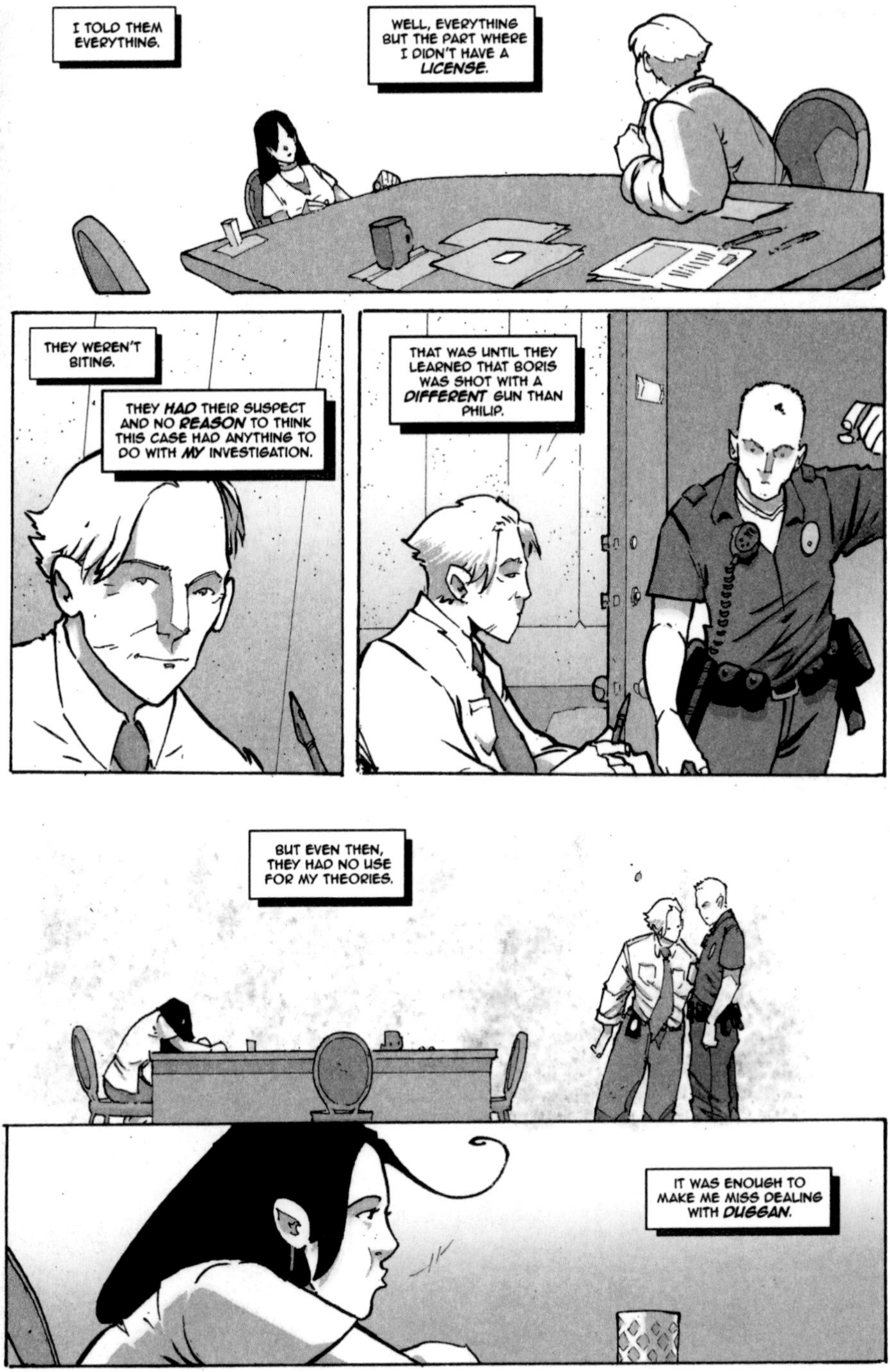
I TOLD THEM EVERYTHING.
WELL, EVERYTHING BUT THE PART WHERE I DIDN'T HAVE A LICENSE.
THEY WEREN'T BITING.
THEY HAD THEIR SUSPECT AND NO REASON TO THINK THIS CASE HAD ANYTHING TO DO WITH MY INVESTIGATION.
THAT WAS UNTIL THEY LEARNED THAT BORIS WAS SHOT WITH A DIFFERENT GUN THAN PHILIP.
BUT EVEN THEN, THEY HAD NO USE FOR MY THEORIES.
IT WAS ENOUGH TO MAKE ME MISS DEALING WITH DUGGAN.

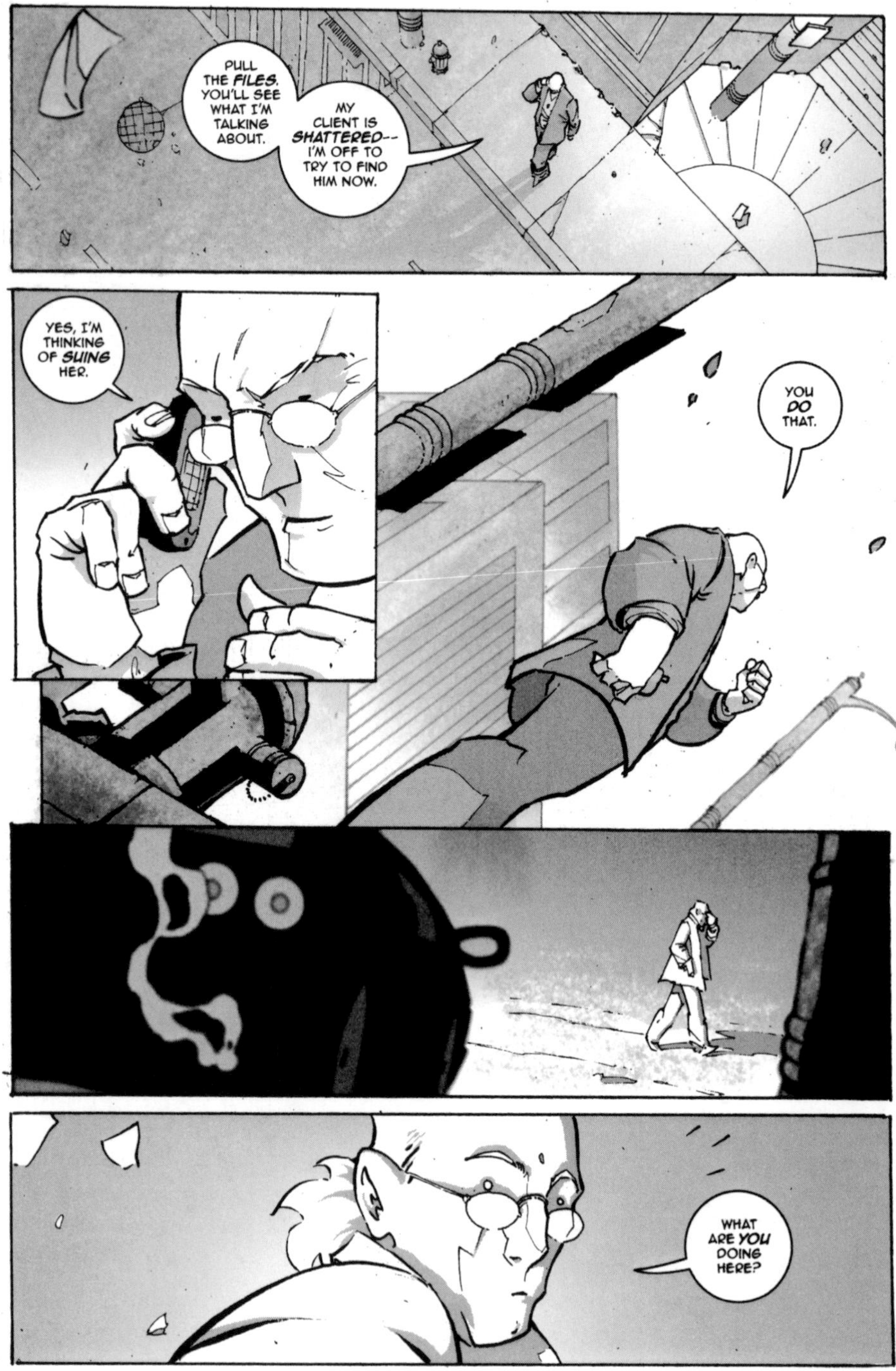
PULL THE FILES. YOU'LL SEE WHAT I'M TALKING ABOUT.
MY CLIENT IS SHATTERED-- I'M OFF TO TRY TO FIND HIM NOW.
YES, I'M THINKING OF SUING HER.
YOU DO THAT.
WHAT ARE YOU DOING HERE?

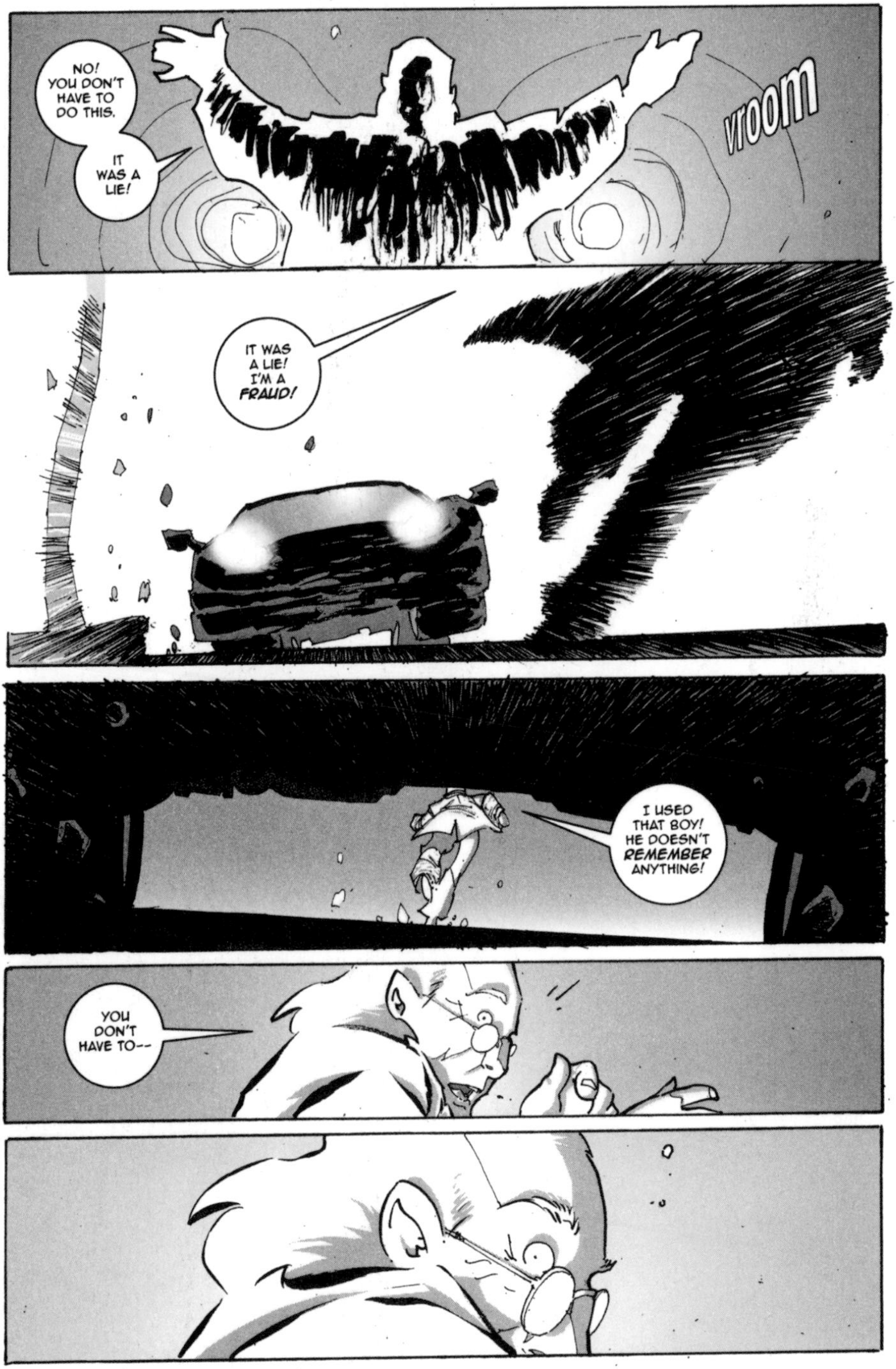
NO! YOU DON'T HAVE TO DO THIS.
IT WAS A LIE!
vroom
IT WAS A LIE! I'M A FRAUD!
I USED THAT BOY! HE DOESN'T REMEMBER ANYTHING!
YOU DON'T HAVE TO--

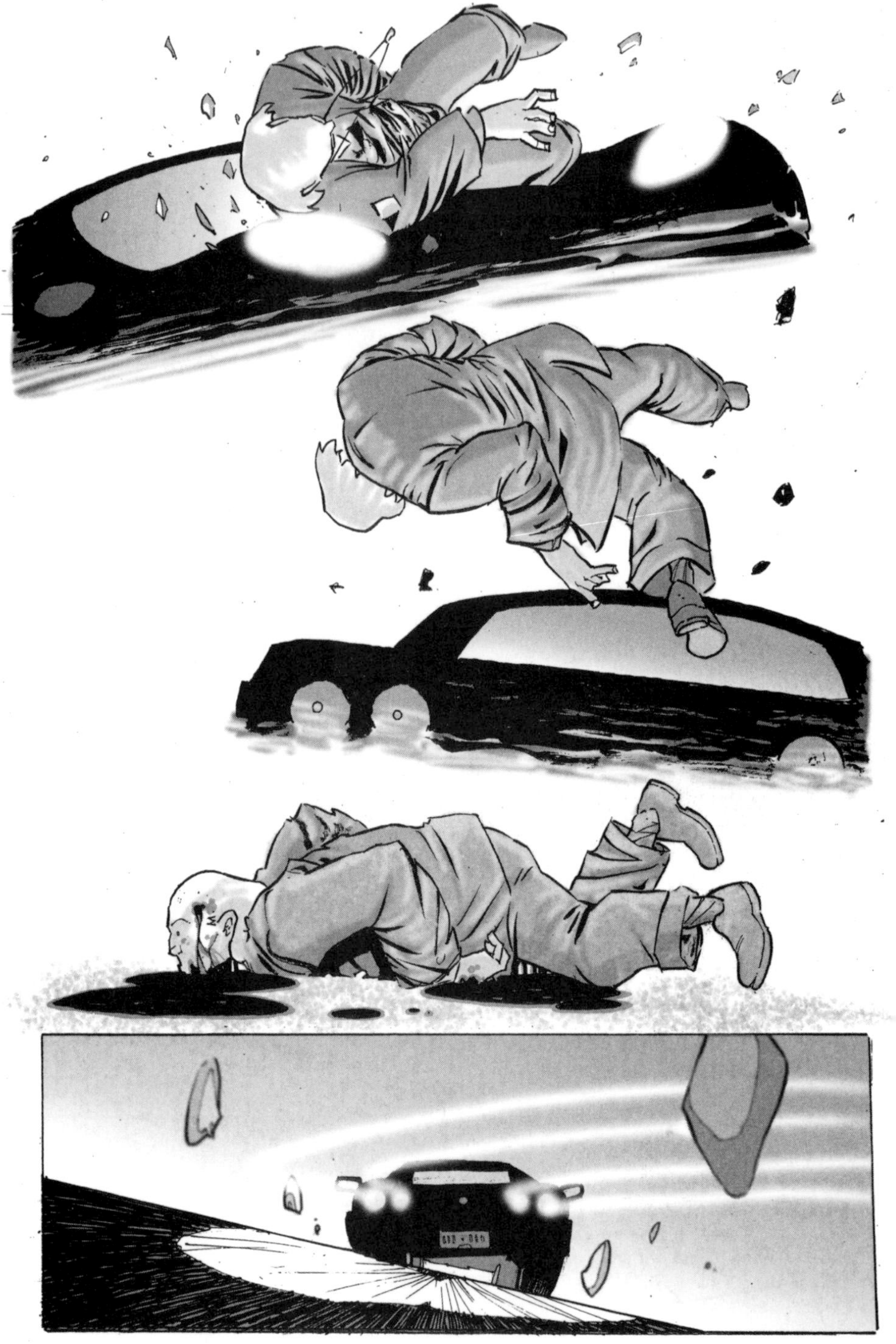

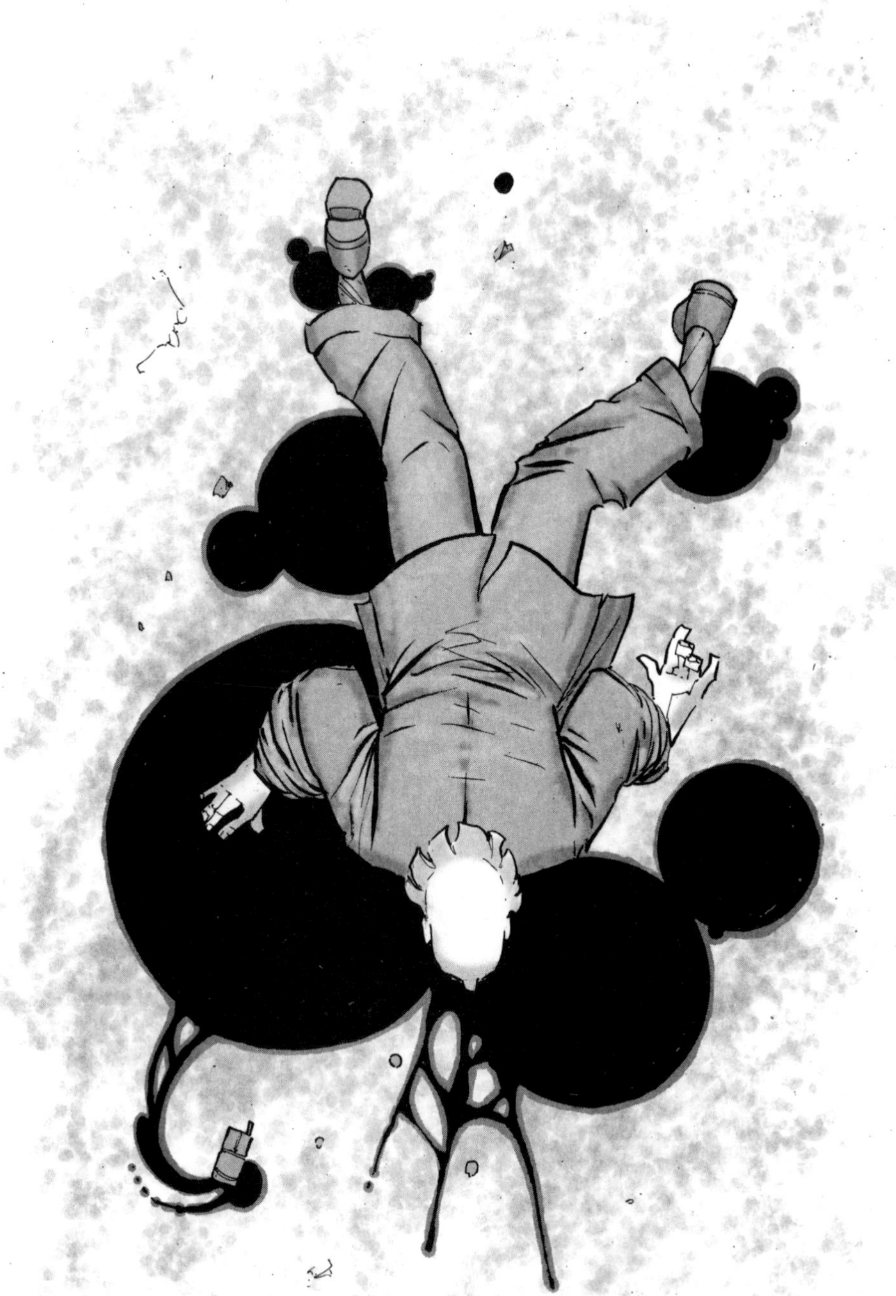

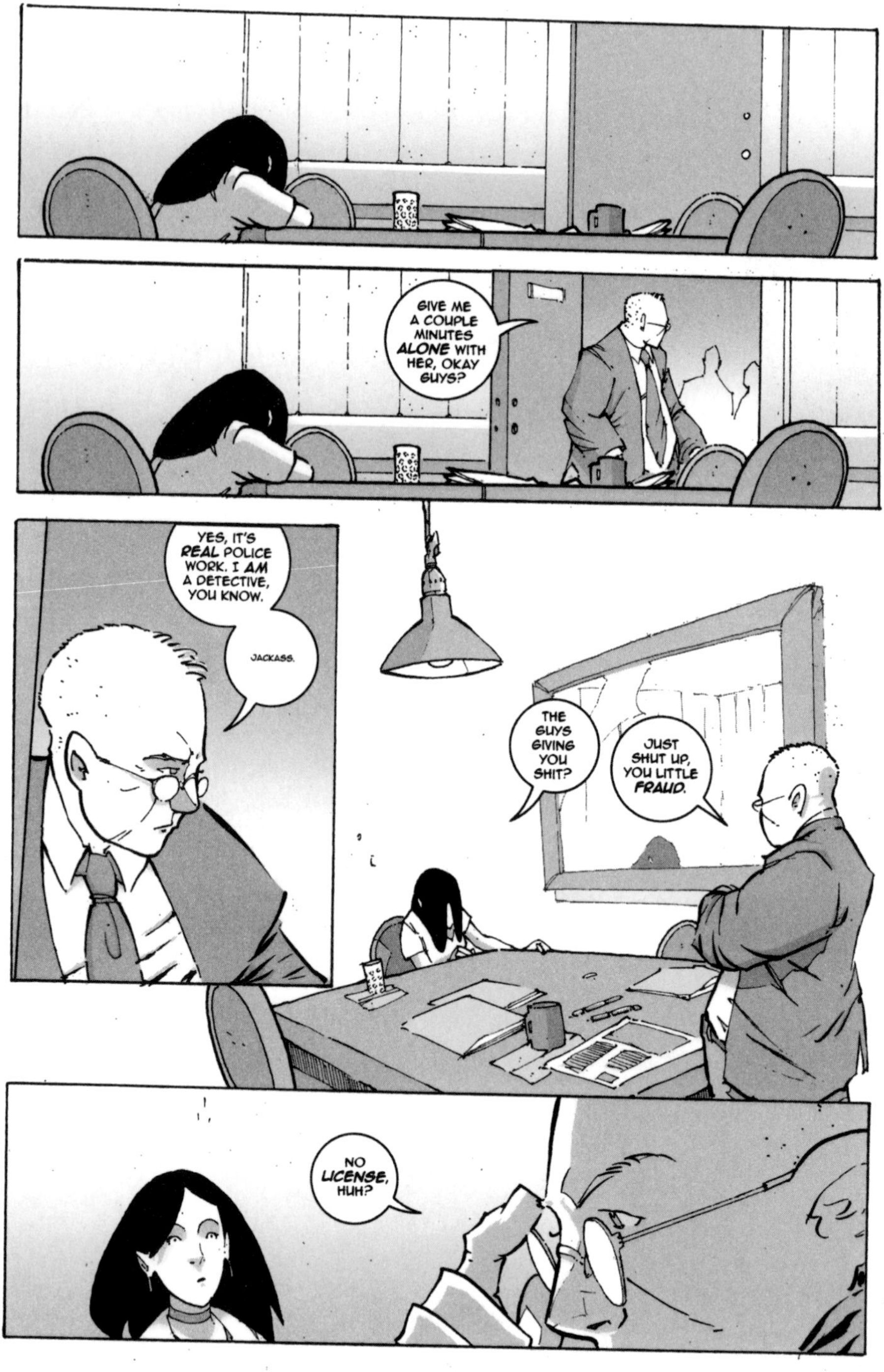
GIVE ME A COUPLE MINUTES ALONE WITH HER, OKAY GUYS?
YES, IT'S REAL POLICE WORK. I AM A DETECTIVE, YOU KNOW.
JACKASS.
THE GUYS GIVING YOU SHIT?
JUST SHUT UP, YOU LITTLE FRAUD.
NO LICENSE, HUH?

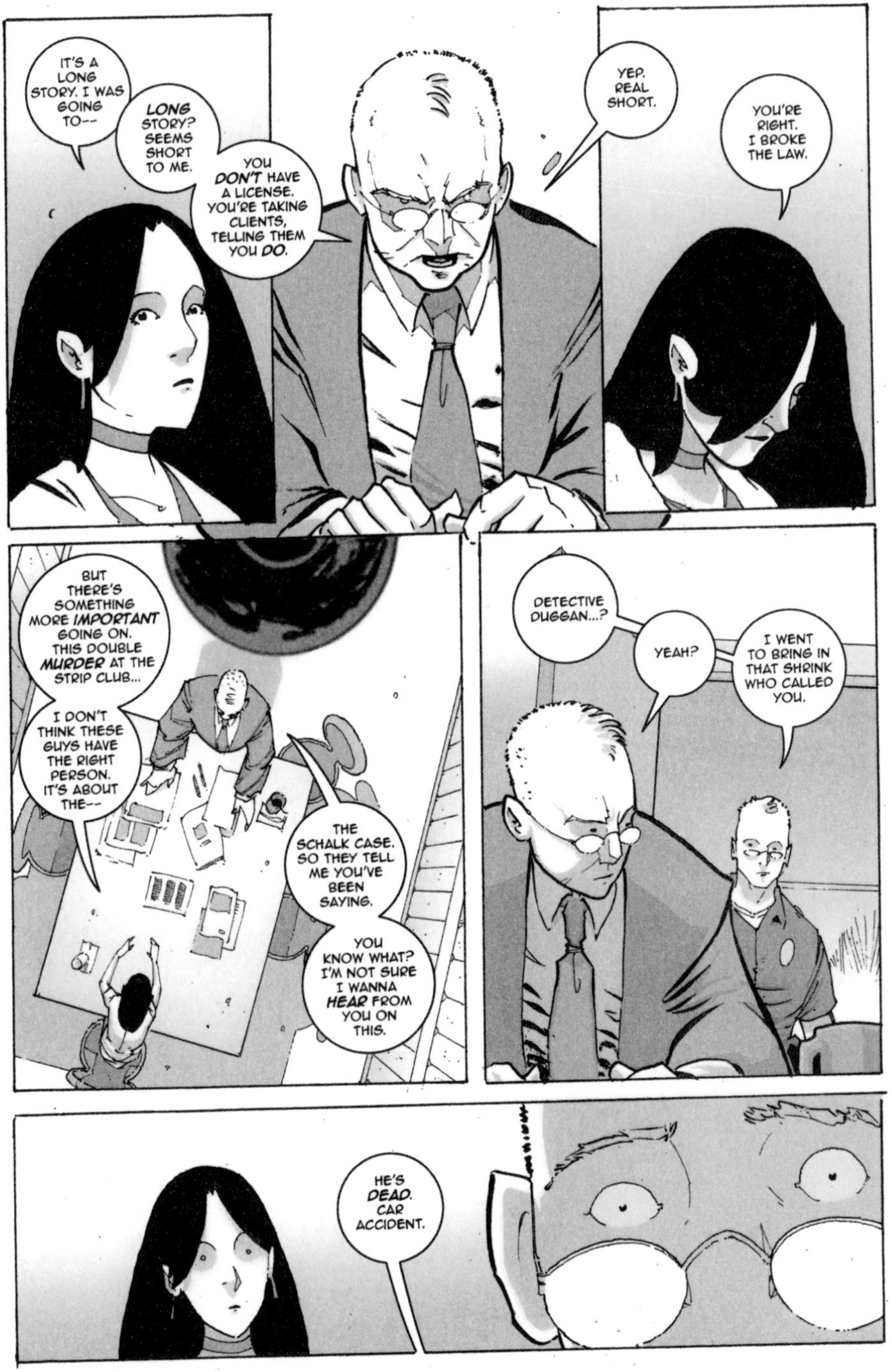
IT'S A LONG STORY. I WAS GOING TO--
LONG STORY? SEEMS SHORT TO ME.
YOU DON'T HAVE A LICENSE. YOU'RE TAKING CLIENTS, TELLING THEM YOU DO.
YEP. REAL SHORT.
YOU'RE RIGHT. I BROKE THE LAW.
BUT THERE'S SOMETHING MORE IMPORTANT GOING ON. THIS DOUBLE MURDER AT THE STRIP CLUB...
I DON'T THINK THESE GUYS HAVE THE RIGHT PERSON. IT'S ABOUT THE--
THE SCHALK CASE. SO THEY TELL ME YOU'VE BEEN SAYING.
YOU KNOW WHAT? I'M NOT SURE I WANNA HEAR FROM YOU ON THIS.
DETECTIVE DUGGAN...?
YEAH?
I WENT TO BRING IN THAT SHRINK WHO CALLED YOU.
HE'S DEAD. CAR ACCIDENT.

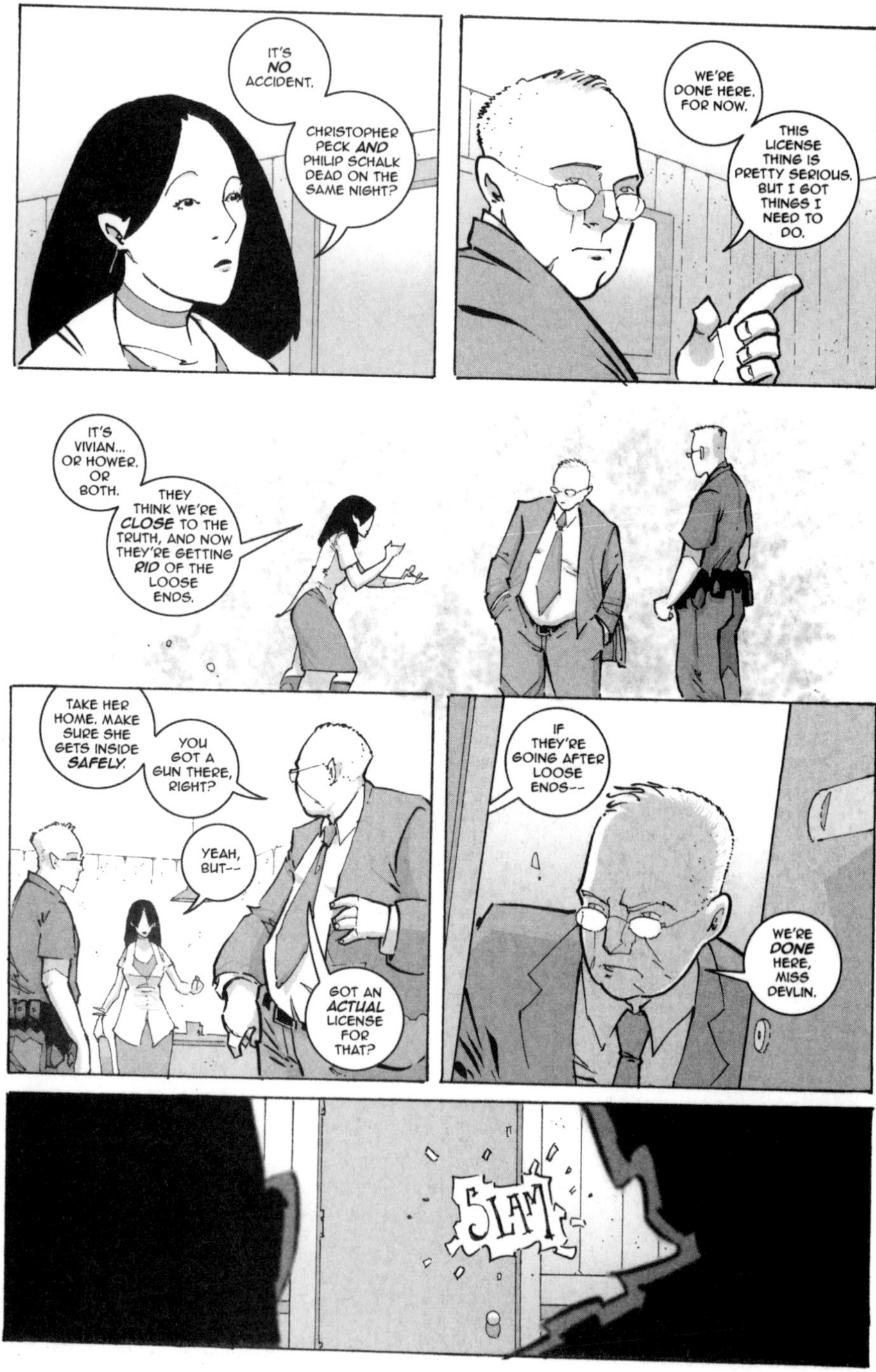
IT'S NO ACCIDENT.
CHRISTOPHER PECK AND PHILIP SCHALK DEAD ON THE SAME NIGHT?
WE'RE DONE HERE. FOR NOW.
THIS LICENSE THING IS PRETTY SERIOUS. BUT I GOT THINGS I NEED TO DO.
IT'S VIVIAN... OR HOWER. OR BOTH.
THEY THINK WE'RE CLOSE TO THE TRUTH, AND NOW THEY'RE GETTING RID OF THE LOOSE ENDS.
TAKE HER HOME. MAKE SURE SHE GETS INSIDE SAFELY.
YOU GOT A GUN THERE, RIGHT?
YEAH, BUT--
GOT AN ACTUAL LICENSE FOR THAT?
IF THEY'RE GOING AFTER LOOSE ENDS--
WE'RE DONE HERE, MISS DEVLIN.
SLAM

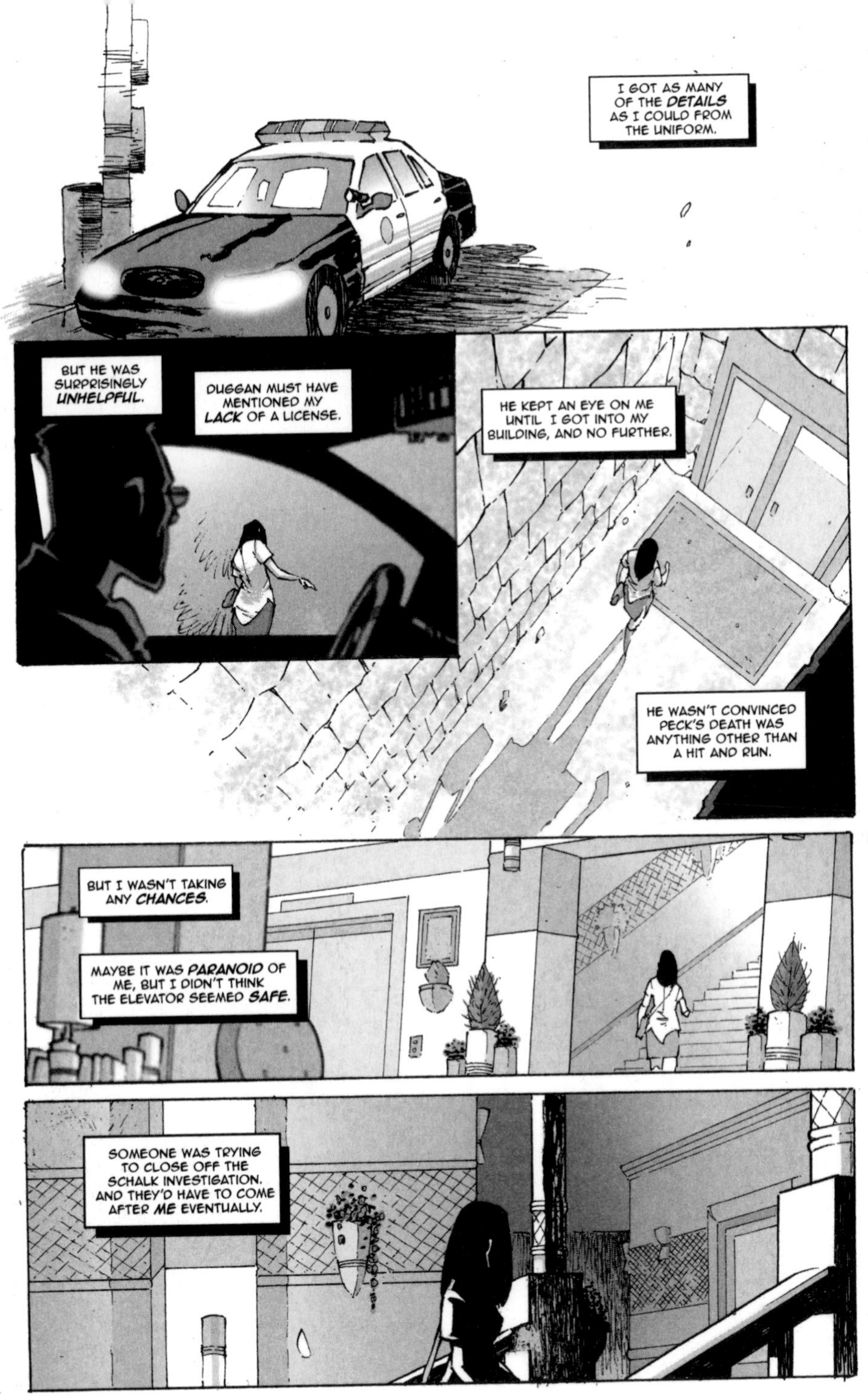
I GOT AS MANY OF THE DETAILS AS I COULD FROM THE UNIFORM.
BUT HE WAS SURPRISINGLY UNHELPFUL.
DUGGAN MUST HAVE MENTIONED MY LACK OF A LICENSE.
HE KEPT AN EYE ON ME UNTIL I GOT INTO MY BUILDING, AND NO FURTHER.
HE WASN'T CONVINCED PECK'S DEATH WAS ANYTHING OTHER THAN A HIT AND RUN.
BUT I WASN'T TAKING ANY CHANCES.
MAYBE IT WAS PARANOID OF ME, BUT I DIDN'T THINK THE ELEVATOR SEEMED SAFE.
SOMEONE WAS TRYING TO CLOSE OFF THE SCHALK INVESTIGATION. AND THEY'D HAVE TO COME AFTER ME EVENTUALLY.

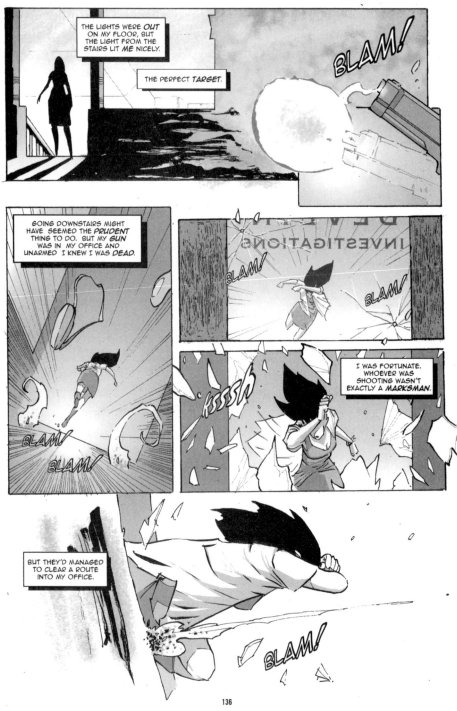

THE LIGHTS WERE *OUT* ON MY FLOOR, BUT THE LIGHT FROM THE STAIRS LIT *ME* NICELY.

THE PERFECT *TARGET*.

BLAM!

GOING DOWNSTAIRS MIGHT HAVE SEEMED THE *PRUDENT* THING TO DO. BUT MY *GUN* WAS IN MY OFFICE AND UNARMED I KNEW I WAS *DEAD*.

BLAM!

BLAM!

BLAM!

BLAM!

I WAS FORTUNATE. WHOEVER WAS SHOOTING WASN'T EXACTLY A *MARKSMAN*.

FSSSSH

BUT THEY'D MANAGED TO CLEAR A ROUTE INTO MY OFFICE.

BLAM!

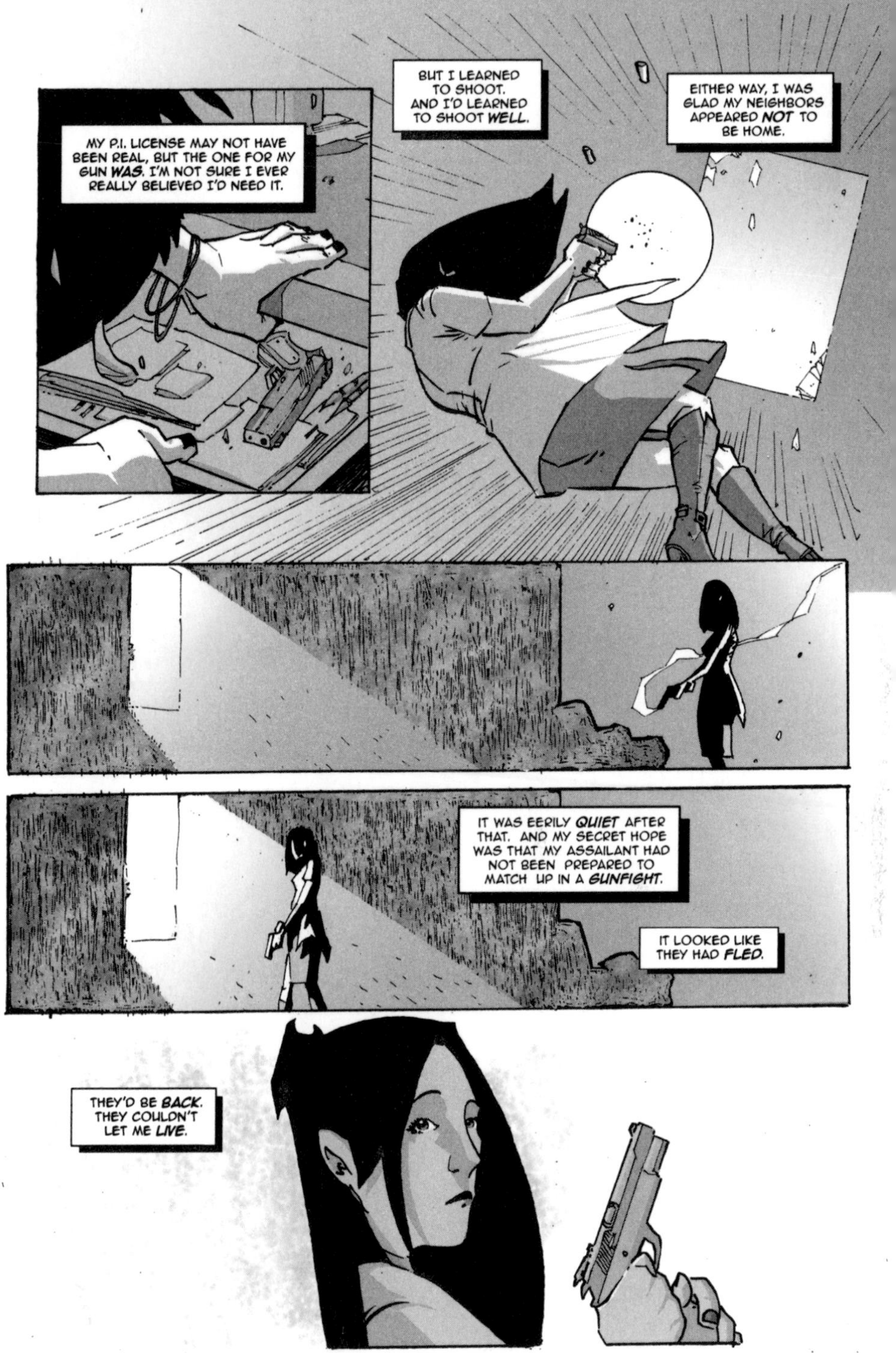
MY P.I. LICENSE MAY NOT HAVE BEEN REAL, BUT THE ONE FOR MY GUN WAS. I'M NOT SURE I EVER REALLY BELIEVED I'D NEED IT.
BUT I LEARNED TO SHOOT. AND I'D LEARNED TO SHOOT WELL.
EITHER WAY, I WAS GLAD MY NEIGHBORS APPEARED NOT TO BE HOME.
IT WAS EERILY QUIET AFTER THAT. AND MY SECRET HOPE WAS THAT MY ASSAILANT HAD NOT BEEN PREPARED TO MATCH UP IN A GUNFIGHT.
IT LOOKED LIKE THEY HAD FLED.
THEY'D BE BACK. THEY COULDN'T LET ME LIVE.

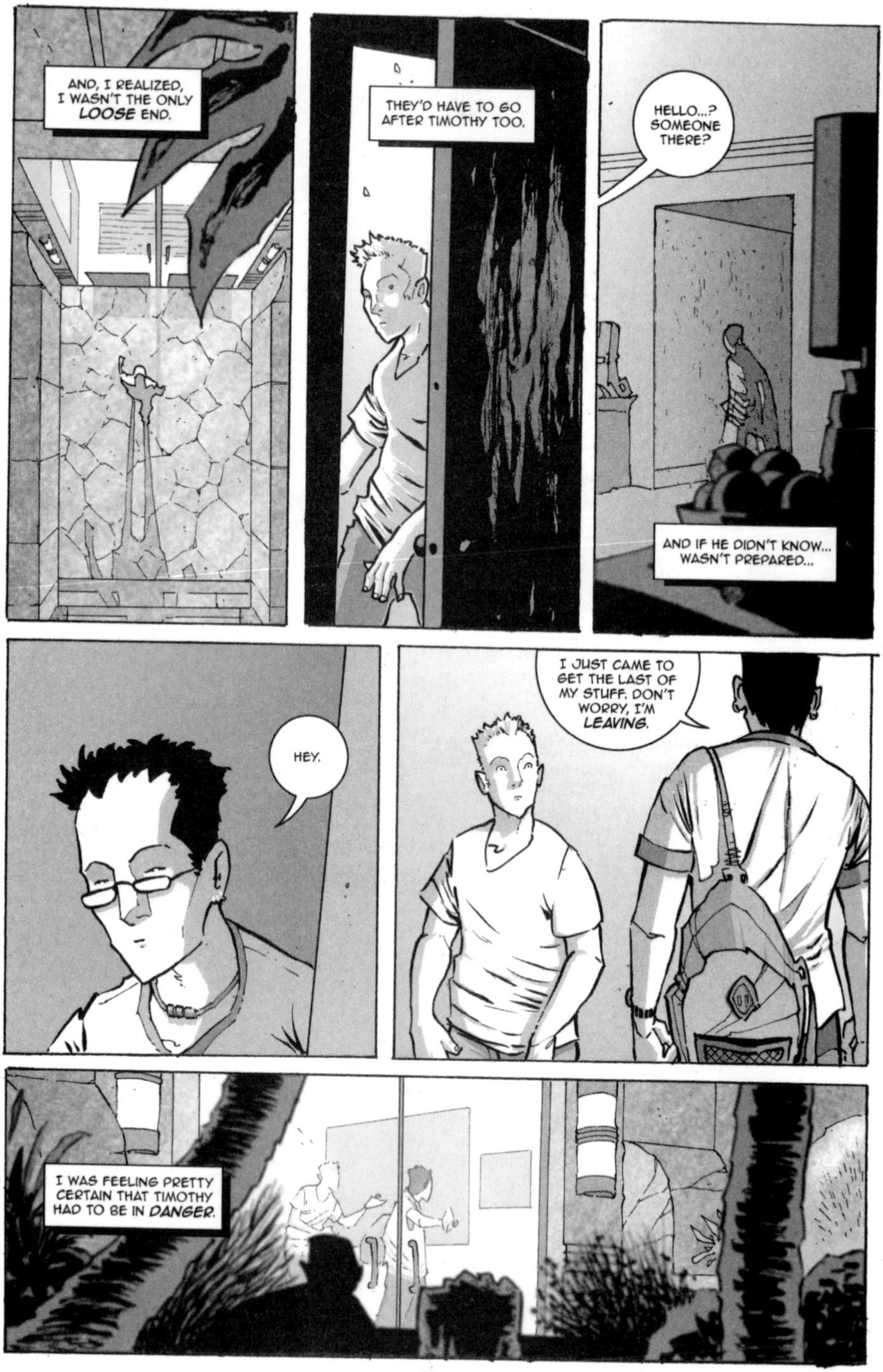
AND, I REALIZED, I WASN'T THE ONLY LOOSE END.
THEY'D HAVE TO GO AFTER TIMOTHY TOO.
HELLO...? SOMEONE THERE?
AND IF HE DIDN'T KNOW... WASN'T PREPARED...
HEY.
I JUST CAME TO GET THE LAST OF MY STUFF. DON'T WORRY, I'M LEAVING.
I WAS FEELING PRETTY CERTAIN THAT TIMOTHY HAD TO BE IN DANGER.

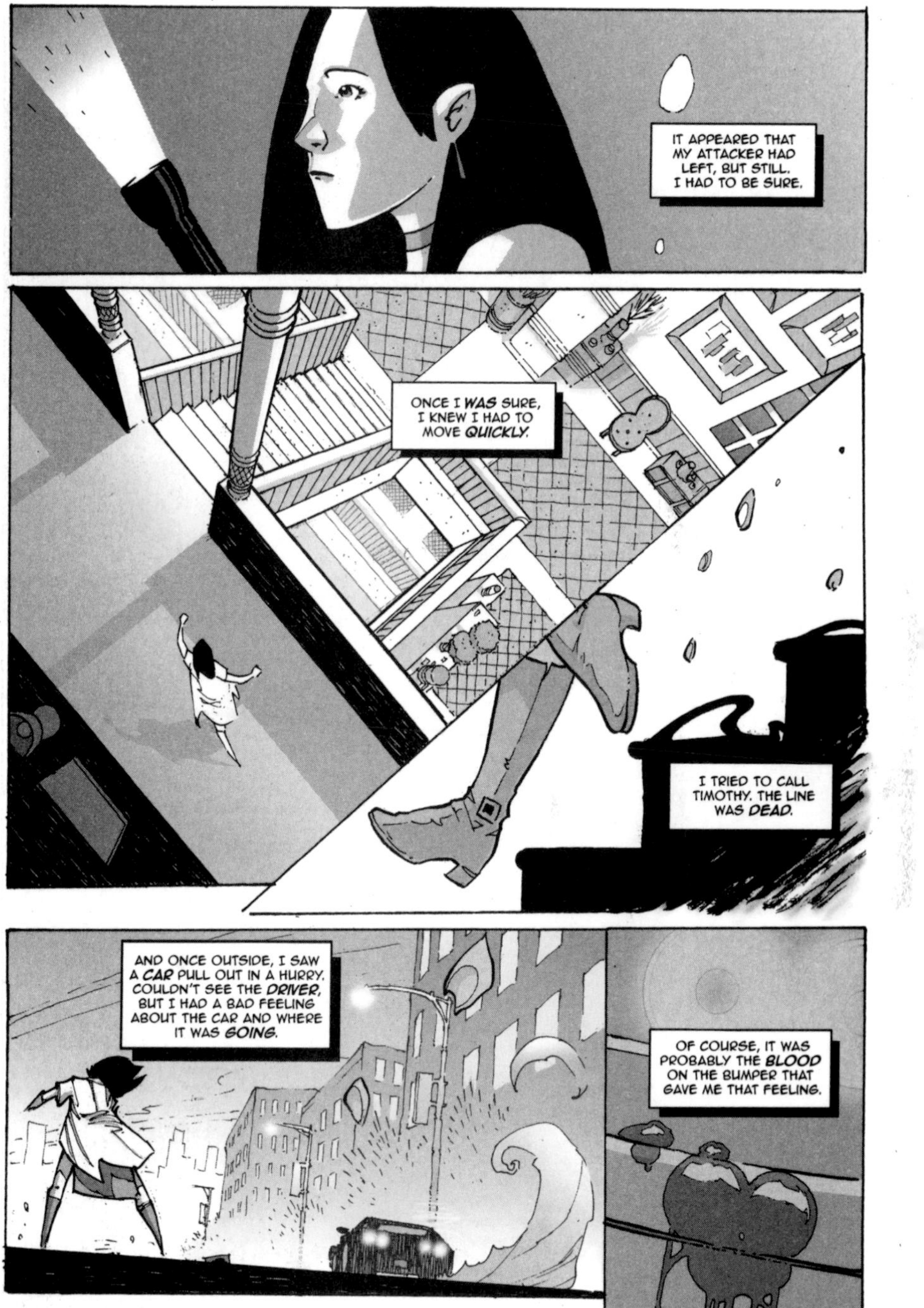
IT APPEARED THAT MY ATTACKER HAD LEFT, BUT STILL. I HAD TO BE SURE.
ONCE I WAS SURE, I KNEW I HAD TO MOVE QUICKLY.
I TRIED TO CALL TIMOTHY. THE LINE WAS DEAD.
AND ONCE OUTSIDE, I SAW A CAR PULL OUT IN A HURRY. COULDN'T SEE THE DRIVER, BUT I HAD A BAD FEELING ABOUT THE CAR AND WHERE IT WAS GOING.
OF COURSE, IT WAS PROBABLY THE BLOOD ON THE BUMPER THAT GAVE ME THAT FEELING.

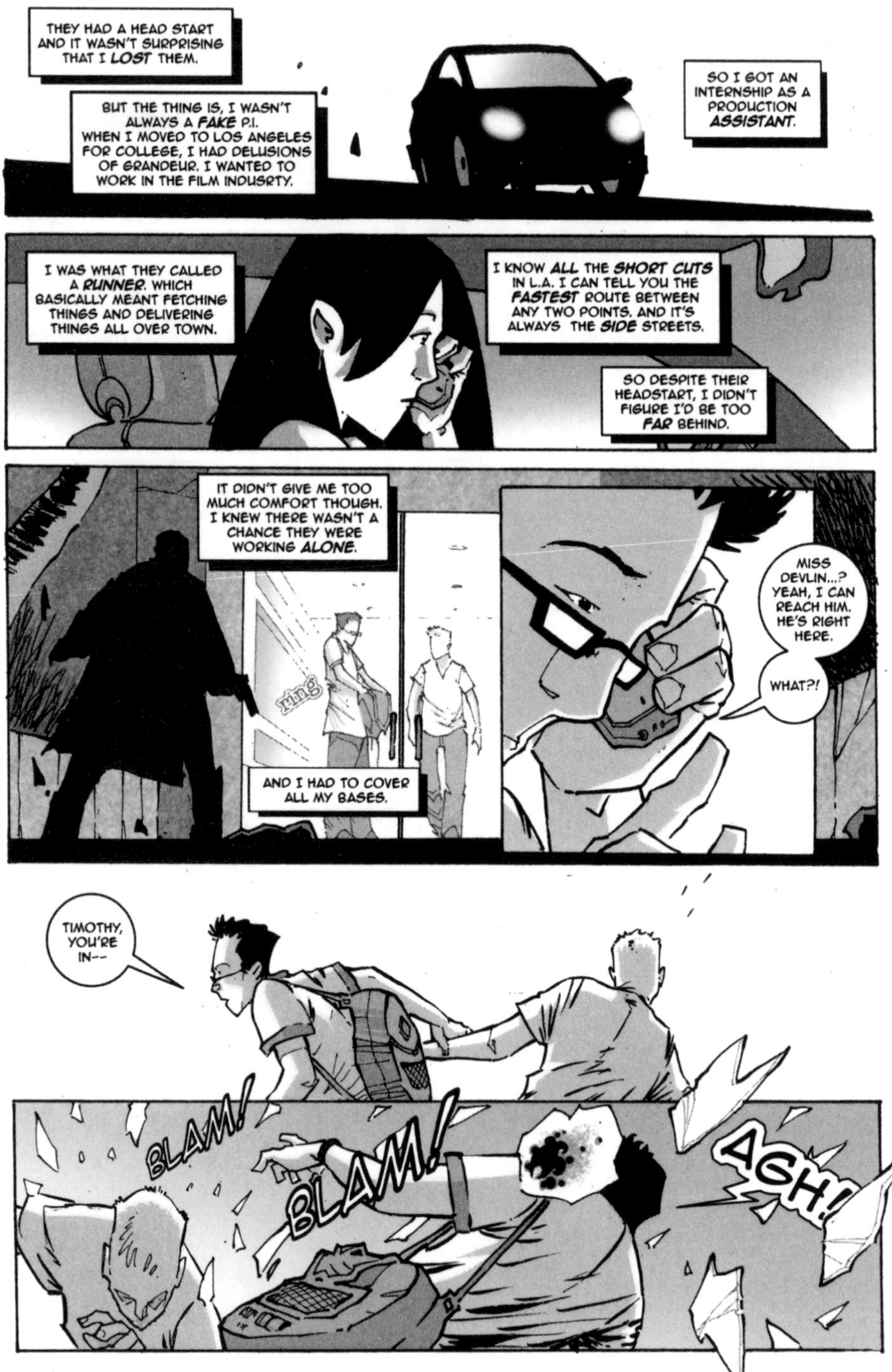
THEY HAD A HEAD START AND IT WASN'T SURPRISING THAT I LOST THEM.
BUT THE THING IS, I WASN'T ALWAYS A FAKE P.I. WHEN I MOVED TO LOS ANGELES FOR COLLEGE, I HAD DELUSIONS OF GRANDEUR. I WANTED TO WORK IN THE FILM INDUSRTY.
SO I GOT AN INTERNSHIP AS A PRODUCTION ASSISTANT.
I WAS WHAT THEY CALLED A RUNNER. WHICH BASICALLY MEANT FETCHING THINGS AND DELIVERING THINGS ALL OVER TOWN.
I KNOW ALL THE SHORT CUTS IN L.A. I CAN TELL YOU THE FASTEST ROUTE BETWEEN ANY TWO POINTS. AND IT'S ALWAYS THE SIDE STREETS.
SO DESPITE THEIR HEADSTART, I DIDN'T FIGURE I'D BE TOO FAR BEHIND.
IT DIDN'T GIVE ME TOO MUCH COMFORT THOUGH. I KNEW THERE WASN'T A CHANCE THEY WERE WORKING ALONE.
ring
AND I HAD TO COVER ALL MY BASES.
MISS DEVLIN...? YEAH, I CAN REACH HIM. HE'S RIGHT HERE.
WHAT?!
TIMOTHY, YOU'RE IN--
BLAM!
BLAM!
AGH!

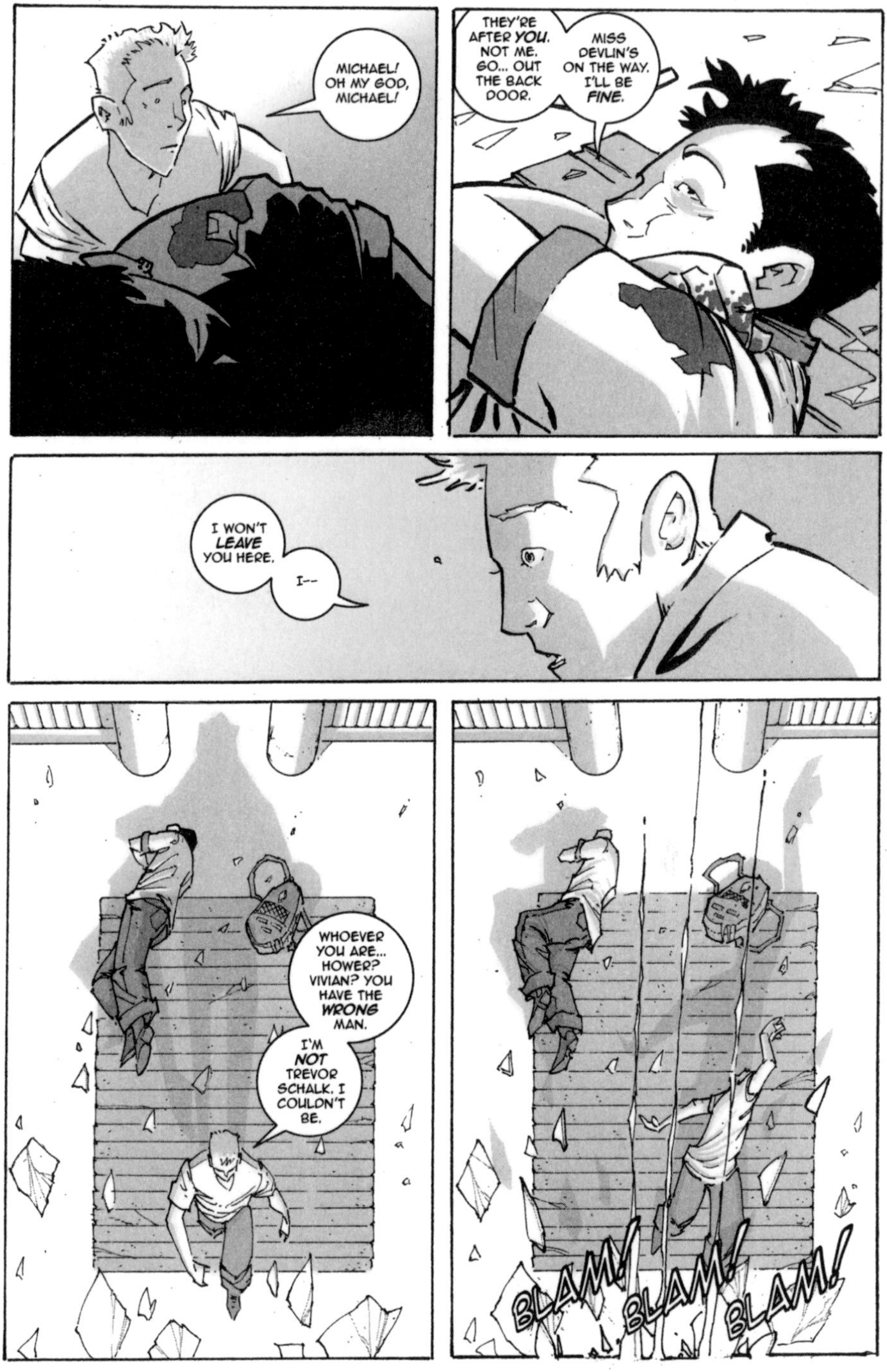
MICHAEL! OH MY GOD, MICHAEL!
THEY'RE AFTER YOU. NOT ME. GO... OUT THE BACK DOOR.
MISS DEVLIN'S ON THE WAY. I'LL BE FINE.
I WON'T LEAVE YOU HERE.
I--
WHOEVER YOU ARE... HOWER? VIVIAN? YOU HAVE THE WRONG MAN.
I'M NOT TREVOR SCHALK. I COULDN'T BE.
BLAM! BLAM! BLAM!

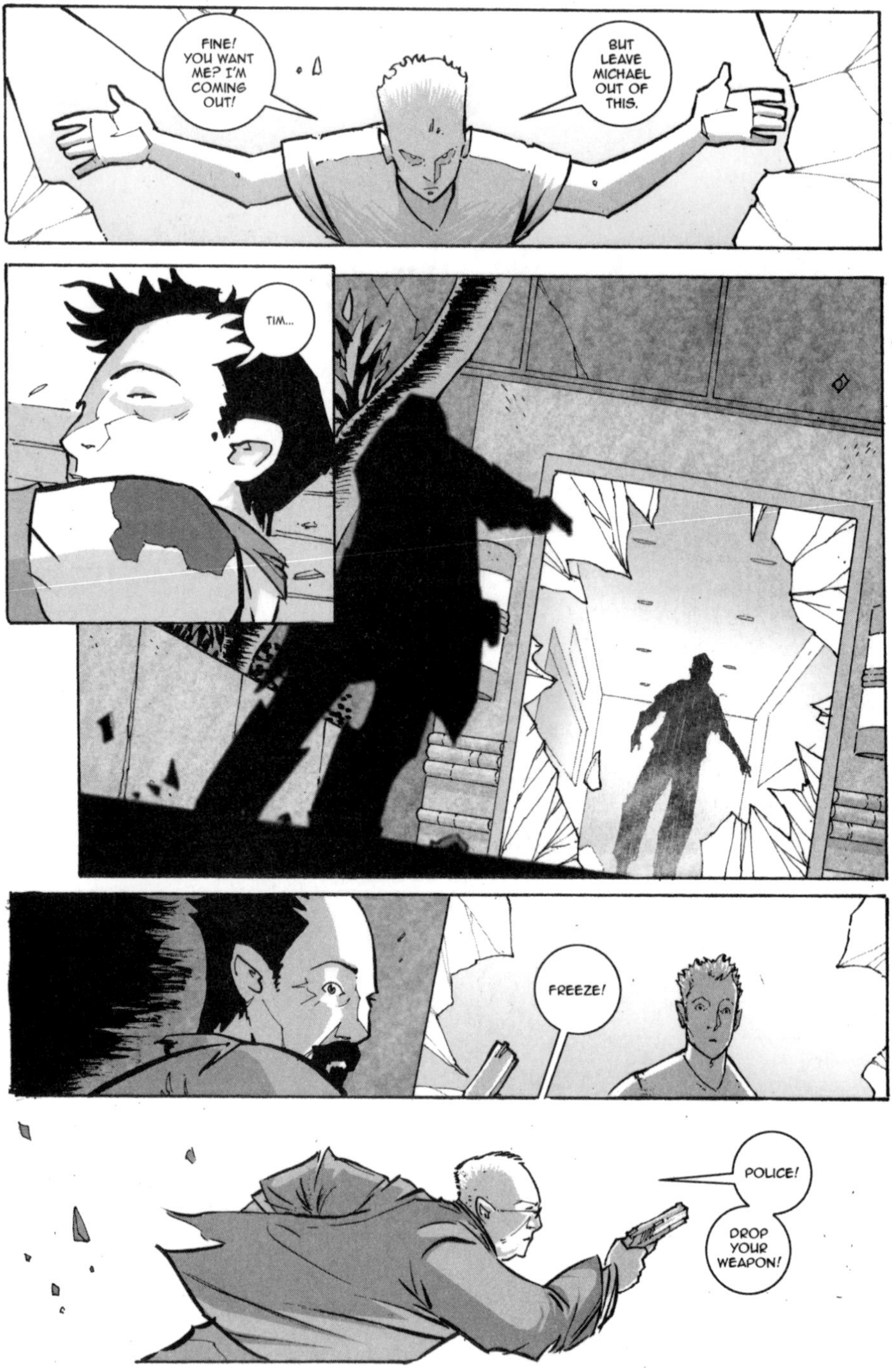
FINE! YOU WANT ME? I'M COMING OUT!
BUT LEAVE MICHAEL OUT OF THIS.
TIM...
FREEZE!
POLICE!
DROP YOUR WEAPON!

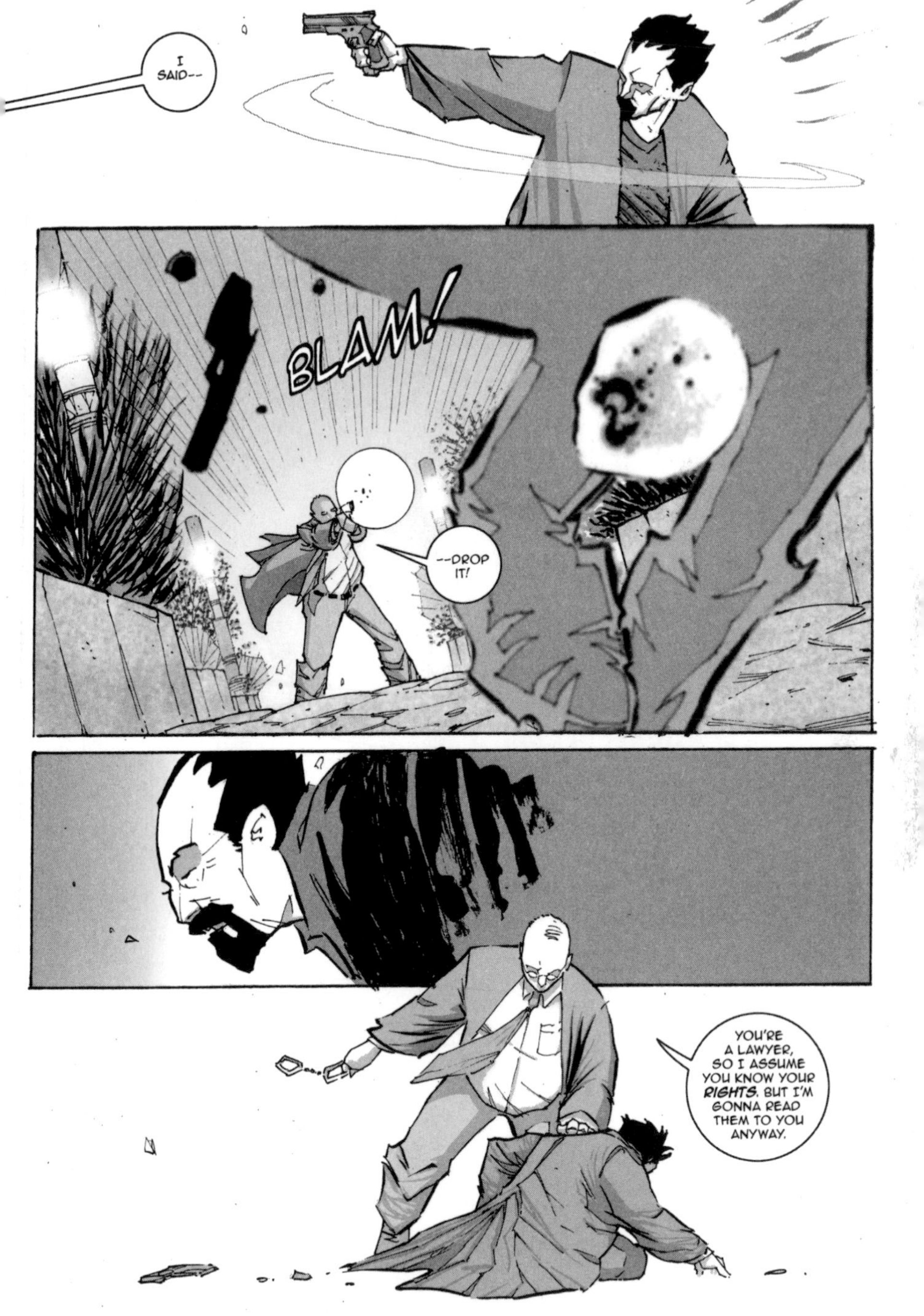
I SAID--
BLAM!
--DROP IT!
YOU'RE A LAWYER, SO I ASSUME YOU KNOW YOUR RIGHTS. BUT I'M GONNA READ THEM TO YOU ANYWAY.

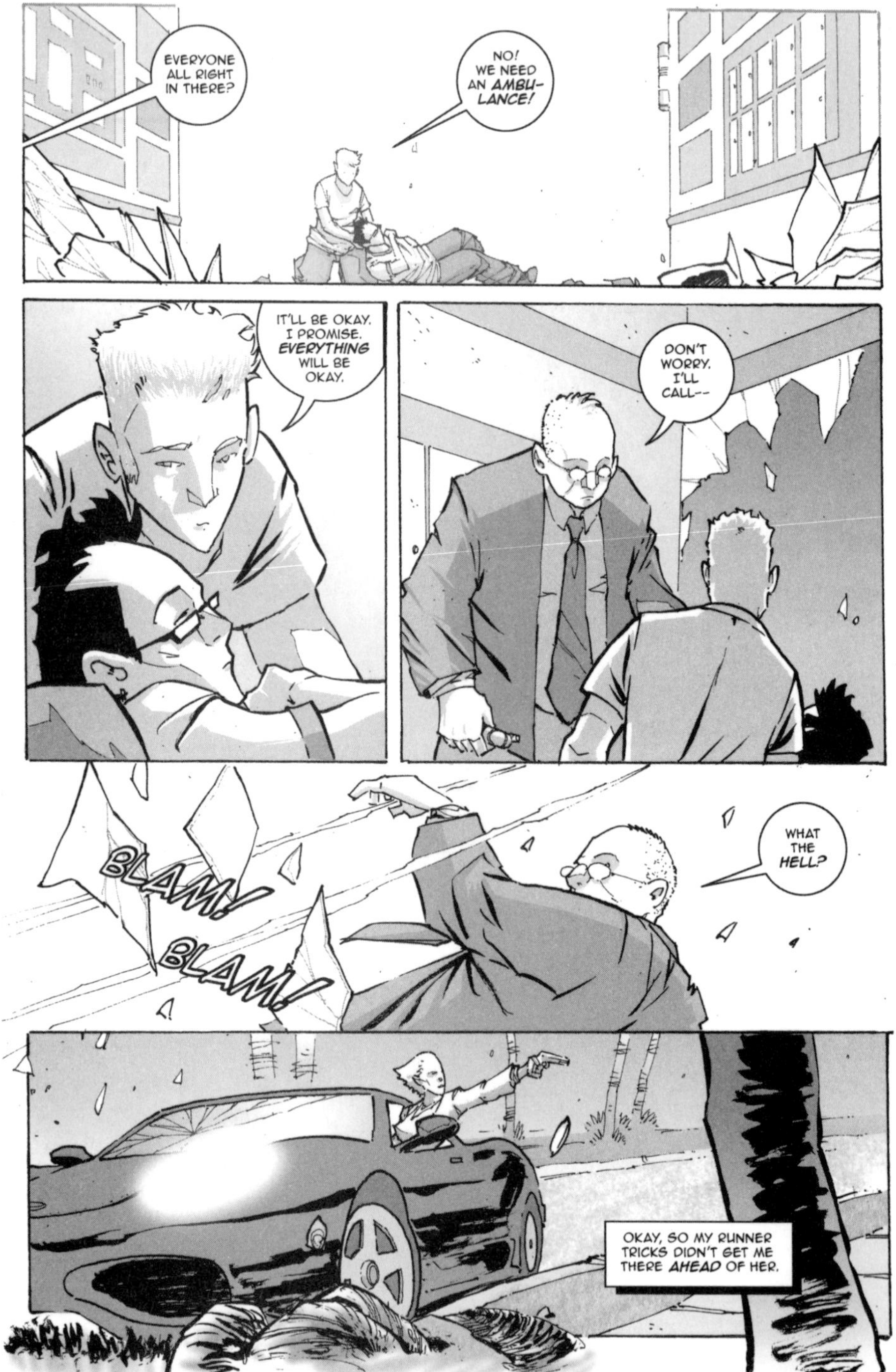
EVERYONE ALL RIGHT IN THERE?
NO! WE NEED AN AMBU-LANCE!
IT'LL BE OKAY. I PROMISE. EVERYTHING WILL BE OKAY.
DON'T WORRY. I'LL CALL--
BLAM!
BLAM!
WHAT THE HELL?
OKAY, SO MY RUNNER TRICKS DIDN'T GET ME THERE AHEAD OF HER.

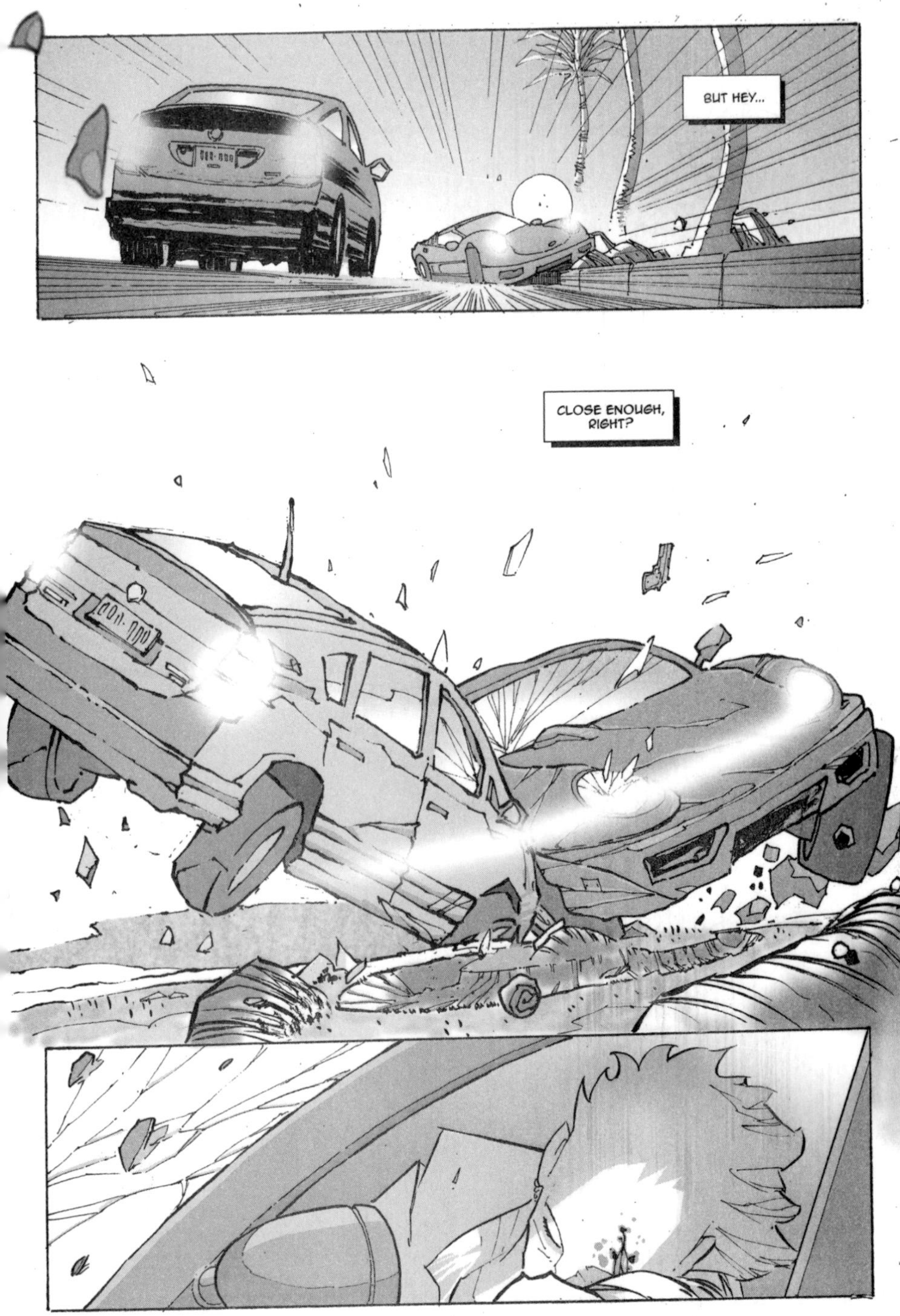
BUT HEY...
CLOSE ENOUGH, RIGHT?

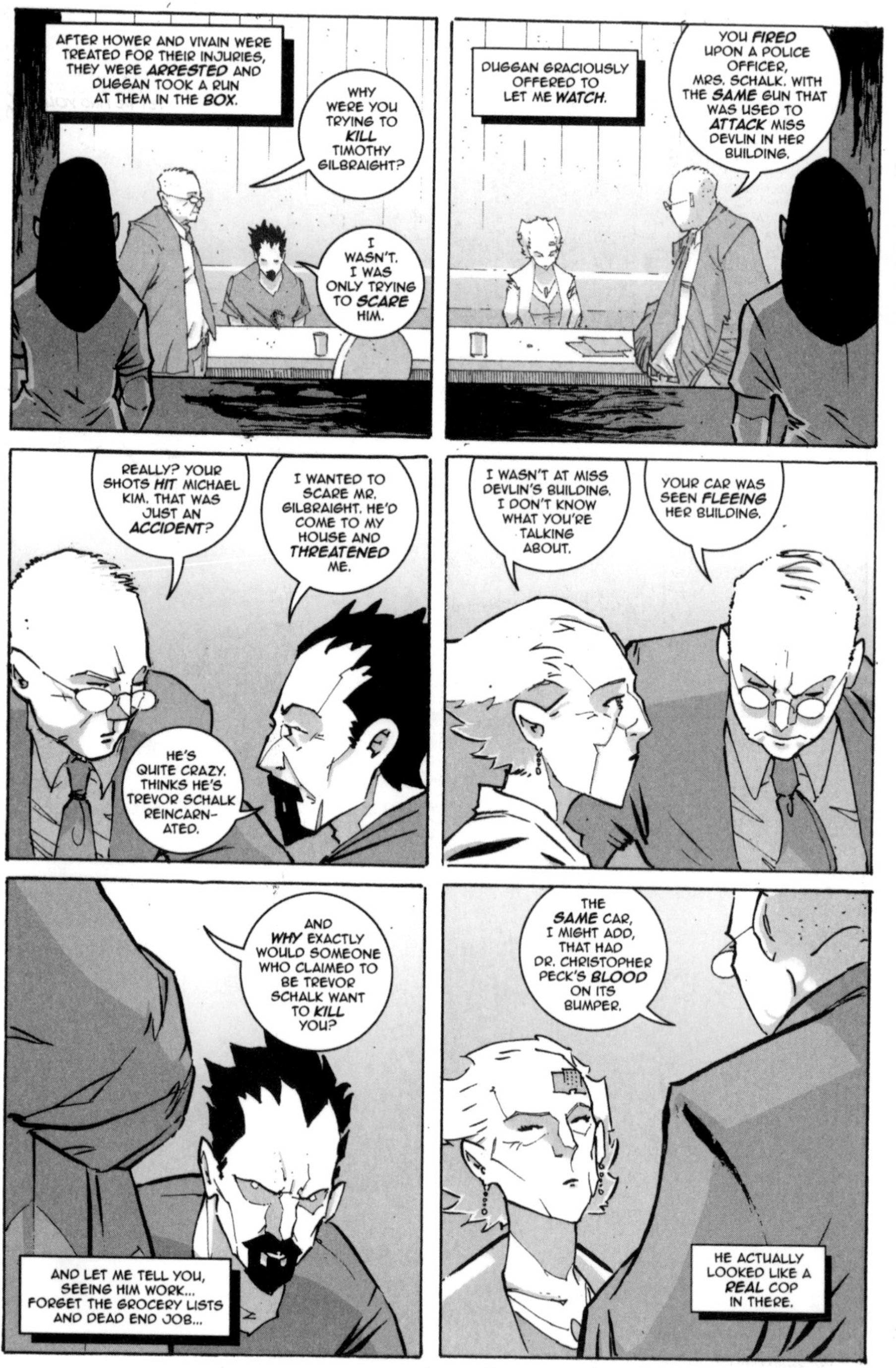
AFTER HOWER AND VIVAIN WERE TREATED FOR THEIR INJURIES, THEY WERE ARRESTED AND DUGGAN TOOK A RUN AT THEM IN THE BOX.
WHY WERE YOU TRYING TO KILL TIMOTHY GILBRAIGHT?
I WASN'T. I WAS ONLY TRYING TO SCARE HIM.
DUGGAN GRACIOUSLY OFFERED TO LET ME WATCH.
YOU FIRED UPON A POLICE OFFICER, MRS. SCHALK, WITH THE SAME GUN THAT WAS USED TO ATTACK MISS DEVLIN IN HER BUILDING.
REALLY? YOUR SHOTS HIT MICHAEL KIM. THAT WAS JUST AN ACCIDENT?
I WANTED TO SCARE MR. GILBRAIGHT. HE'D COME TO MY HOUSE AND THREATENED ME.
HE'S QUITE CRAZY. THINKS HE'S TREVOR SCHALK REINCARNATED.
I WASN'T AT MISS DEVLIN'S BUILDING. I DON'T KNOW WHAT YOU'RE TALKING ABOUT.
YOUR CAR WAS SEEN FLEEING HER BUILDING.
AND WHY EXACTLY WOULD SOMEONE WHO CLAIMED TO BE TREVOR SCHALK WANT TO KILL YOU?
AND LET ME TELL YOU, SEEING HIM WORK... FORGET THE GROCERY LISTS AND DEAD END JOB...
THE SAME CAR, I MIGHT ADD, THAT HAD DR. CHRISTOPHER PECK'S BLOOD ON ITS BUMPER.
HE ACTUALLY LOOKED LIKE A REAL COP IN THERE.

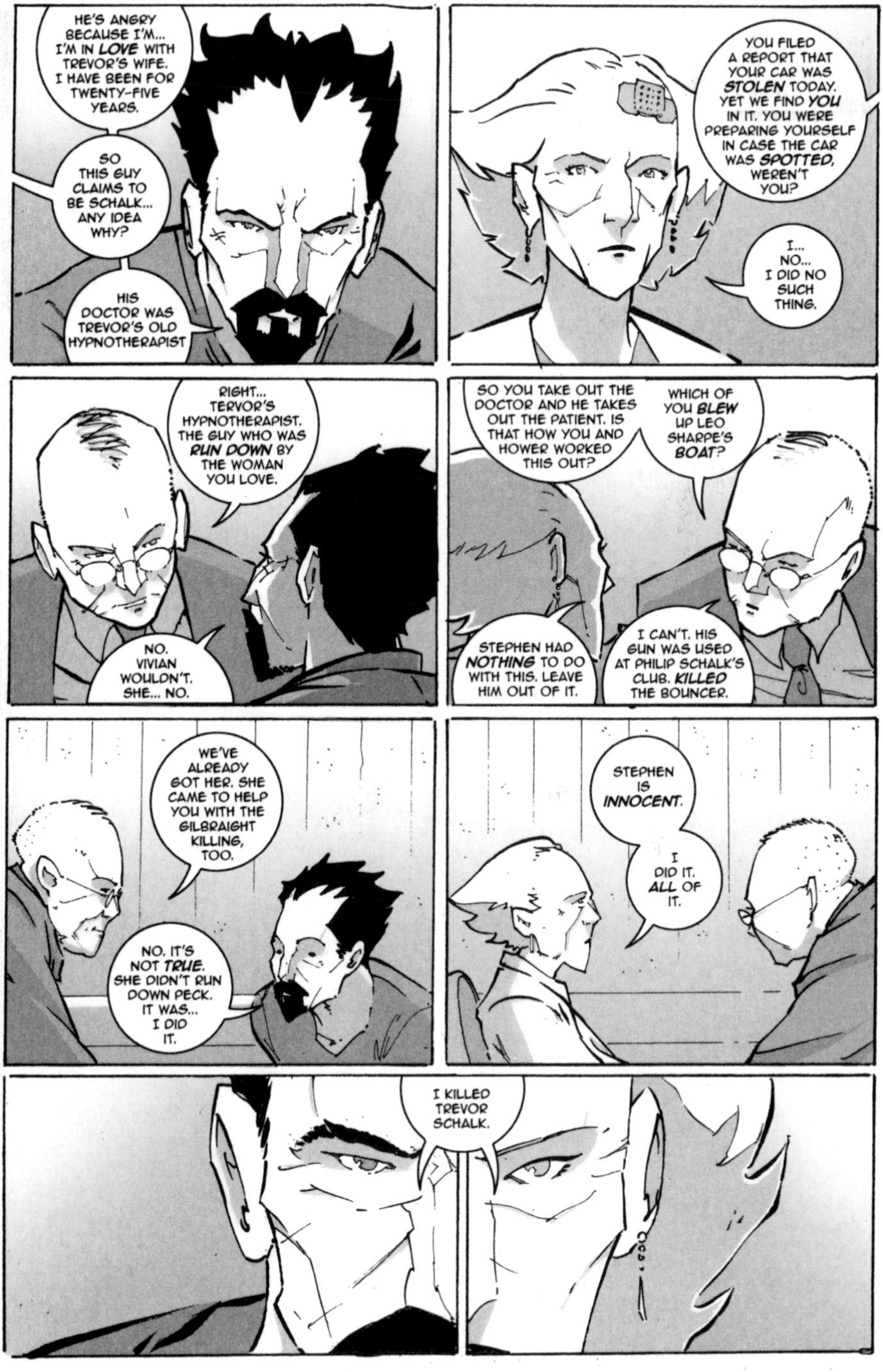
HE'S ANGRY BECAUSE I'M... I'M IN LOVE WITH TREVOR'S WIFE. I HAVE BEEN FOR TWENTY-FIVE YEARS.
SO THIS GUY CLAIMS TO BE SCHALK... ANY IDEA WHY?
HIS DOCTOR WAS TREVOR'S OLD HYPNOTHERAPIST
YOU FILED A REPORT THAT YOUR CAR WAS STOLEN TODAY. YET WE FIND YOU IN IT. YOU WERE PREPARING YOURSELF IN CASE THE CAR WAS SPOTTED, WEREN'T YOU?
I... NO... I DID NO SUCH THING.
RIGHT... TREVOR'S HYPNOTHERAPIST. THE GUY WHO WAS RUN DOWN BY THE WOMAN YOU LOVE.
NO. VIVIAN WOULDN'T. SHE... NO.
SO YOU TAKE OUT THE DOCTOR AND HE TAKES OUT THE PATIENT. IS THAT HOW YOU AND HOWER WORKED THIS OUT?
WHICH OF YOU BLEW UP LEO SHARPE'S BOAT?
STEPHEN HAD NOTHING TO DO WITH THIS. LEAVE HIM OUT OF IT.
I CAN'T. HIS GUN WAS USED AT PHILIP SCHALK'S CLUB. KILLED THE BOUNCER.
WE'VE ALREADY GOT HER. SHE CAME TO HELP YOU WITH THE GILBRAIGHT KILLING, TOO.
NO. IT'S NOT TRUE. SHE DIDN'T RUN DOWN PECK. IT WAS... I DID IT.
STEPHEN IS INNOCENT.
I DID IT. ALL OF IT.
I KILLED TREVOR SCHALK.

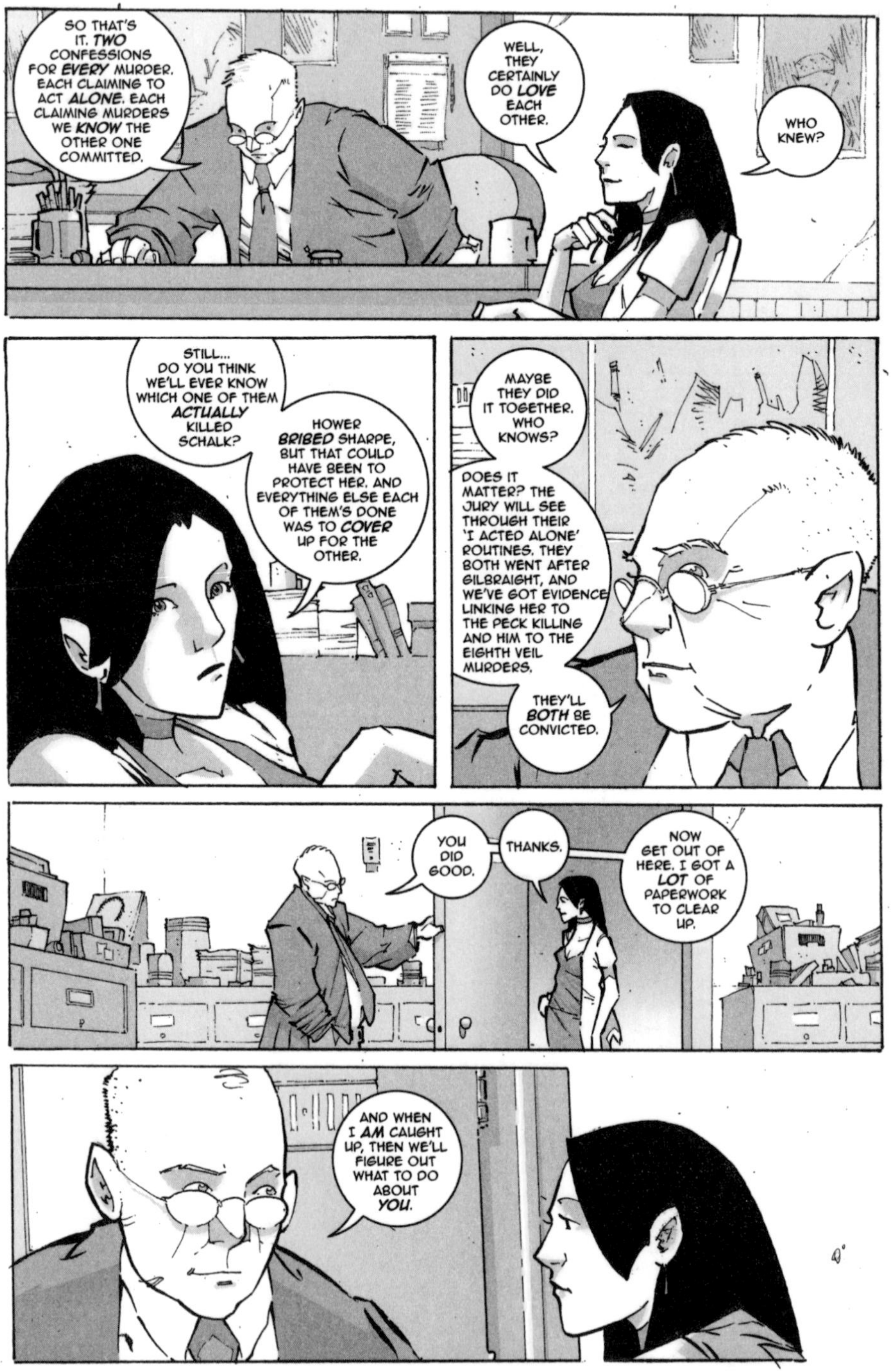
SO THAT'S IT. TWO CONFESSIONS FOR EVERY MURDER. EACH CLAIMING TO ACT ALONE. EACH CLAIMING MURDERS WE KNOW THE OTHER ONE COMMITTED.
WELL, THEY CERTAINLY DO LOVE EACH OTHER.
WHO KNEW?
STILL... DO YOU THINK WE'LL EVER KNOW WHICH ONE OF THEM ACTUALLY KILLED SCHALK?
HOWER BRIBED SHARPE, BUT THAT COULD HAVE BEEN TO PROTECT HER. AND EVERYTHING ELSE EACH OF THEM'S DONE WAS TO COVER UP FOR THE OTHER.
MAYBE THEY DID IT TOGETHER. WHO KNOWS?
DOES IT MATTER? THE JURY WILL SEE THROUGH THEIR 'I ACTED ALONE' ROUTINES. THEY BOTH WENT AFTER GILBRAIGHT, AND WE'VE GOT EVIDENCE LINKING HER TO THE PECK KILLING AND HIM TO THE EIGHTH VEIL MURDERS.
THEY'LL BOTH BE CONVICTED.
YOU DID GOOD.
THANKS.
NOW GET OUT OF HERE. I GOT A LOT OF PAPERWORK TO CLEAR UP.
AND WHEN I AM CAUGHT UP, THEN WE'LL FIGURE OUT WHAT TO DO ABOUT YOU.

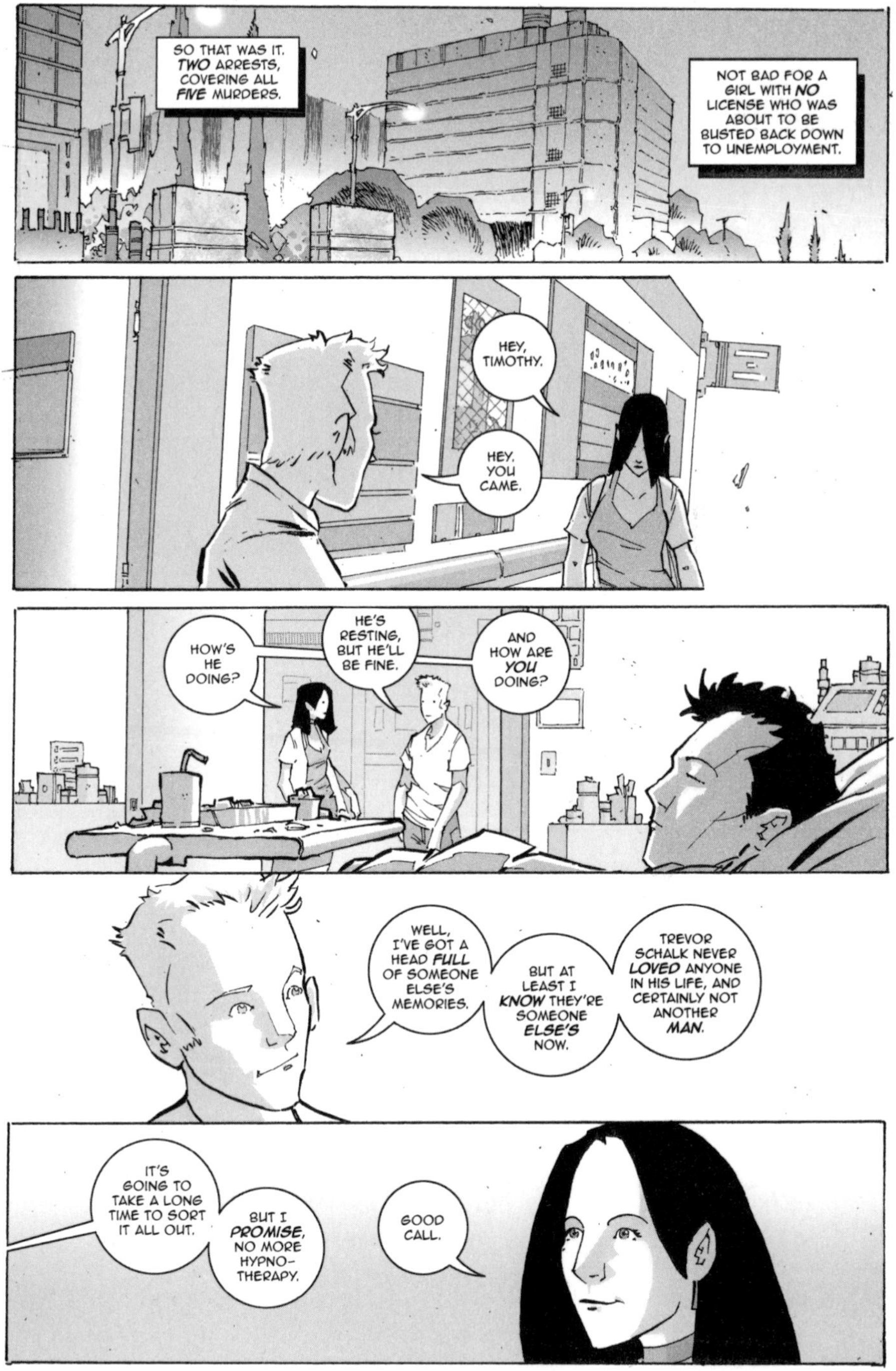
SO THAT WAS IT. TWO ARRESTS, COVERING ALL FIVE MURDERS.
NOT BAD FOR A GIRL WITH NO LICENSE WHO WAS ABOUT TO BE BUSTED BACK DOWN TO UNEMPLOYMENT.
HEY, TIMOTHY.
HEY. YOU CAME.
HOW'S HE DOING?
HE'S RESTING, BUT HE'LL BE FINE.
AND HOW ARE YOU DOING?
WELL, I'VE GOT A HEAD FULL OF SOMEONE ELSE'S MEMORIES.
BUT AT LEAST I KNOW THEY'RE SOMEONE ELSE'S NOW.
TREVOR SCHALK NEVER LOVED ANYONE IN HIS LIFE, AND CERTAINLY NOT ANOTHER MAN.
IT'S GOING TO TAKE A LONG TIME TO SORT IT ALL OUT.
BUT I PROMISE, NO MORE HYPNO-THERAPY.
GOOD CALL.

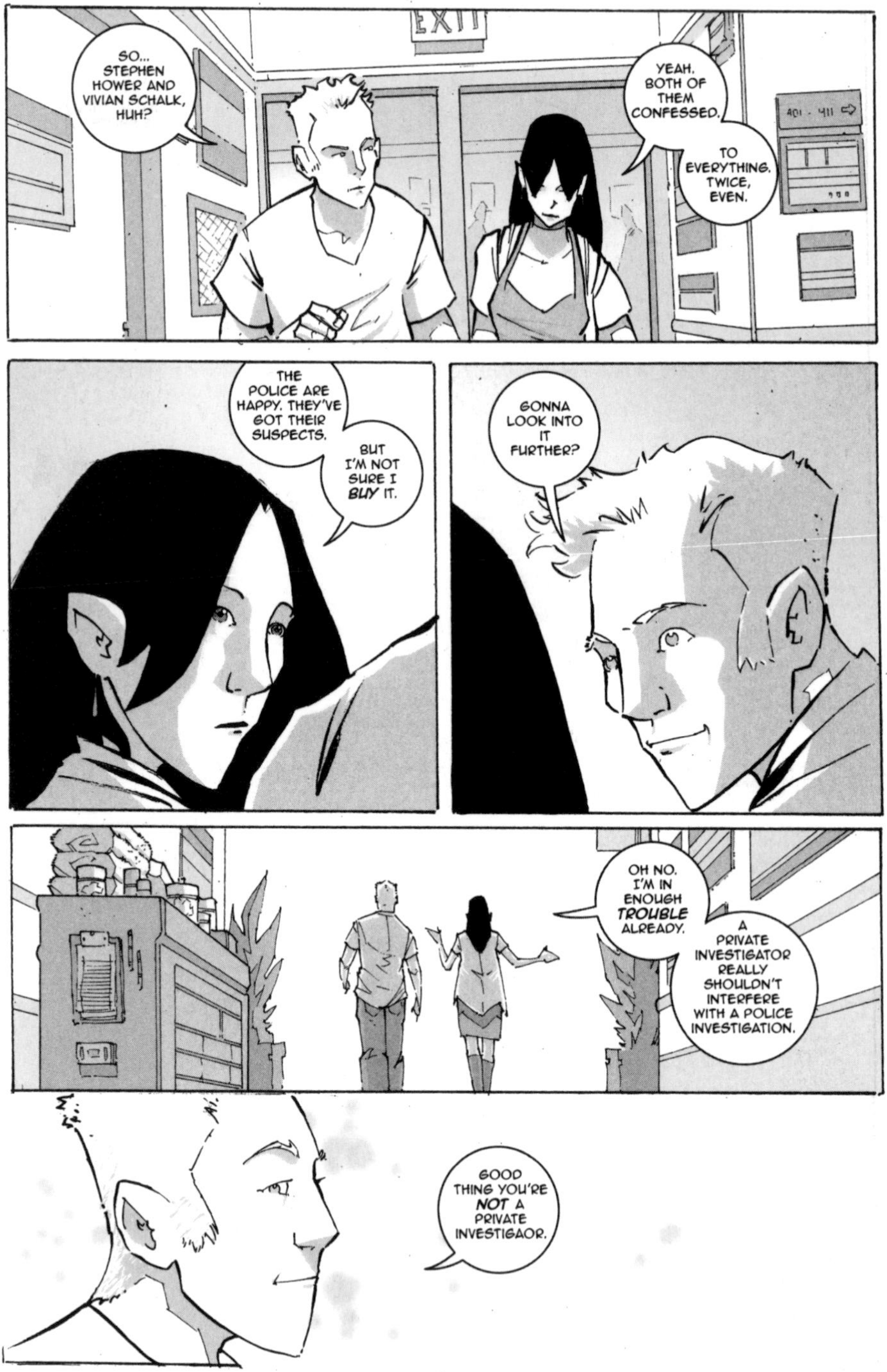

SO... STEPHEN HOWER AND VIVIAN SCHALK, HUH?
YEAH. BOTH OF THEM CONFESSED.
TO EVERYTHING. TWICE, EVEN.
EXIT
401 - 411
THE POLICE ARE HAPPY. THEY'VE GOT THEIR SUSPECTS.
BUT I'M NOT SURE I *BUY* IT.
GONNA LOOK INTO IT FURTHER?
OH NO. I'M IN ENOUGH *TROUBLE* ALREADY.
A PRIVATE INVESTIGATOR REALLY SHOULDN'T INTERFERE WITH A POLICE INVESTIGATION.
GOOD THING YOU'RE *NOT* A PRIVATE INVESTIGAOR.

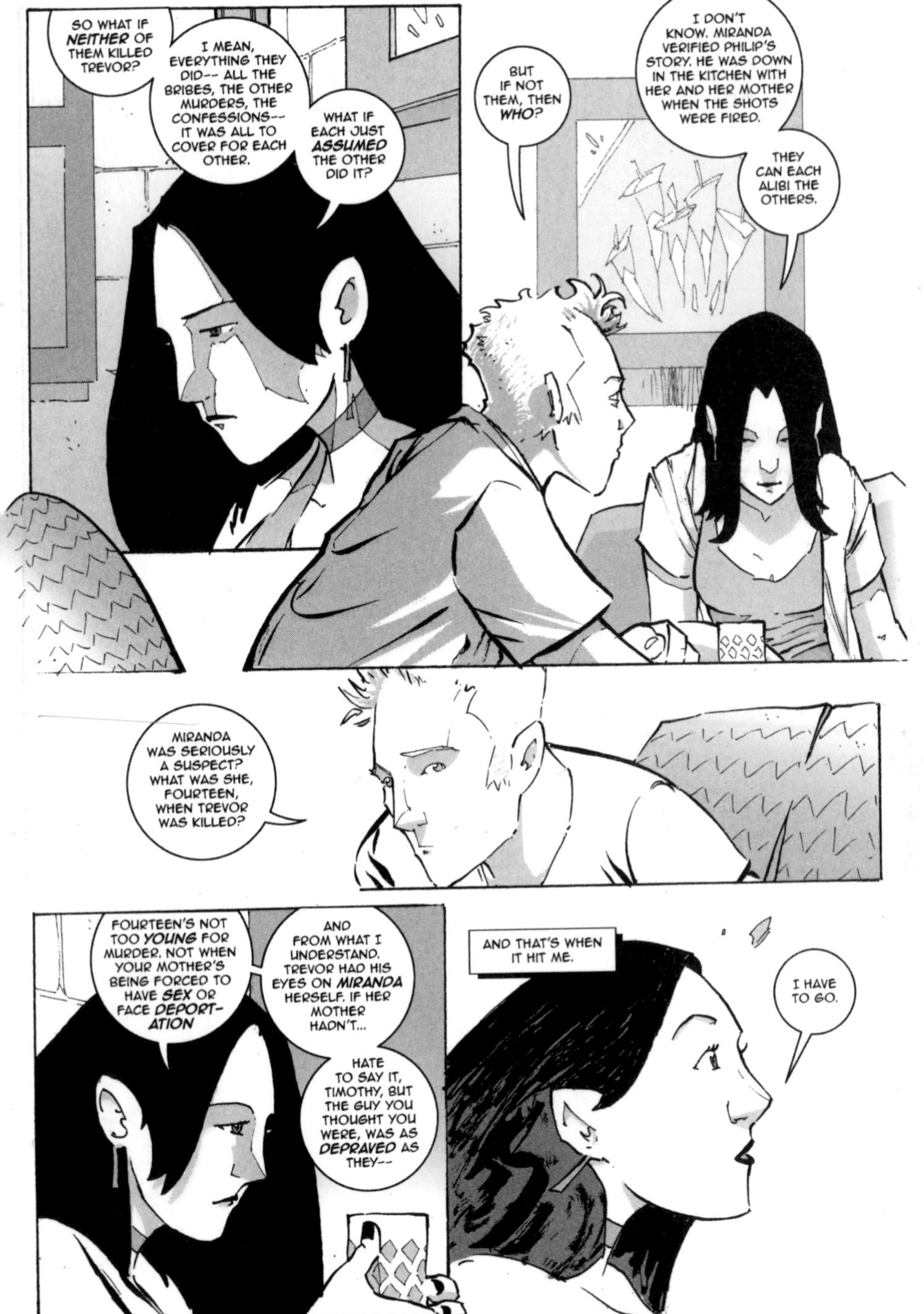
SO WHAT IF NEITHER OF THEM KILLED TREVOR?
I MEAN, EVERYTHING THEY DID-- ALL THE BRIBES, THE OTHER MURDERS, THE CONFESSIONS-- IT WAS ALL TO COVER FOR EACH OTHER.
WHAT IF EACH JUST ASSUMED THE OTHER DID IT?
BUT IF NOT THEM, THEN WHO?
I DON'T KNOW. MIRANDA VERIFIED PHILIP'S STORY. HE WAS DOWN IN THE KITCHEN WITH HER AND HER MOTHER WHEN THE SHOTS WERE FIRED.
THEY CAN EACH ALIBI THE OTHERS.
MIRANDA WAS SERIOUSLY A SUSPECT? WHAT WAS SHE, FOURTEEN, WHEN TREVOR WAS KILLED?
FOURTEEN'S NOT TOO YOUNG FOR MURDER. NOT WHEN YOUR MOTHER'S BEING FORCED TO HAVE SEX OR FACE DEPORT-ATION
AND FROM WHAT I UNDERSTAND. TREVOR HAD HIS EYES ON MIRANDA HERSELF. IF HER MOTHER HADN'T...
HATE TO SAY IT, TIMOTHY, BUT THE GUY YOU THOUGHT YOU WERE, WAS AS DEPRAVED AS THEY--
AND THAT'S WHEN IT HIT ME.
I HAVE TO GO.

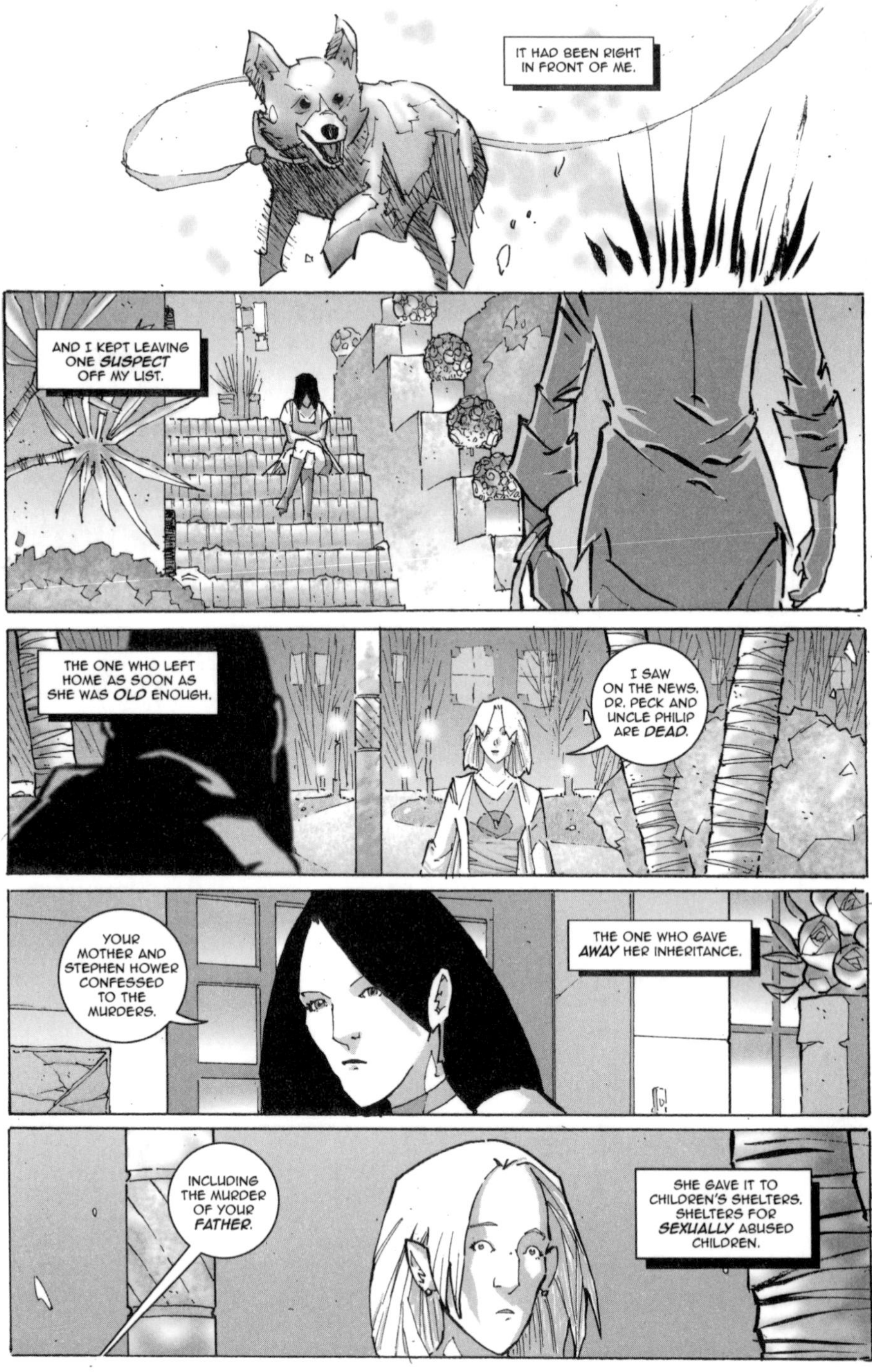
IT HAD BEEN RIGHT IN FRONT OF ME.
AND I KEPT LEAVING ONE SUSPECT OFF MY LIST.
THE ONE WHO LEFT HOME AS SOON AS SHE WAS OLD ENOUGH.
I SAW ON THE NEWS. DR. PECK AND UNCLE PHILIP ARE DEAD.
YOUR MOTHER AND STEPHEN HOWER CONFESSED TO THE MURDERS.
THE ONE WHO GAVE AWAY HER INHERITANCE.
INCLUDING THE MURDER OF YOUR FATHER.
SHE GAVE IT TO CHILDREN'S SHELTERS. SHELTERS FOR SEXUALLY ABUSED CHILDREN.

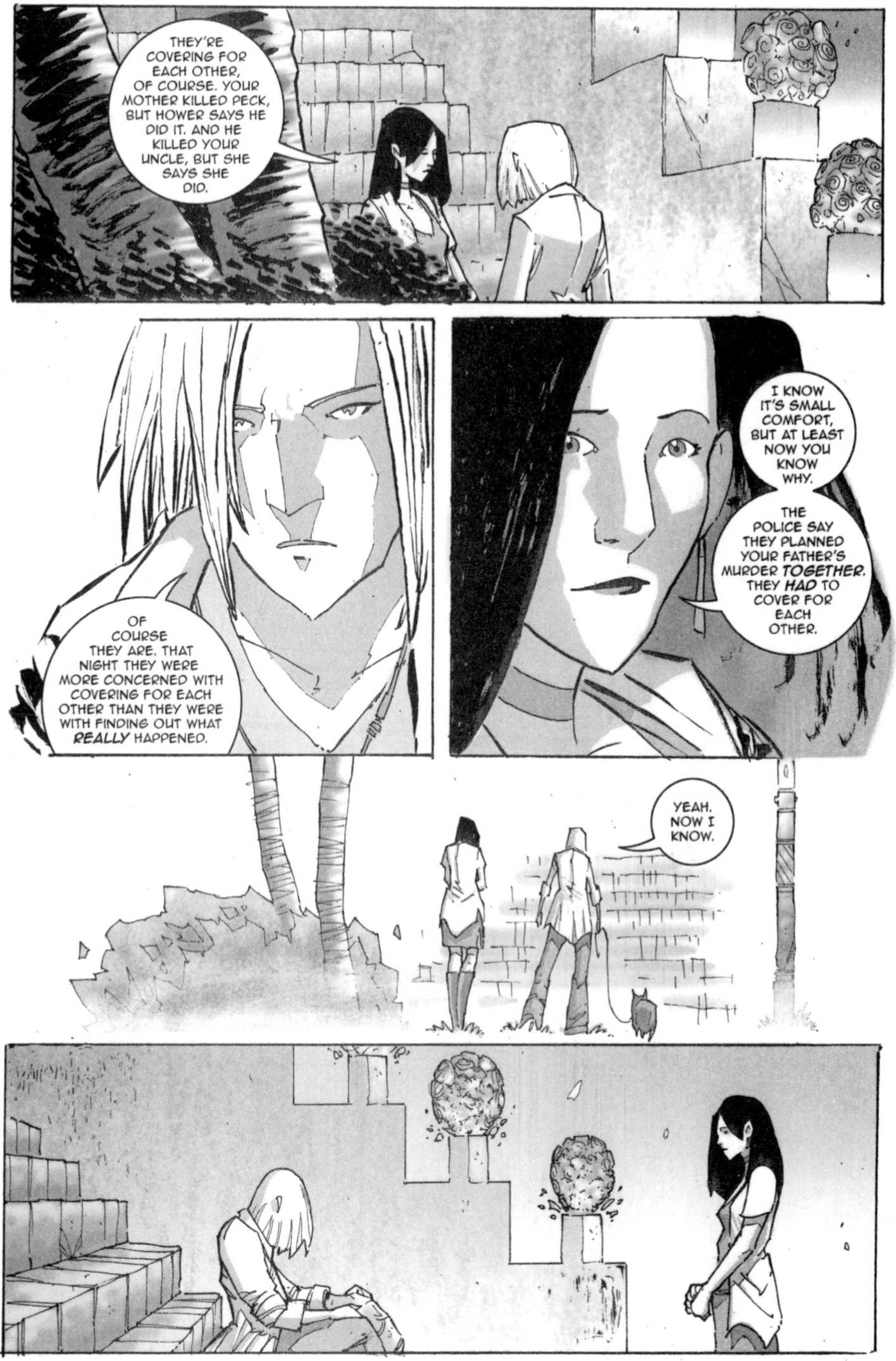
THEY'RE COVERING FOR EACH OTHER, OF COURSE. YOUR MOTHER KILLED PECK, BUT HOWER SAYS HE DID IT. AND HE KILLED YOUR UNCLE, BUT SHE SAYS SHE DID.
OF COURSE THEY ARE. THAT NIGHT THEY WERE MORE CONCERNED WITH COVERING FOR EACH OTHER THAN THEY WERE WITH FINDING OUT WHAT ***REALLY*** HAPPENED.
I KNOW IT'S SMALL COMFORT, BUT AT LEAST NOW YOU KNOW WHY.
THE POLICE SAY THEY PLANNED YOUR FATHER'S MURDER ***TOGETHER.*** THEY ***HAD*** TO COVER FOR EACH OTHER.
YEAH. NOW I KNOW.

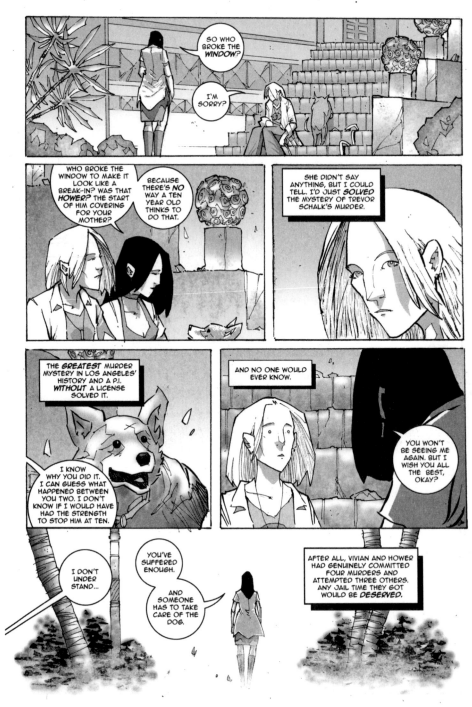

SO WHO BROKE THE *WINDOW*?

I'M SORRY?

WHO BROKE THE WINDOW TO MAKE IT LOOK LIKE A BREAK-IN? WAS THAT *HOWER*? THE START OF HIM COVERING FOR YOUR MOTHER?

BECAUSE THERE'S *NO* WAY A TEN YEAR OLD THINKS TO DO THAT.

SHE DIDN'T SAY ANYTHING, BUT I COULD TELL. I'D JUST *SOLVED* THE MYSTERY OF TREVOR SCHALK'S MURDER.

THE *GREATEST* MURDER MYSTERY IN LOS ANGELES' HISTORY AND A P.I. *WITHOUT* A LICENSE SOLVED IT.

AND NO ONE WOULD EVER KNOW.

I KNOW WHY YOU DID IT. I CAN GUESS WHAT HAPPENED BETWEEN YOU TWO. I DON'T KNOW IF I WOULD HAVE HAD THE STRENGTH TO STOP HIM AT TEN.

YOU WON'T BE SEEING ME AGAIN. BUT I WISH YOU ALL THE BEST, OKAY?

I DON'T UNDER STAND...

YOU'VE SUFFERED ENOUGH.

AND SOMEONE HAS TO TAKE CARE OF THE DOG.

AFTER ALL, VIVIAN AND HOWER HAD GENUINELY COMMITTED FOUR MURDERS AND ATTEMPTED THREE OTHERS. ANY JAIL TIME THEY GOT WOULD BE *DESERVED*.

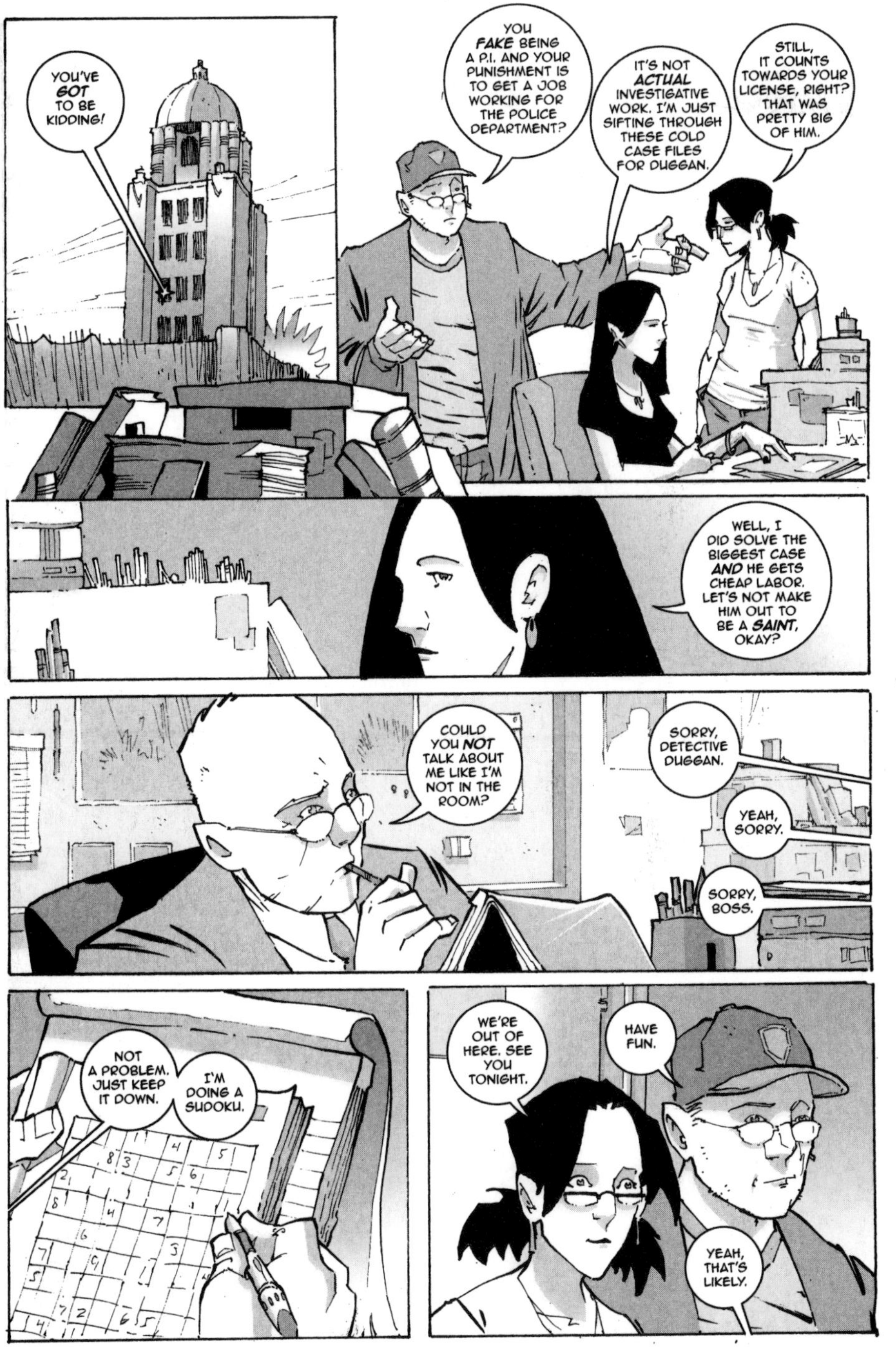
YOU'VE GOT TO BE KIDDING!
YOU FAKE BEING A P.I. AND YOUR PUNISHMENT IS TO GET A JOB WORKING FOR THE POLICE DEPARTMENT?
IT'S NOT ACTUAL INVESTIGATIVE WORK. I'M JUST SIFTING THROUGH THESE COLD CASE FILES FOR DUGGAN.
STILL, IT COUNTS TOWARDS YOUR LICENSE, RIGHT? THAT WAS PRETTY BIG OF HIM.
WELL, I DID SOLVE THE BIGGEST CASE AND HE GETS CHEAP LABOR. LET'S NOT MAKE HIM OUT TO BE A SAINT, OKAY?
COULD YOU NOT TALK ABOUT ME LIKE I'M NOT IN THE ROOM?
SORRY, DETECTIVE DUGGAN.
YEAH, SORRY.
SORRY, BOSS.
NOT A PROBLEM. JUST KEEP IT DOWN.
I'M DOING A SUDOKU.
WE'RE OUT OF HERE. SEE YOU TONIGHT.
HAVE FUN.
YEAH, THAT'S LIKELY.

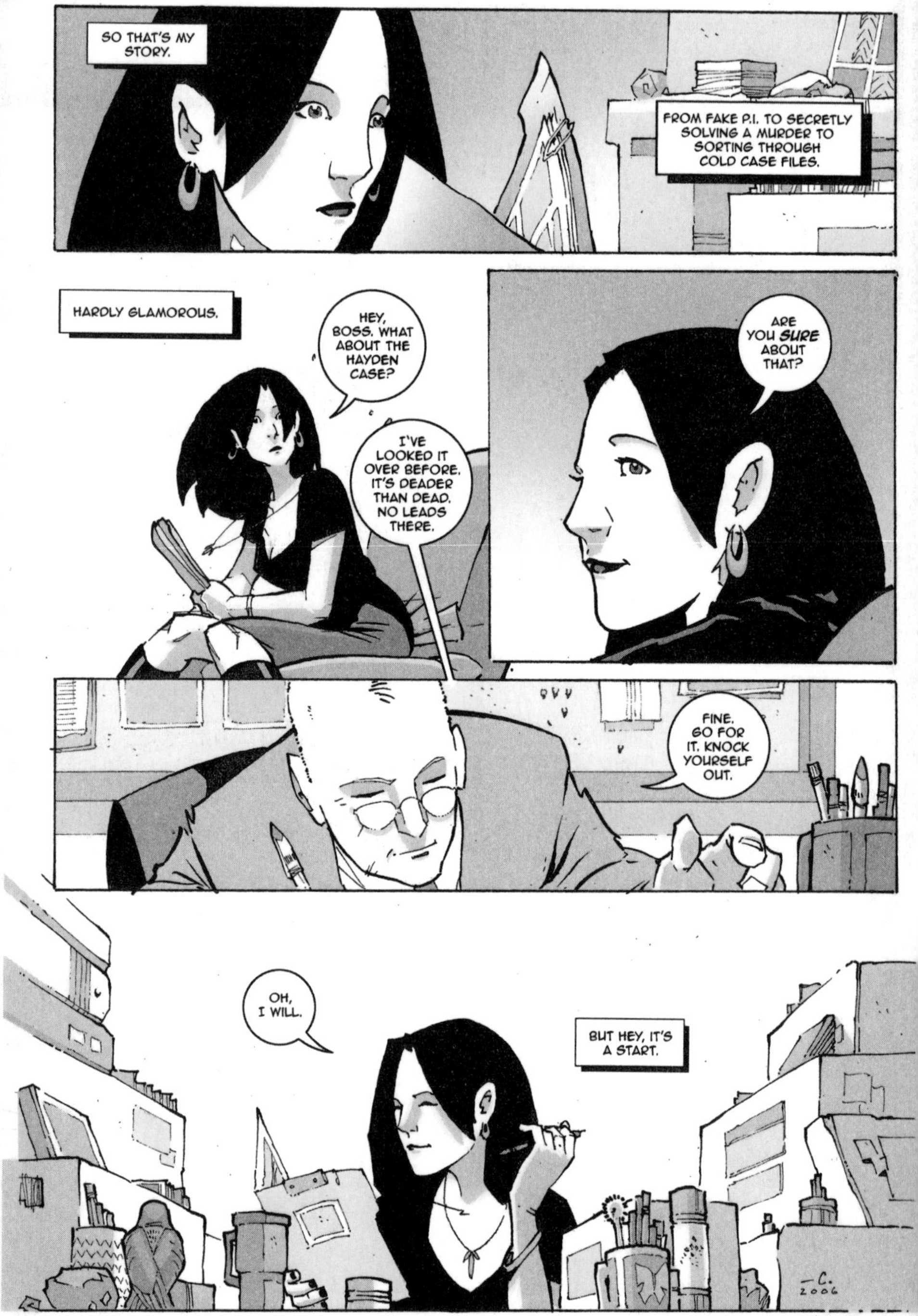
SO THAT'S MY STORY.
FROM FAKE P.I. TO SECRETLY SOLVING A MURDER TO SORTING THROUGH COLD CASE FILES.
HARDLY GLAMOROUS.
HEY, BOSS. WHAT ABOUT THE HAYDEN CASE?
I'VE LOOKED IT OVER BEFORE. IT'S DEADER THAN DEAD. NO LEADS THERE.
ARE YOU SURE ABOUT THAT?
FINE. GO FOR IT. KNOCK YOURSELF OUT.
OH, I WILL.
BUT HEY, IT'S A START.
—C. 2006

NUNZIO DEFILIPPIS & CHRISTINA WEIR are a writing team who have worked in comics, television, videogames and film. Trained as screenwriters (DeFilippis at USC's Screenwriting Program and Weir at Emerson's Television Program), they began writing together as a team on HBO's *Arliss*, where they worked for two seasons. They've also contributed two stories for Disney's *Kim Possible*. In comics, they have written *Skinwalker*, *Three Strikes*, *Maria's Wedding*, *Once In A Blue Moon* and *The Tomb* for Oni Press, and spent 3 years in the world of Marvel's mutants writing *New Mutants*, *Hellions* and *New X-men*. They have also written for *Wonder Woman*, *Adventures Of Superman* and *Detective Comics*. In the world of manga, they have created *Amazing Agent Luna* and *Destiny's Hand* and have adapted several Japanese series for Del Rey. Their first video game project is awaiting a title and release date.

This is their second collaboration with Christopher Mitten, their co-creator on *The Tomb*.

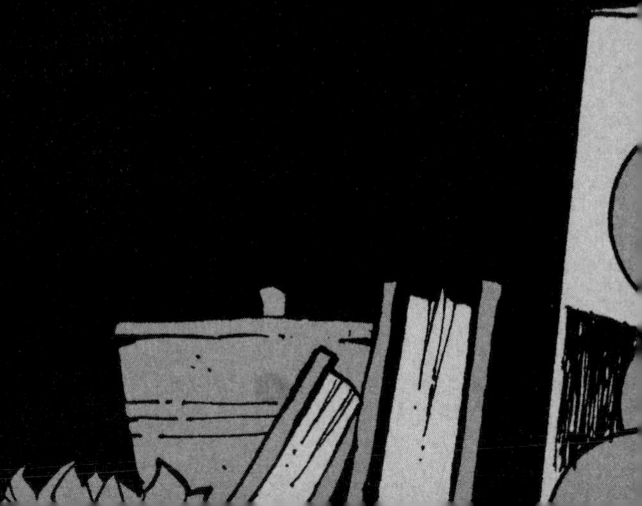

CHRISTOPHER MITTEN is the accomplished illustrator of the graphic novels *Last Exit Before Toll* and *The Tomb* as well as the third volume of *Queen & Country*'s *Declassified* series of spin-offs. He resides just outside of Chicago, Illinois where he currently splits his time between work on his new ongoing comic series, *Wasteland*, with writer Antony Johnston and denying his intense desire to shoot caffeine directly into his eyeballs.

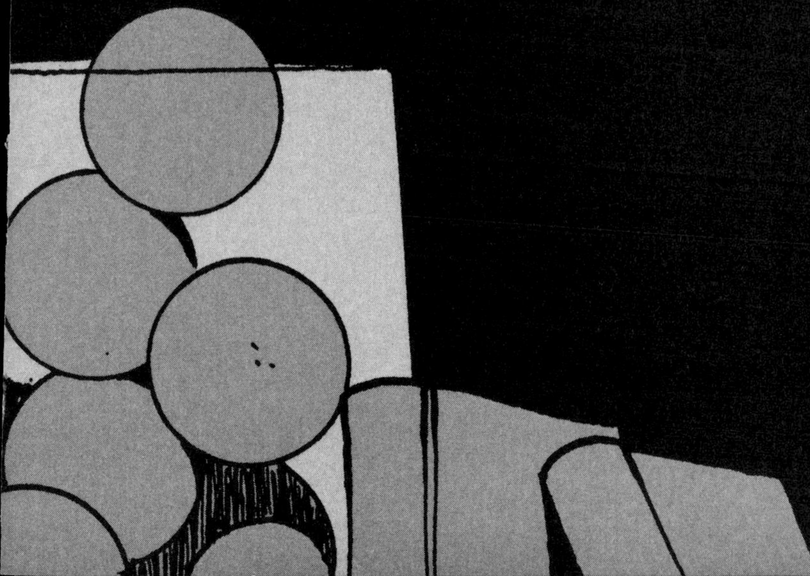